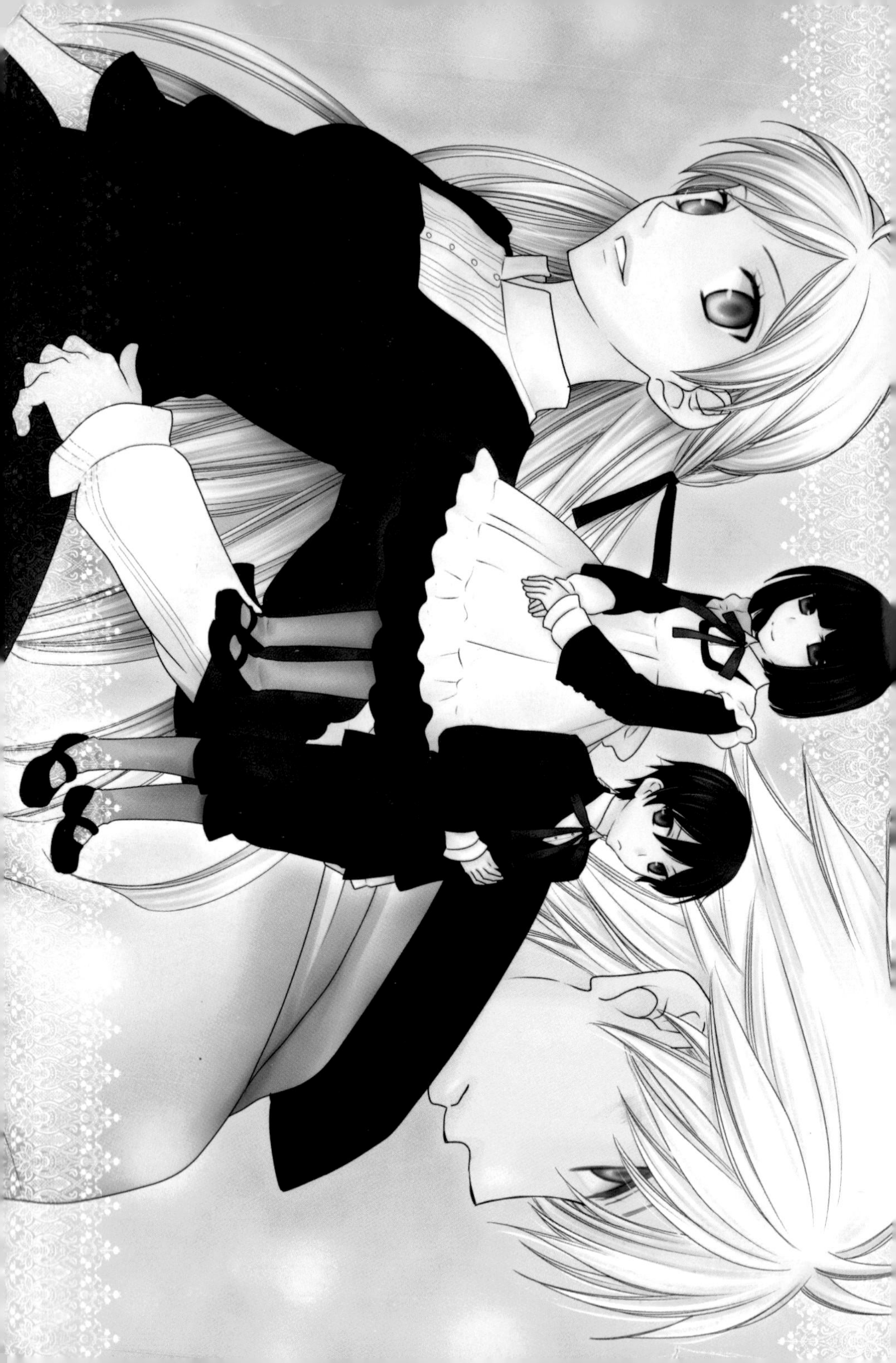

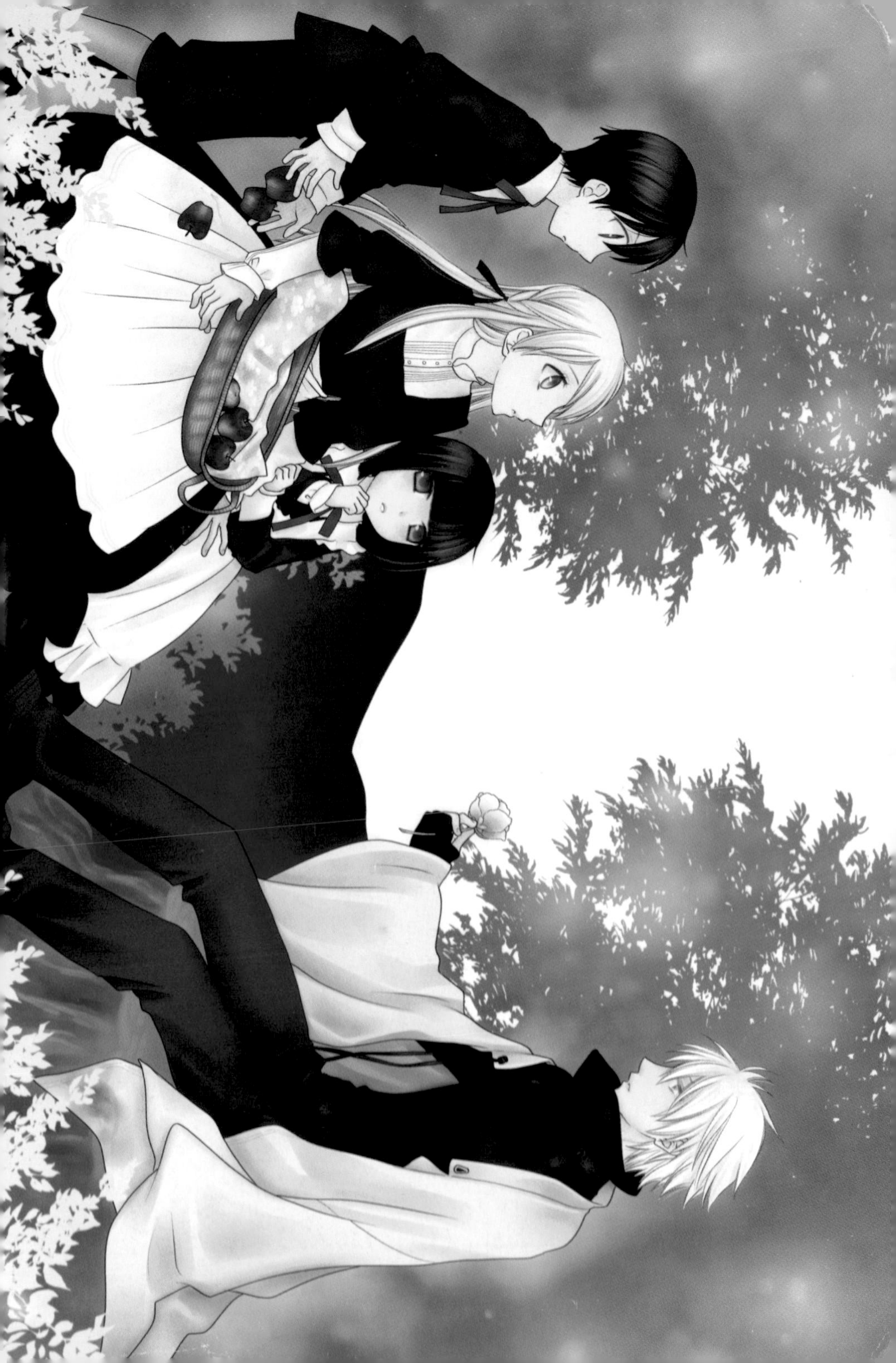

Liselotte & Witch's Forest

1

NATSUKI TAKAYA

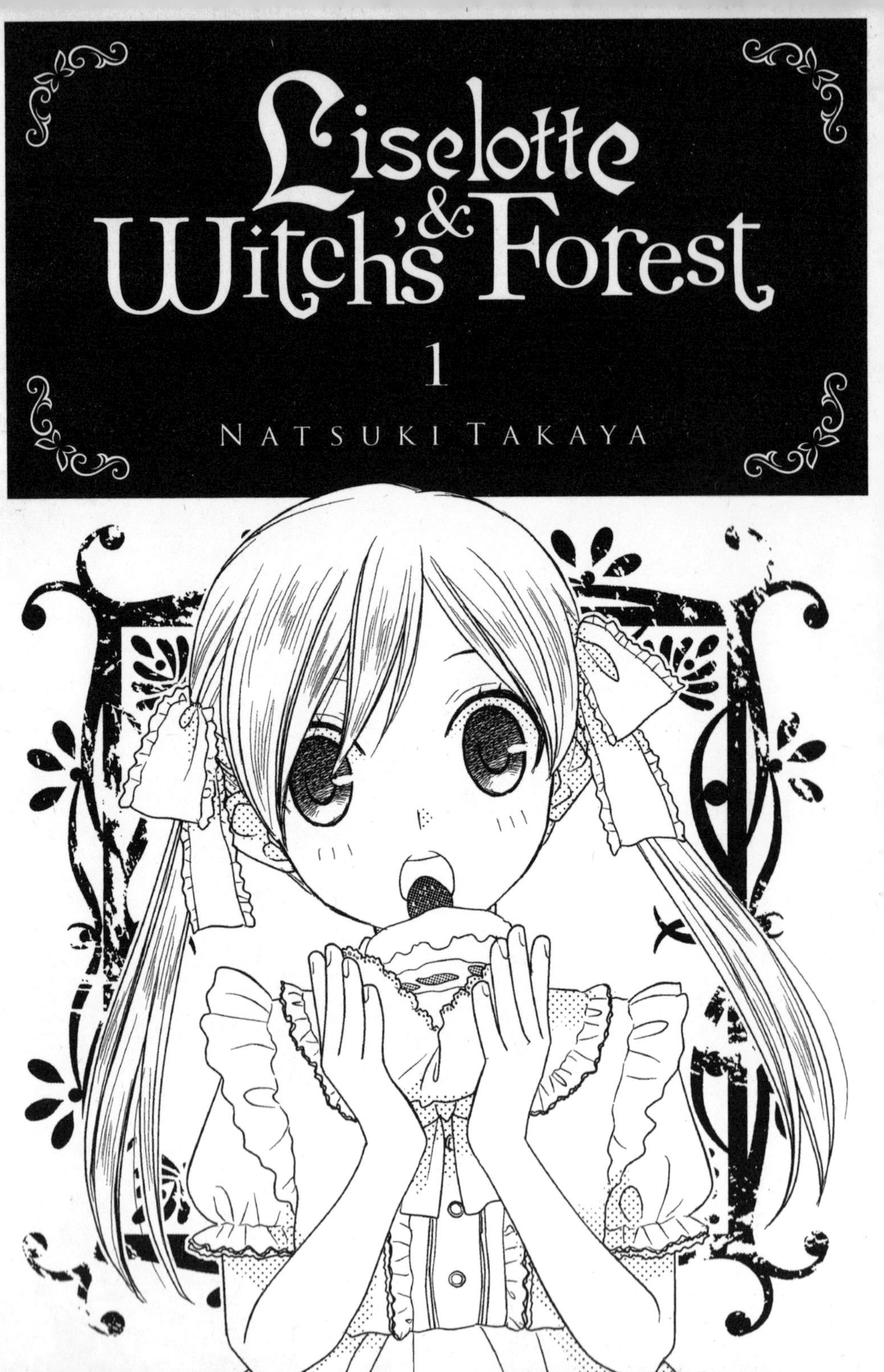

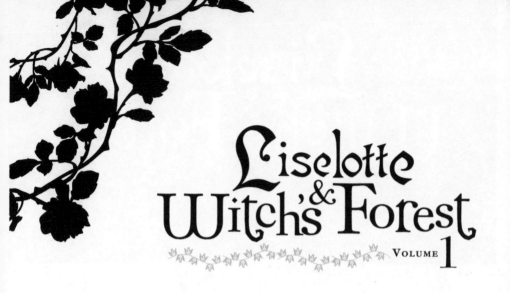

Liselotte & Witch's Forest

VOLUME 1

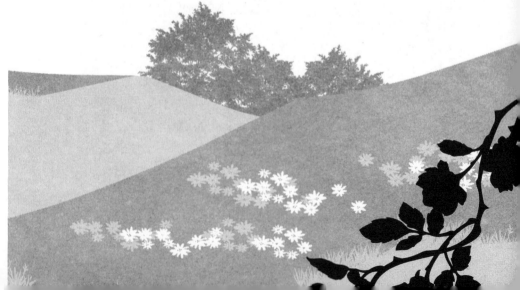

THIS TALE TAKES PLACE IN A FARAWAY LAND,

EAST OF THE EAST OF THE EAST.

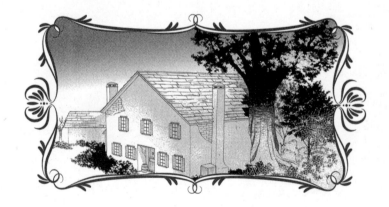

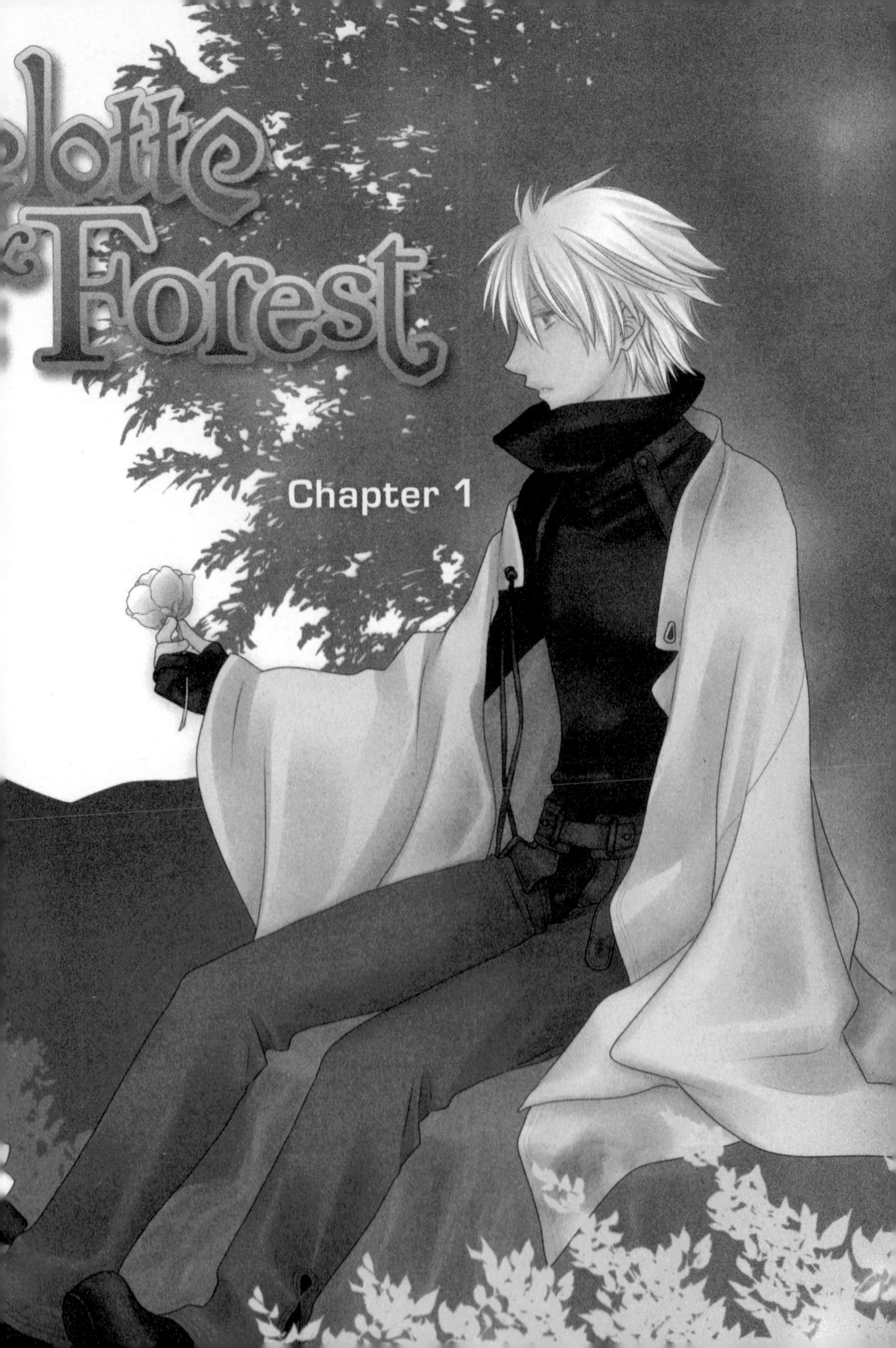
lotte
Forest
Chapter 1

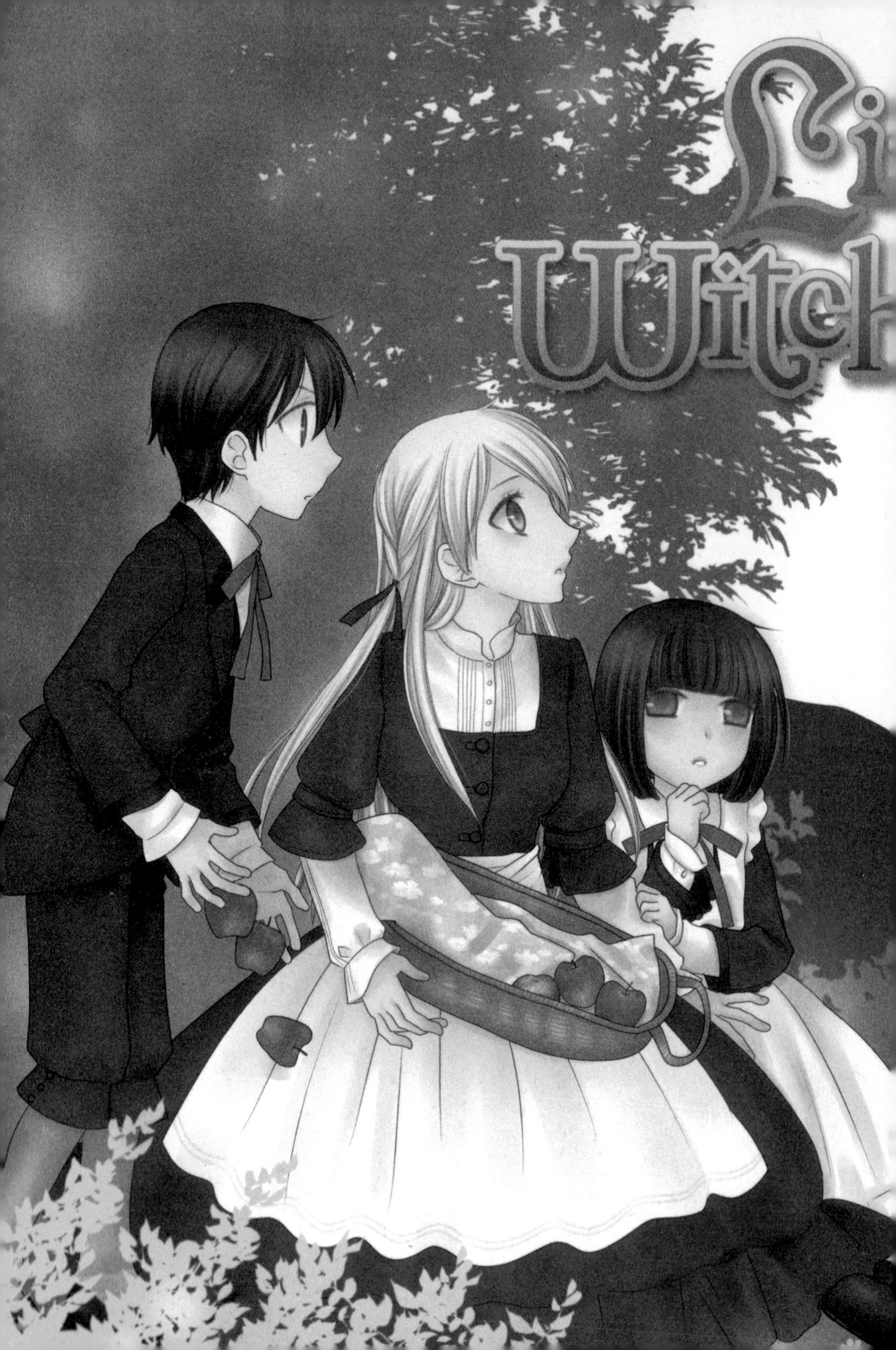

Li
Witc

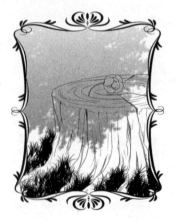

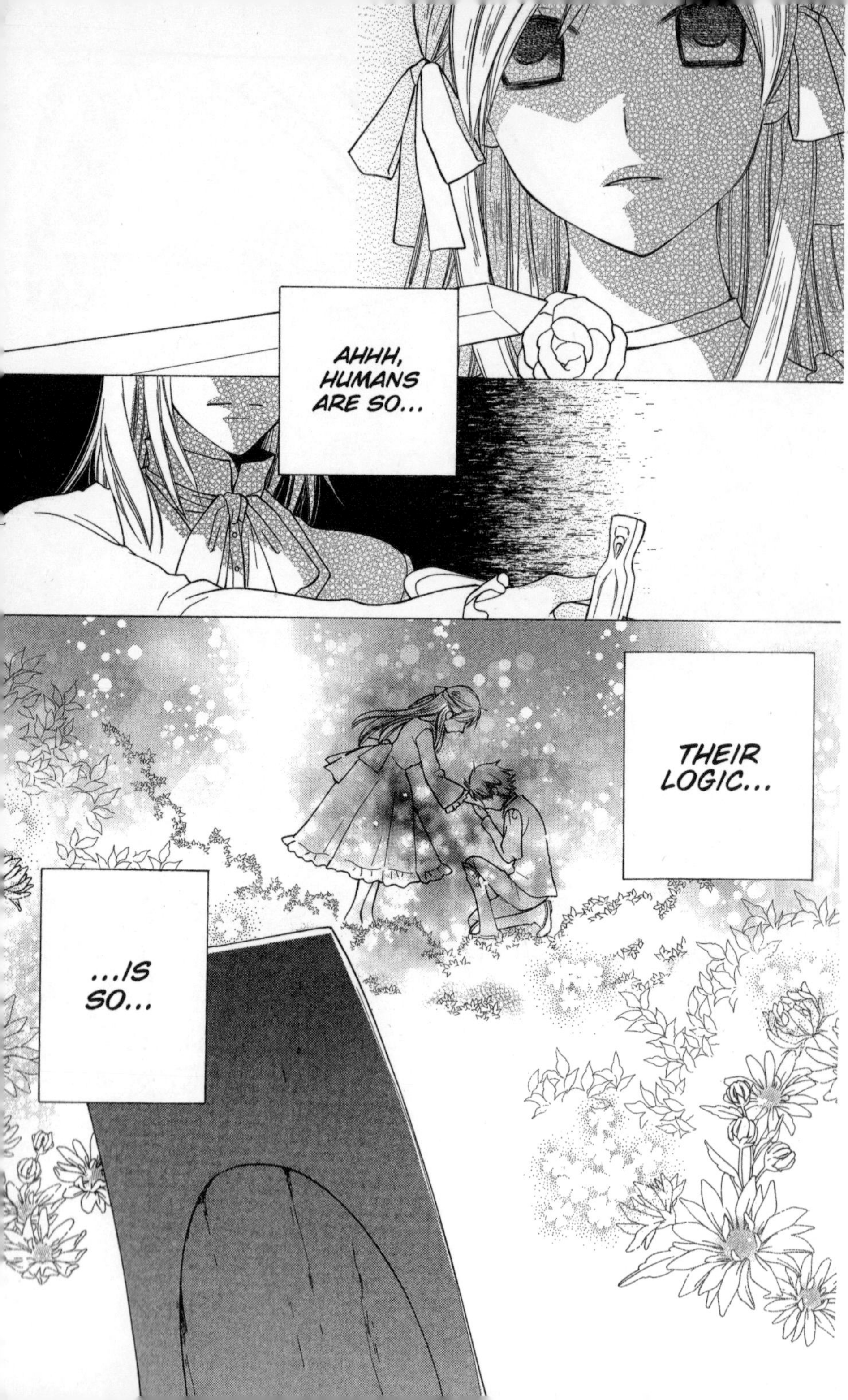
AHHH, HUMANS ARE SO...
THEIR LOGIC...
...IS SO...

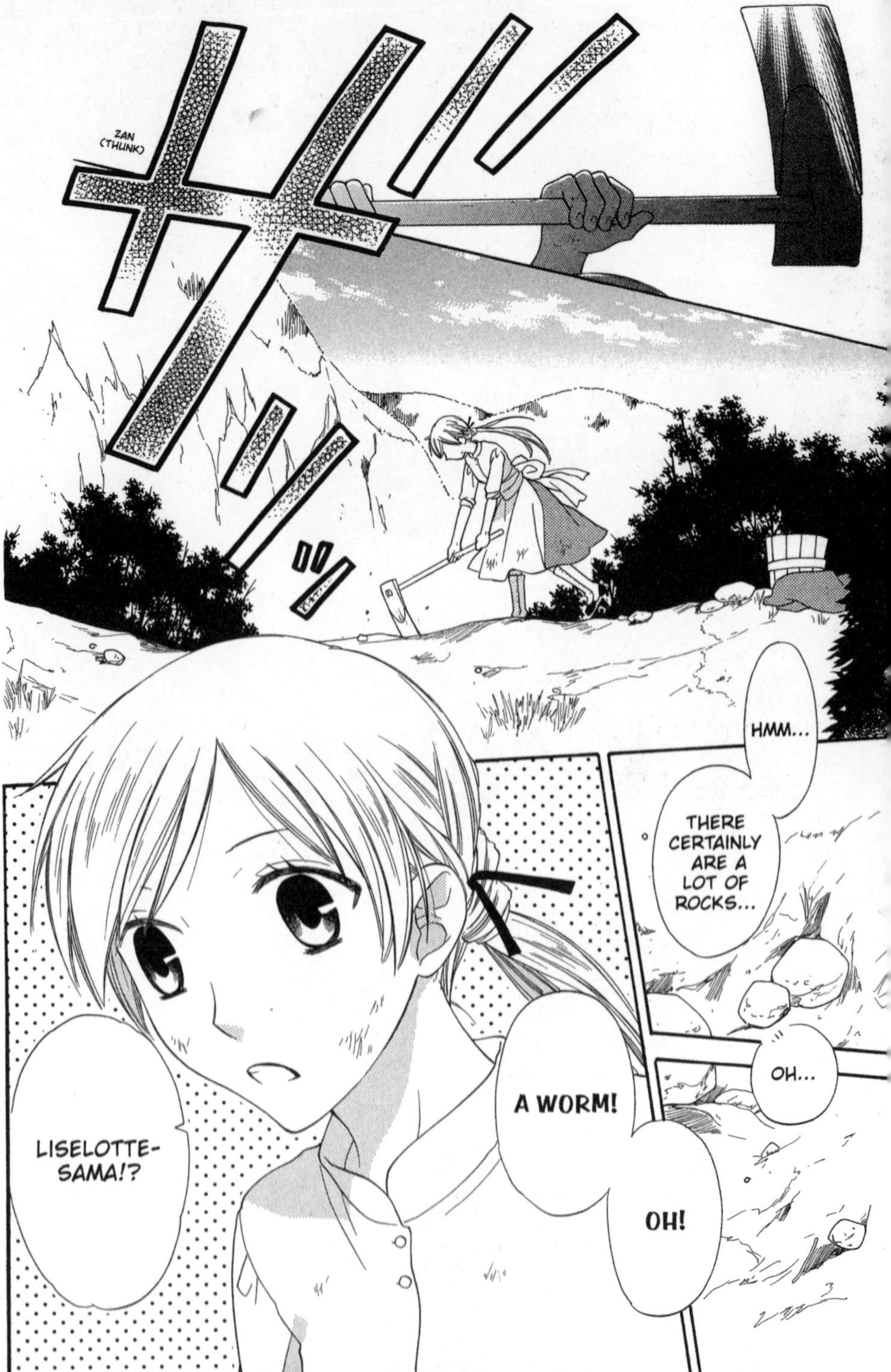
ZAN (THUNK)
HMM...
THERE CERTAINLY ARE A LOT OF ROCKS...
OH...
OH!
A WORM!
LISELOTTE-SAMA!?

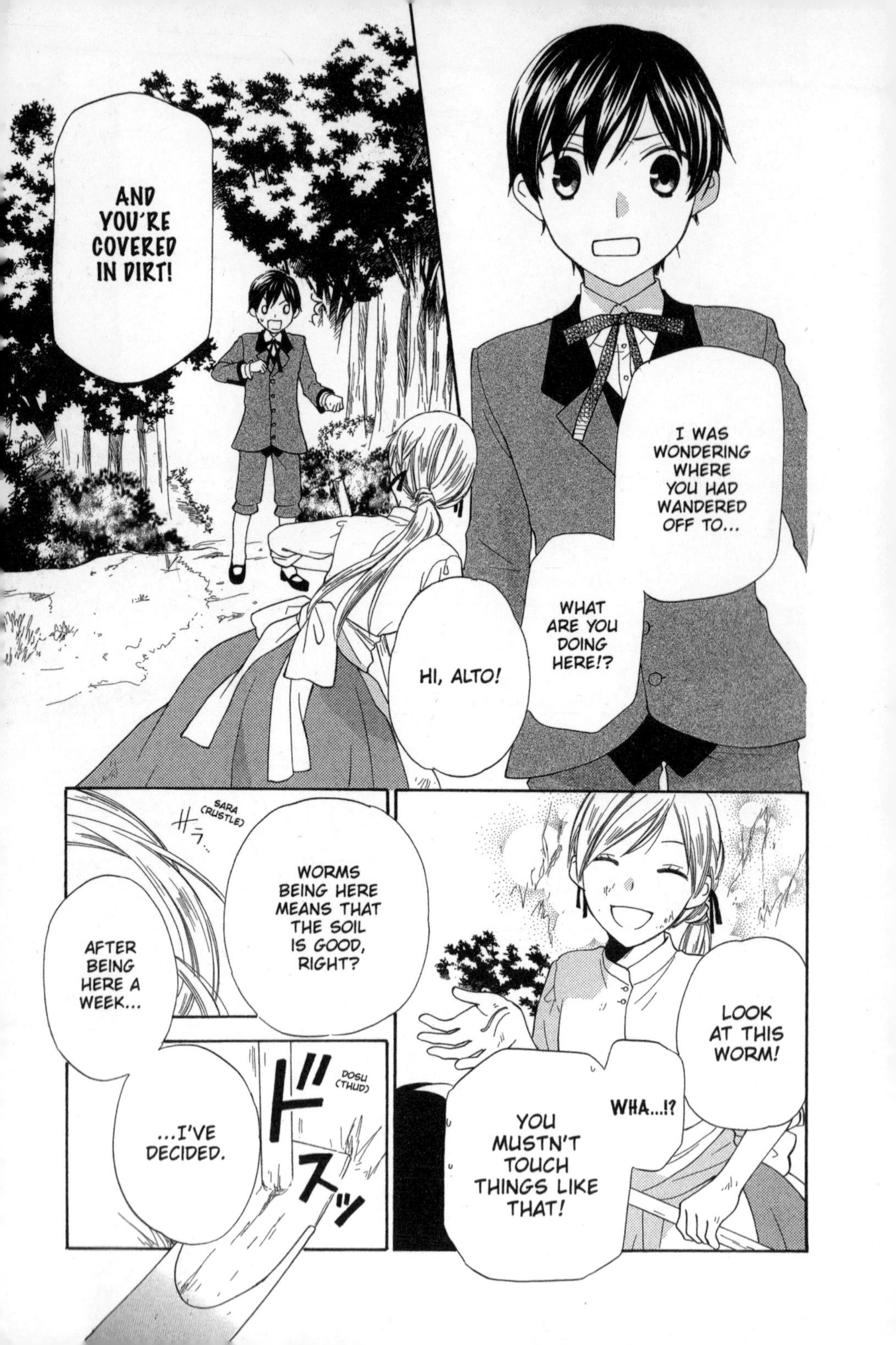
I WAS WONDERING WHERE YOU HAD WANDERED OFF TO...
WHAT ARE YOU DOING HERE!?
HI, ALTO!
AND YOU'RE COVERED IN DIRT!
LOOK AT THIS WORM!
WHA...!?
YOU MUSTN'T TOUCH THINGS LIKE THAT!
ザラ..
SARA (RUSTLE)
WORMS BEING HERE MEANS THAT THE SOIL IS GOOD, RIGHT?
AFTER BEING HERE A WEEK...
ドスッ
DOSU (THUD)
...I'VE DECIDED.

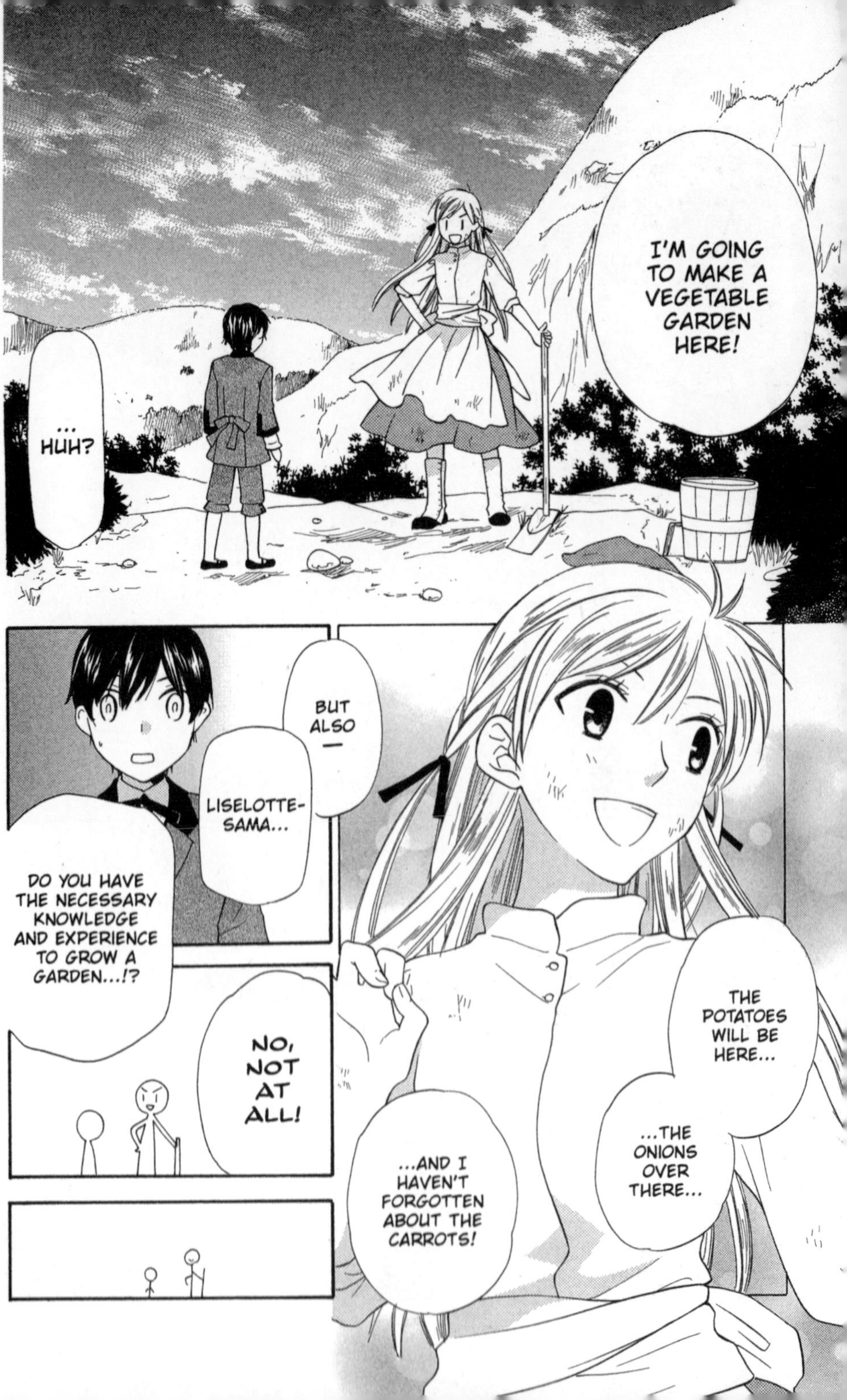
I'M GOING TO MAKE A VEGETABLE GARDEN HERE!
... HUH?
THE POTATOES WILL BE HERE...
...THE ONIONS OVER THERE...
...AND I HAVEN'T FORGOTTEN ABOUT THE CARROTS!
BUT ALSO—
LISELOTTE-SAMA...
DO YOU HAVE THE NECESSARY KNOWLEDGE AND EXPERIENCE TO GROW A GARDEN...!?
NO, NOT AT ALL!

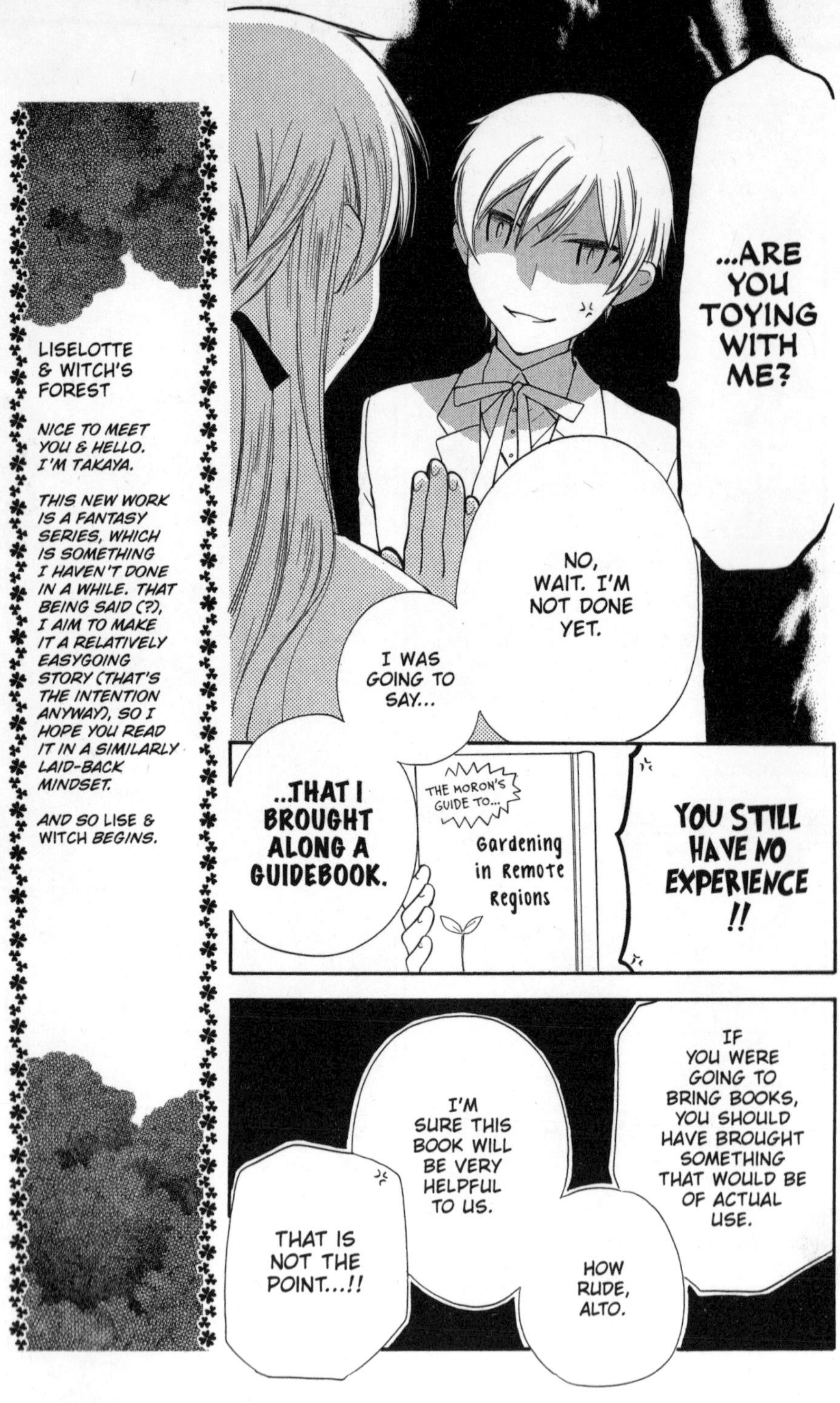
...ARE YOU TOYING WITH ME?
NO, WAIT. I'M NOT DONE YET.
I WAS GOING TO SAY...
...THAT I BROUGHT ALONG A GUIDEBOOK.
THE MORON'S GUIDE TO...
Gardening in Remote Regions
YOU STILL HAVE NO EXPERIENCE!!
IF YOU WERE GOING TO BRING BOOKS, YOU SHOULD HAVE BROUGHT SOMETHING THAT WOULD BE OF ACTUAL USE.
I'M SURE THIS BOOK WILL BE VERY HELPFUL TO US.
HOW RUDE, ALTO.
THAT IS NOT THE POINT...!!

LISELOTTE & WITCH'S FOREST

NICE TO MEET YOU & HELLO. I'M TAKAYA.

THIS NEW WORK IS A FANTASY SERIES, WHICH IS SOMETHING I HAVEN'T DONE IN A WHILE. THAT BEING SAID (?), I AIM TO MAKE IT A RELATIVELY EASYGOING STORY (THAT'S THE INTENTION ANYWAY), SO I HOPE YOU READ IT IN A SIMILARLY LAID-BACK MINDSET.

AND SO LISE & WITCH BEGINS.

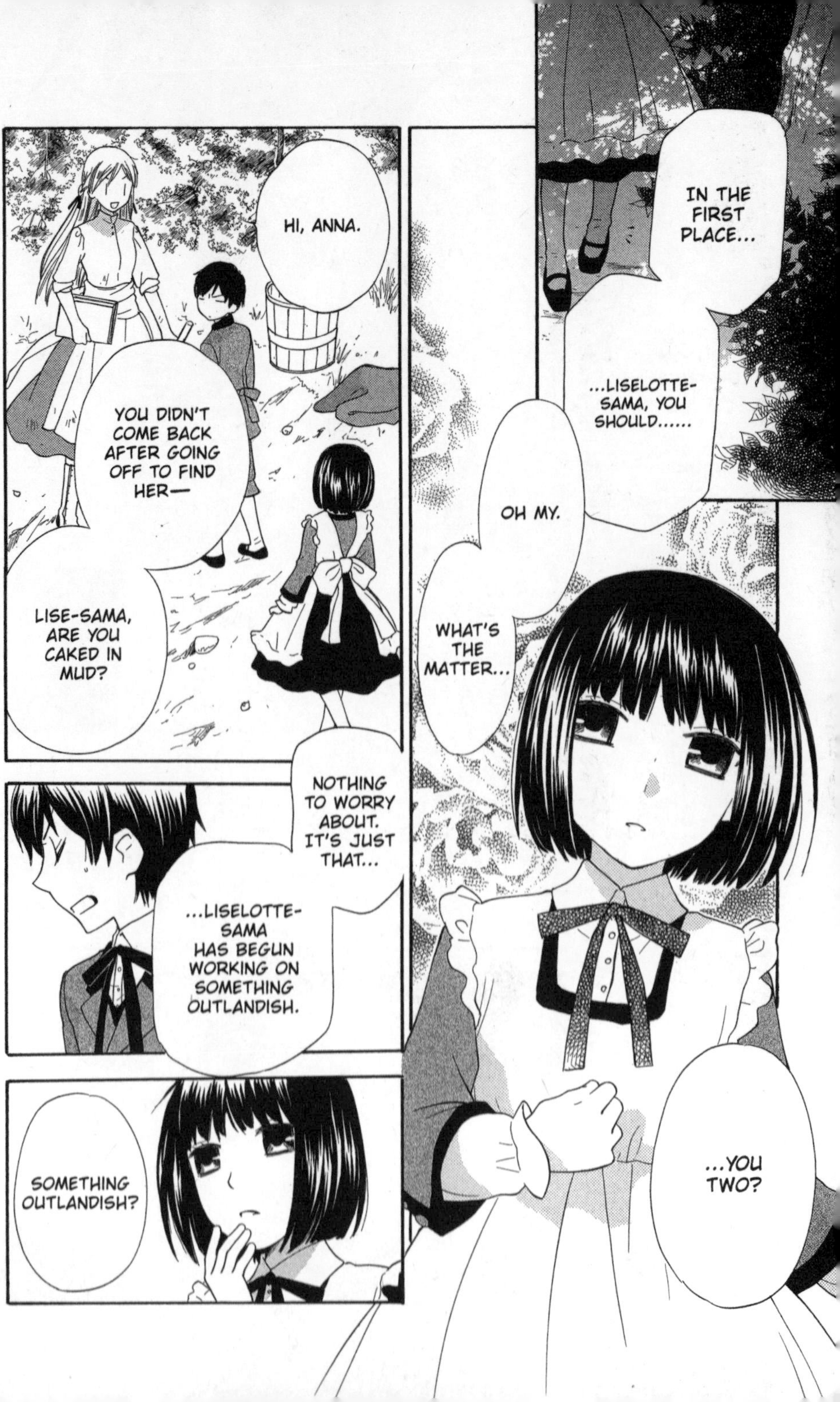
IN THE FIRST PLACE...
...LISELOTTE-SAMA, YOU SHOULD......
OH MY.
WHAT'S THE MATTER...
...YOU TWO?
HI, ANNA.
YOU DIDN'T COME BACK AFTER GOING OFF TO FIND HER—
LISE-SAMA, ARE YOU CAKED IN MUD?
NOTHING TO WORRY ABOUT. IT'S JUST THAT...
...LISELOTTE-SAMA HAS BEGUN WORKING ON SOMETHING OUTLANDISH.
SOMETHING OUTLANDISH?

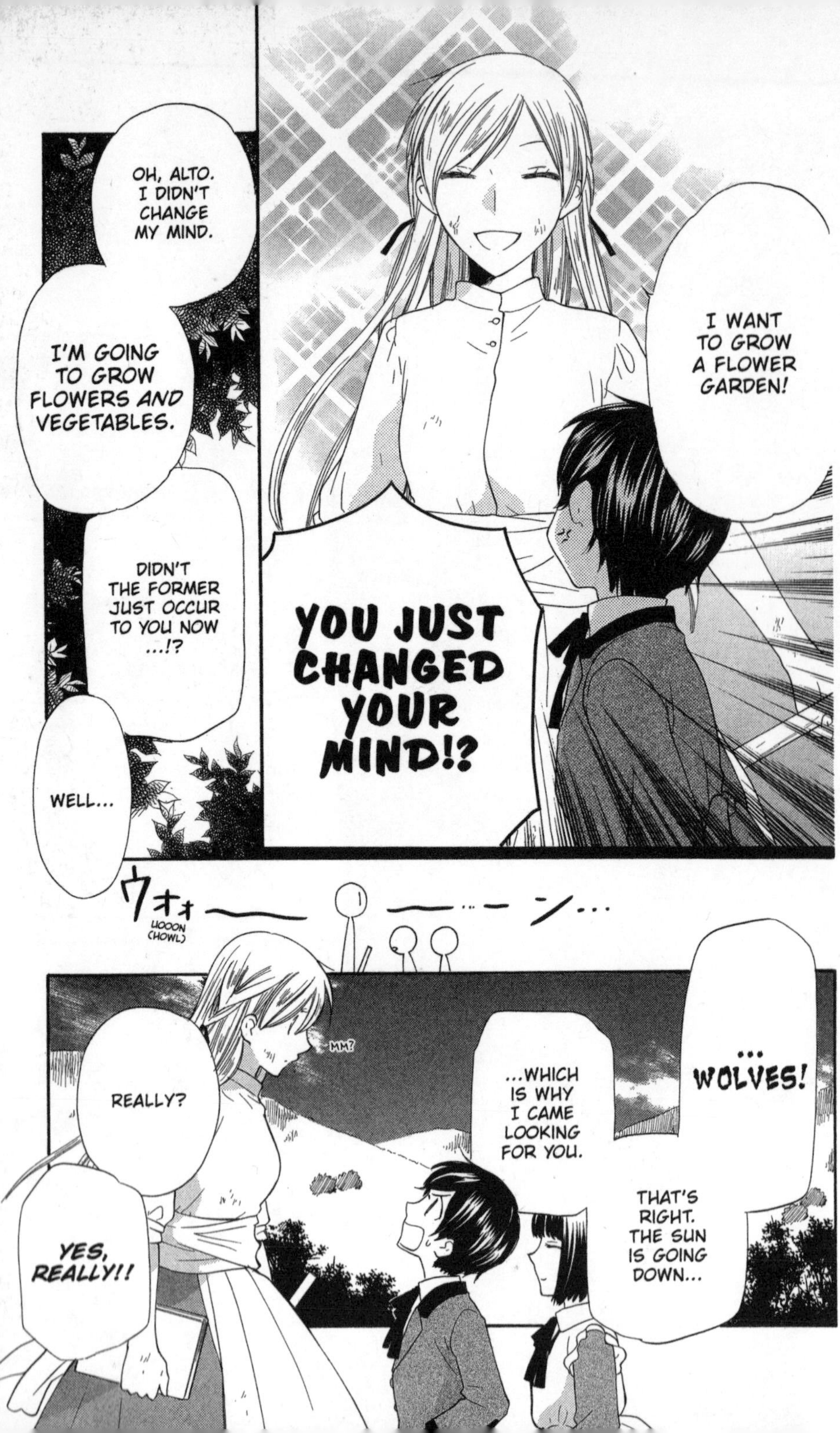
I WANT TO GROW A FLOWER GARDEN!
YOU JUST CHANGED YOUR MIND!?
OH, ALTO. I DIDN'T CHANGE MY MIND.
I'M GOING TO GROW FLOWERS AND VEGETABLES.
DIDN'T THE FORMER JUST OCCUR TO YOU NOW ...!?
WELL...
ウオォー…ン…
UOOON (HOWL)
...WOLVES!
...WHICH IS WHY I CAME LOOKING FOR YOU.
THAT'S RIGHT. THE SUN IS GOING DOWN...
MM?
REALLY?
YES, REALLY!!

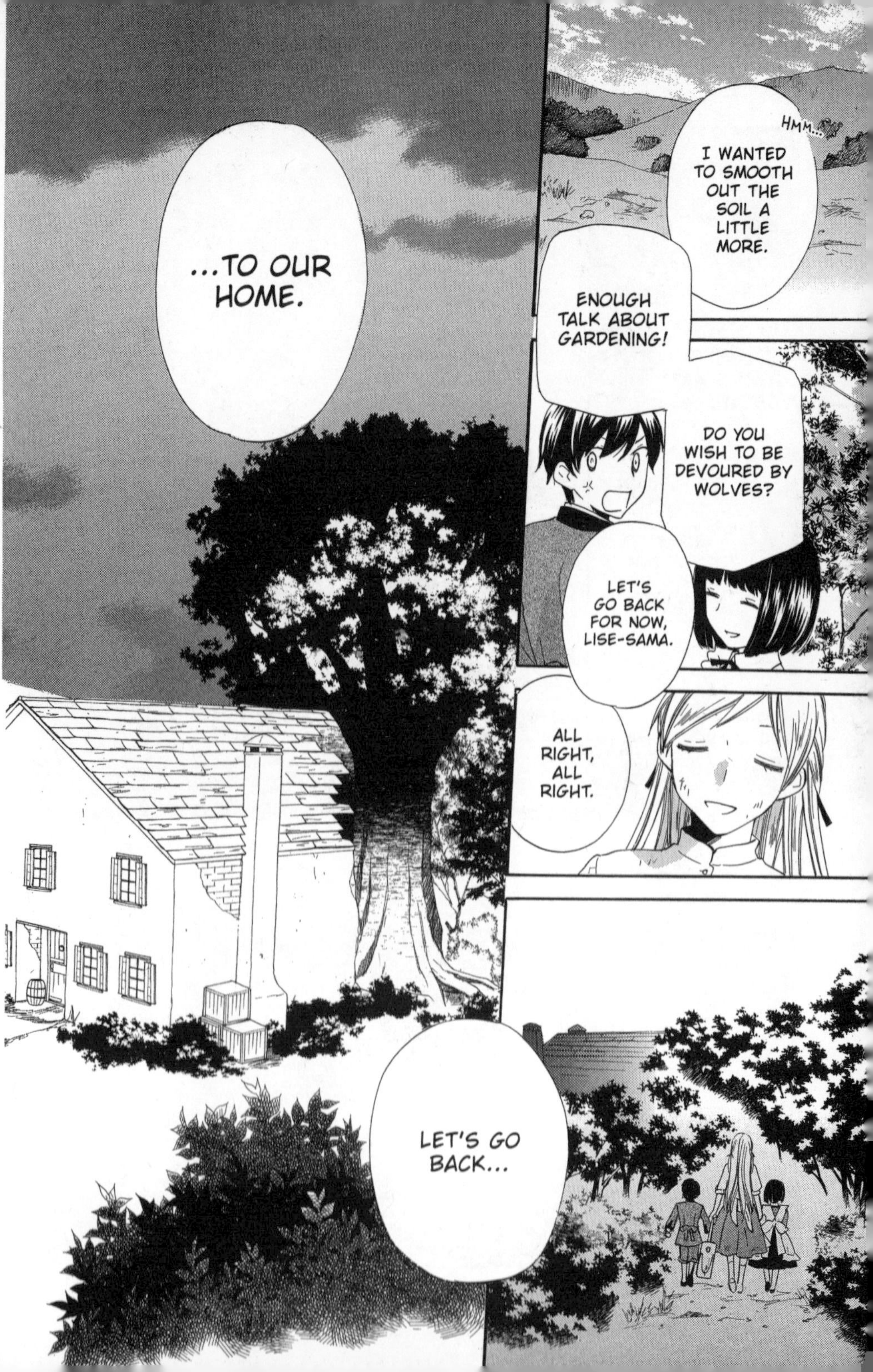
HMM...
I WANTED TO SMOOTH OUT THE SOIL A LITTLE MORE.
ENOUGH TALK ABOUT GARDENING!
DO YOU WISH TO BE DEVOURED BY WOLVES?
LET'S GO BACK FOR NOW, LISE-SAMA.
ALL RIGHT, ALL RIGHT.
LET'S GO BACK...
...TO OUR HOME.

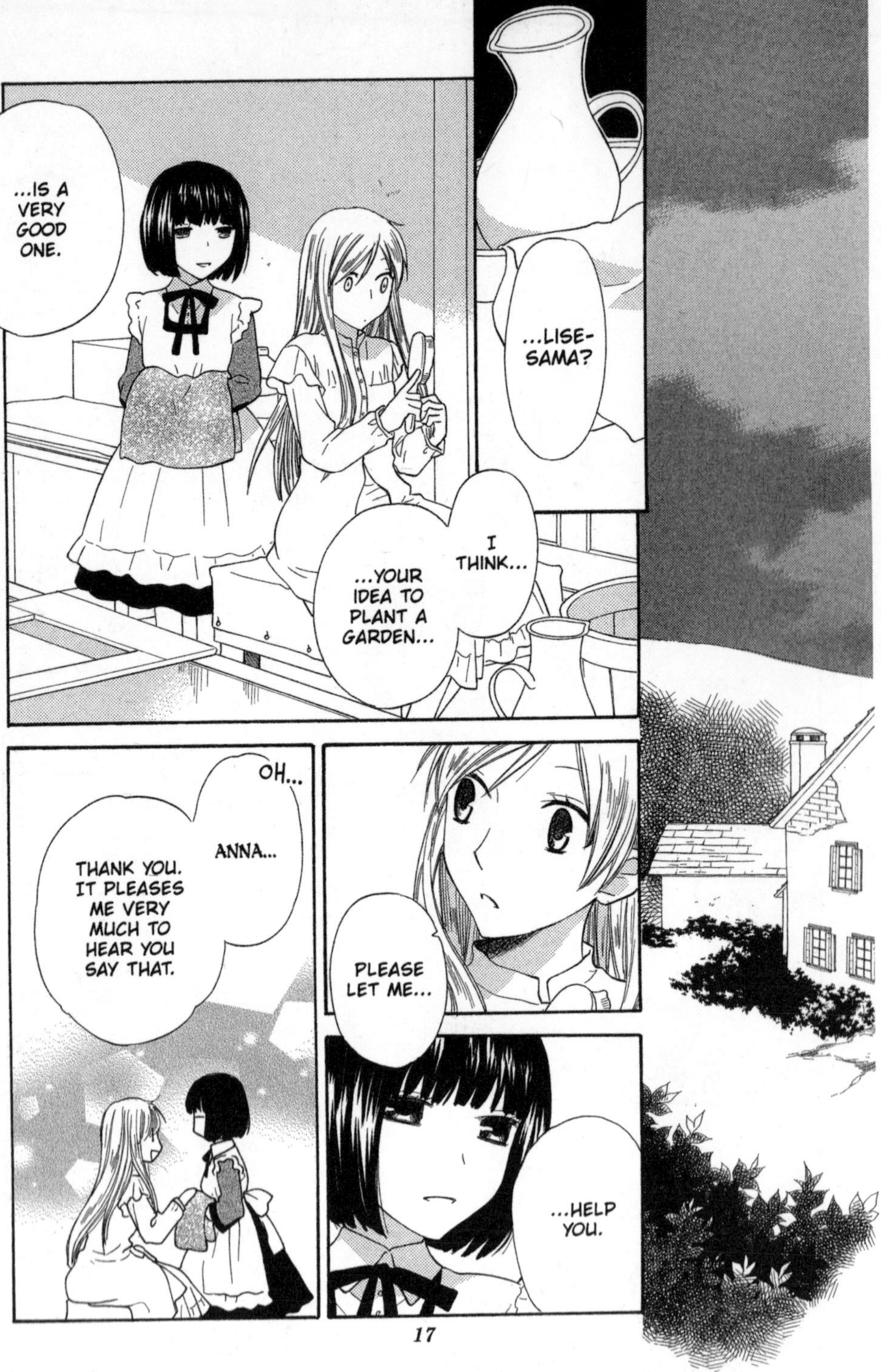
...LISE-SAMA?
I THINK...
...YOUR IDEA TO PLANT A GARDEN...
...IS A VERY GOOD ONE.
PLEASE LET ME...
...HELP YOU.
OH...
ANNA...
THANK YOU. IT PLEASES ME VERY MUCH TO HEAR YOU SAY THAT.

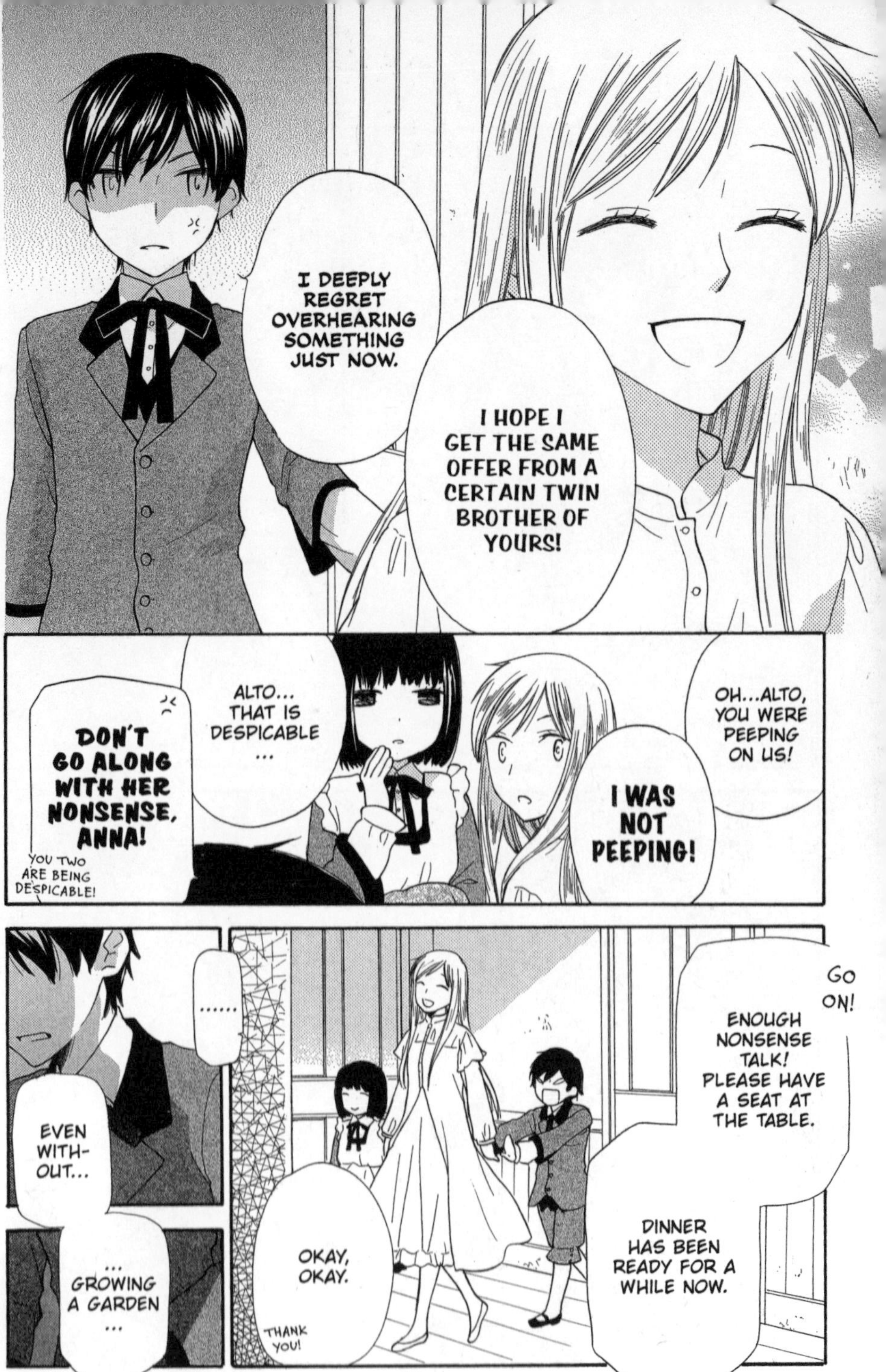
I DEEPLY REGRET OVERHEARING SOMETHING JUST NOW.
I HOPE I GET THE SAME OFFER FROM A CERTAIN TWIN BROTHER OF YOURS!
OH...ALTO, YOU WERE PEEPING ON US!
I WAS NOT PEEPING!
ALTO... THAT IS DESPICABLE ...
DON'T GO ALONG WITH HER NONSENSE, ANNA!
YOU TWO ARE BEING DESPICABLE!
GO ON!
ENOUGH NONSENSE TALK! PLEASE HAVE A SEAT AT THE TABLE.
DINNER HAS BEEN READY FOR A WHILE NOW.
OKAY, OKAY.
THANK YOU!
....
EVEN WITH-OUT...
... GROWING A GARDEN ...

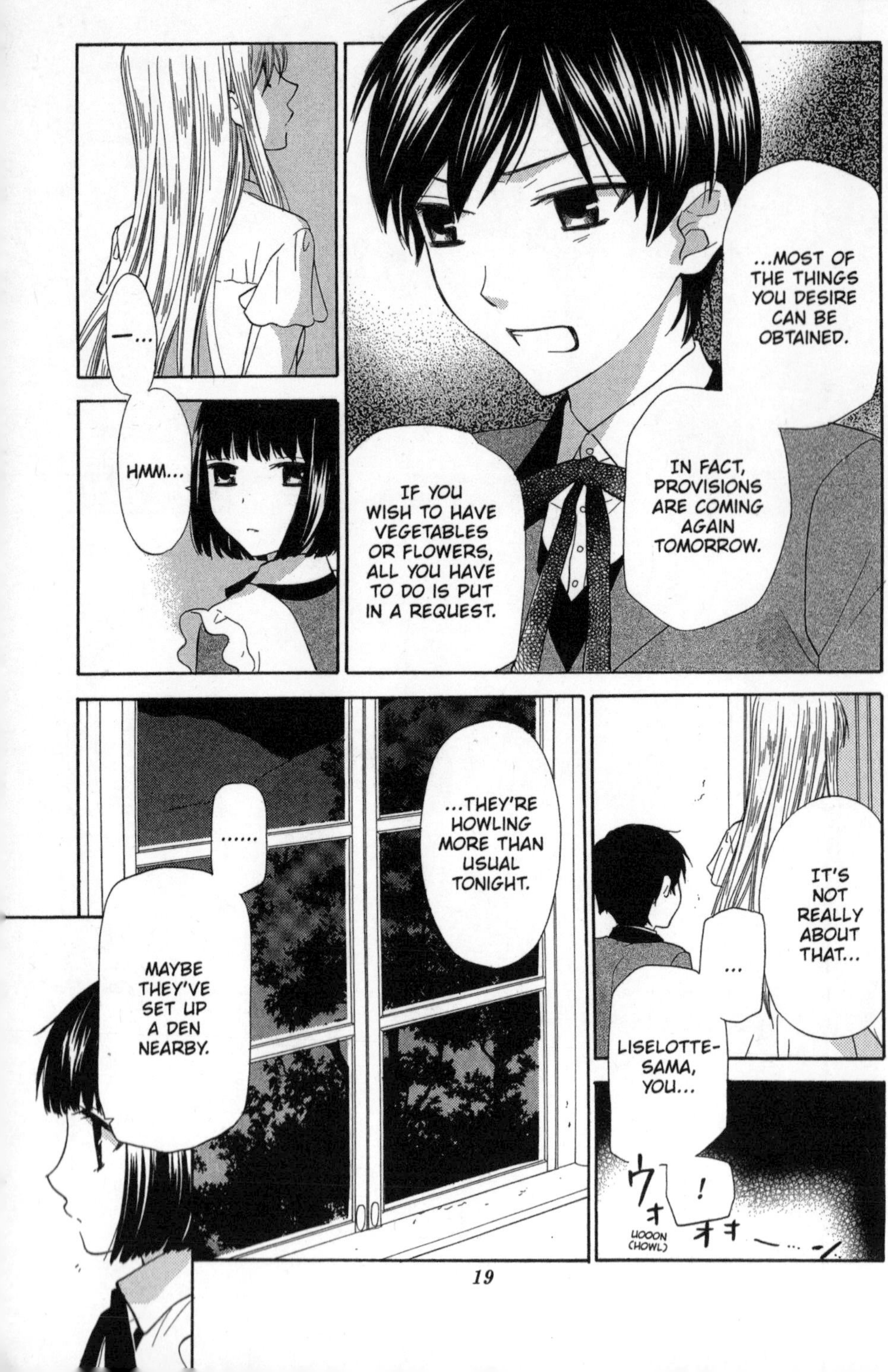
...MOST OF THE THINGS YOU DESIRE CAN BE OBTAINED.
IN FACT, PROVISIONS ARE COMING AGAIN TOMORROW.
IF YOU WISH TO HAVE VEGETABLES OR FLOWERS, ALL YOU HAVE TO DO IS PUT IN A REQUEST.
—...
HMM...
IT'S NOT REALLY ABOUT THAT...
...
LISELOTTE-SAMA, YOU...
UOOON (HOWL)
...THEY'RE HOWLING MORE THAN USUAL TONIGHT.
......
MAYBE THEY'VE SET UP A DEN NEARBY.

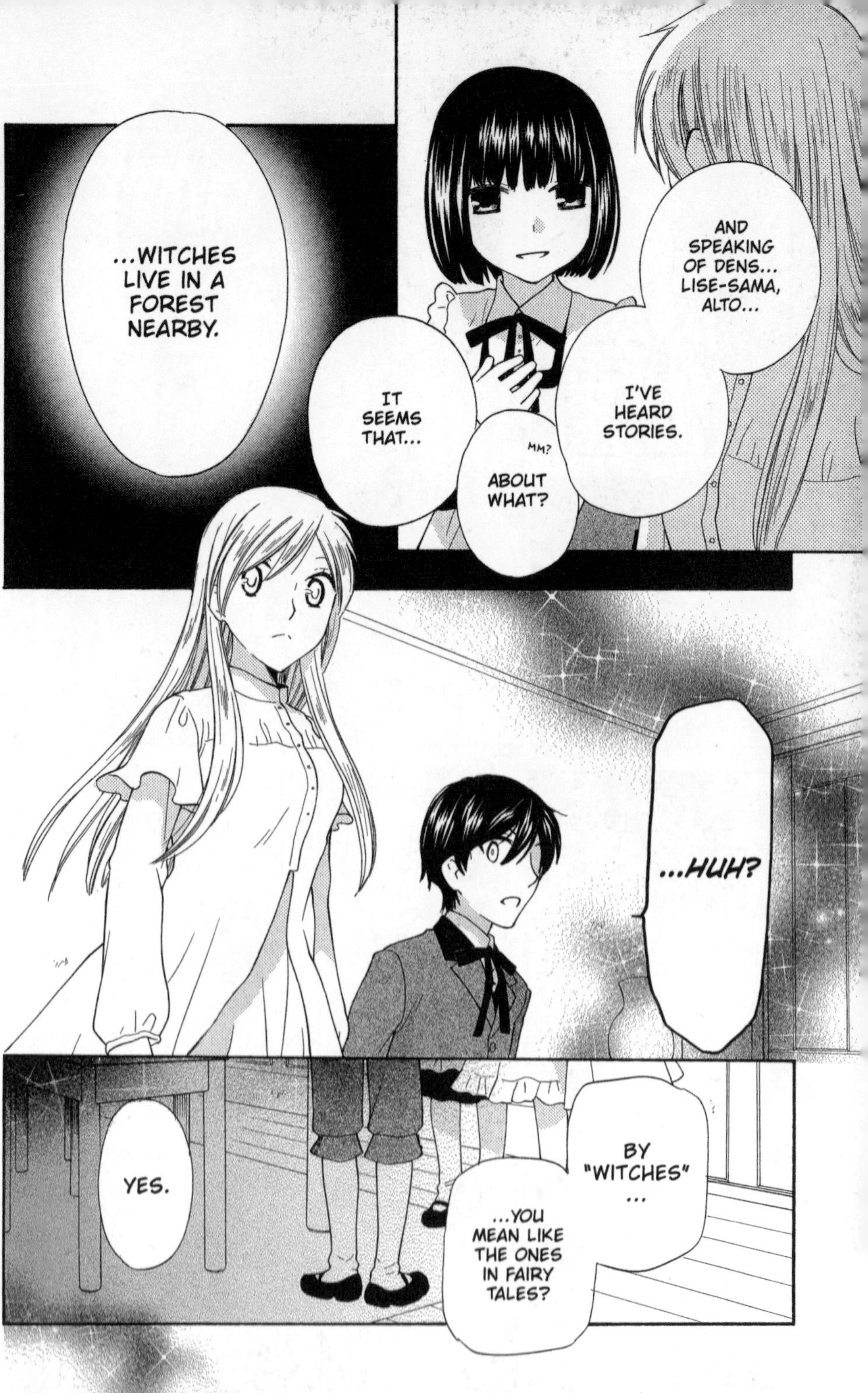
AND SPEAKING OF DENS... LISE-SAMA, ALTO...
I'VE HEARD STORIES.
MM?
ABOUT WHAT?
IT SEEMS THAT...
...WITCHES LIVE IN A FOREST NEARBY.
...HUH?
BY "WITCHES"...
...YOU MEAN LIKE THE ONES IN FAIRY TALES?
YES.

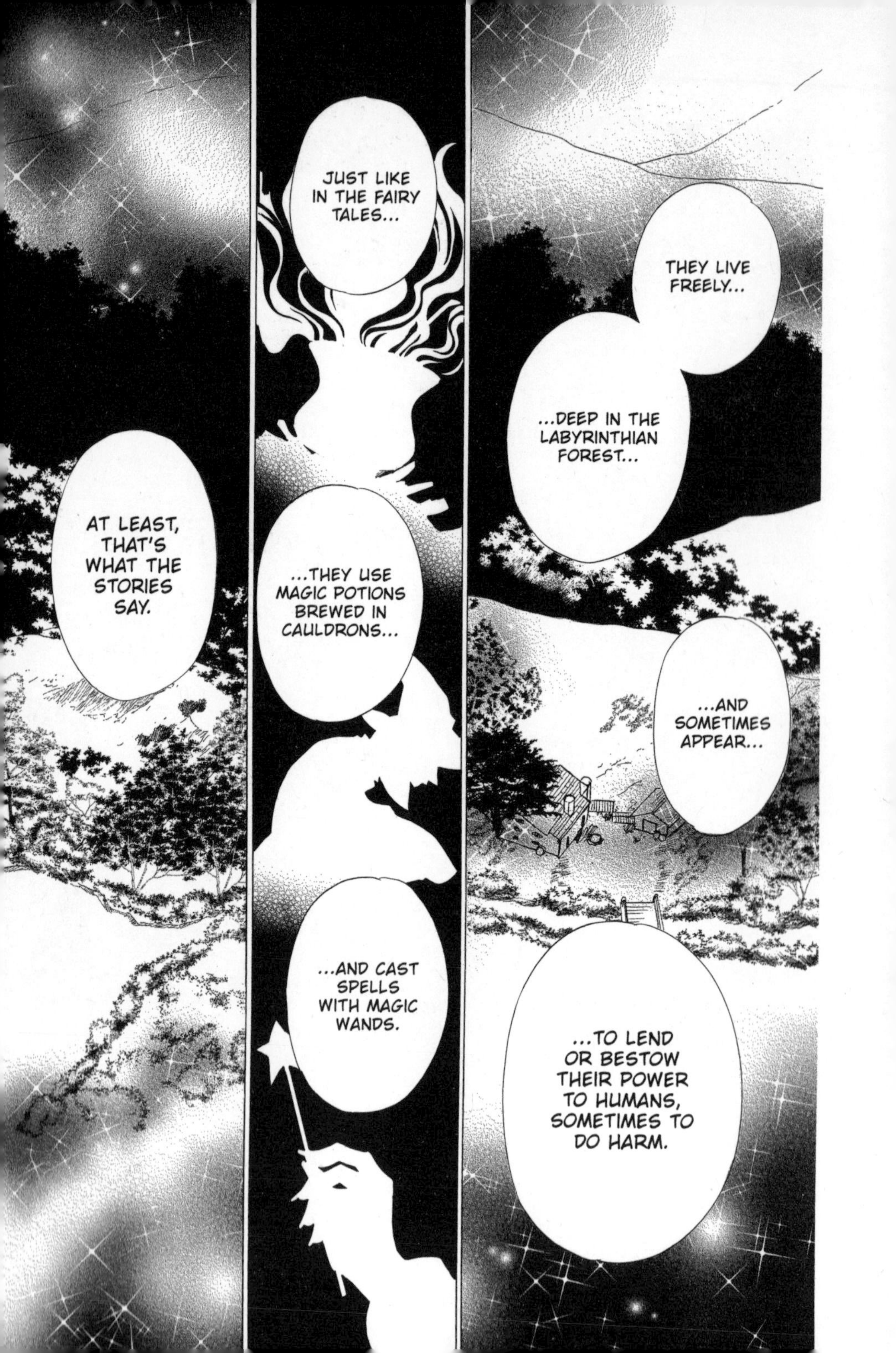
THEY LIVE FREELY...
...DEEP IN THE LABYRINTHIAN FOREST...
...AND SOMETIMES APPEAR...
...TO LEND OR BESTOW THEIR POWER TO HUMANS, SOMETIMES TO DO HARM.
JUST LIKE IN THE FAIRY TALES...
...THEY USE MAGIC POTIONS BREWED IN CAULDRONS...
...AND CAST SPELLS WITH MAGIC WANDS.
AT LEAST, THAT'S WHAT THE STORIES SAY.

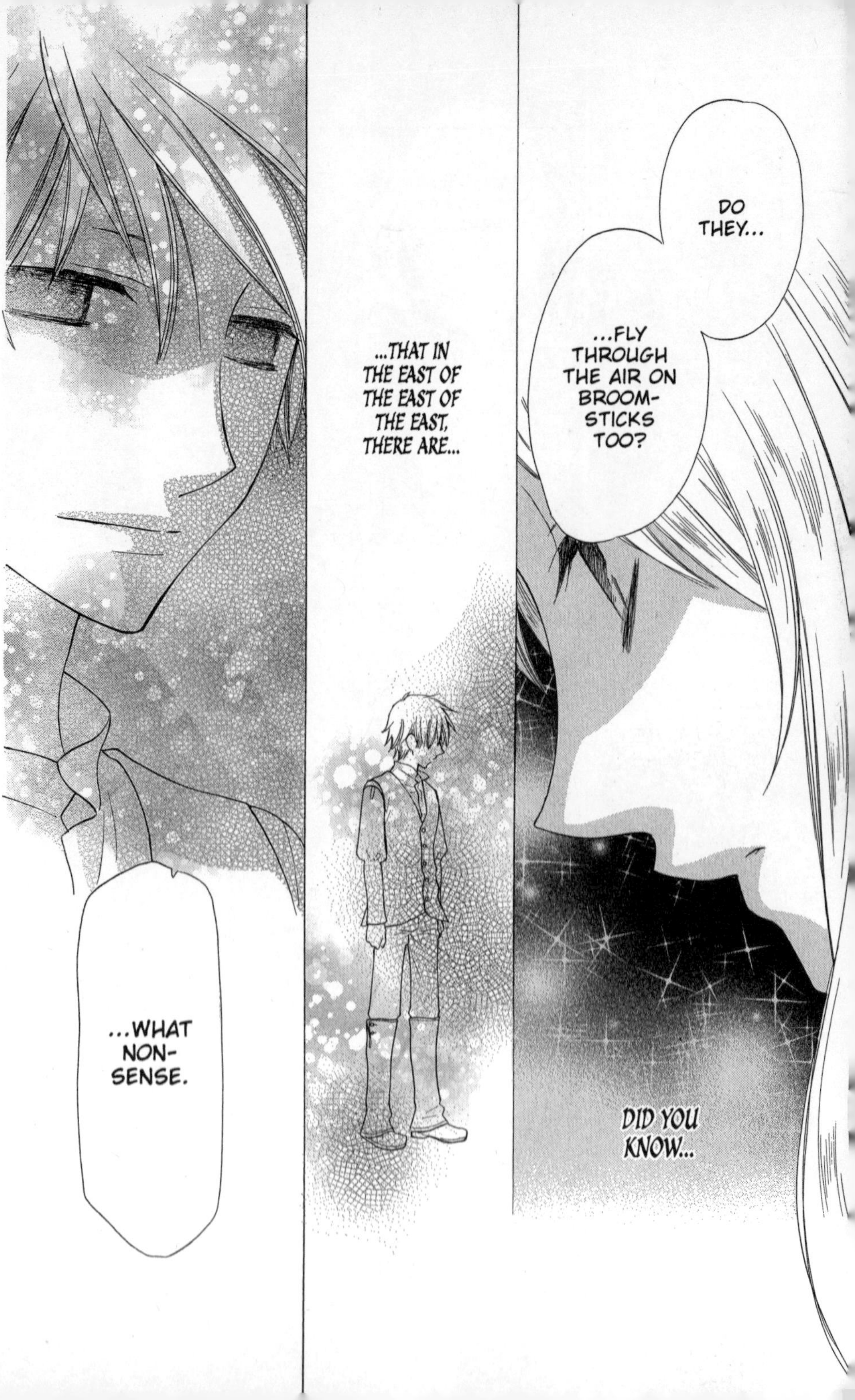
DID YOU KNOW...
DO THEY...
...FLY THROUGH THE AIR ON BROOM-STICKS TOO?
...THAT IN THE EAST OF THE EAST OF THE EAST, THERE ARE...
...WHAT NON-SENSE.

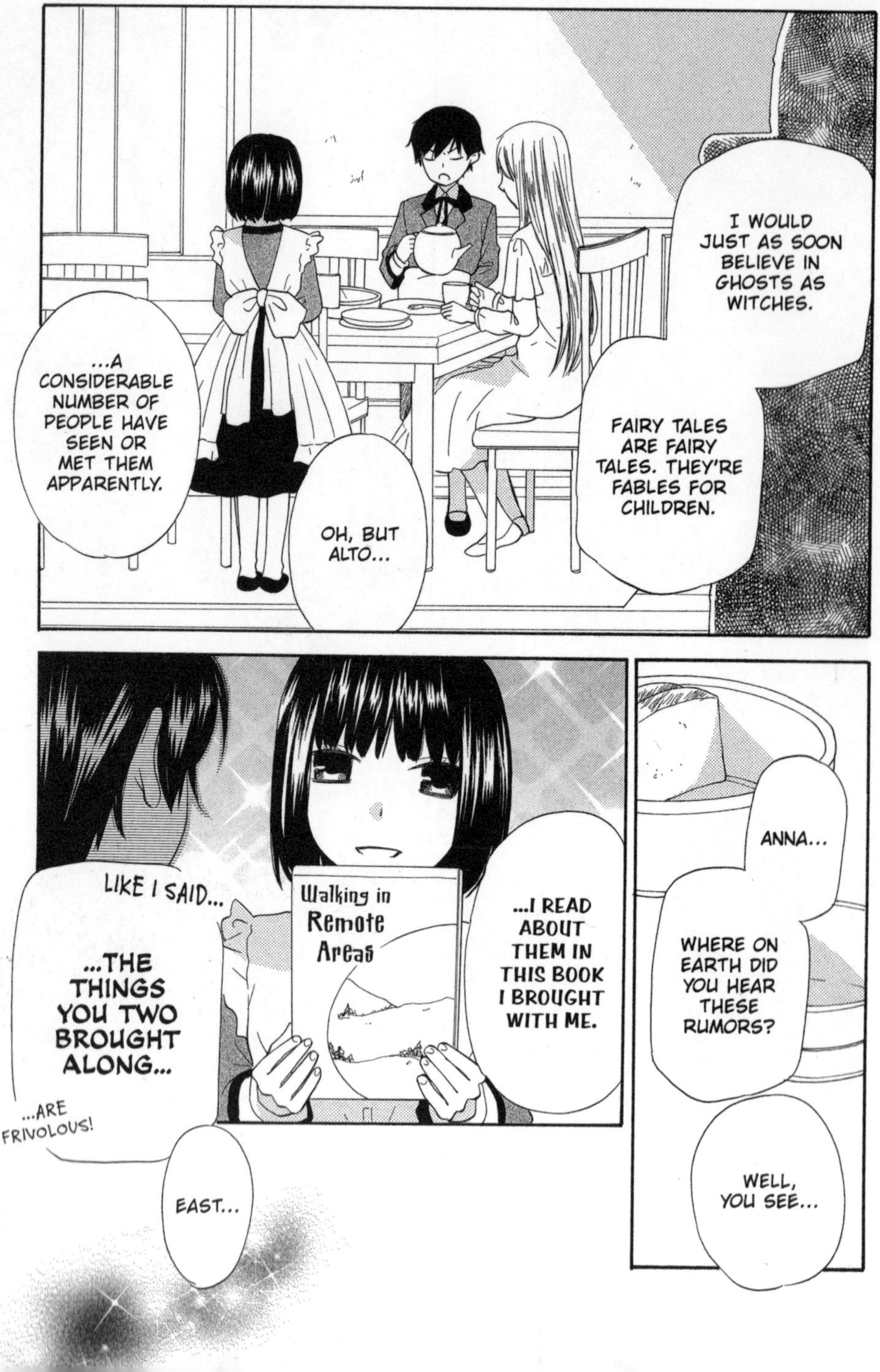
I WOULD JUST AS SOON BELIEVE IN GHOSTS AS WITCHES.
FAIRY TALES ARE FAIRY TALES. THEY'RE FABLES FOR CHILDREN.
OH, BUT ALTO...
...A CONSIDERABLE NUMBER OF PEOPLE HAVE SEEN OR MET THEM APPARENTLY.
ANNA...
WHERE ON EARTH DID YOU HEAR THESE RUMORS?
WELL, YOU SEE...
...I READ ABOUT THEM IN THIS BOOK I BROUGHT WITH ME.
Walking in Remote Areas
LIKE I SAID...
...THE THINGS YOU TWO BROUGHT ALONG...
...ARE FRIVOLOUS!
EAST...

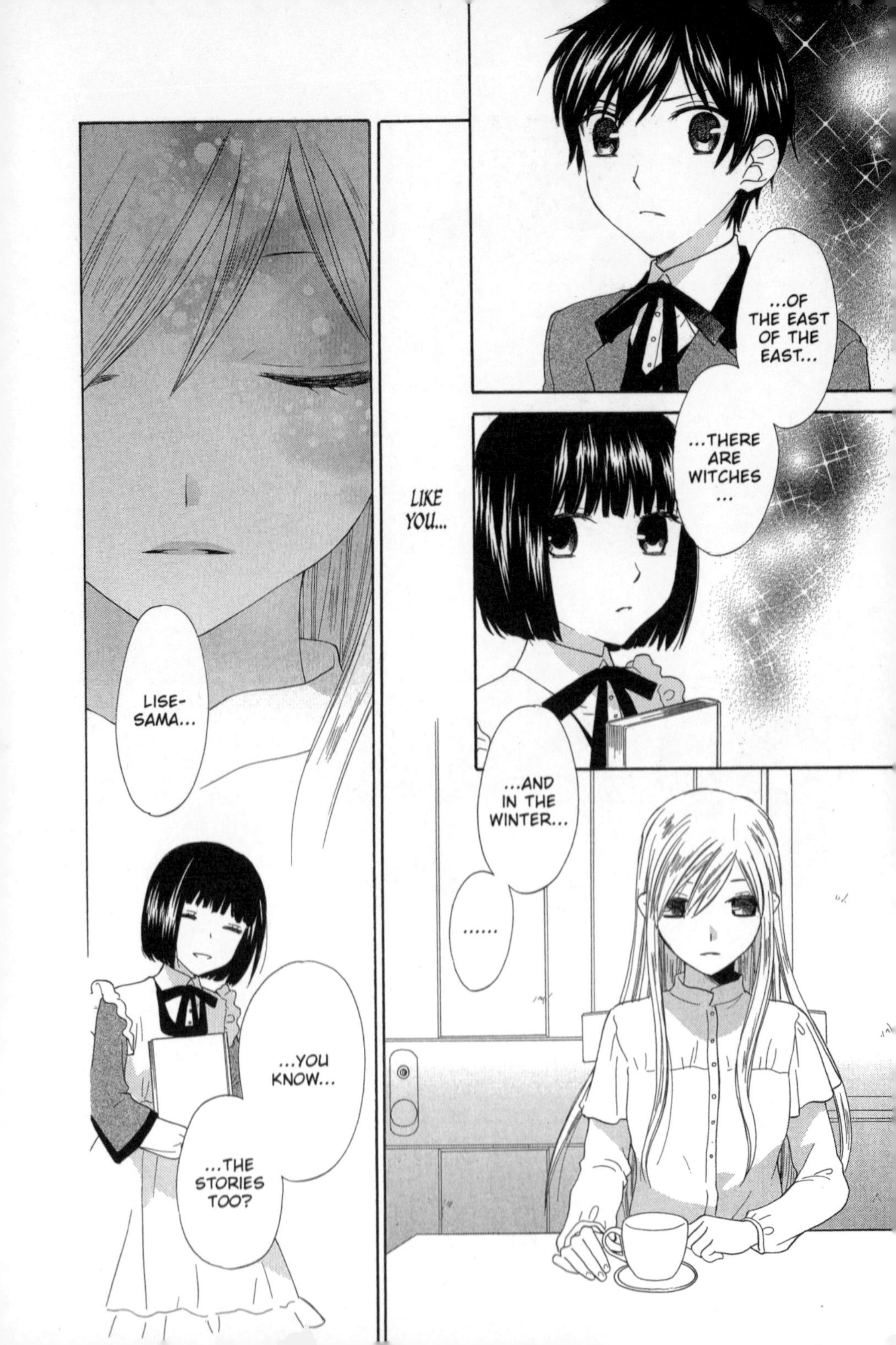
...OF THE EAST OF THE EAST...
...THERE ARE WITCHES...
LIKE YOU...
...AND IN THE WINTER...
......
LISE-SAMA...
...YOU KNOW...
...THE STORIES TOO?

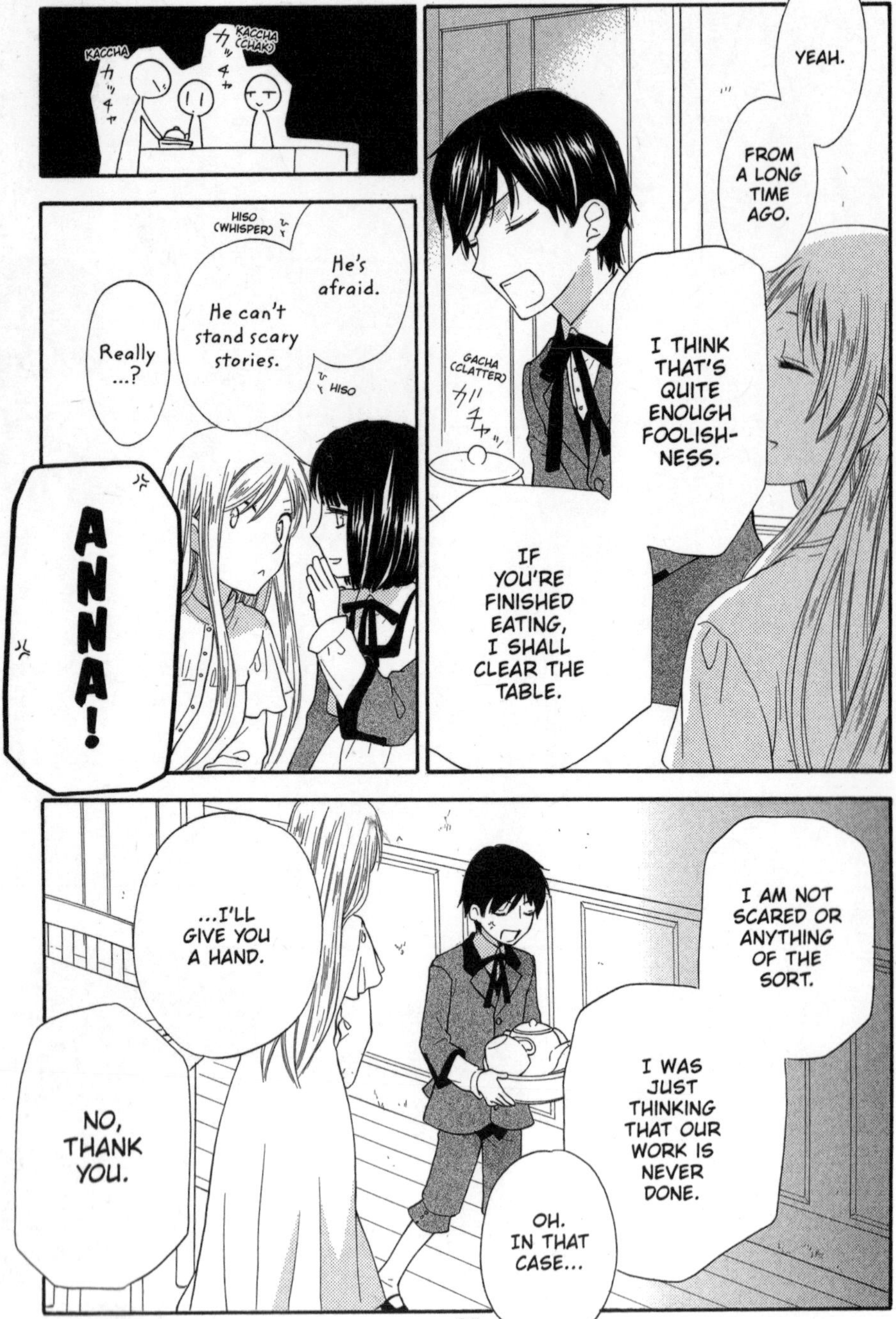
YEAH.
FROM A LONG TIME AGO.
I THINK THAT'S QUITE ENOUGH FOOLISHNESS.
GACHA (CLATTER)
IF YOU'RE FINISHED EATING, I SHALL CLEAR THE TABLE.
KACCHA (CHAK)
KACCHA
HISO (WHISPER)
He's afraid.
He can't stand scary stories.
HISO
Really ...?
ANNA!
I AM NOT SCARED OR ANYTHING OF THE SORT.
I WAS JUST THINKING THAT OUR WORK IS NEVER DONE.
OH. IN THAT CASE...
...I'LL GIVE YOU A HAND.
NO, THANK YOU.

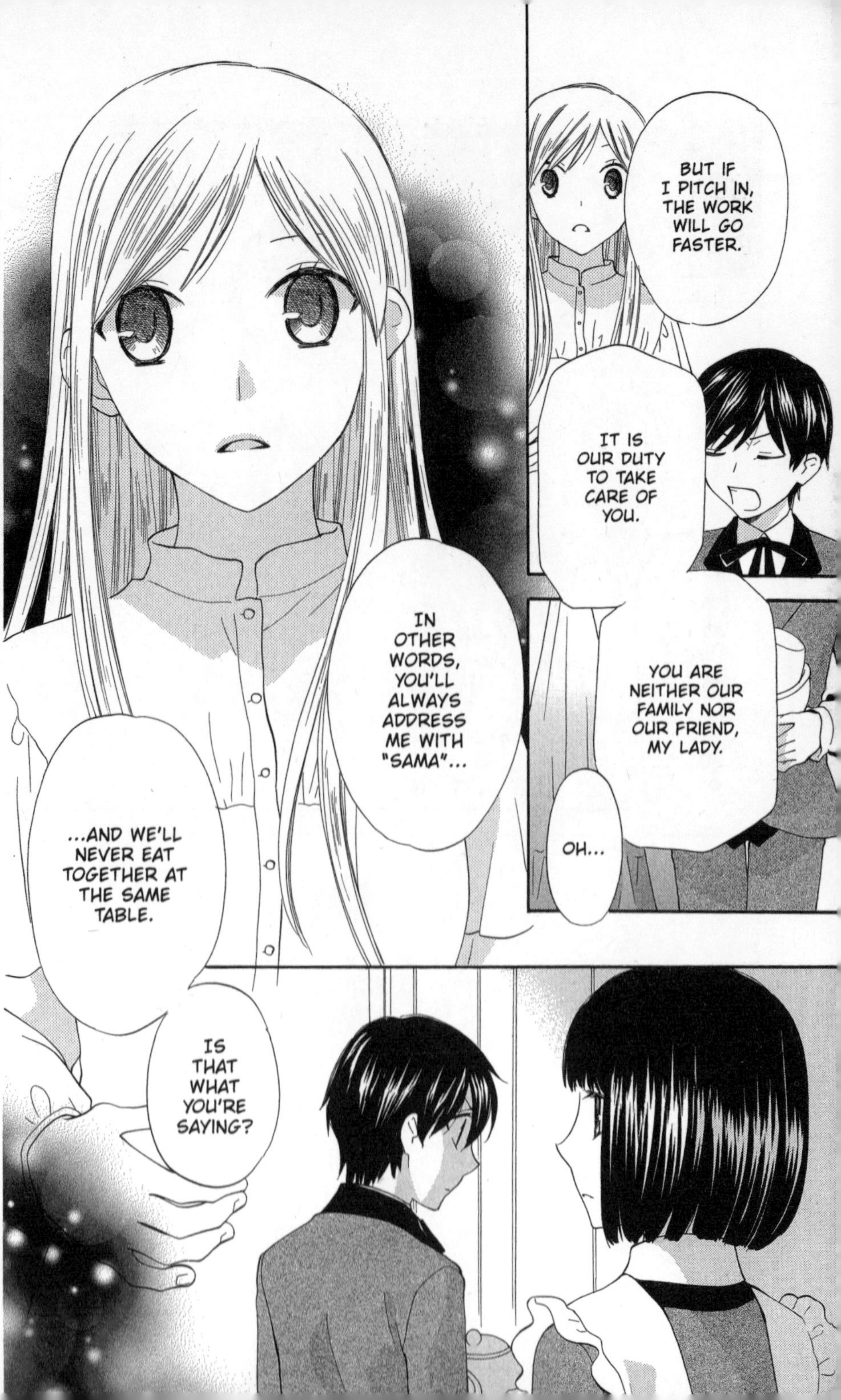
BUT IF I PITCH IN, THE WORK WILL GO FASTER.
IT IS OUR DUTY TO TAKE CARE OF YOU.
YOU ARE NEITHER OUR FAMILY NOR OUR FRIEND, MY LADY.
OH...
IN OTHER WORDS, YOU'LL ALWAYS ADDRESS ME WITH "SAMA"...
...AND WE'LL NEVER EAT TOGETHER AT THE SAME TABLE.
IS THAT WHAT YOU'RE SAYING?

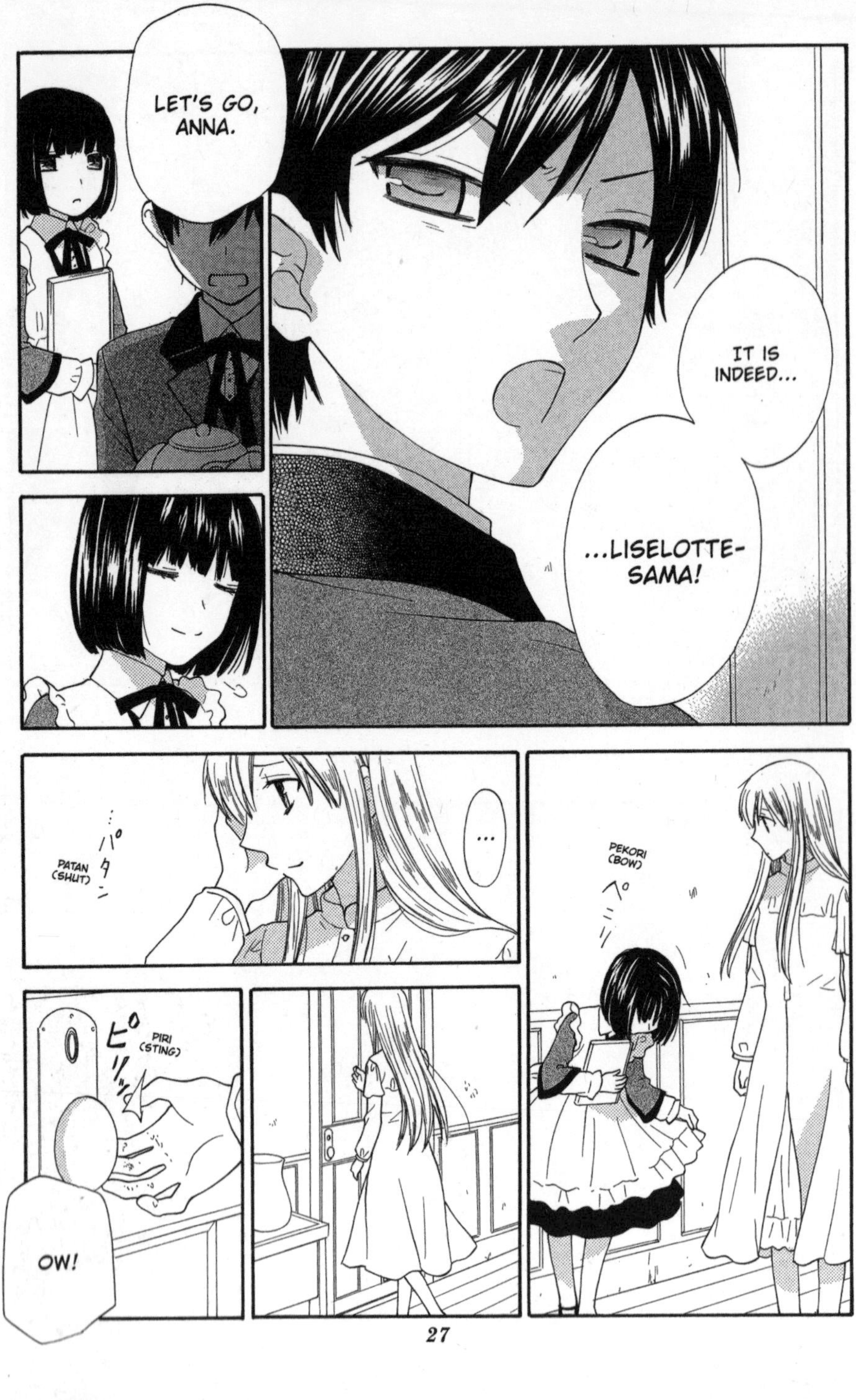
IT IS INDEED...
...LISELOTTE-SAMA!
LET'S GO, ANNA.
PEKORI (BOW)
ペこ
...
パタン
PATAN (SHUT)
ピリッ
PIRI (STING)
OW!

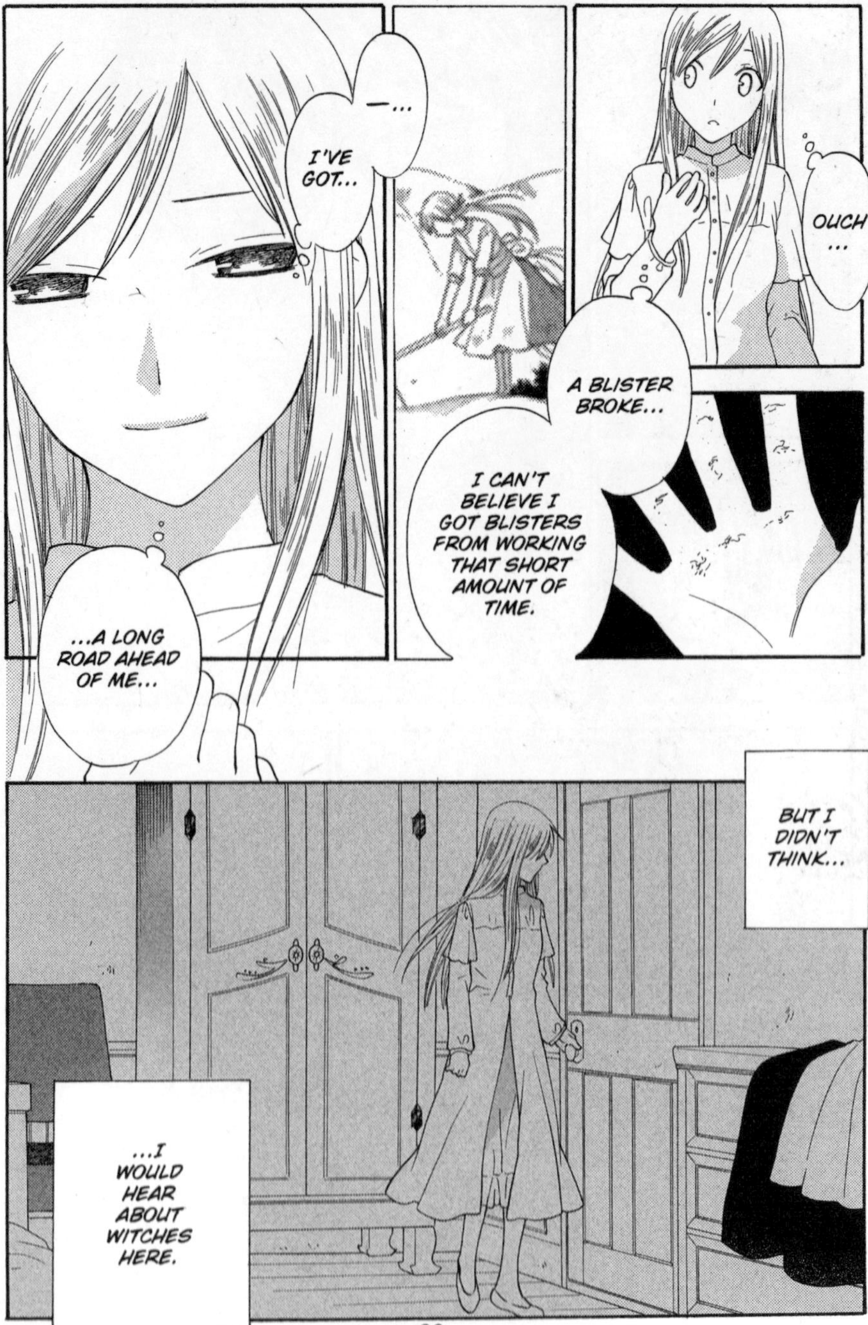
OUCH...
A BLISTER BROKE...
I CAN'T BELIEVE I GOT BLISTERS FROM WORKING THAT SHORT AMOUNT OF TIME.
—...
I'VE GOT...
...A LONG ROAD AHEAD OF ME...
BUT I DIDN'T THINK...
...I WOULD HEAR ABOUT WITCHES HERE.

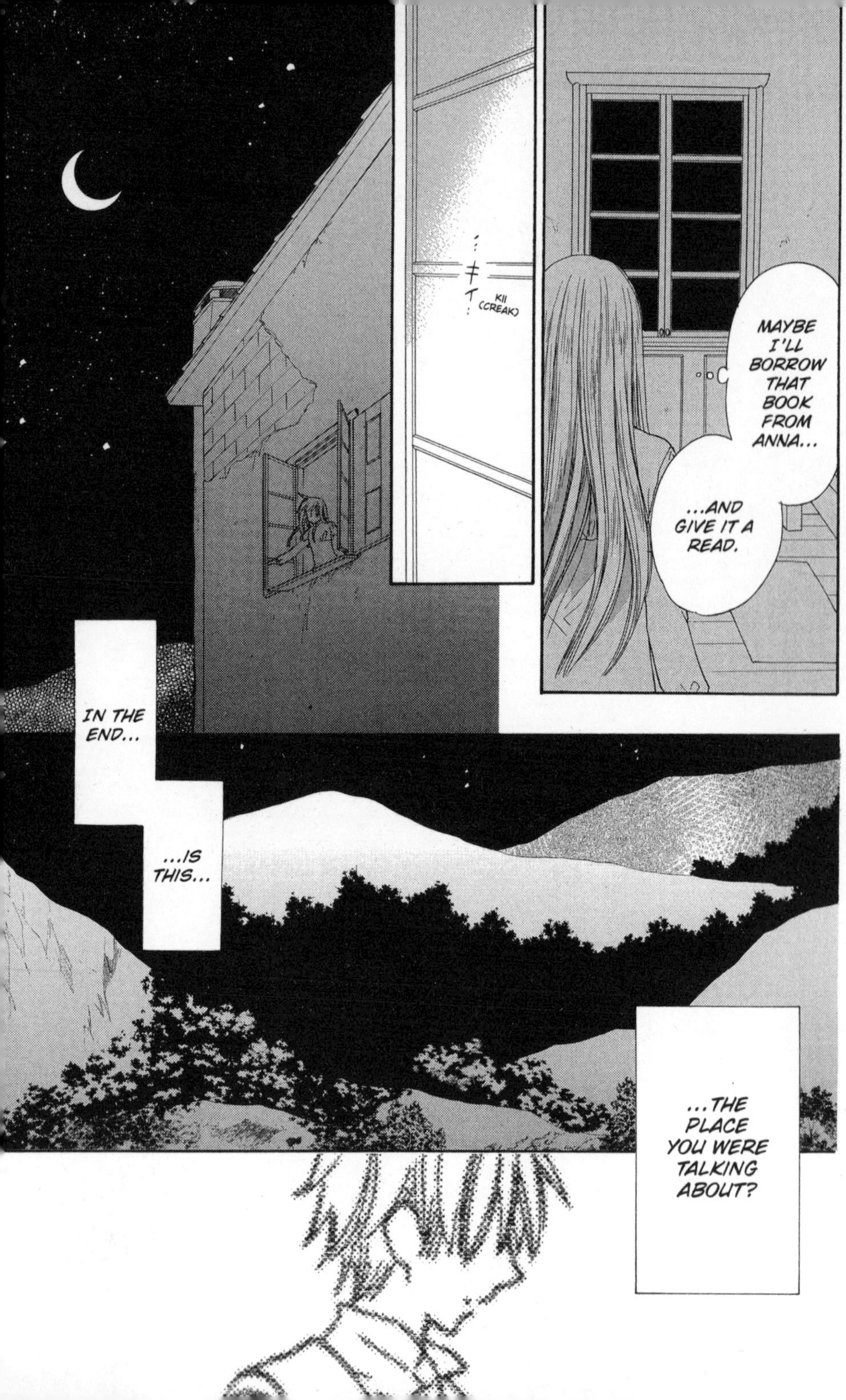
MAYBE I'LL BORROW THAT BOOK FROM ANNA...
...AND GIVE IT A READ.
KII (CREAK)
IN THE END...
...IS THIS...
...THE PLACE YOU WERE TALKING ABOUT?

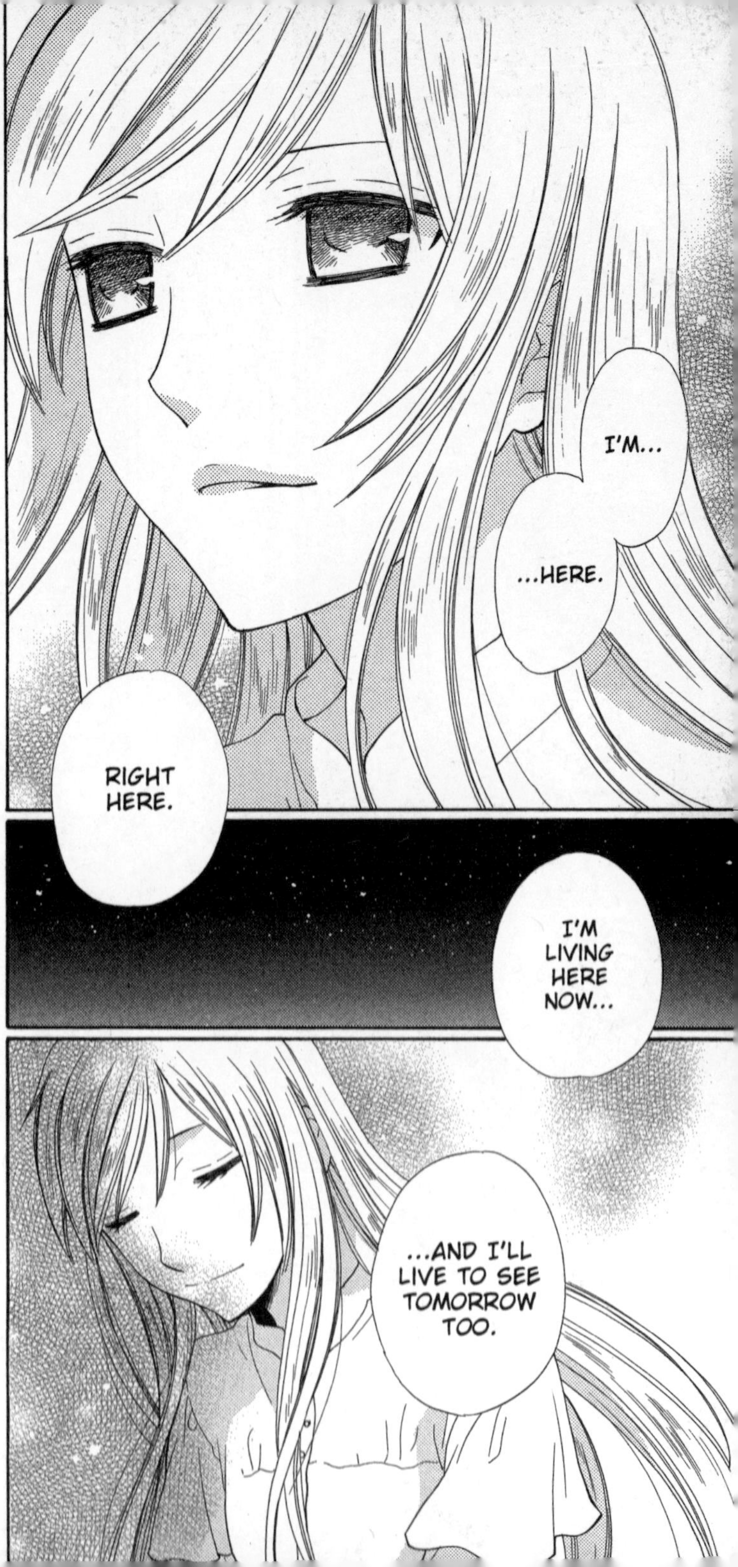
I'M...
...HERE.
RIGHT HERE.
I'M LIVING HERE NOW...
...AND I'LL LIVE TO SEE TOMORROW TOO.

HOW ABOUT YOU?

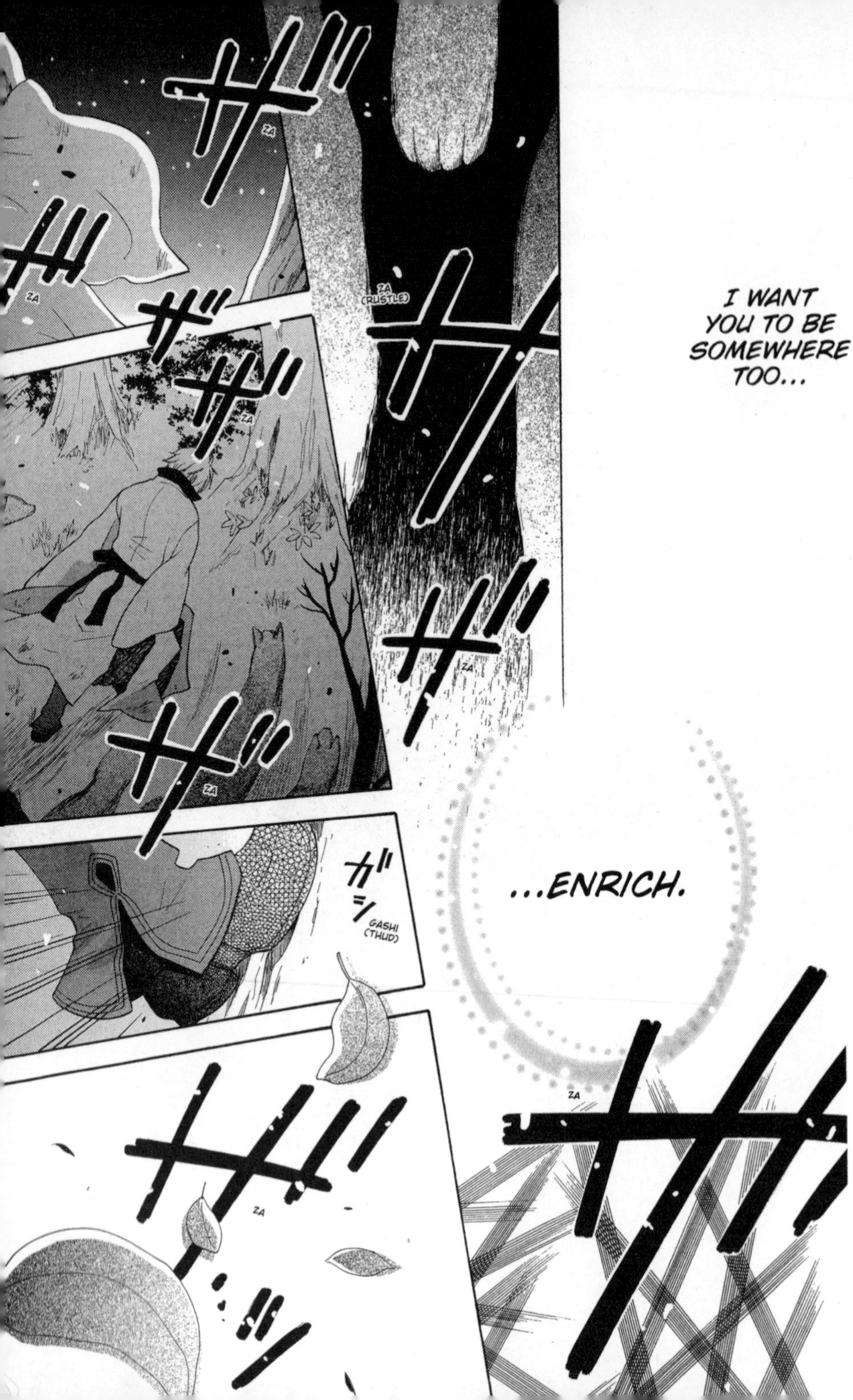
I WANT YOU TO BE SOMEWHERE TOO...
ZA (RUSTLE)
ZA
ZA
ZA
ZA
ZA
ZA
ZA
ガシ GASHI (THUD)
...ENRICH.
ZA
ZA

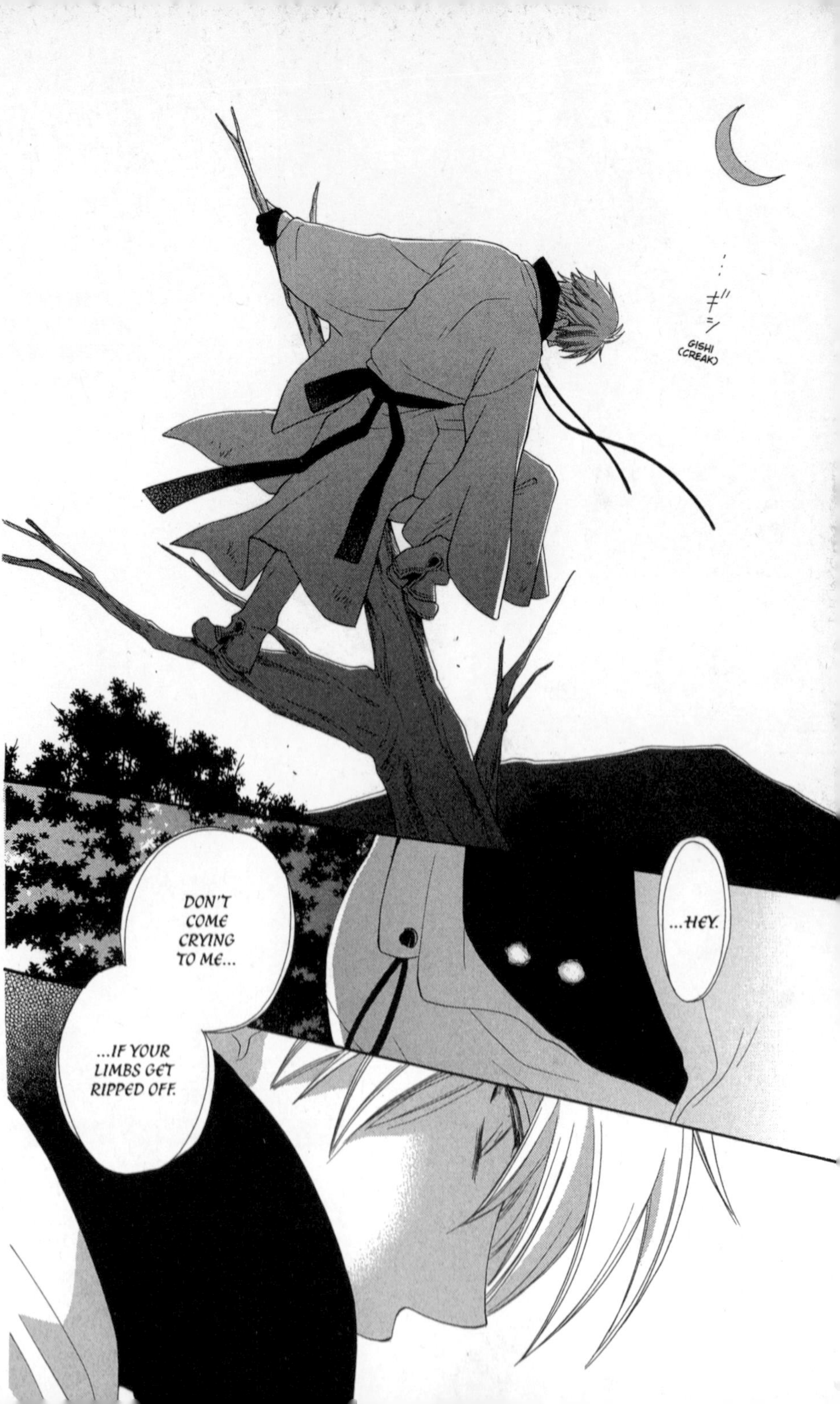

...ギシ
GISHI (CREAK)
...HEY.
DON'T COME CRYING TO ME...
...IF YOUR LIMBS GET RIPPED OFF.

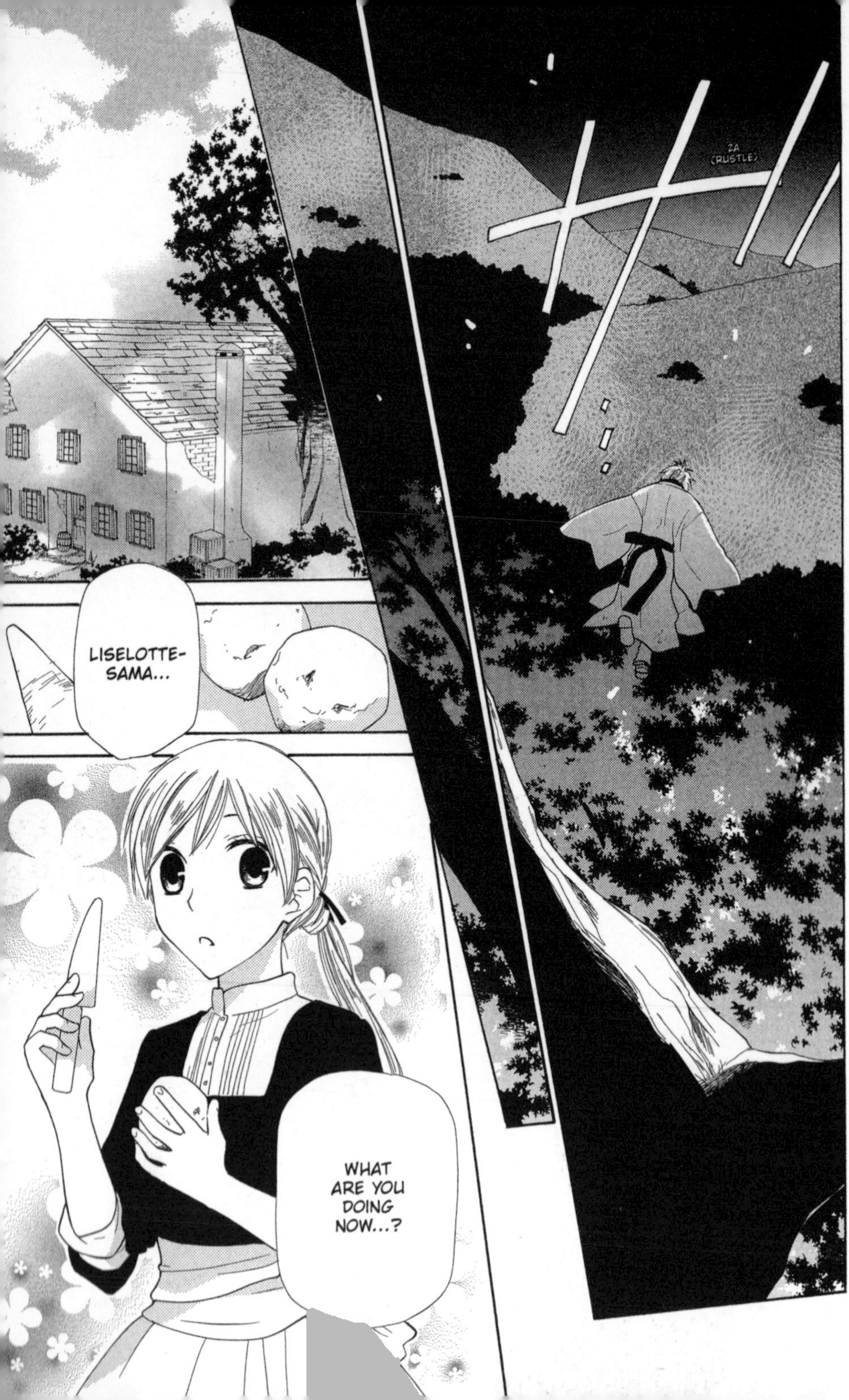
ZA (RUSTLE)
LISELOTTE-SAMA...
WHAT ARE YOU DOING NOW...?

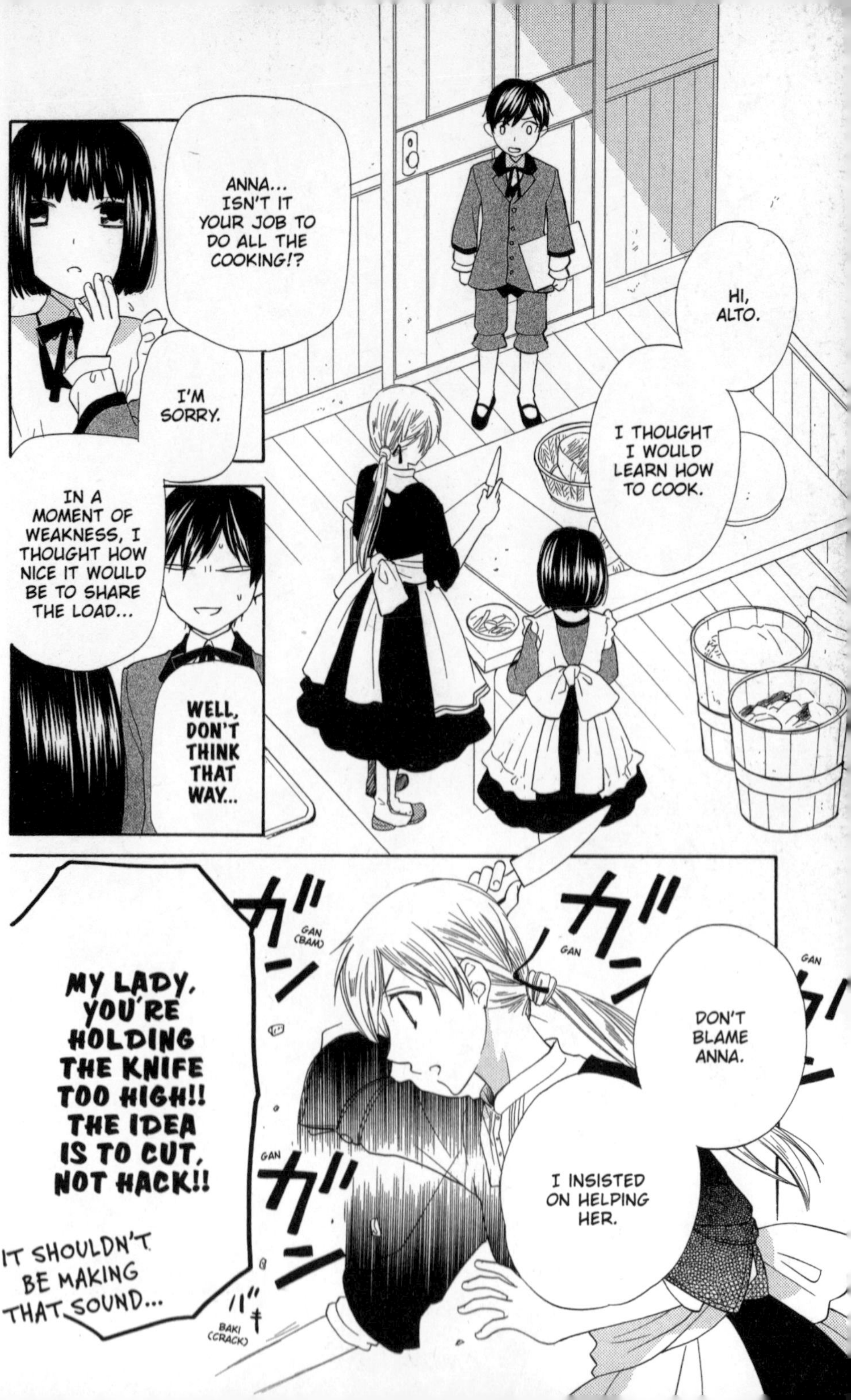
HI, ALTO.
I THOUGHT I WOULD LEARN HOW TO COOK.
ANNA... ISN'T IT YOUR JOB TO DO ALL THE COOKING!?
I'M SORRY.
IN A MOMENT OF WEAKNESS, I THOUGHT HOW NICE IT WOULD BE TO SHARE THE LOAD...
WELL, DON'T THINK THAT WAY...
GAN
GAN
GAN (BAM)
DON'T BLAME ANNA.
I INSISTED ON HELPING HER.
MY LADY, YOU'RE HOLDING THE KNIFE TOO HIGH!! THE IDEA IS TO CUT, NOT HACK!!
GAN
BAKI (CRACK)
IT SHOULDN'T BE MAKING THAT SOUND...

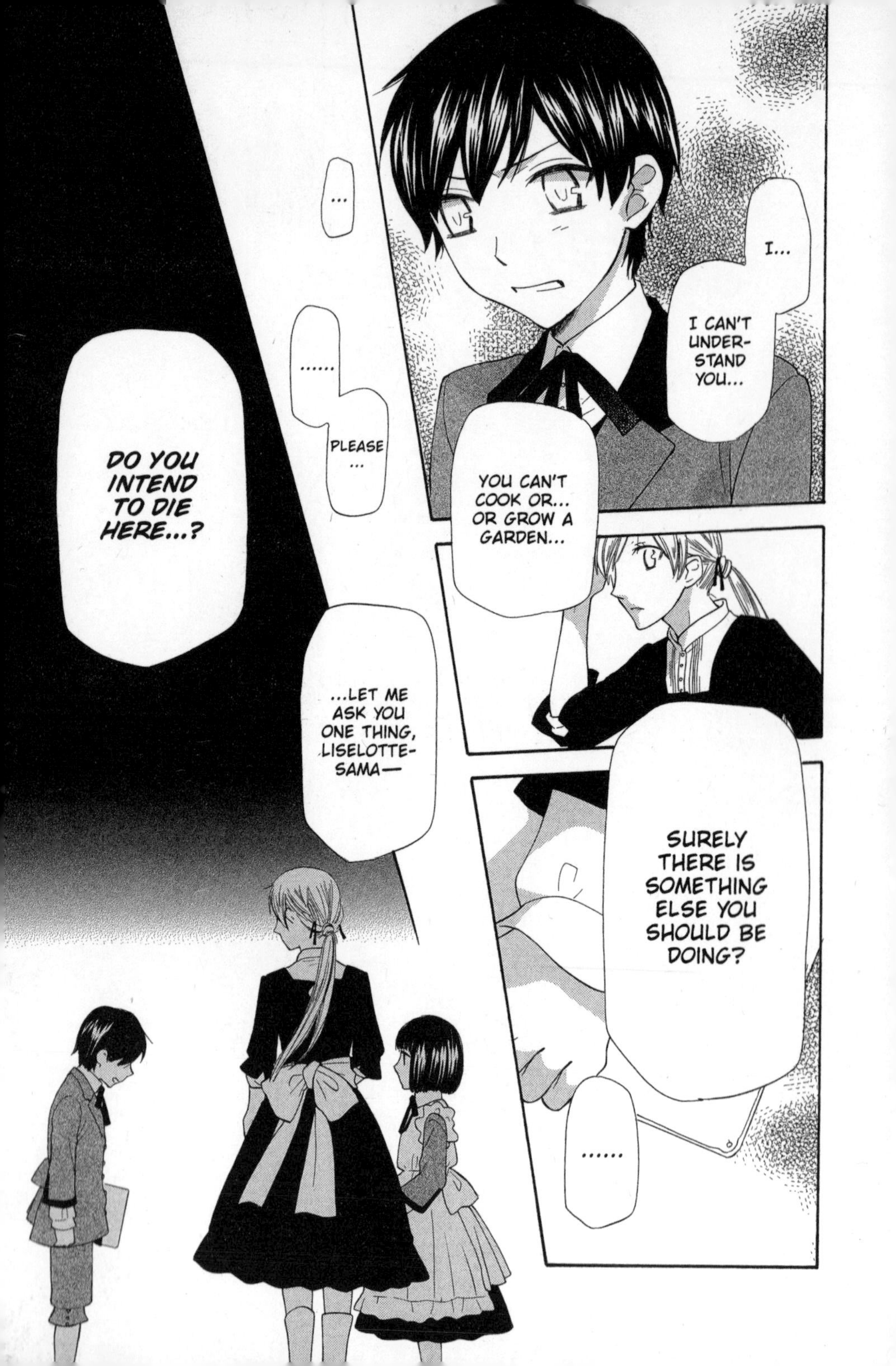
I...
I CAN'T UNDER-STAND YOU...
YOU CAN'T COOK OR... OR GROW A GARDEN...
SURELY THERE IS SOMETHING ELSE YOU SHOULD BE DOING?
......
...
......
PLEASE ...
...LET ME ASK YOU ONE THING, LISELOTTE-SAMA—
DO YOU INTEND TO DIE HERE...?

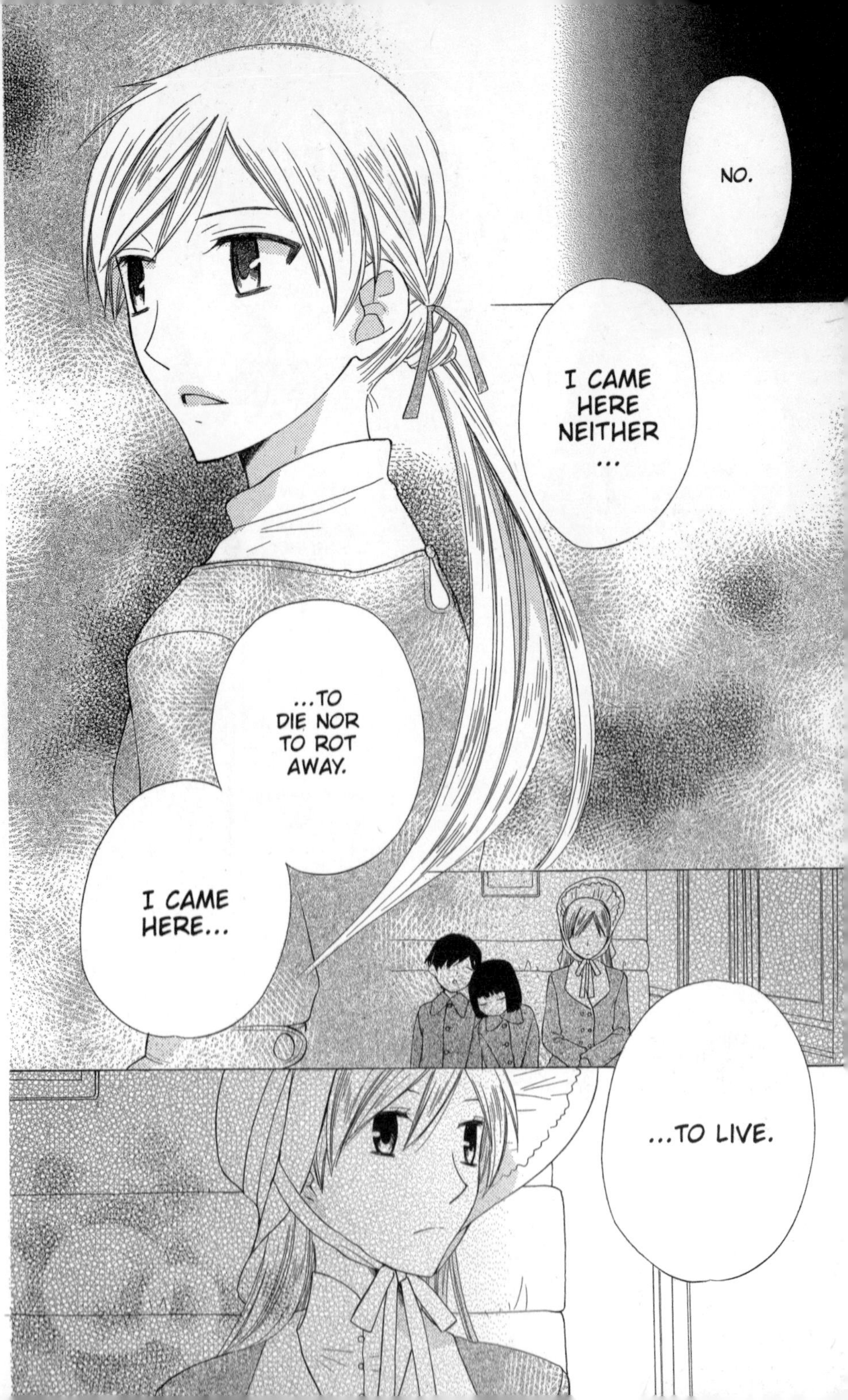
NO.
I CAME HERE NEITHER...
...TO DIE NOR TO ROT AWAY.
I CAME HERE...
...TO LIVE.

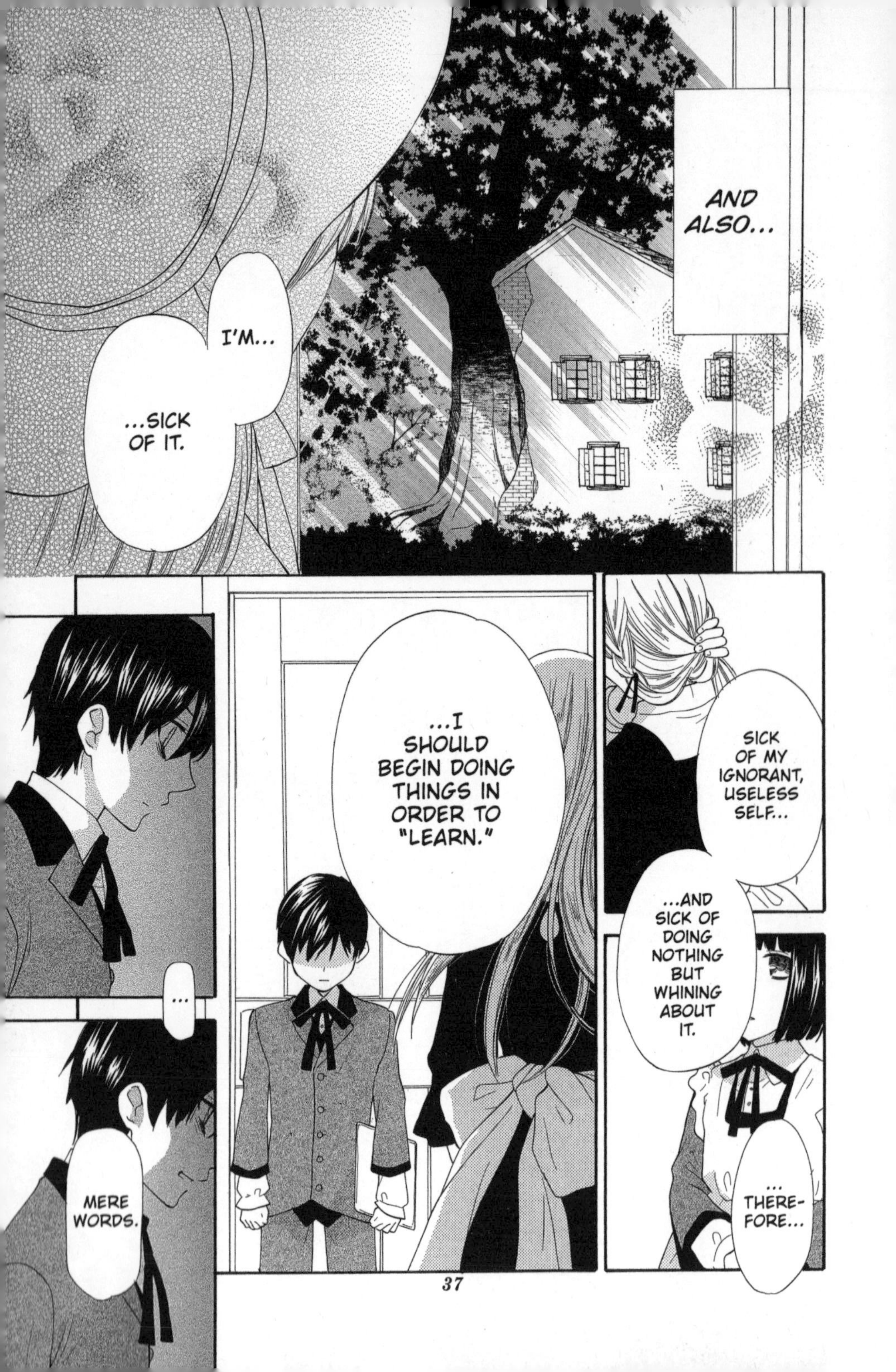
AND ALSO...
I'M...
...SICK OF IT.
SICK OF MY IGNORANT, USELESS SELF...
...AND SICK OF DOING NOTHING BUT WHINING ABOUT IT.
...THEREFORE...
...I SHOULD BEGIN DOING THINGS IN ORDER TO "LEARN."
...
MERE WORDS.

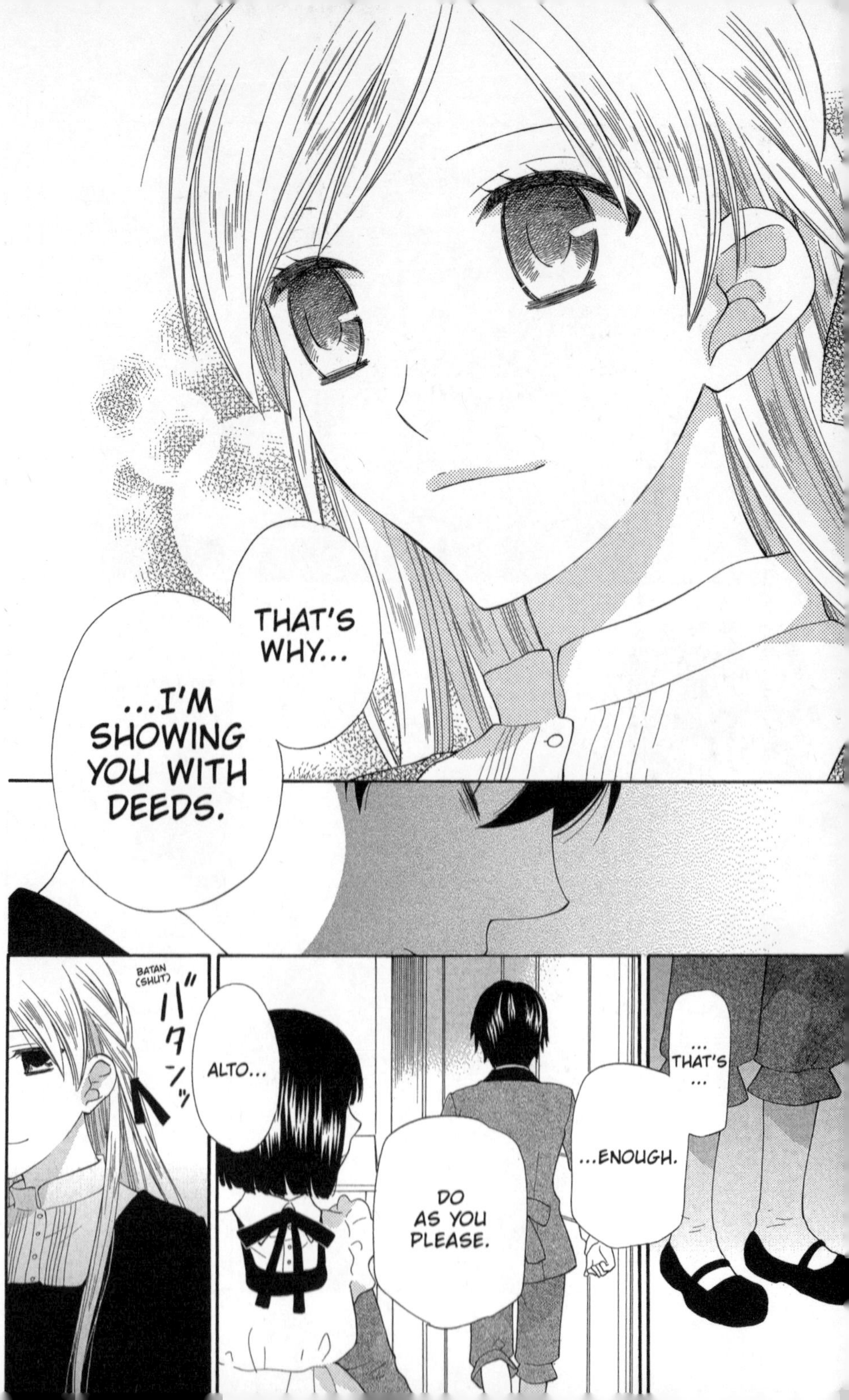
THAT'S WHY...
...I'M SHOWING YOU WITH DEEDS.
...THAT'S...
...ENOUGH.
DO AS YOU PLEASE.
ALTO...
BATAN (SHUT)
バタンッ

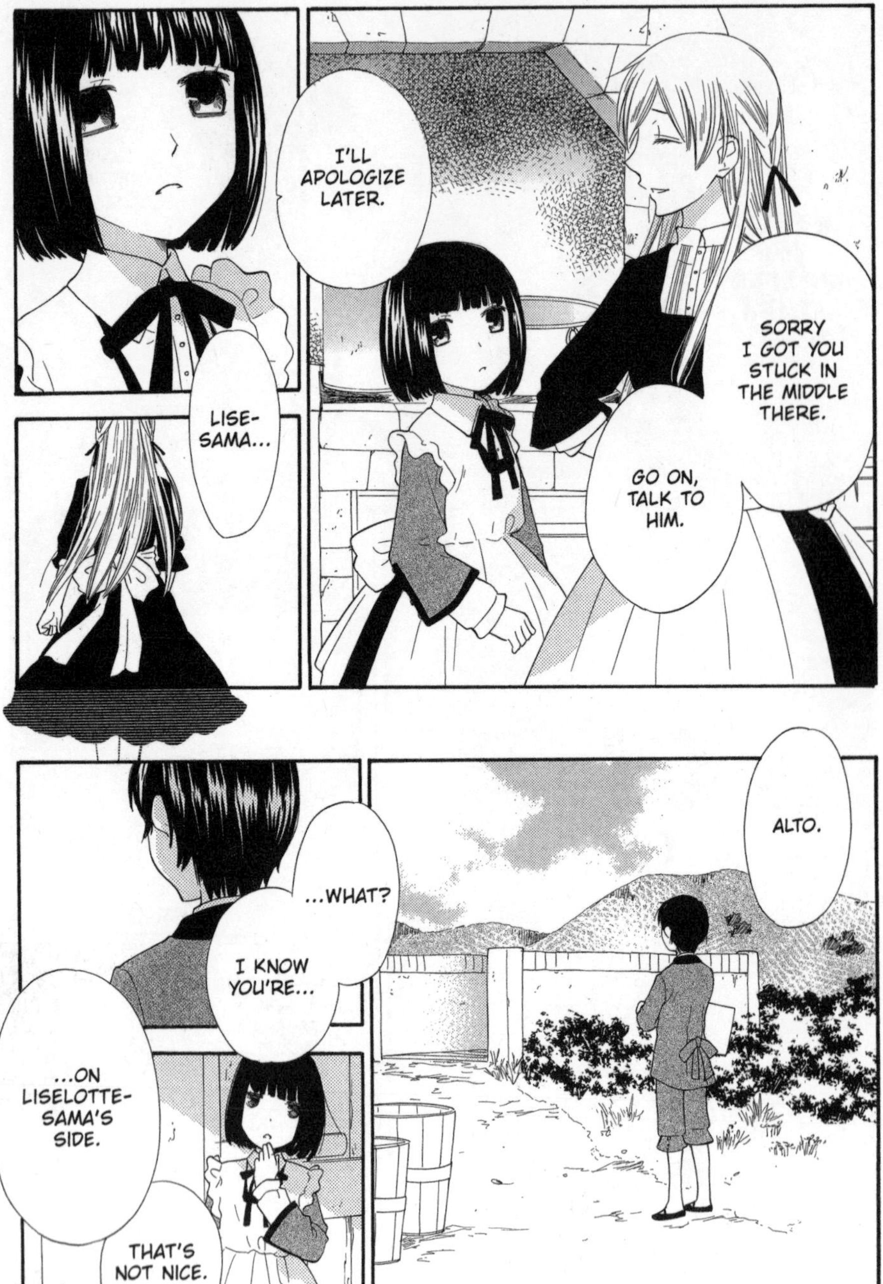
SORRY I GOT YOU STUCK IN THE MIDDLE THERE.
I'LL APOLOGIZE LATER.
GO ON, TALK TO HIM.
LISE-SAMA...
ALTO.
...WHAT?
I KNOW YOU'RE...
...ON LISELOTTE-SAMA'S SIDE.
THAT'S NOT NICE.

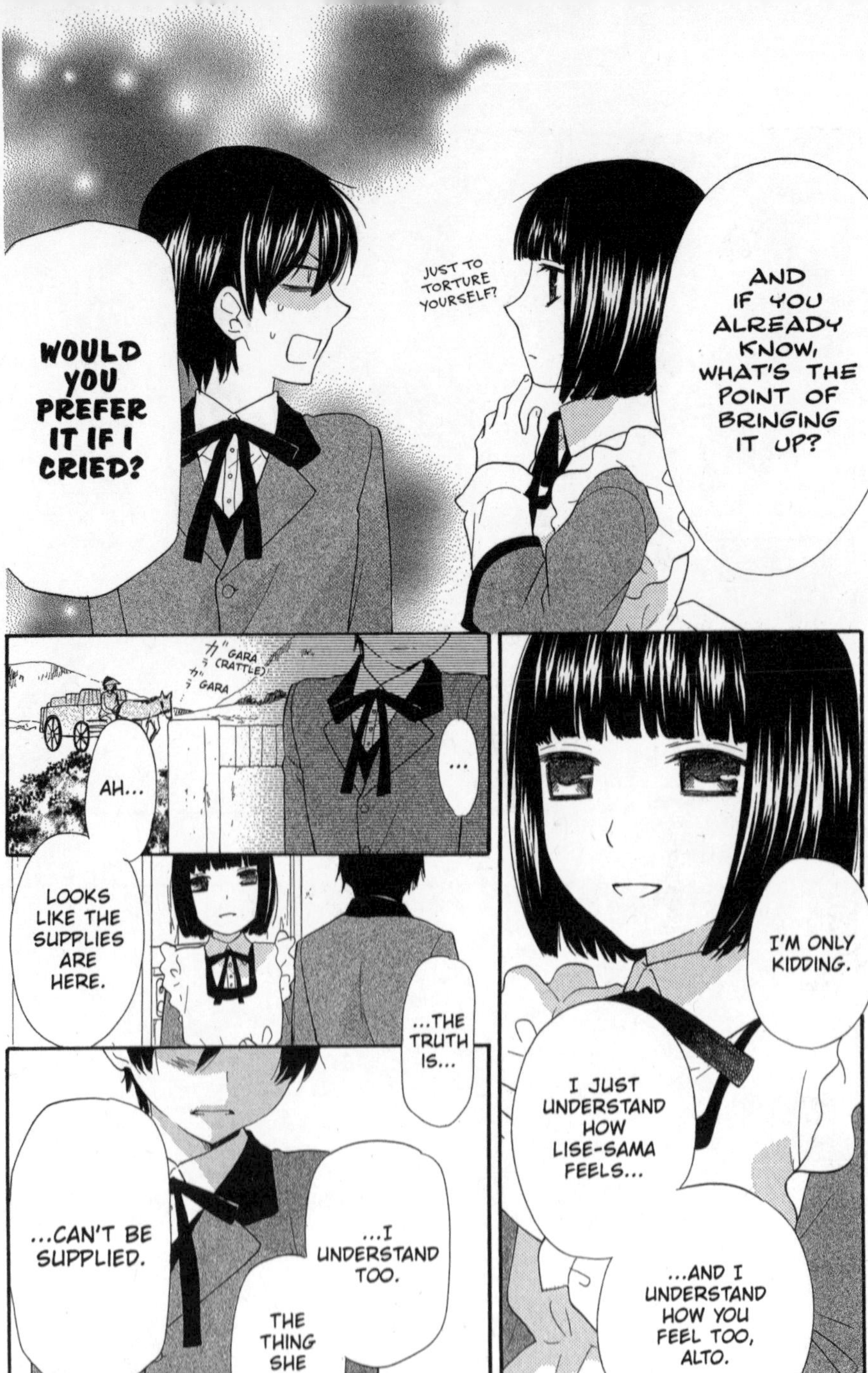
AND IF YOU ALREADY KNOW, WHAT'S THE POINT OF BRINGING IT UP?
JUST TO TORTURE YOURSELF?
WOULD YOU PREFER IT IF I CRIED?
I'M ONLY KIDDING.
I JUST UNDERSTAND HOW LISE-SAMA FEELS...
...AND I UNDERSTAND HOW YOU FEEL TOO, ALTO.
GARA (RATTLE)
GARA
...
AH...
LOOKS LIKE THE SUPPLIES ARE HERE.
...THE TRUTH IS...
...I UNDERSTAND TOO.
THE THING SHE WISHES FOR...
...CAN'T BE SUPPLIED.

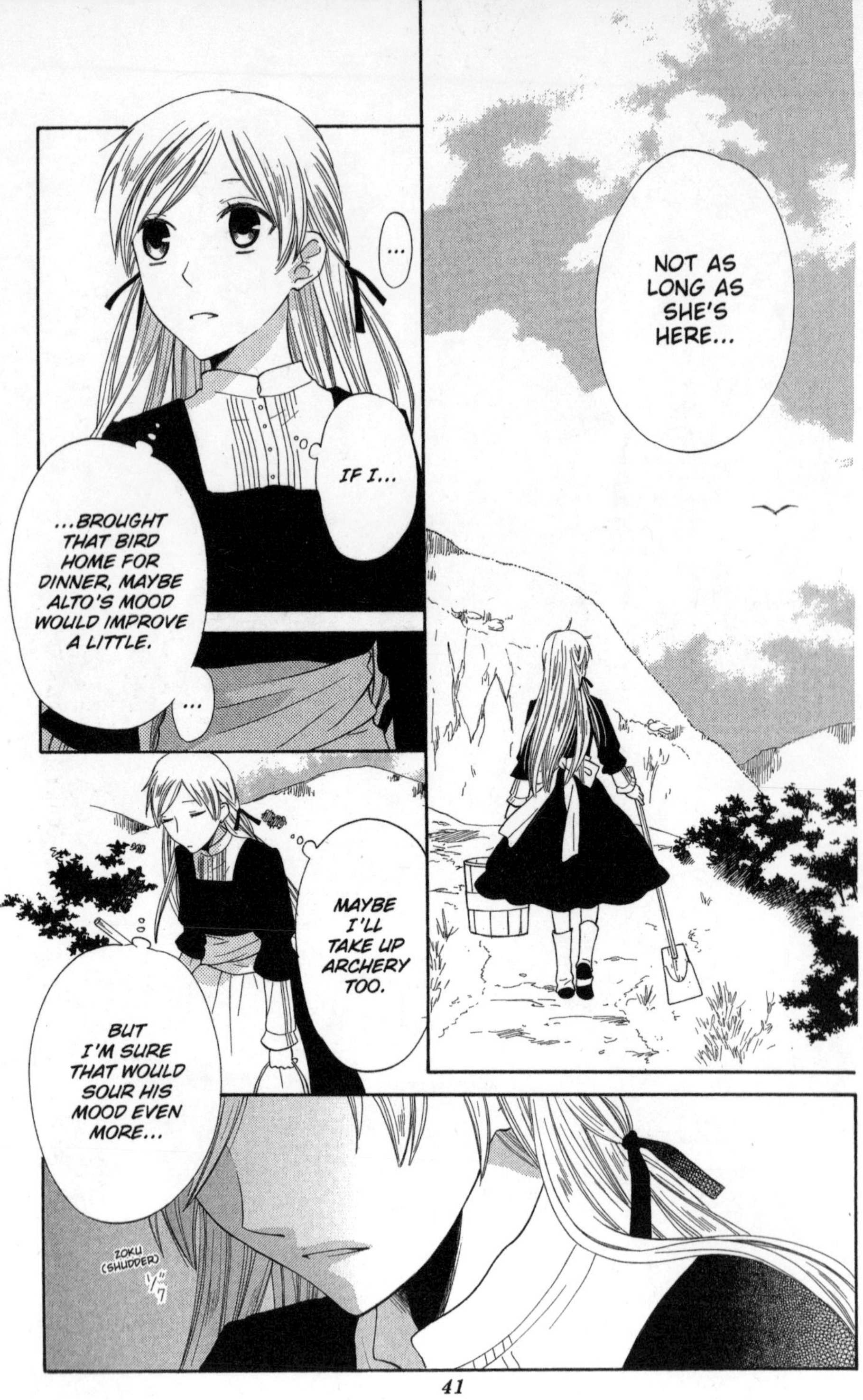
NOT AS LONG AS SHE'S HERE...
...
IF I...
...BROUGHT THAT BIRD HOME FOR DINNER, MAYBE ALTO'S MOOD WOULD IMPROVE A LITTLE.
...
MAYBE I'LL TAKE UP ARCHERY TOO.
BUT I'M SURE THAT WOULD SOUR HIS MOOD EVEN MORE...
ZOKU (SHUDDER)

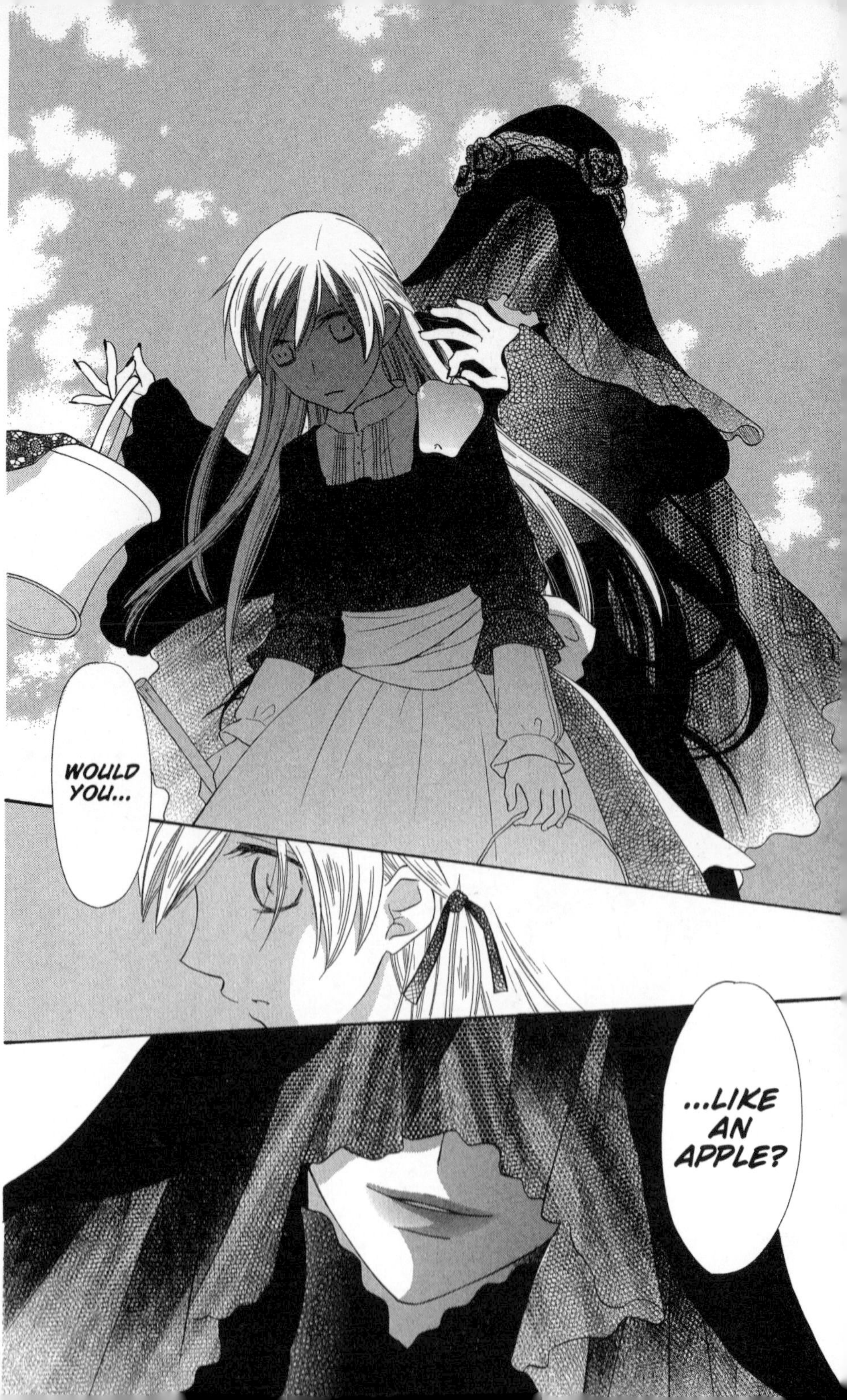
WOULD YOU...
...LIKE AN APPLE?

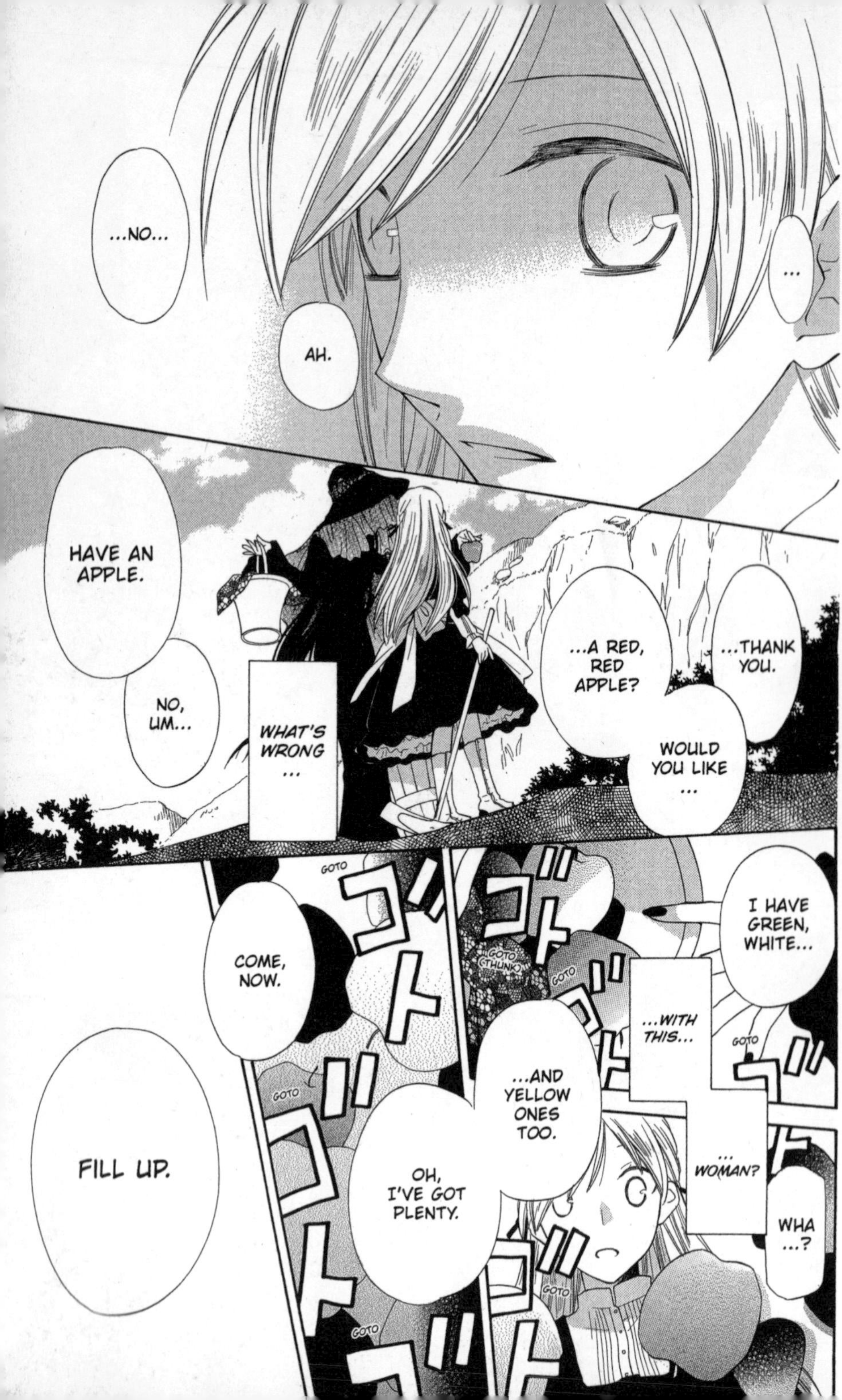
...
AH.
...NO...
...THANK YOU.
WOULD YOU LIKE ...
...A RED, RED APPLE?
WHAT'S WRONG ...
HAVE AN APPLE.
NO, UM...
I HAVE GREEN, WHITE...
GOTO
...WITH THIS...
WHA ...?
... WOMAN?
...AND YELLOW ONES TOO.
OH, I'VE GOT PLENTY.
GOTO (THUNK)
GOTO
GOTO
GOTO
COME, NOW.
GOTO
GOTO
FILL UP.

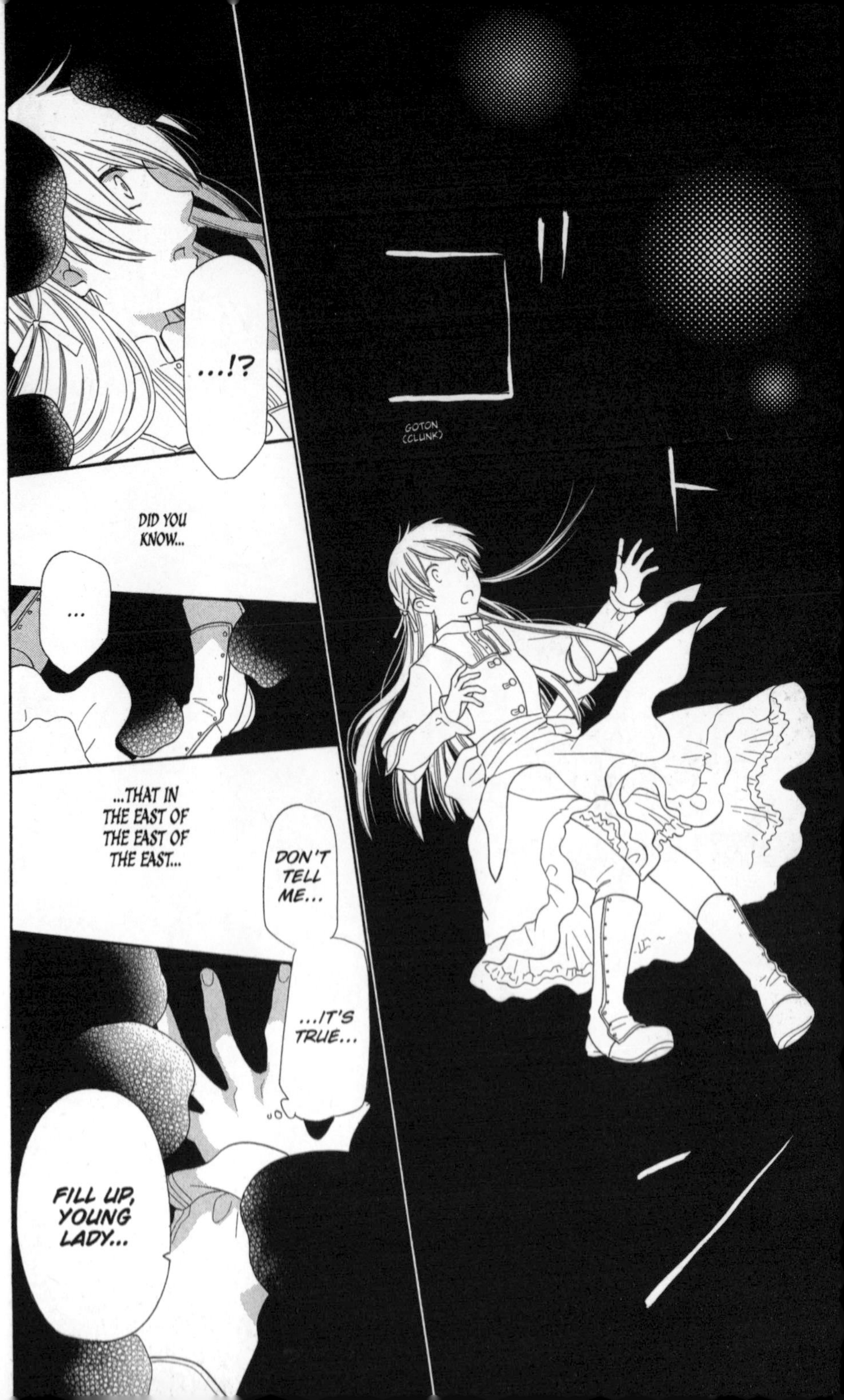
GOTON (CLUNK)
...!?
DID YOU KNOW...
...
...THAT IN THE EAST OF THE EAST OF THE EAST...
DON'T TELL ME...
...IT'S TRUE...
FILL UP, YOUNG LADY...

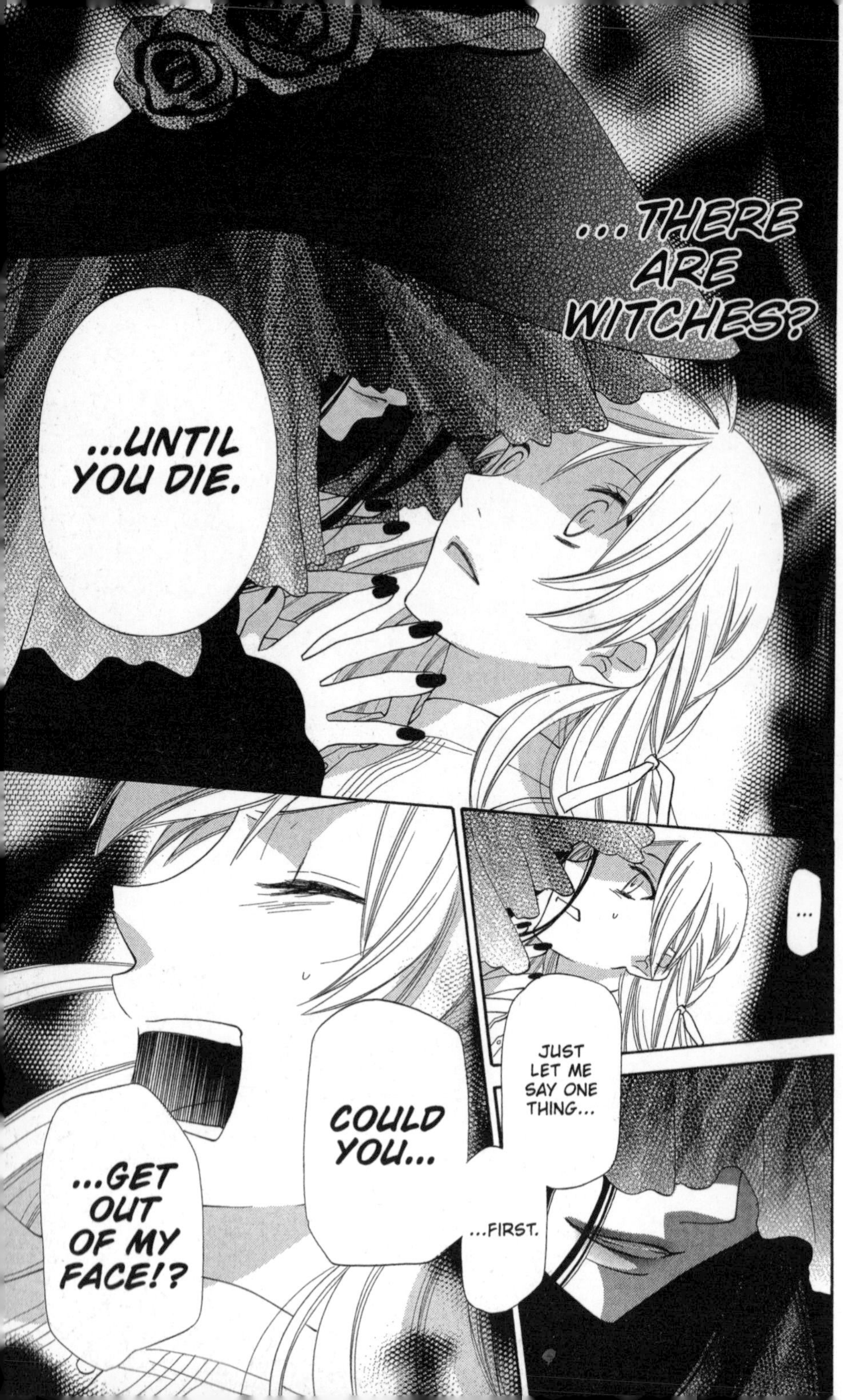
...THERE ARE WITCHES?
...UNTIL YOU DIE.
...
JUST LET ME SAY ONE THING...
...FIRST.
COULD YOU...
...GET OUT OF MY FACE!?

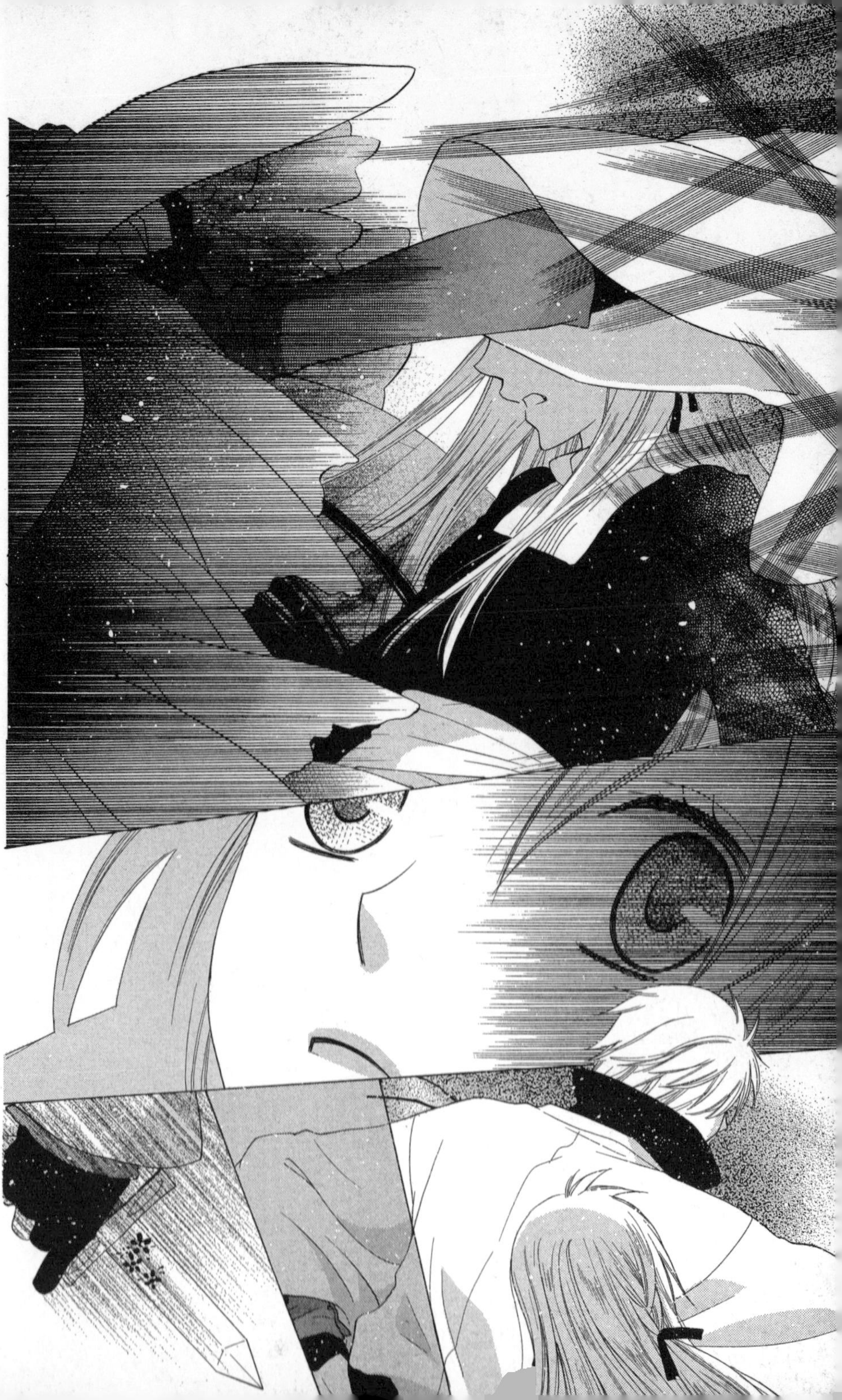

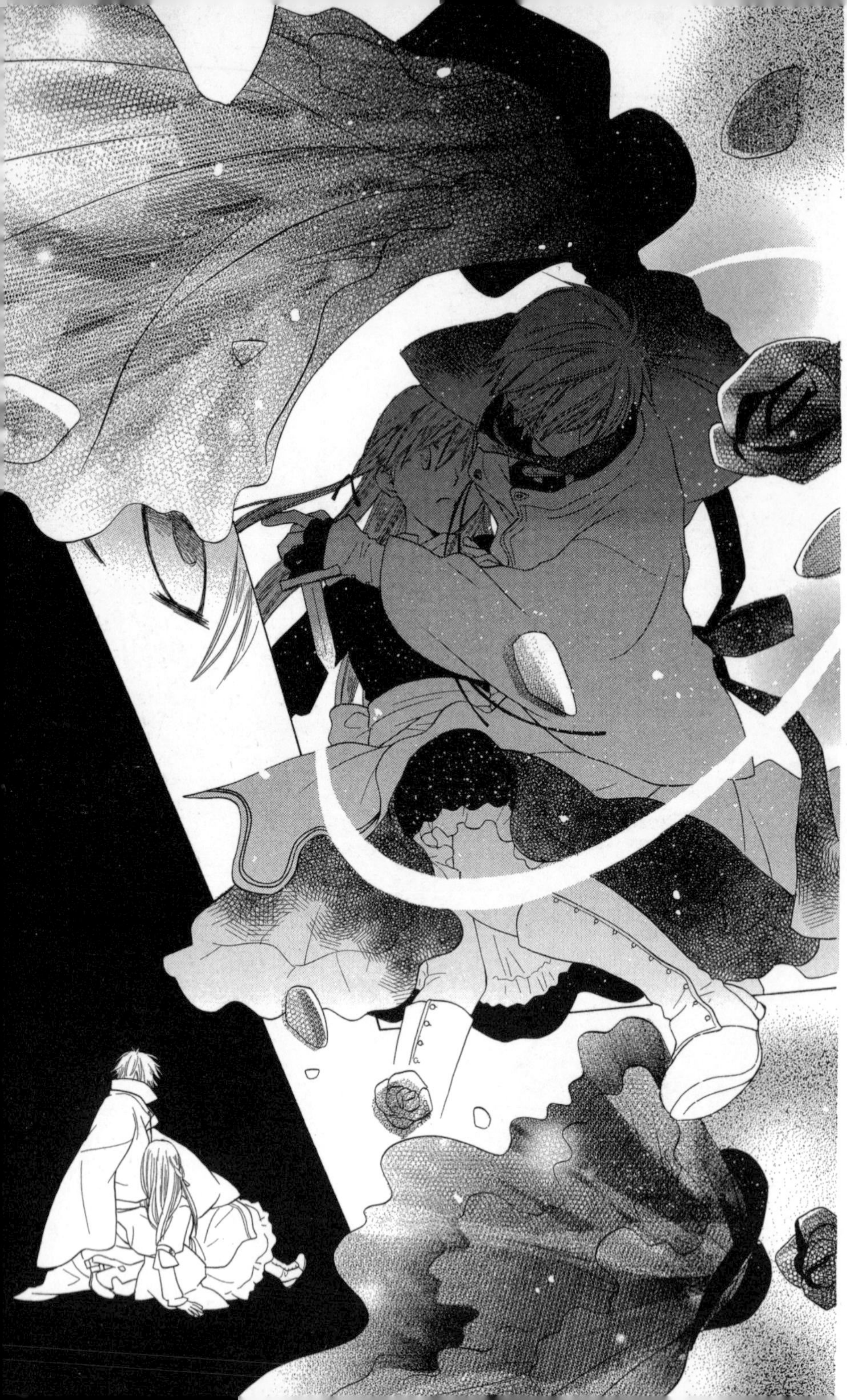

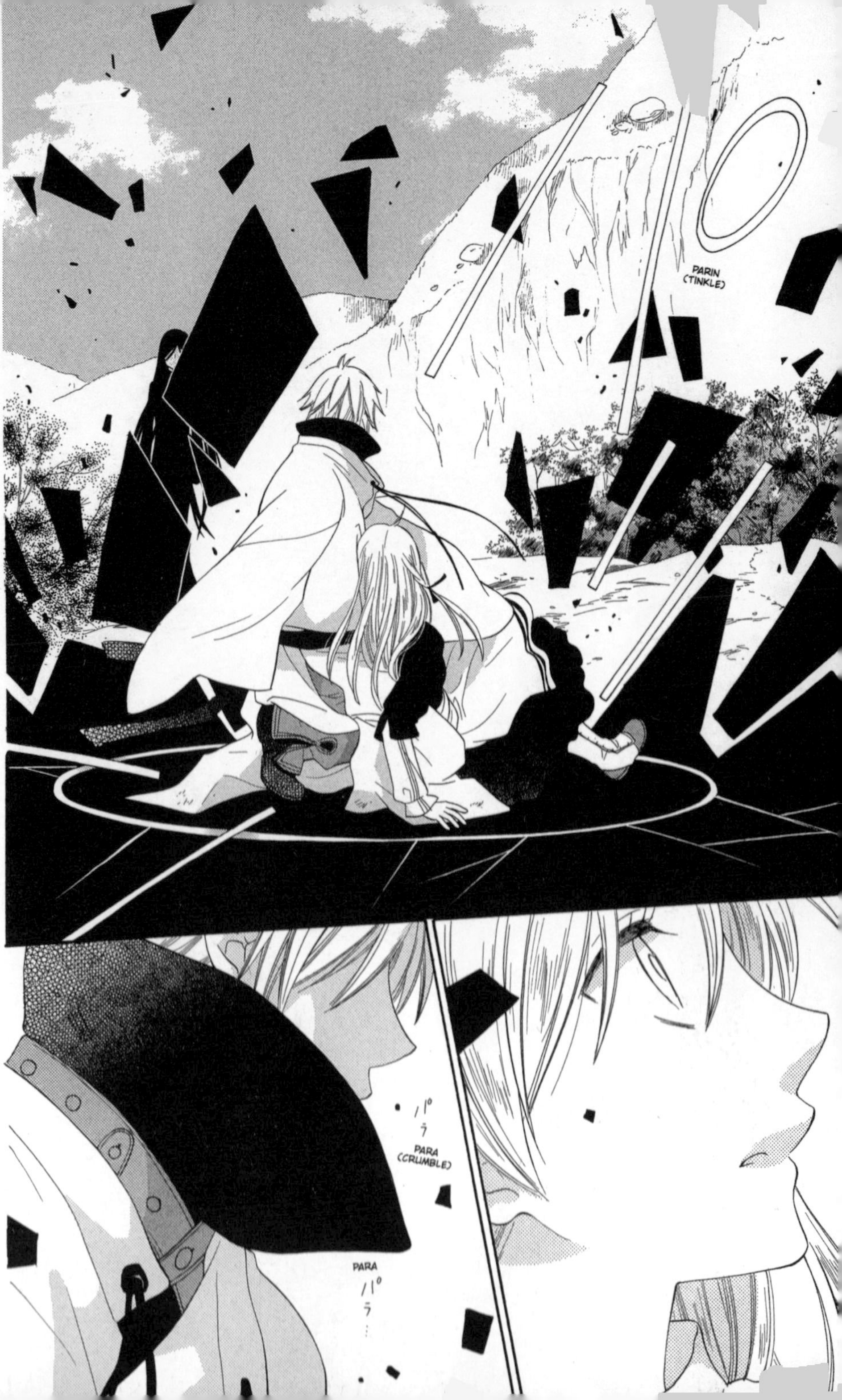
PARIN
(TINKLE)
パ
ラ
PARA
(CRUMBLE)
PARA
パ
ラ…

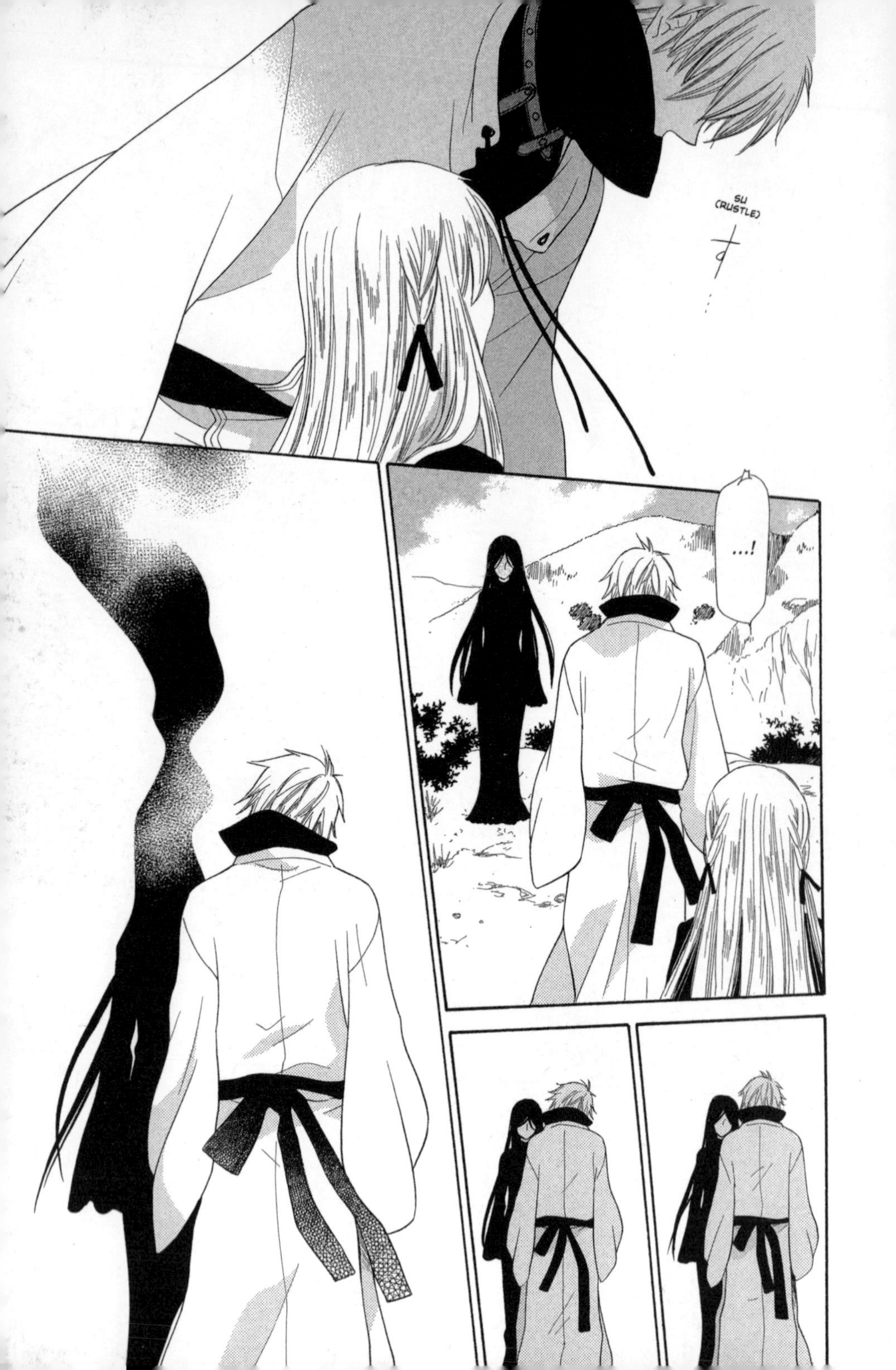
SU (RUSTLE)
す
...!

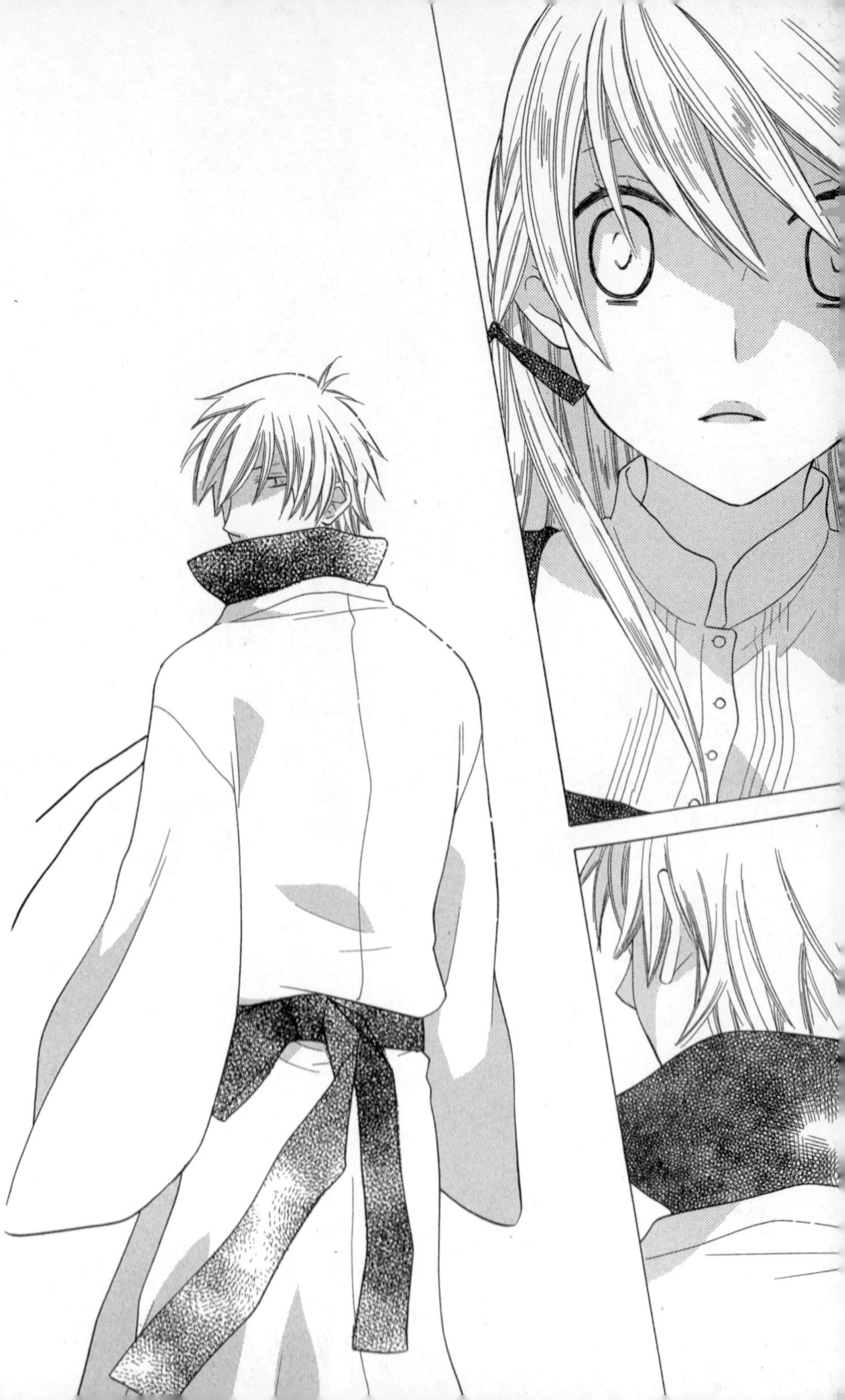

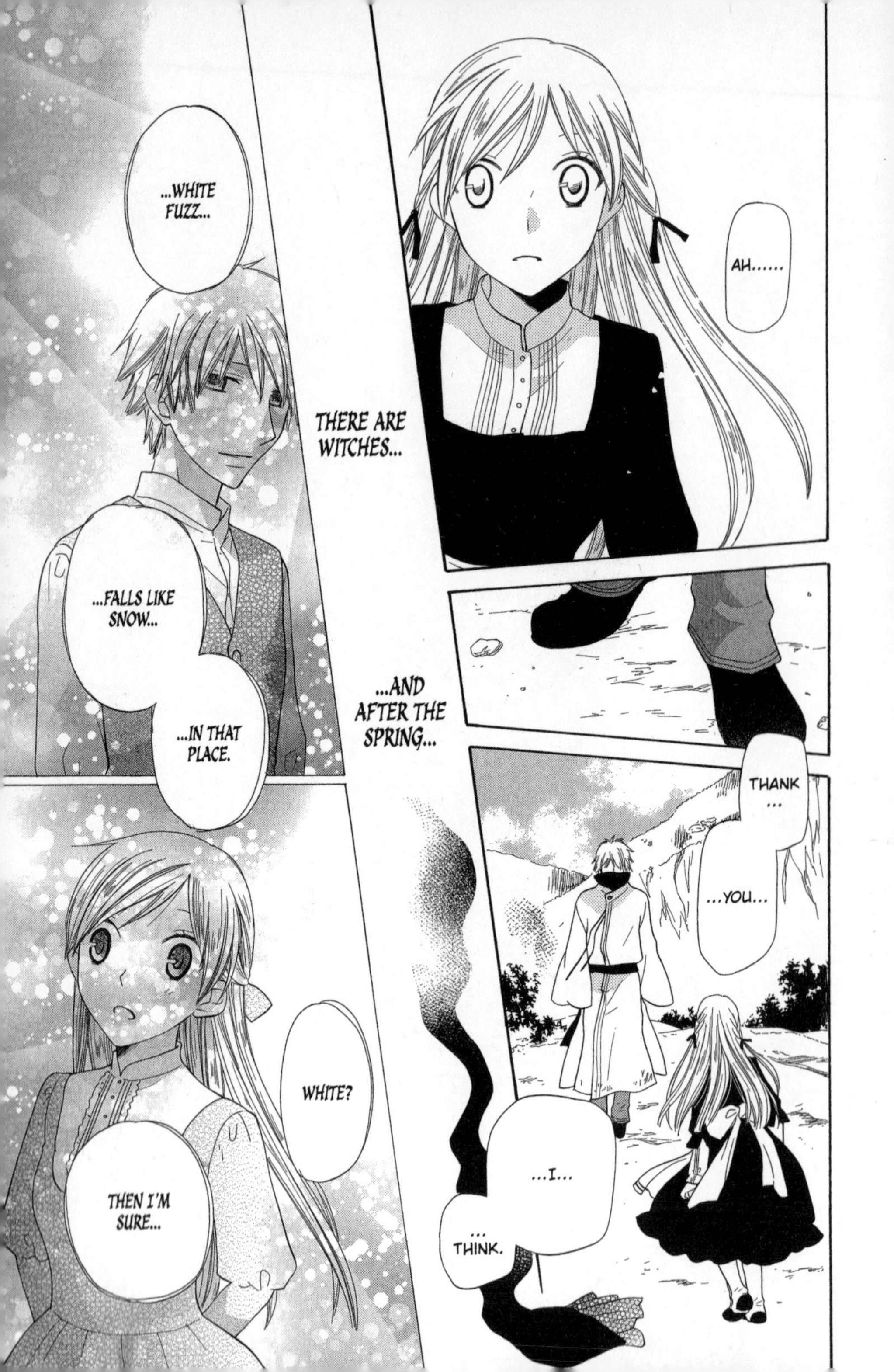
AH......
THERE ARE WITCHES...
...AND AFTER THE SPRING...
THANK ...
...YOU...
...I...
... THINK.
...WHITE FUZZ...
...FALLS LIKE SNOW...
...IN THAT PLACE.
WHITE?
THEN I'M SURE...

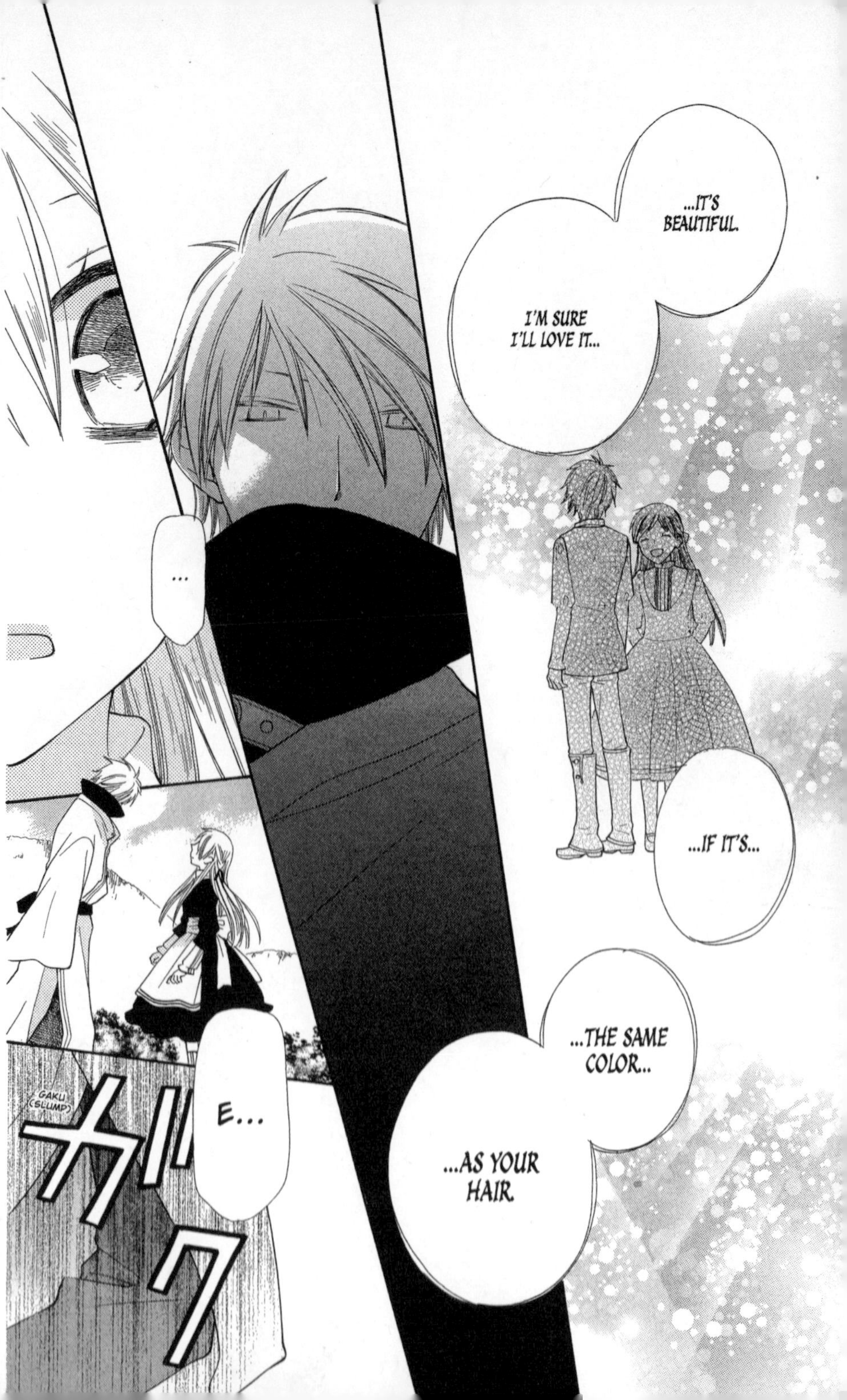
...IT'S BEAUTIFUL.
I'M SURE I'LL LOVE IT...
...IF IT'S...
...THE SAME COLOR...
...AS YOUR HAIR.
...
E...
GAKU (SLUMP)

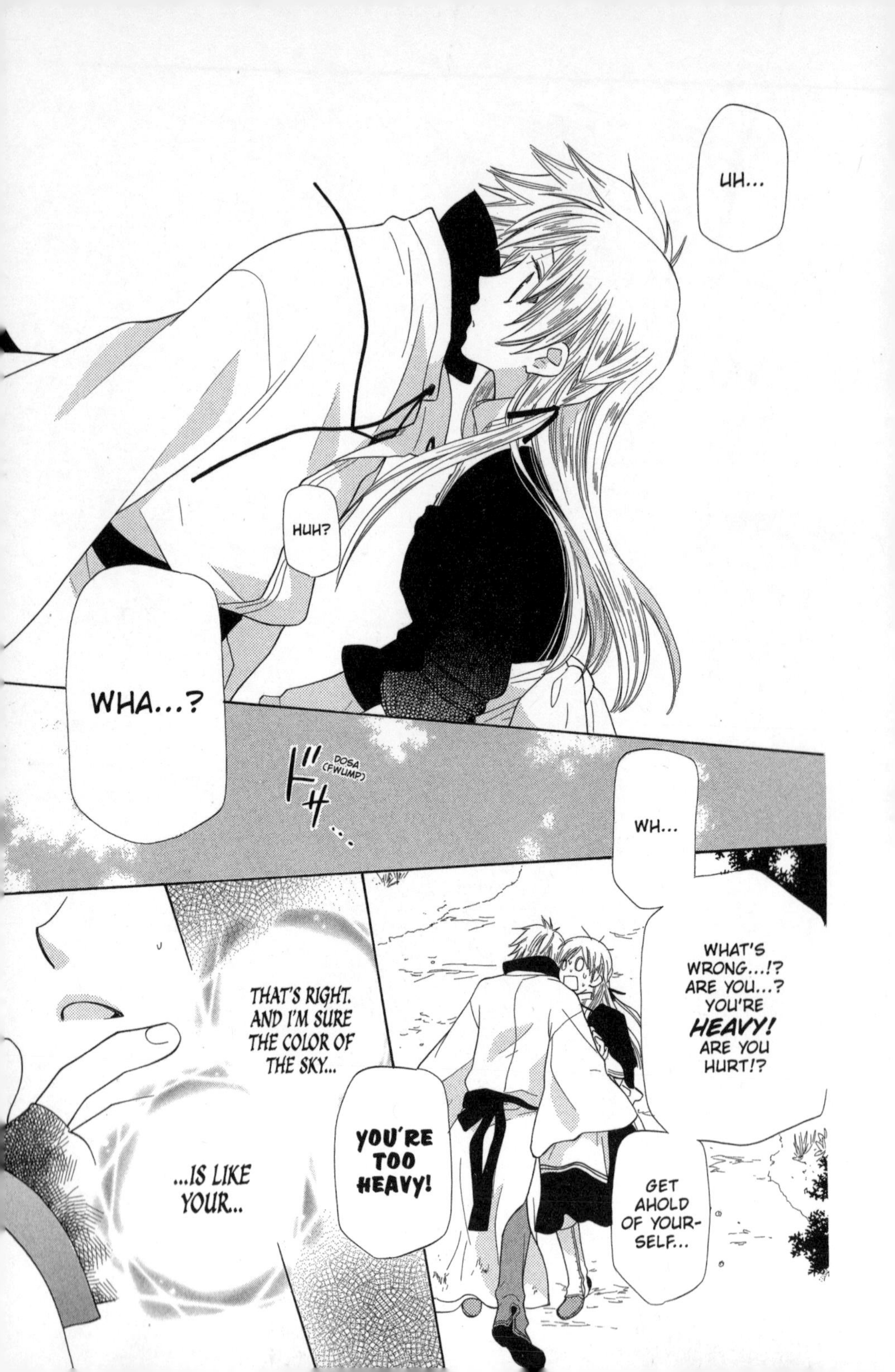
UH...
HUH?
WHA...?
WH...
ドサ...
DOSA (FWUMP)
WHAT'S WRONG...!? ARE YOU...? YOU'RE HEAVY! ARE YOU HURT!?
GET AHOLD OF YOUR-SELF...
YOU'RE TOO HEAVY!
THAT'S RIGHT. AND I'M SURE THE COLOR OF THE SKY...
...IS LIKE YOUR...

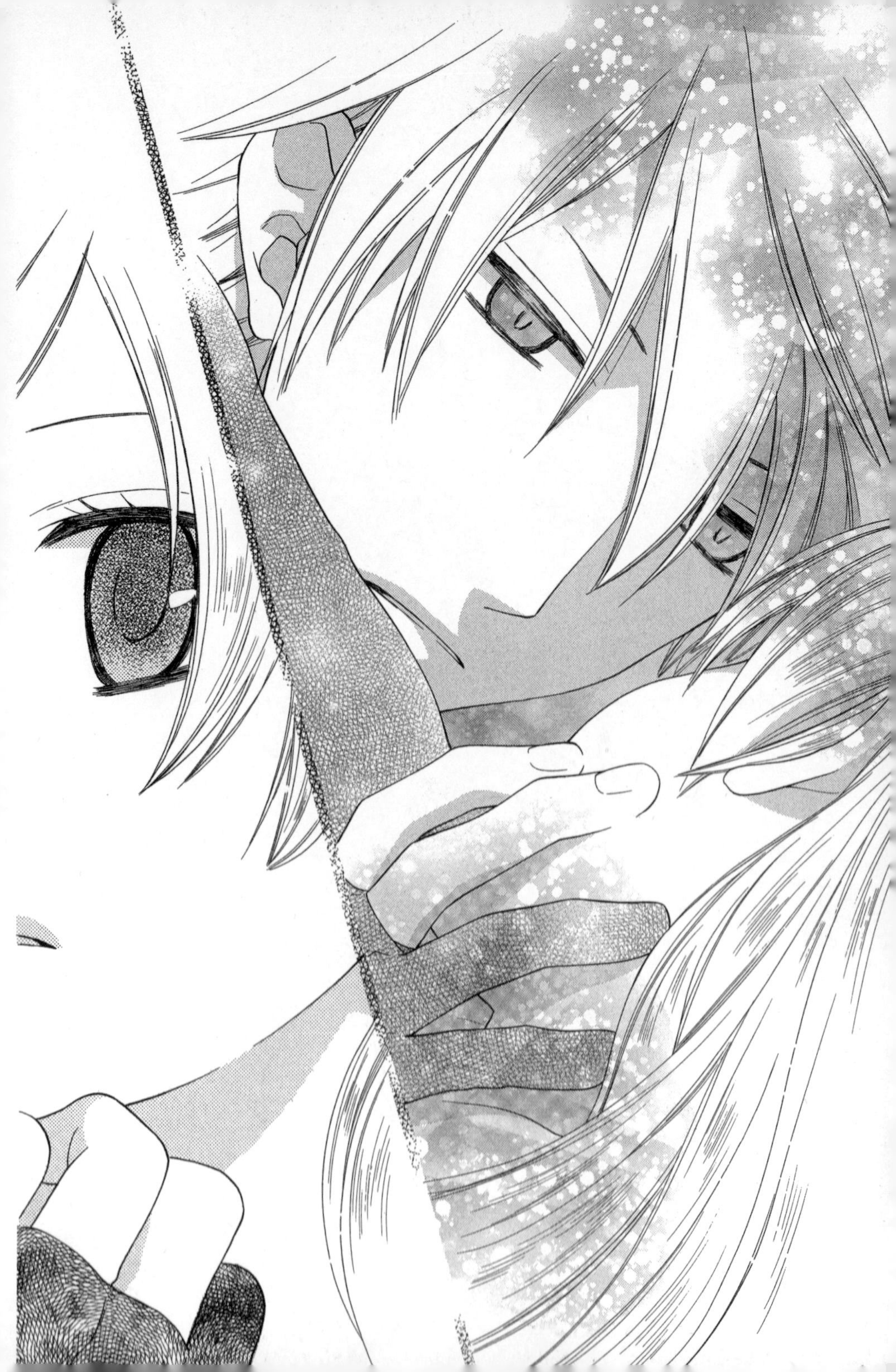

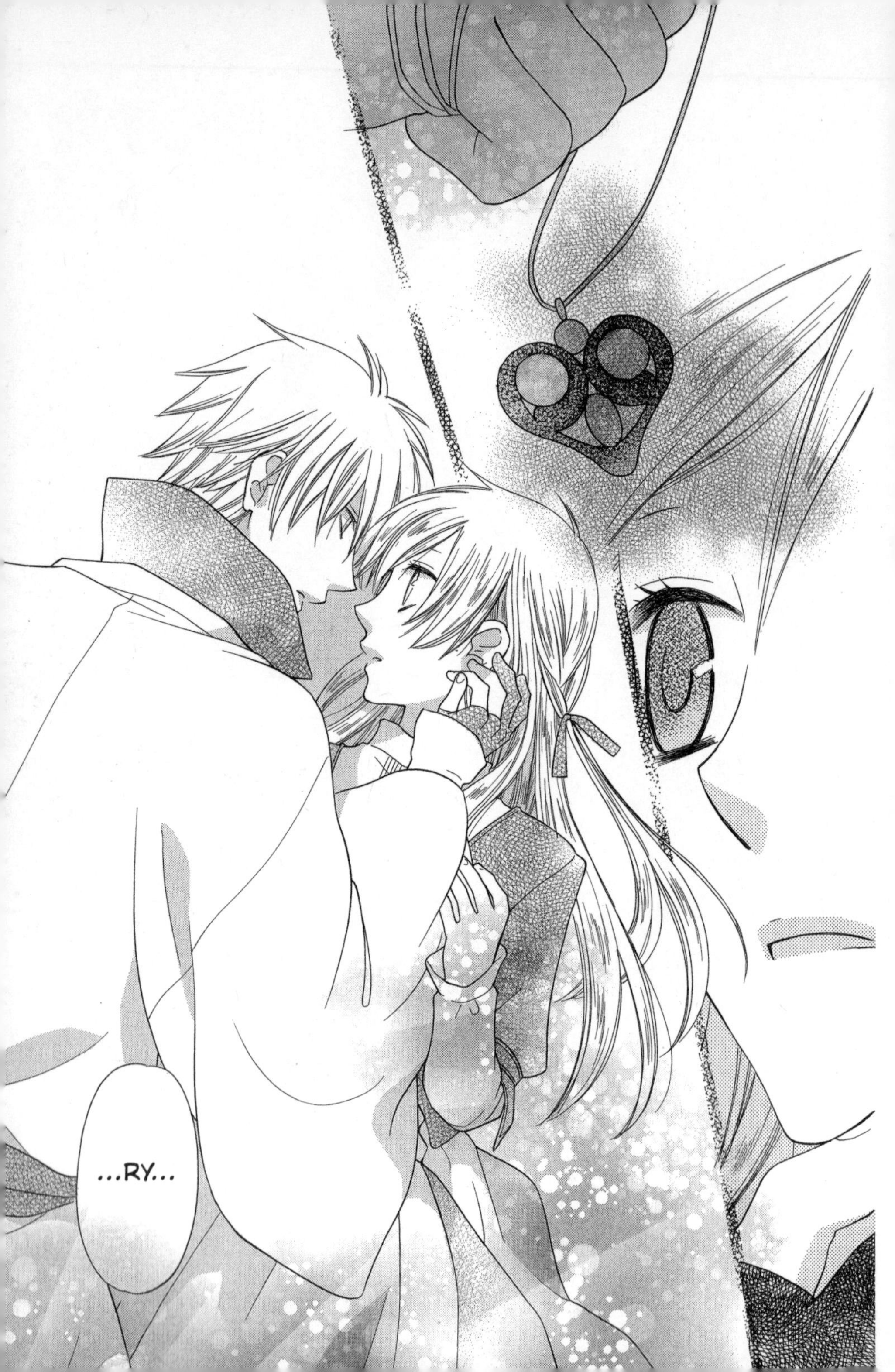
...RY...

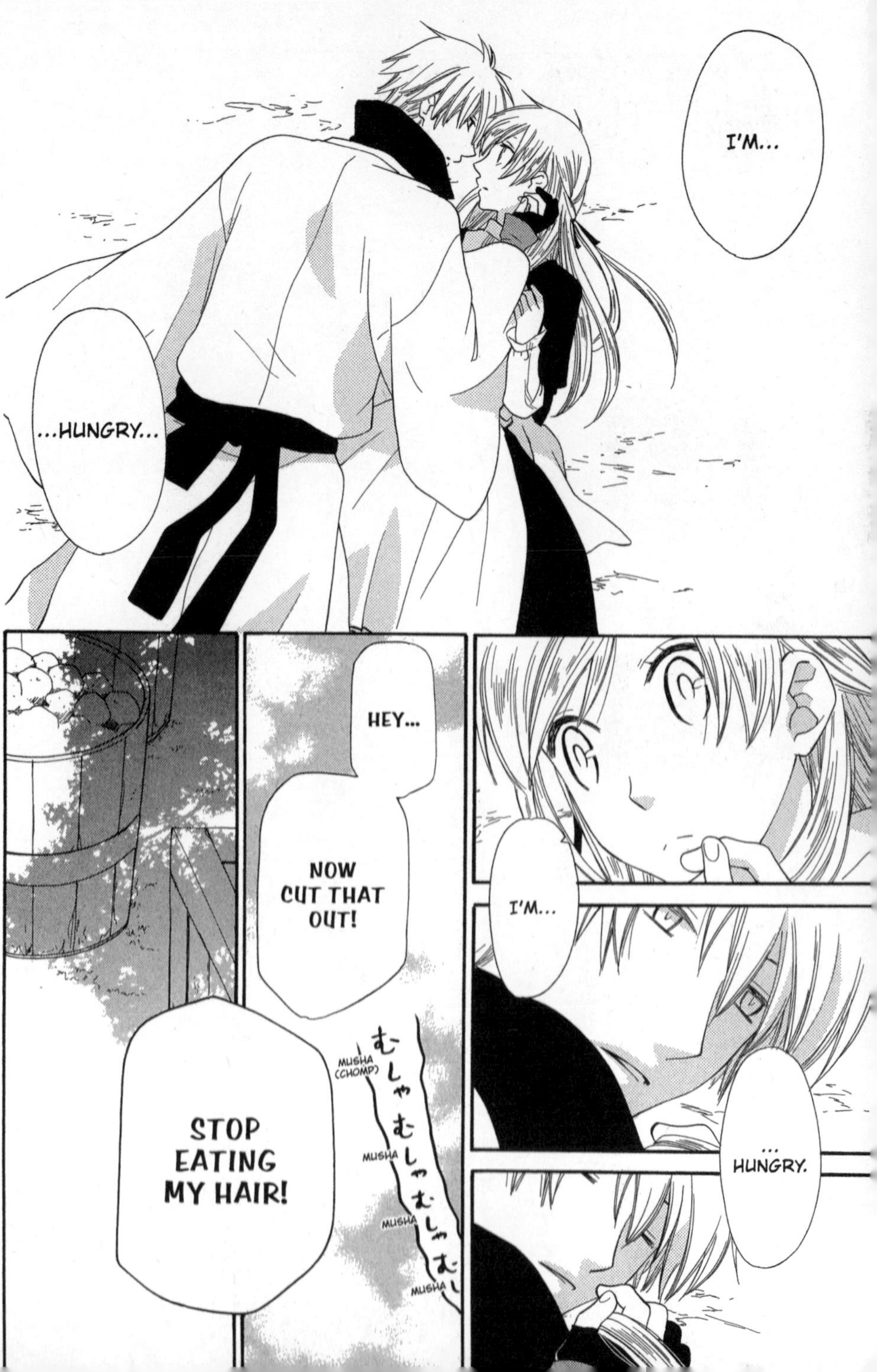
I'M...
...HUNGRY...
I'M...
...HUNGRY.
HEY...
NOW CUT THAT OUT!
むしゃむしゃむしゃむし
MUSHA (CHOMP)
MUSHA
MUSHA
MUSHA
STOP EATING MY HAIR!

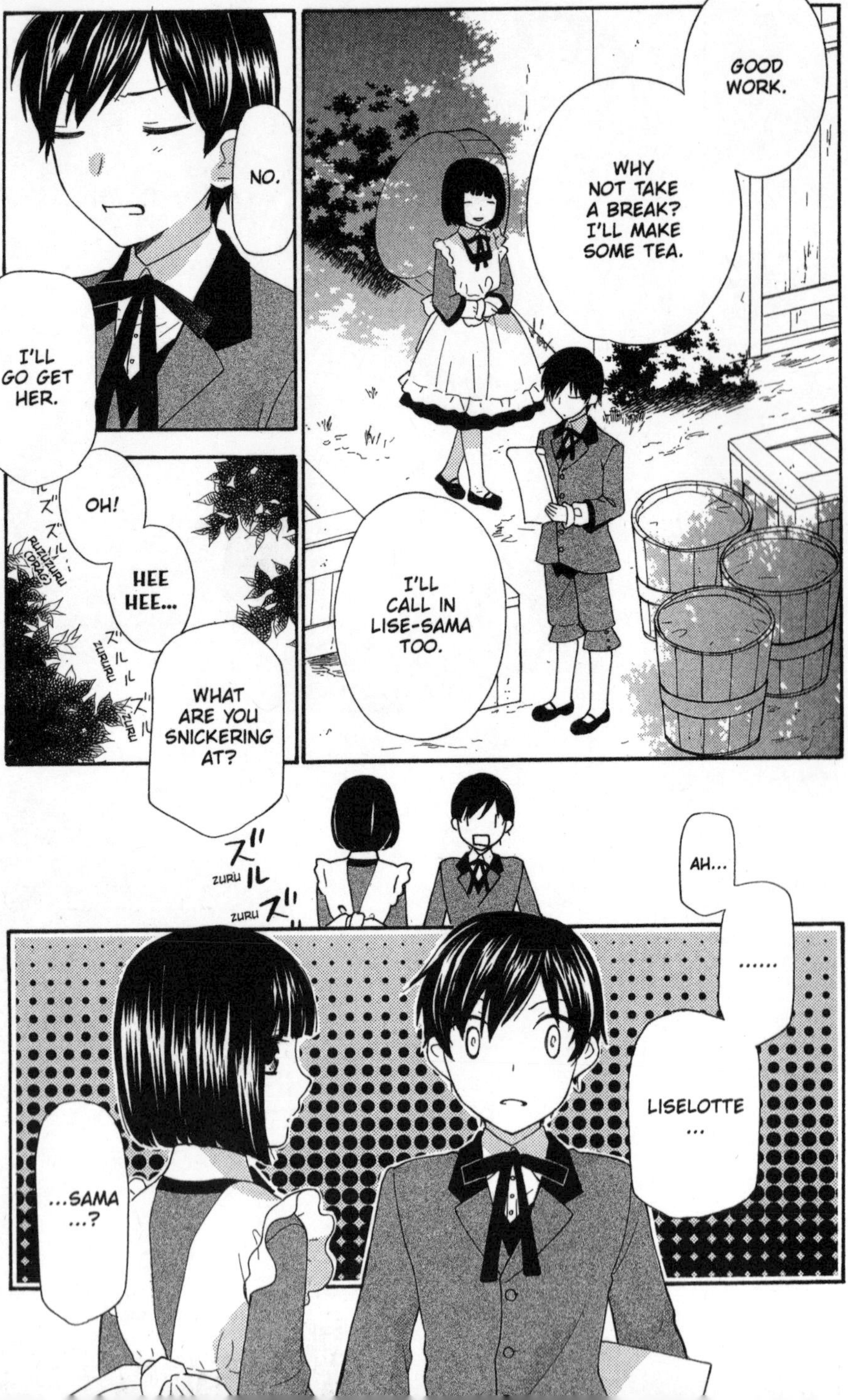
GOOD WORK.
WHY NOT TAKE A BREAK? I'LL MAKE SOME TEA.
I'LL CALL IN LISE-SAMA TOO.
NO.
I'LL GO GET HER.
ズルズル
ZUZUZURU (DRAG)
OH!
HEE HEE...
ズルズル
ZURUZURU
WHAT ARE YOU SNICKERING AT?
AH...
ズル
ZURU
ZURU
......
LISELOTTE ...
...SAMA ...?

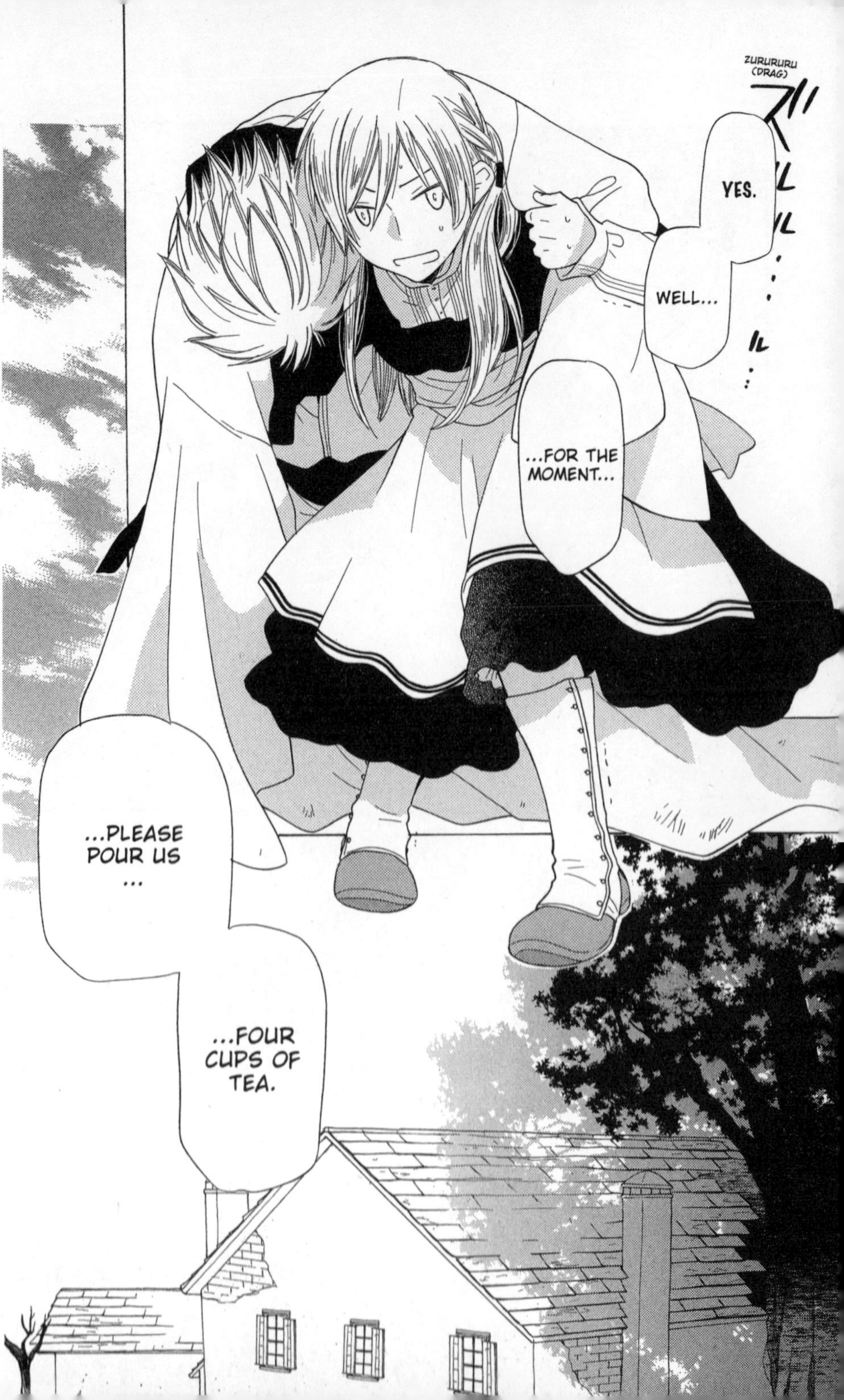
ZURURURU (DRAG)
ズルルル・・・ル・・・
YES.
WELL...
...FOR THE MOMENT...
...PLEASE POUR US ...
...FOUR CUPS OF TEA.

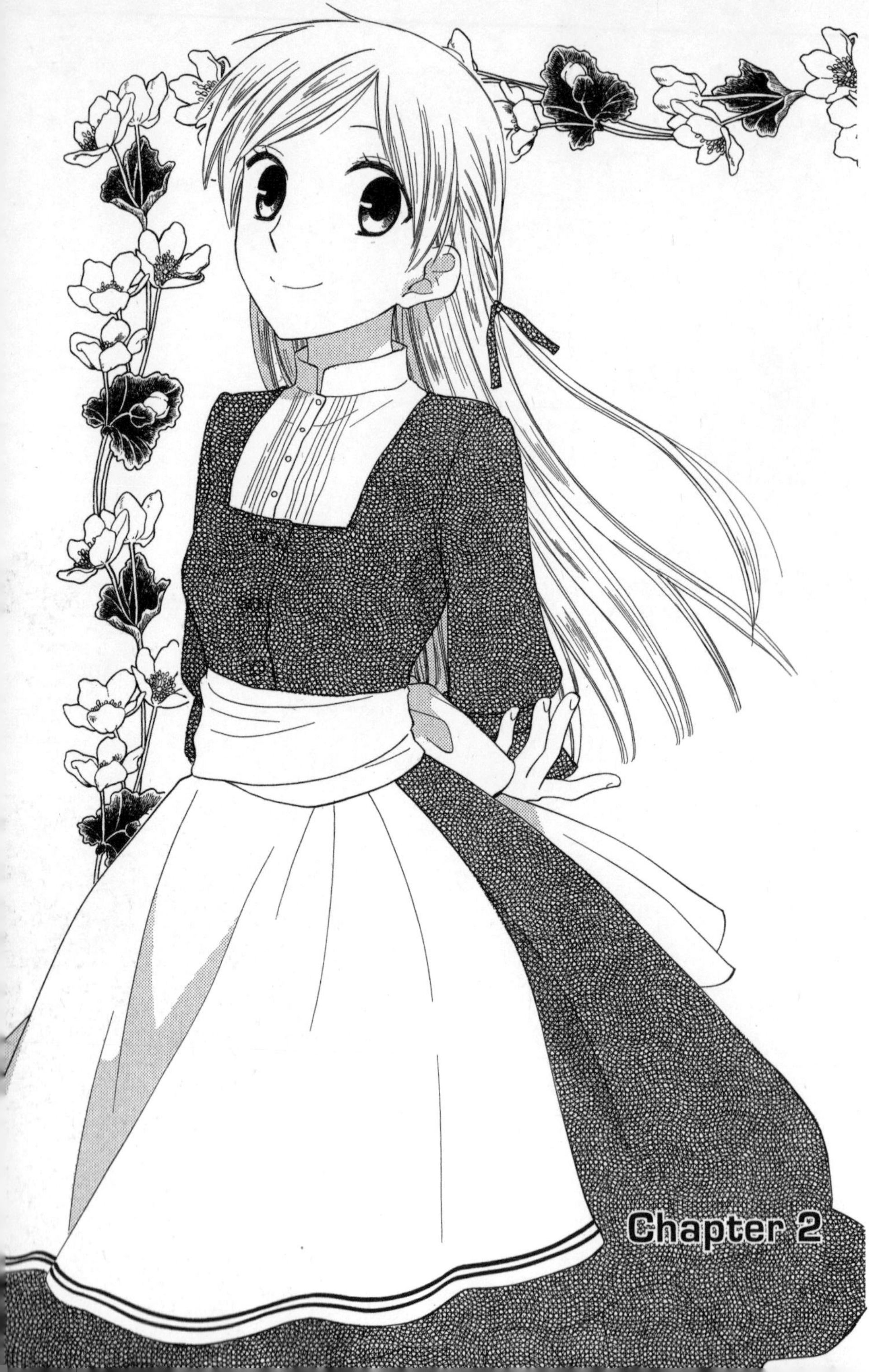
Chapter 2

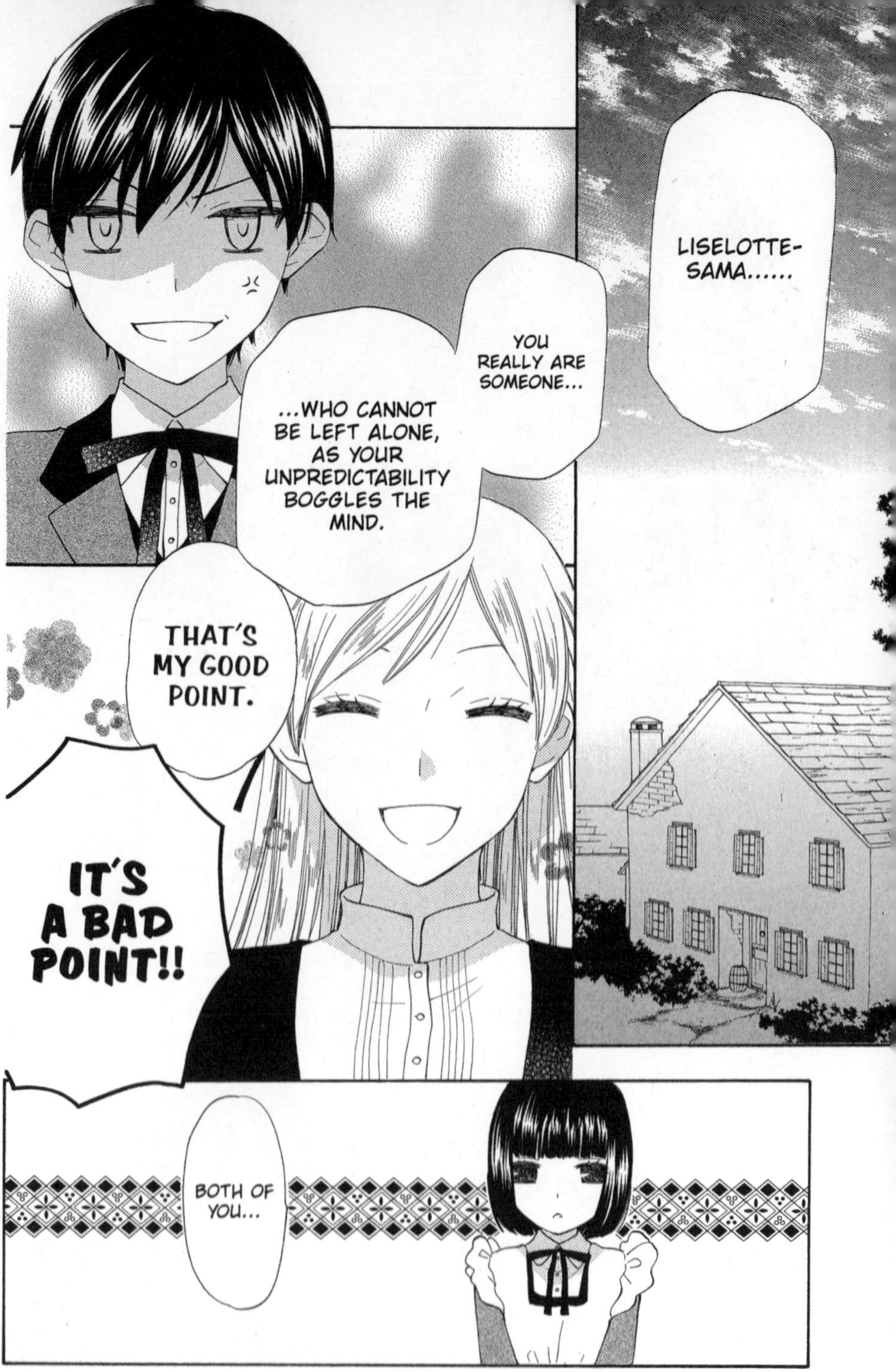
LISELOTTE-SAMA......
YOU REALLY ARE SOMEONE...
...WHO CANNOT BE LEFT ALONE, AS YOUR UNPREDICTABILITY BOGGLES THE MIND.
THAT'S MY GOOD POINT.
IT'S A BAD POINT!!
BOTH OF YOU...

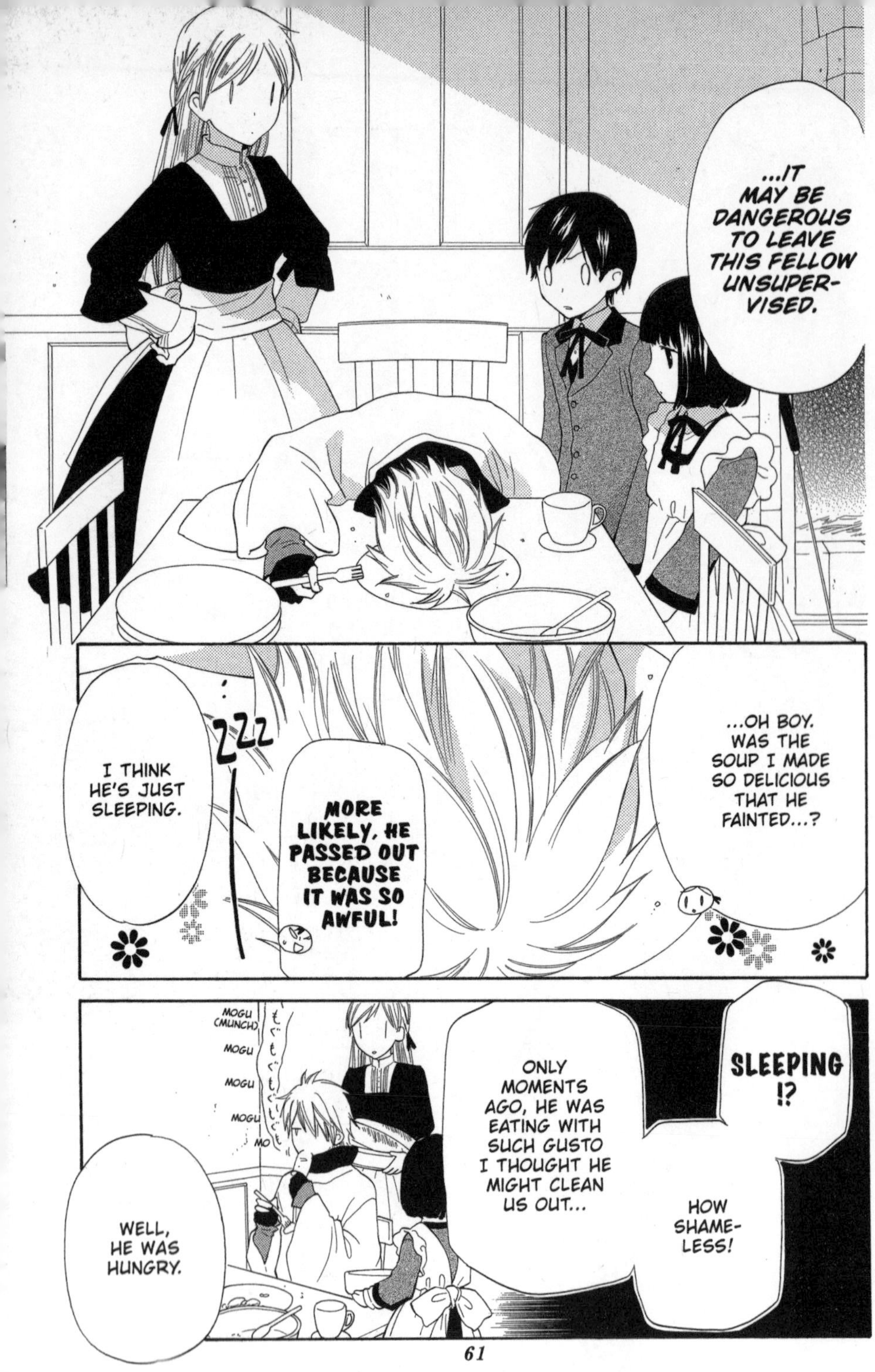
...IT MAY BE DANGEROUS TO LEAVE THIS FELLOW UNSUPER-VISED.
...OH BOY. WAS THE SOUP I MADE SO DELICIOUS THAT HE FAINTED...?
MORE LIKELY, HE PASSED OUT BECAUSE IT WAS SO AWFUL!
ZZZ
I THINK HE'S JUST SLEEPING.
SLEEPING!?
ONLY MOMENTS AGO, HE WAS EATING WITH SUCH GUSTO I THOUGHT HE MIGHT CLEAN US OUT...
HOW SHAME-LESS!
MOGU (MUNCH)
MOGU
MOGU
MOGU
MO
WELL, HE WAS HUNGRY.

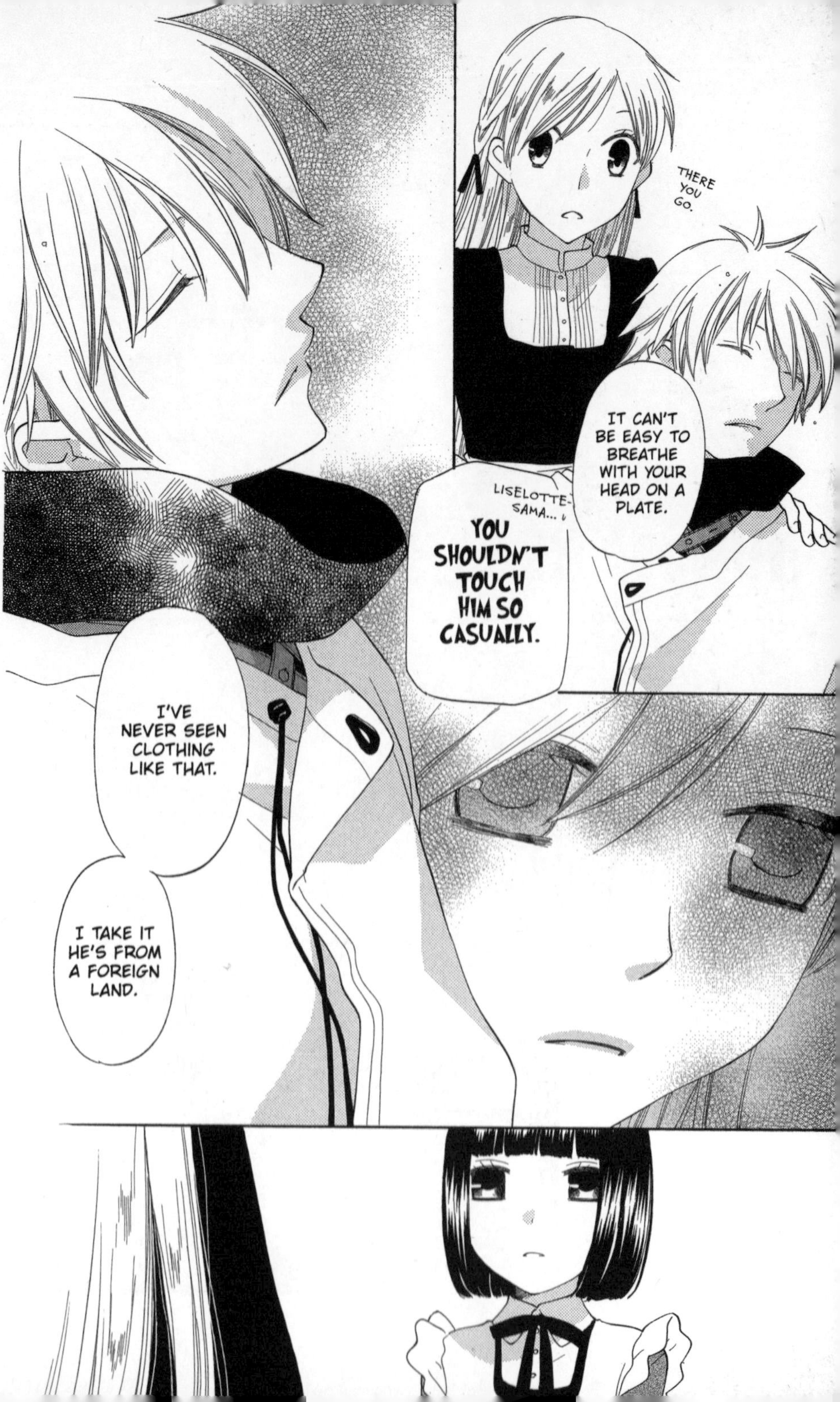
THERE YOU GO.
IT CAN'T BE EASY TO BREATHE WITH YOUR HEAD ON A PLATE.
LISELOTTE-SAMA...
YOU SHOULDN'T TOUCH HIM SO CASUALLY.
I'VE NEVER SEEN CLOTHING LIKE THAT.
I TAKE IT HE'S FROM A FOREIGN LAND.

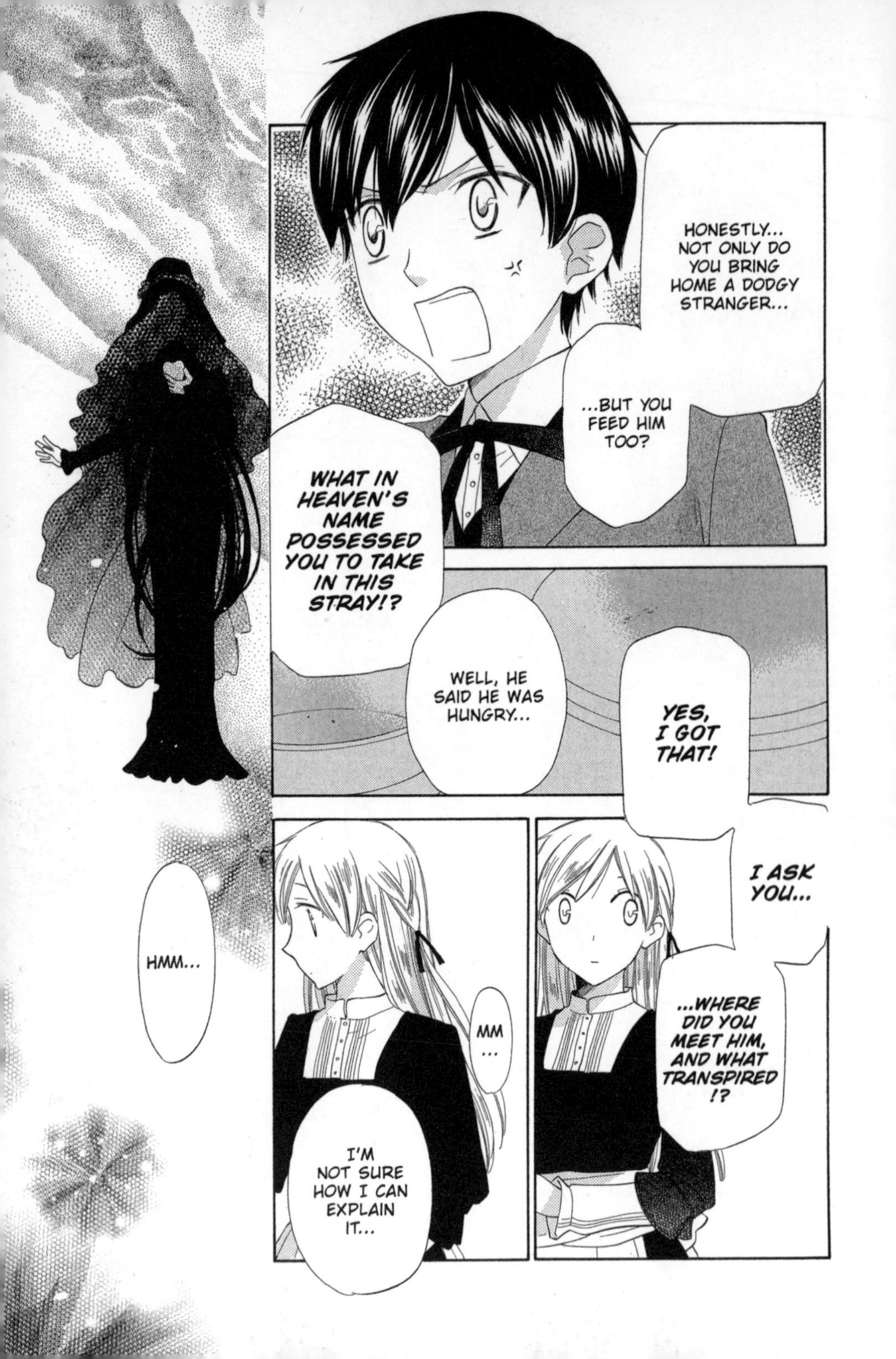
HONESTLY... NOT ONLY DO YOU BRING HOME A DODGY STRANGER...
...BUT YOU FEED HIM TOO?
WHAT IN HEAVEN'S NAME POSSESSED YOU TO TAKE IN THIS STRAY!?
WELL, HE SAID HE WAS HUNGRY...
YES, I GOT THAT!
I ASK YOU...
...WHERE DID YOU MEET HIM, AND WHAT TRANSPIRED!?
MM...
I'M NOT SURE HOW I CAN EXPLAIN IT...
HMM...

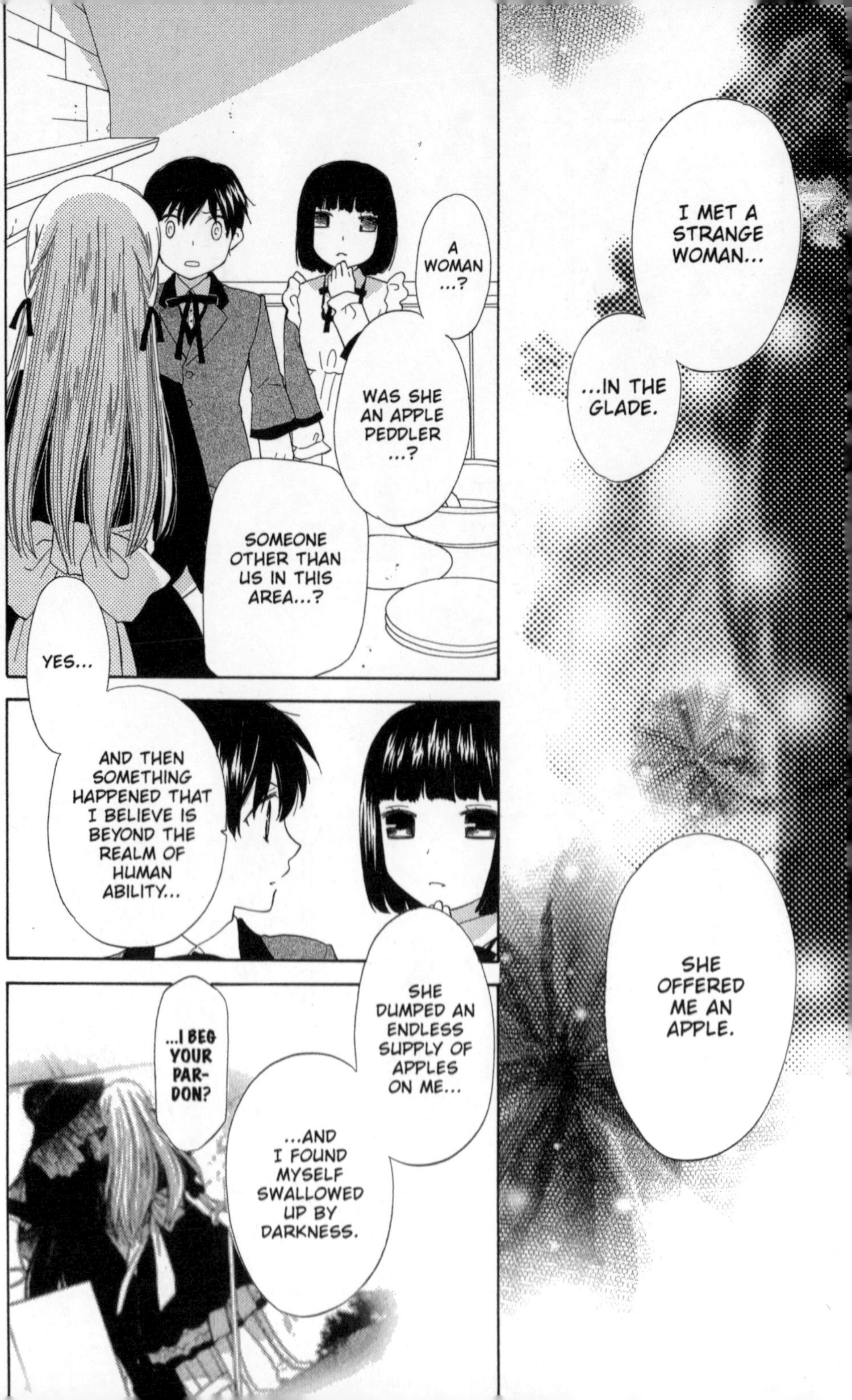
I MET A STRANGE WOMAN...
...IN THE GLADE.
SHE OFFERED ME AN APPLE.
A WOMAN...?
WAS SHE AN APPLE PEDDLER...?
SOMEONE OTHER THAN US IN THIS AREA...?
YES...
AND THEN SOMETHING HAPPENED THAT I BELIEVE IS BEYOND THE REALM OF HUMAN ABILITY...
SHE DUMPED AN ENDLESS SUPPLY OF APPLES ON ME...
...AND I FOUND MYSELF SWALLOWED UP BY DARKNESS.
...I BEG YOUR PARDON?

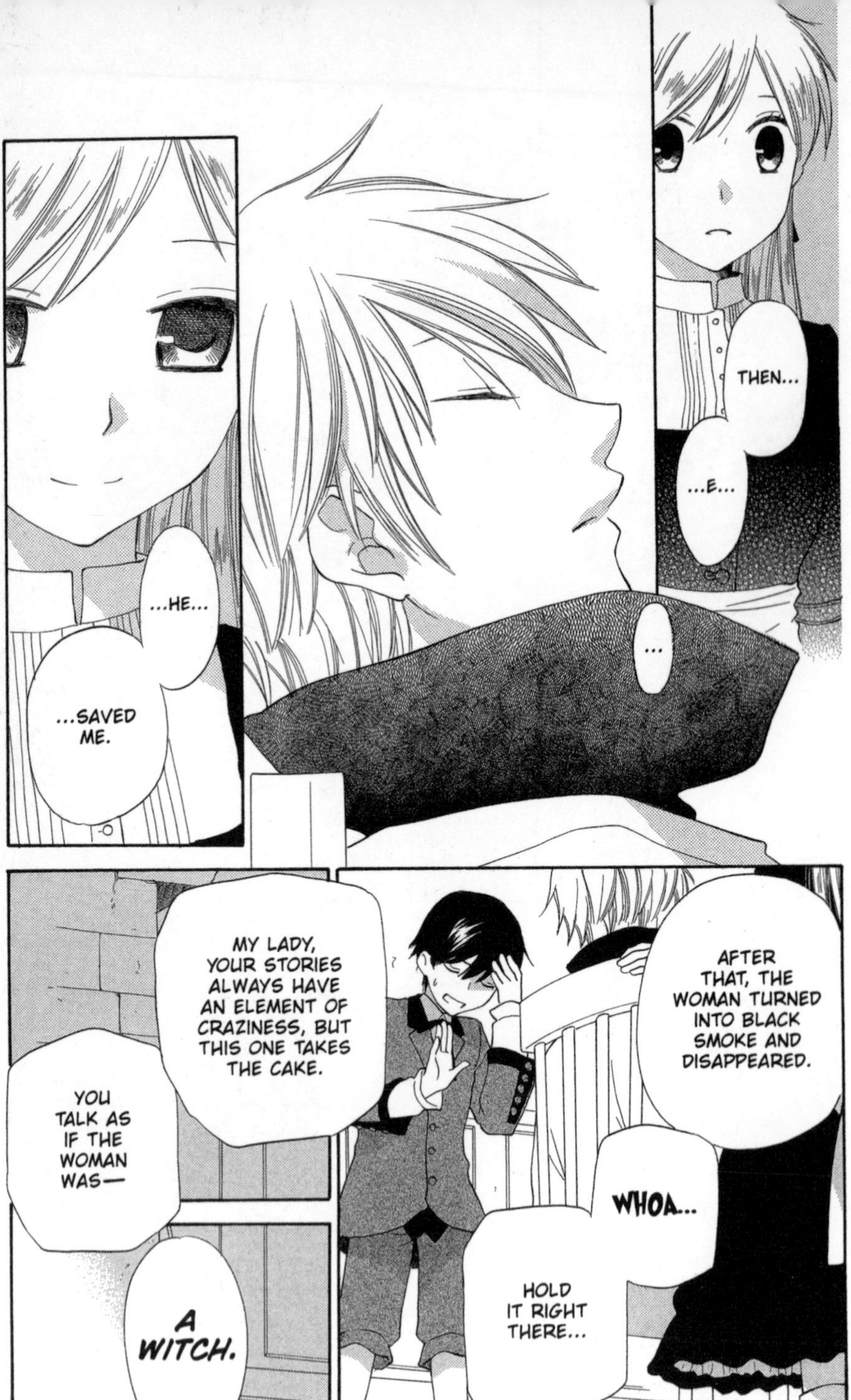
THEN...
...E...
...
...HE...
...SAVED ME.
AFTER THAT, THE WOMAN TURNED INTO BLACK SMOKE AND DISAPPEARED.
WHOA...
HOLD IT RIGHT THERE...
MY LADY, YOUR STORIES ALWAYS HAVE AN ELEMENT OF CRAZINESS, BUT THIS ONE TAKES THE CAKE.
YOU TALK AS IF THE WOMAN WAS—
A WITCH.

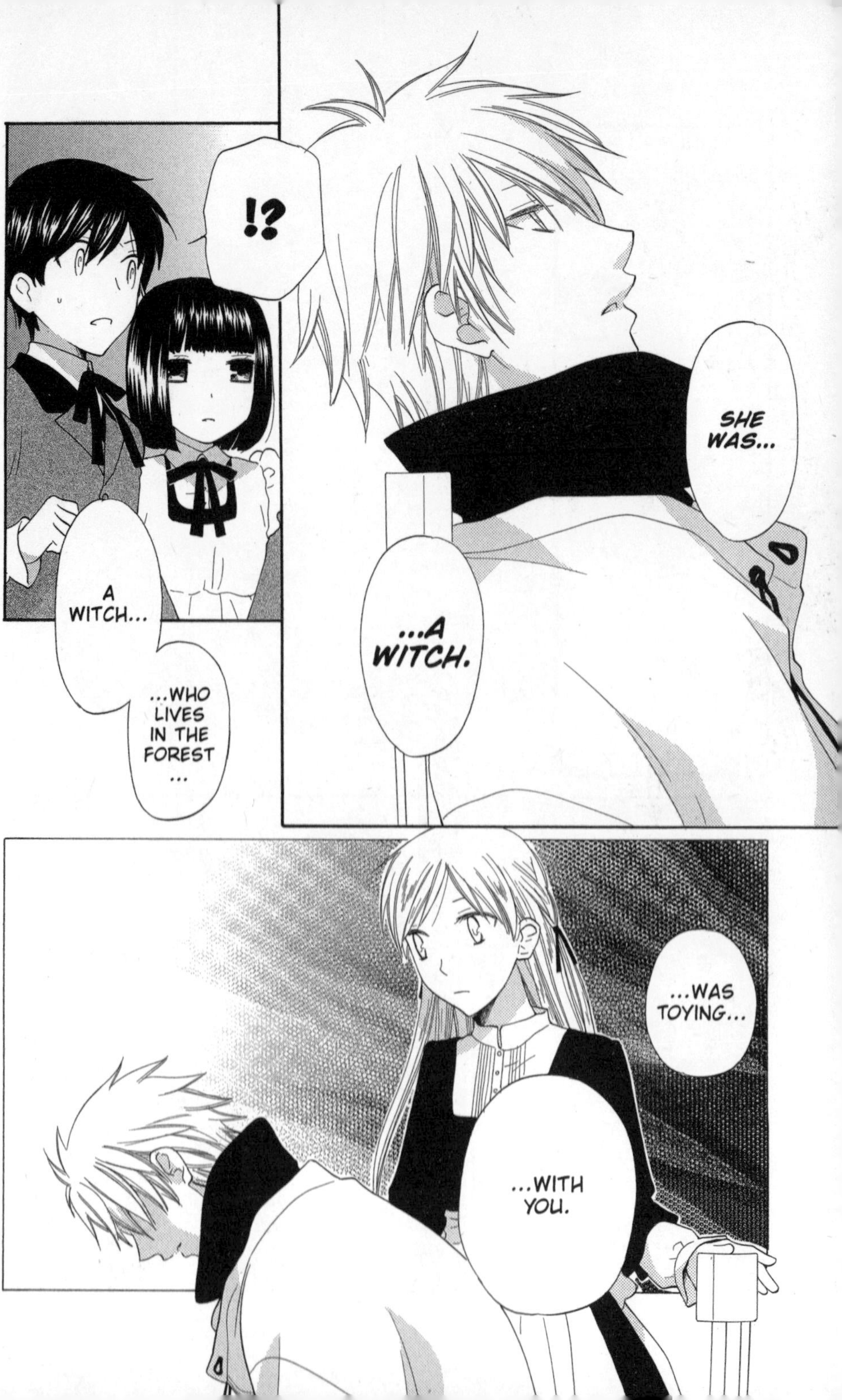
SHE WAS...
...A WITCH.
!?
A WITCH...
...WHO LIVES IN THE FOREST...
...WAS TOYING...
...WITH YOU.

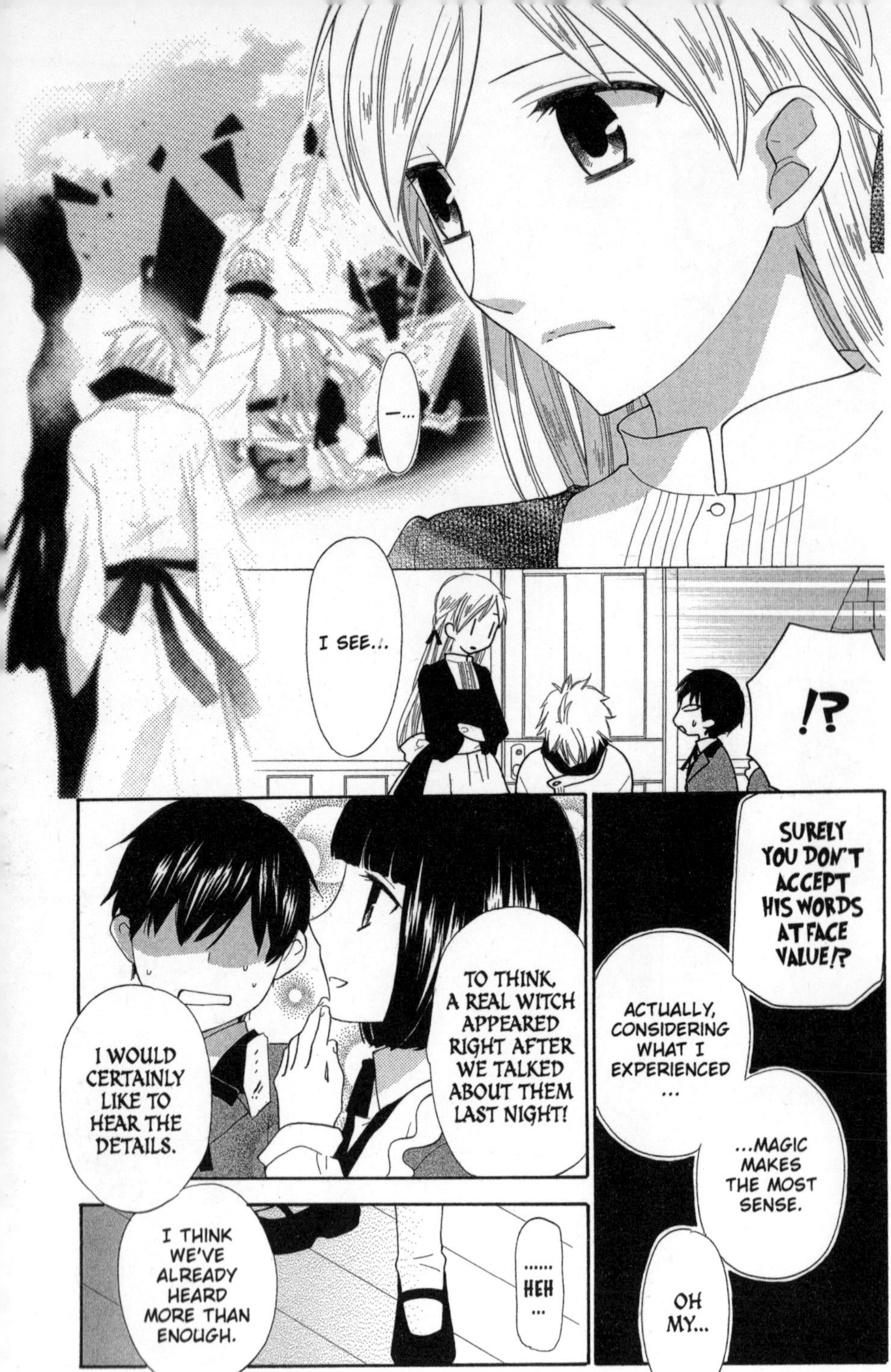
—...
I SEE...
!?
SURELY YOU DON'T ACCEPT HIS WORDS AT FACE VALUE!?
ACTUALLY, CONSIDERING WHAT I EXPERIENCED ...
...MAGIC MAKES THE MOST SENSE.
OH MY...
TO THINK, A REAL WITCH APPEARED RIGHT AFTER WE TALKED ABOUT THEM LAST NIGHT!
I WOULD CERTAINLY LIKE TO HEAR THE DETAILS.
......HEH...
I THINK WE'VE ALREADY HEARD MORE THAN ENOUGH.

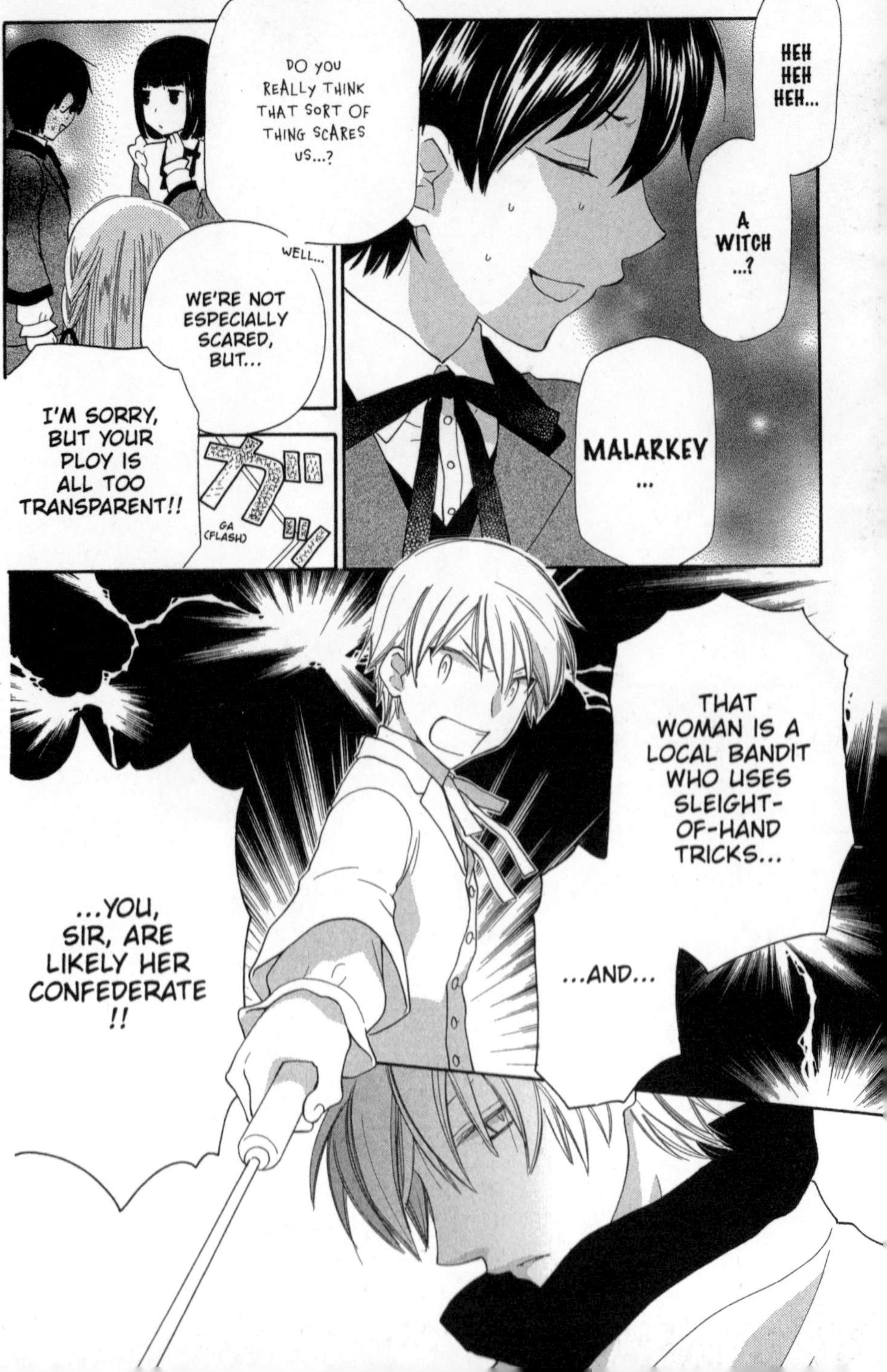
HEH HEH HEH...
A WITCH ...?
MALARKEY ...
DO YOU REALLY THINK THAT SORT OF THING SCARES US...?
WELL...
WE'RE NOT ESPECIALLY SCARED, BUT...
I'M SORRY, BUT YOUR PLOY IS ALL TOO TRANSPARENT!!
GA (FLASH)
THAT WOMAN IS A LOCAL BANDIT WHO USES SLEIGHT-OF-HAND TRICKS...
...AND...
...YOU, SIR, ARE LIKELY HER CONFEDERATE !!

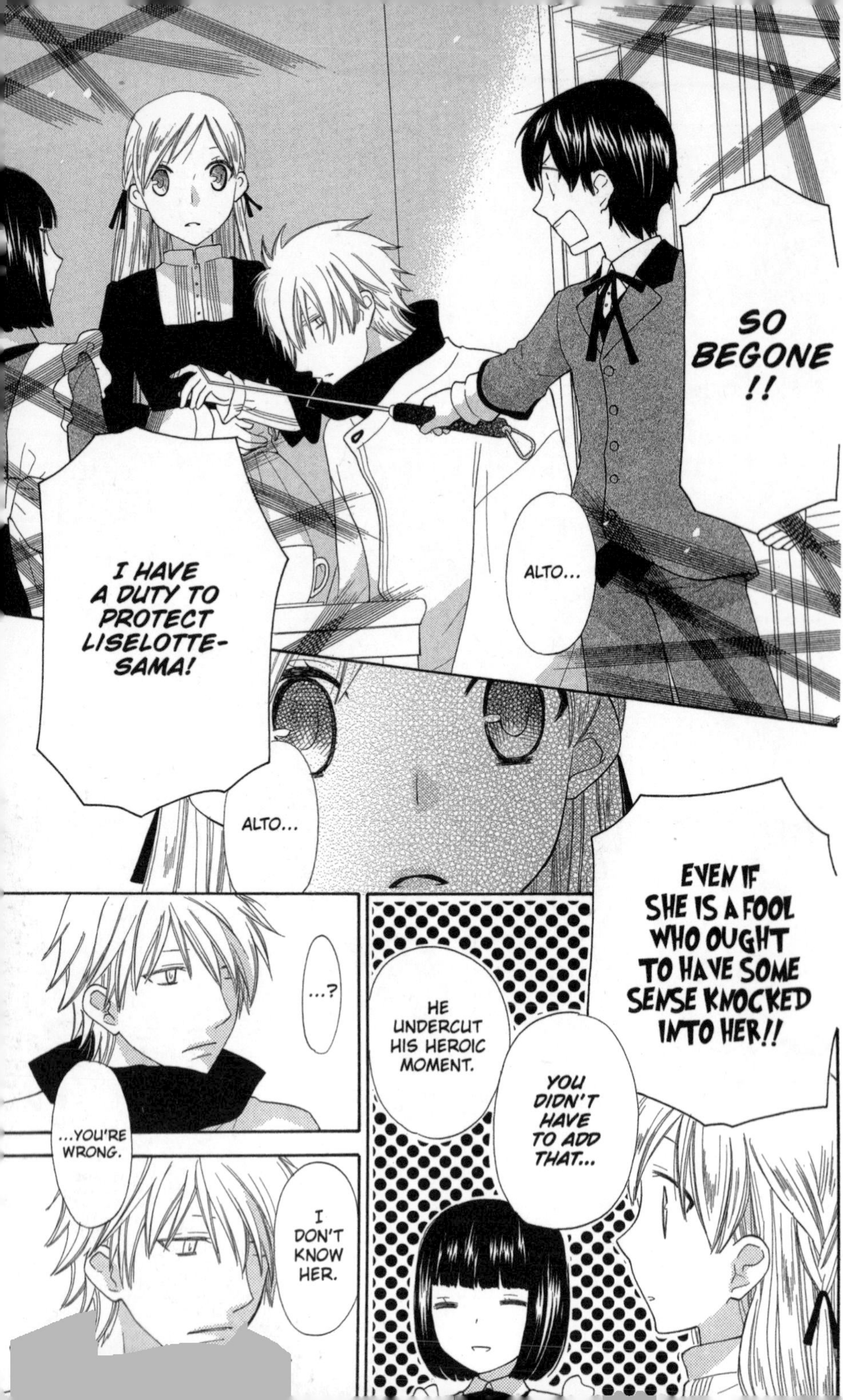
SO BEGONE !!
ALTO...
I HAVE A DUTY TO PROTECT LISELOTTE-SAMA!
EVEN IF SHE IS A FOOL WHO OUGHT TO HAVE SOME SENSE KNOCKED INTO HER!!
ALTO...
YOU DIDN'T HAVE TO ADD THAT...
HE UNDERCUT HIS HEROIC MOMENT.
...?
...YOU'RE WRONG.
I DON'T KNOW HER.

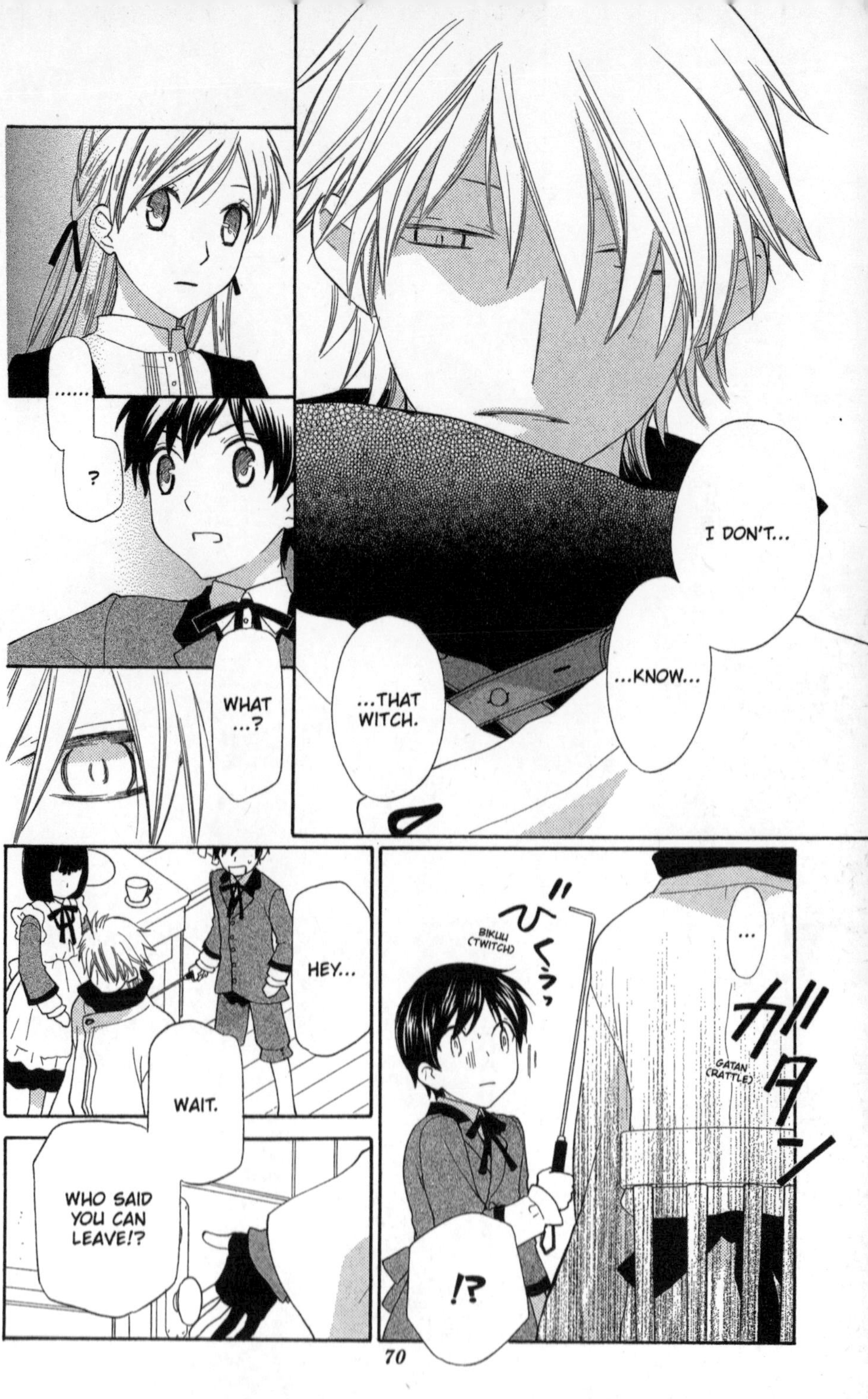
I DON'T...
...KNOW...
...THAT WITCH.
......
?
WHAT ...?
...
ガタン
GATAN (RATTLE)
びくっ
BIKUU (TWITCH)
!?
HEY...
WAIT.
WHO SAID YOU CAN LEAVE!?

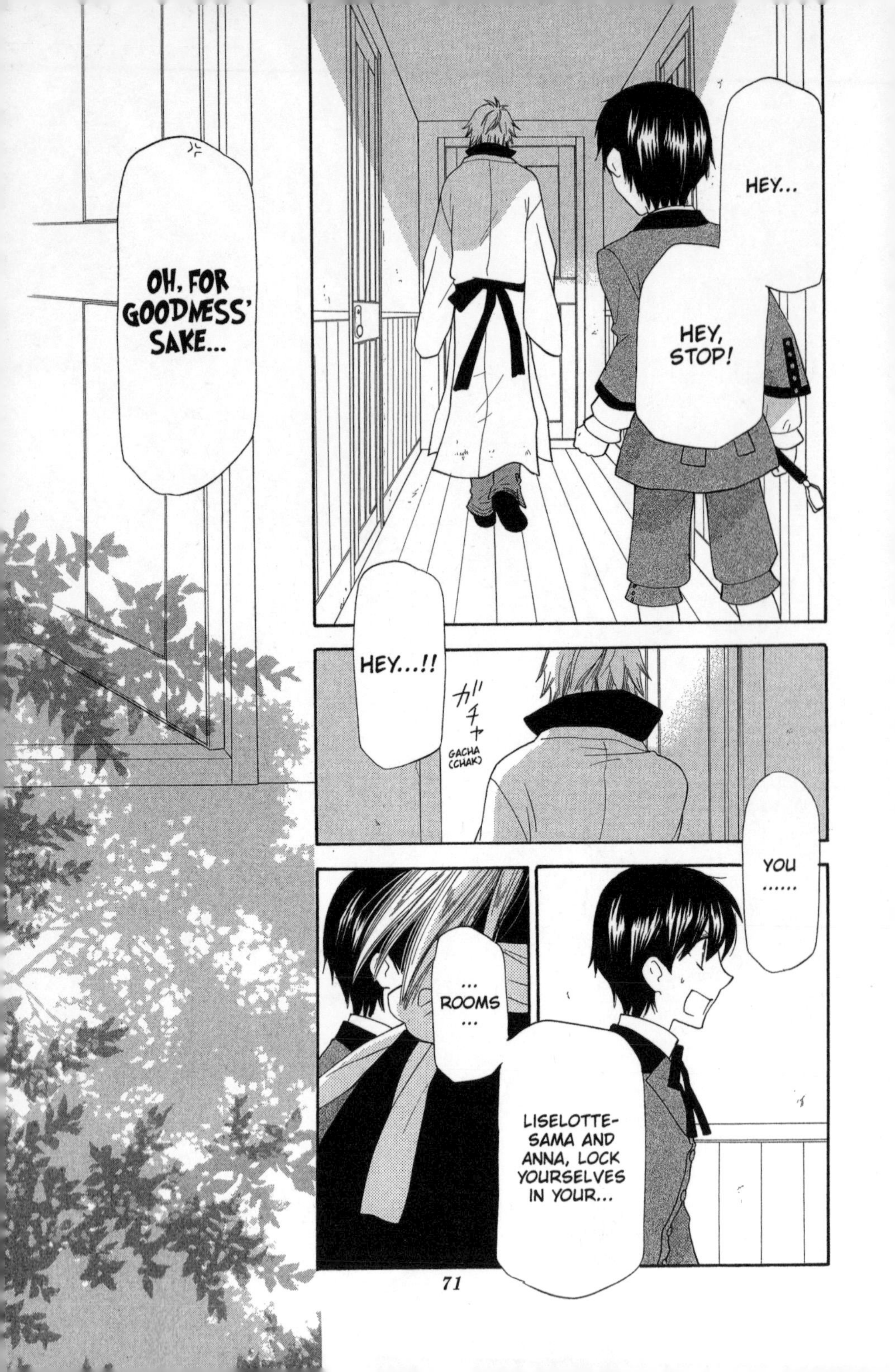
HEY...
HEY, STOP!
HEY...!!
ガチャ
GACHA (CHAK)
YOU ......
LISELOTTE-SAMA AND ANNA, LOCK YOURSELVES IN YOUR...
... ROOMS ...
OH, FOR GOODNESS' SAKE...

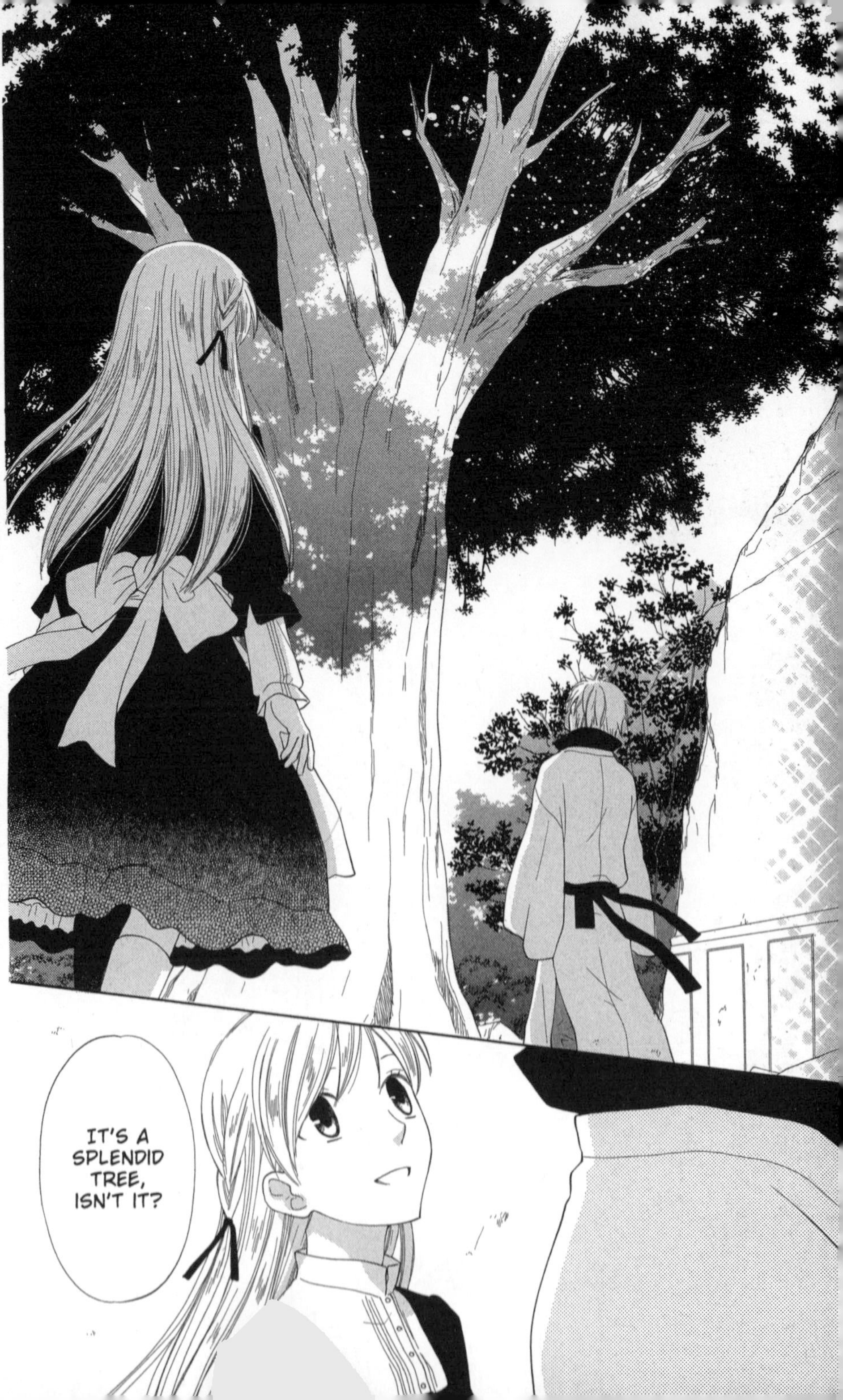
IT'S A SPLENDID TREE, ISN'T IT?

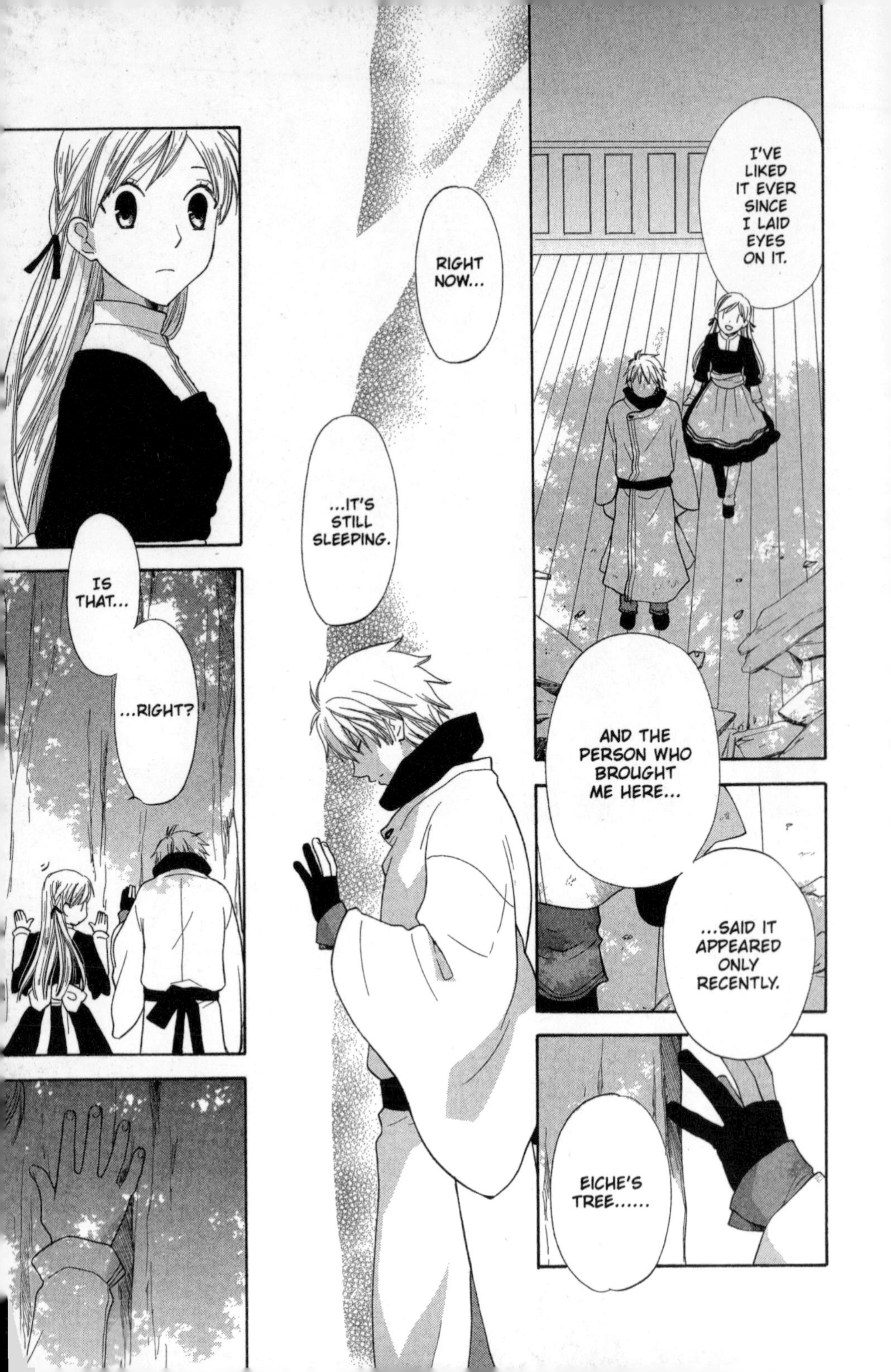
I'VE LIKED IT EVER SINCE I LAID EYES ON IT.
AND THE PERSON WHO BROUGHT ME HERE...
...SAID IT APPEARED ONLY RECENTLY.
EICHE'S TREE......
RIGHT NOW...
...IT'S STILL SLEEPING.
IS THAT...
...RIGHT?

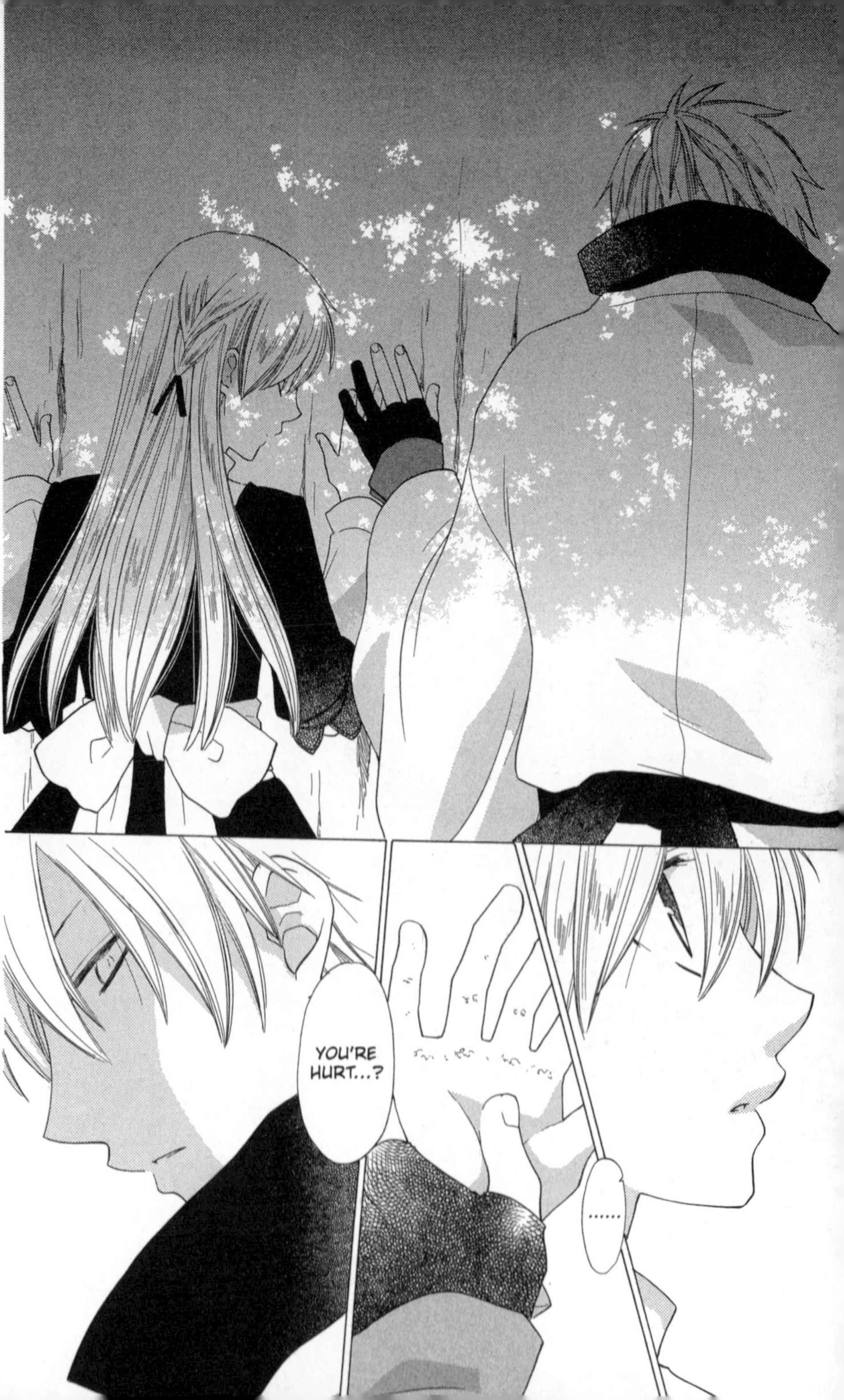
......
YOU'RE HURT...?

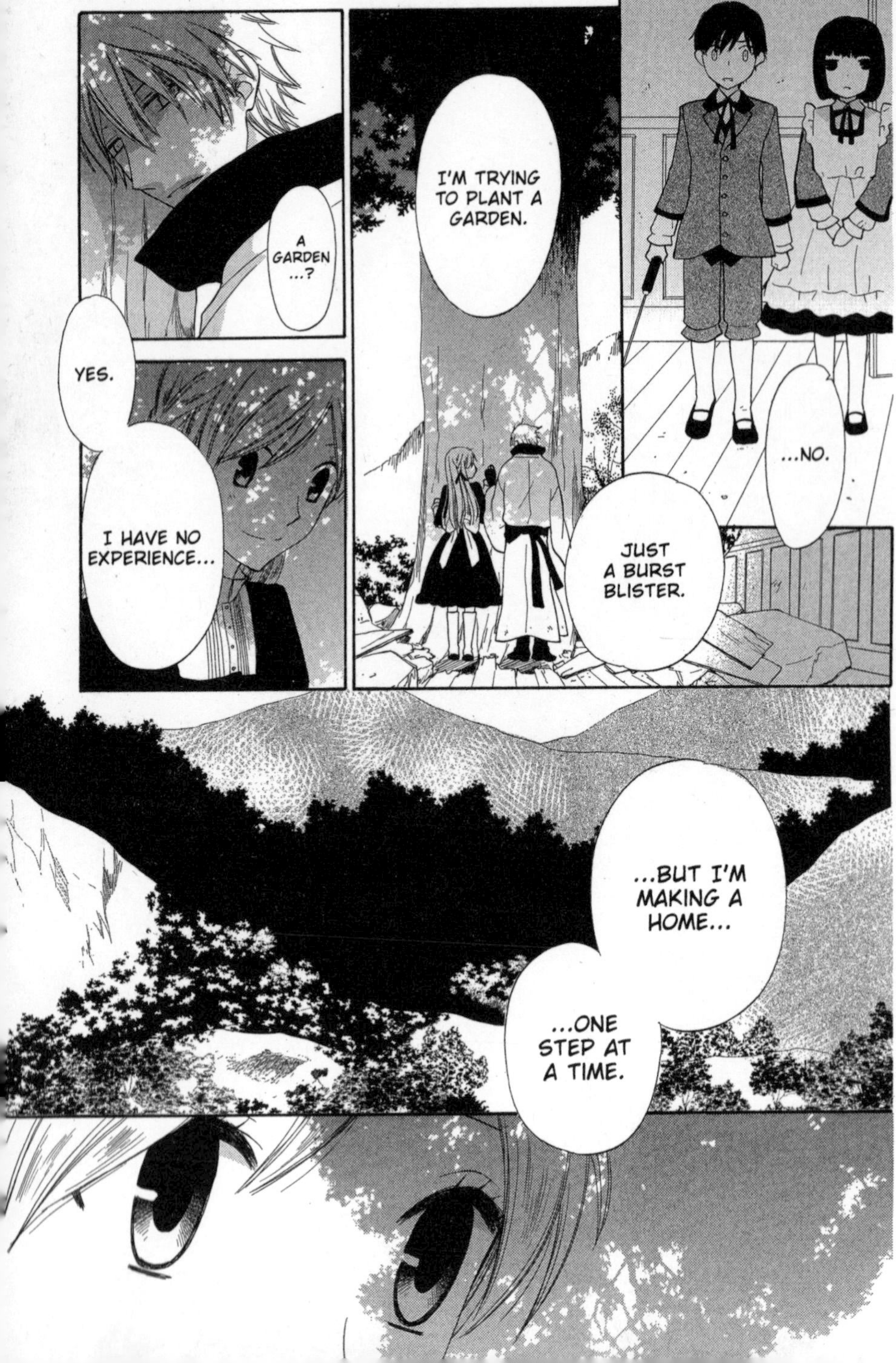
...NO.
JUST A BURST BLISTER.
I'M TRYING TO PLANT A GARDEN.
A GARDEN...?
YES.
I HAVE NO EXPERIENCE...
...BUT I'M MAKING A HOME...
...ONE STEP AT A TIME.

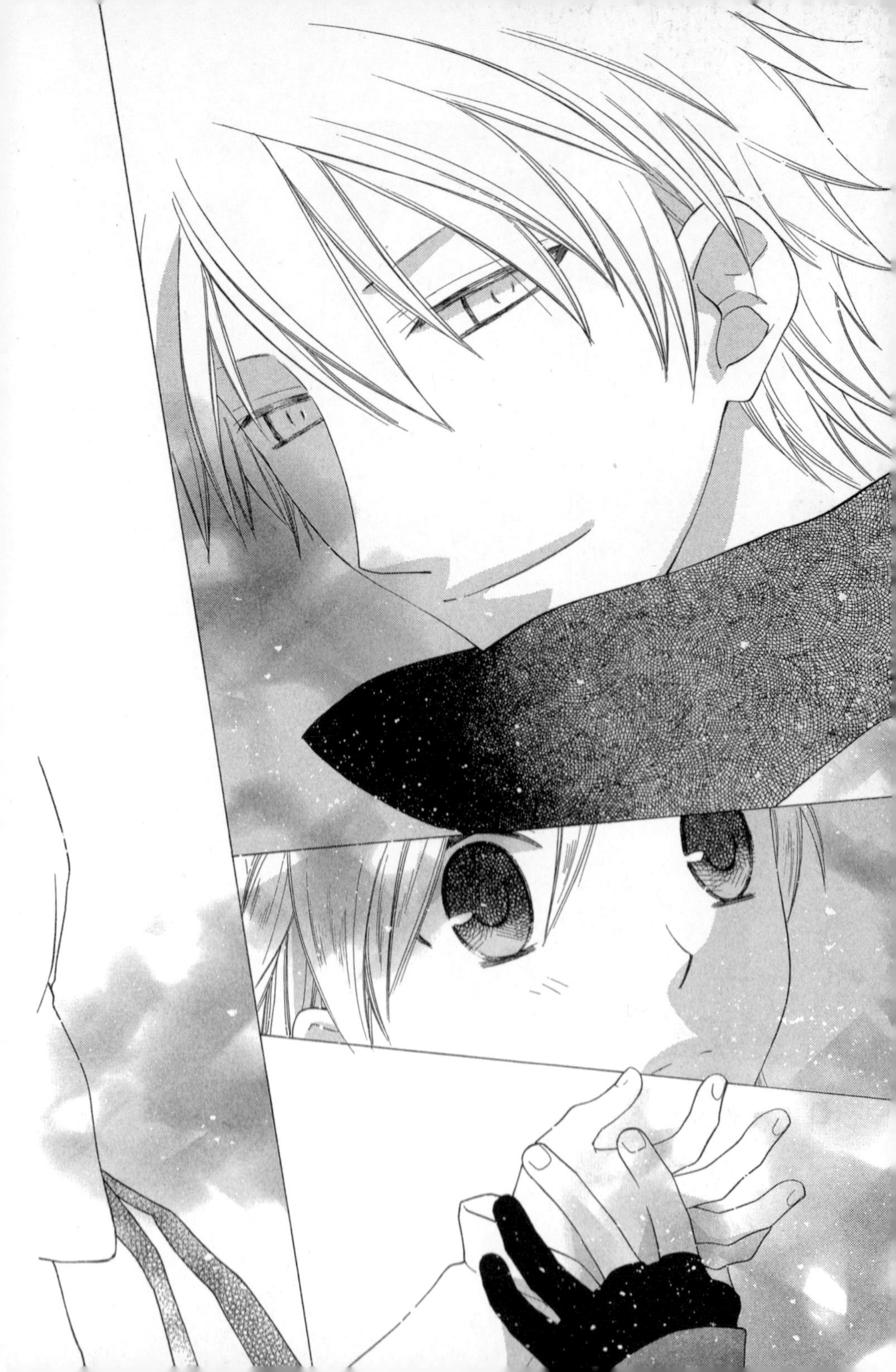

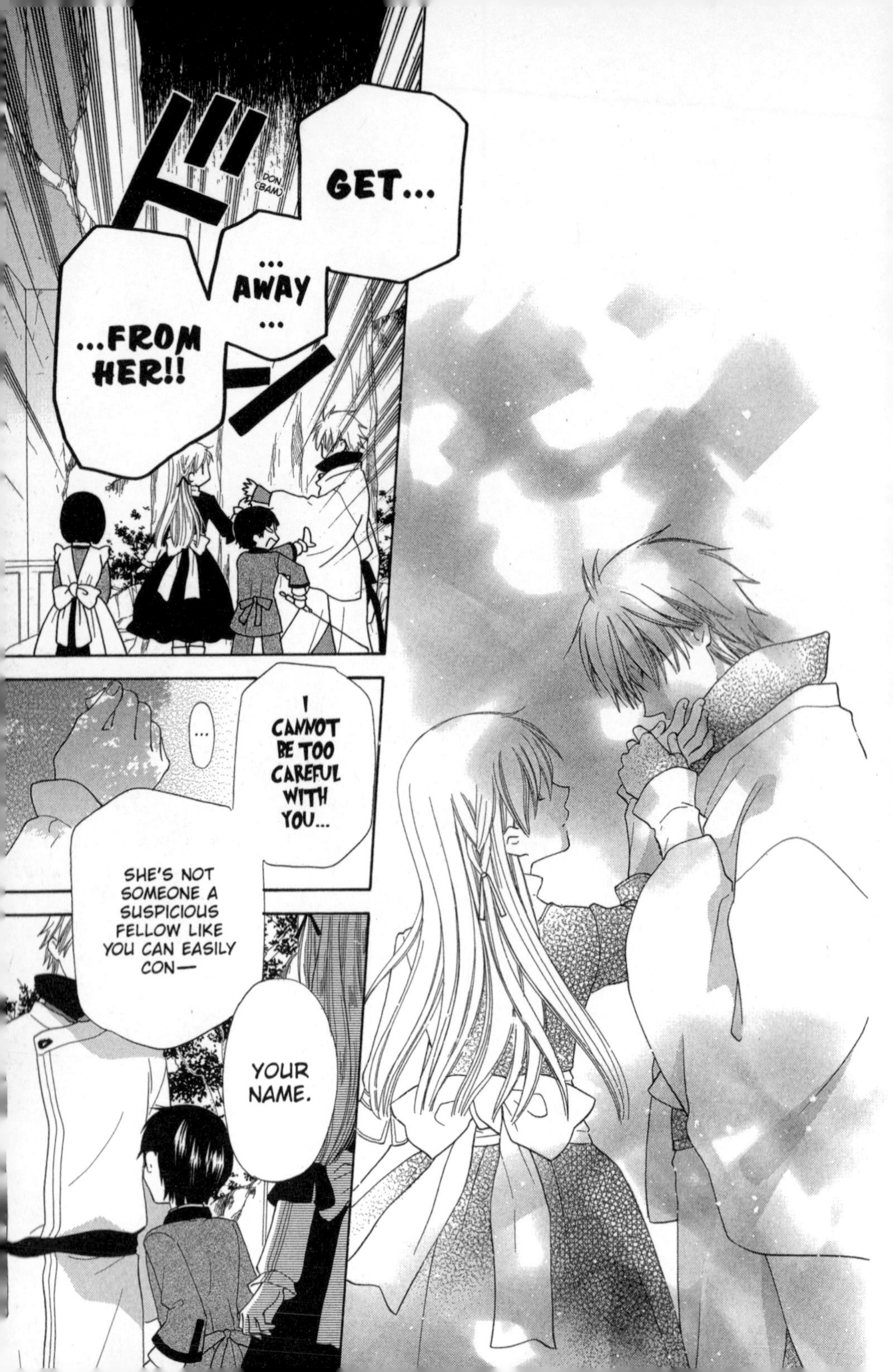
GET...
... AWAY ...
...FROM HER!!
DON (BAM)
...
I CANNOT BE TOO CAREFUL WITH YOU...
SHE'S NOT SOMEONE A SUSPICIOUS FELLOW LIKE YOU CAN EASILY CON—
YOUR NAME.

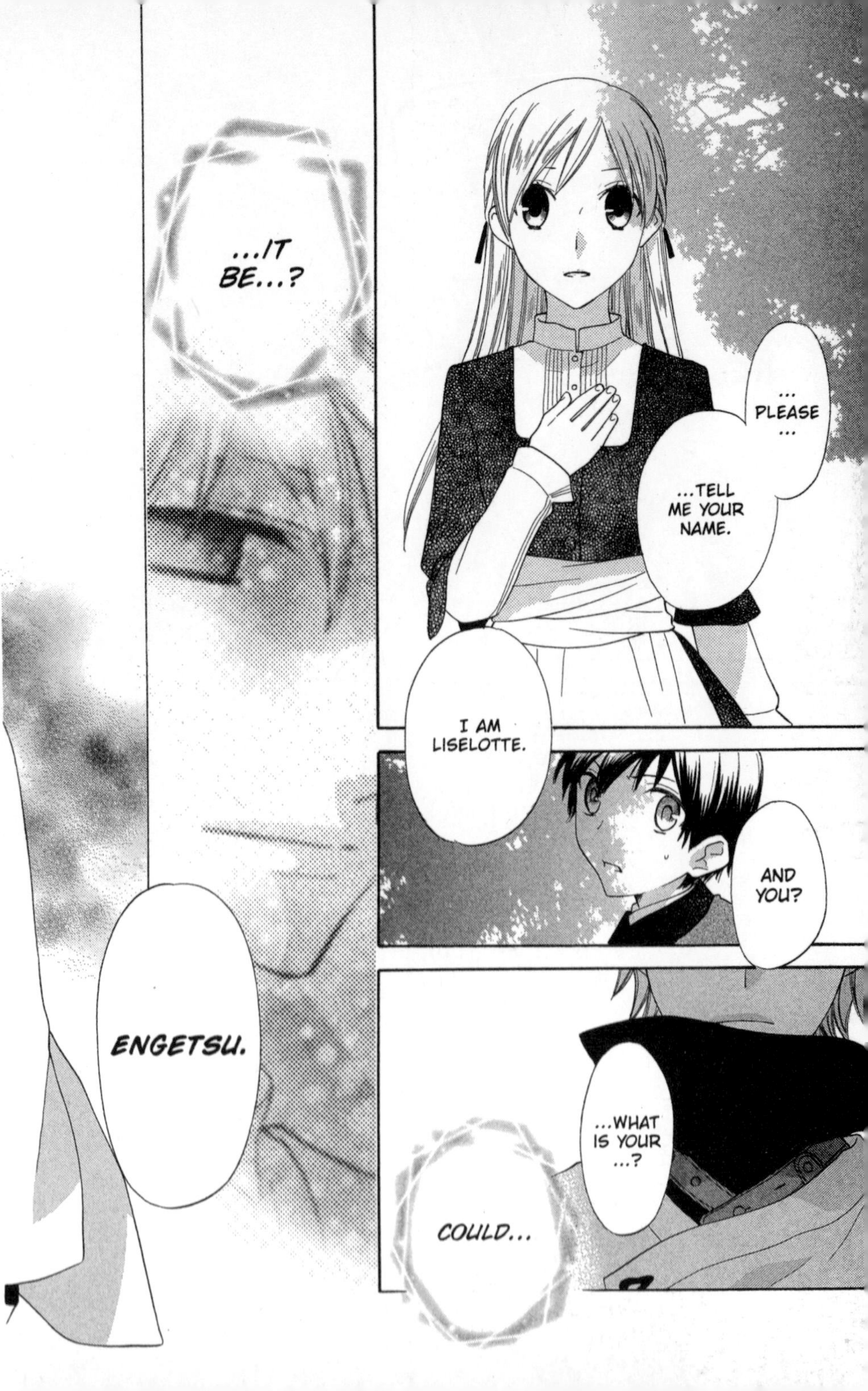
...PLEASE...
...TELL ME YOUR NAME.
I AM LISELOTTE.
AND YOU?
...WHAT IS YOUR ...?
COULD...
...IT BE...?
ENGETSU.

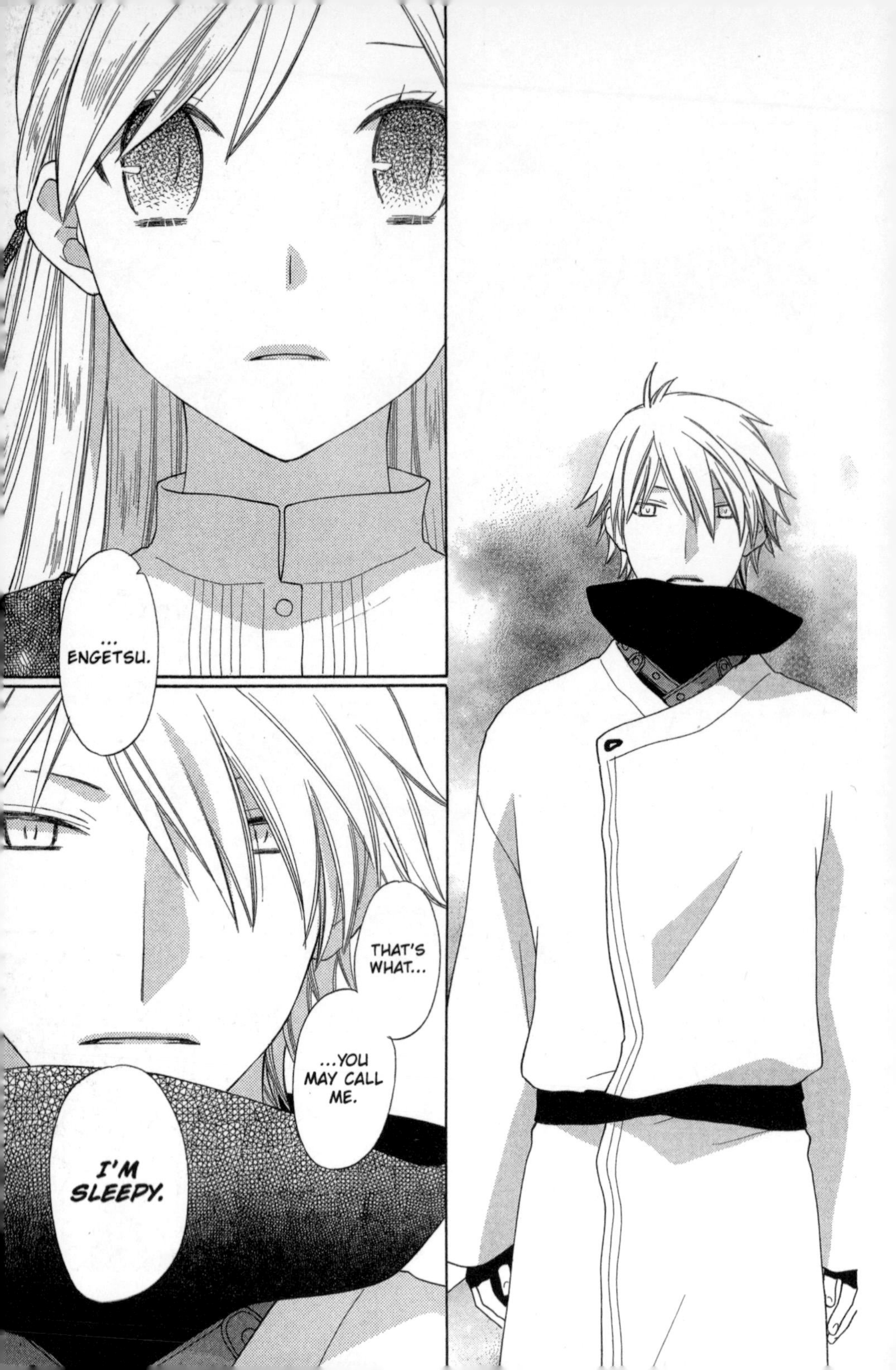
... ENGETSU.
THAT'S WHAT...
...YOU MAY CALL ME.
I'M SLEEPY.

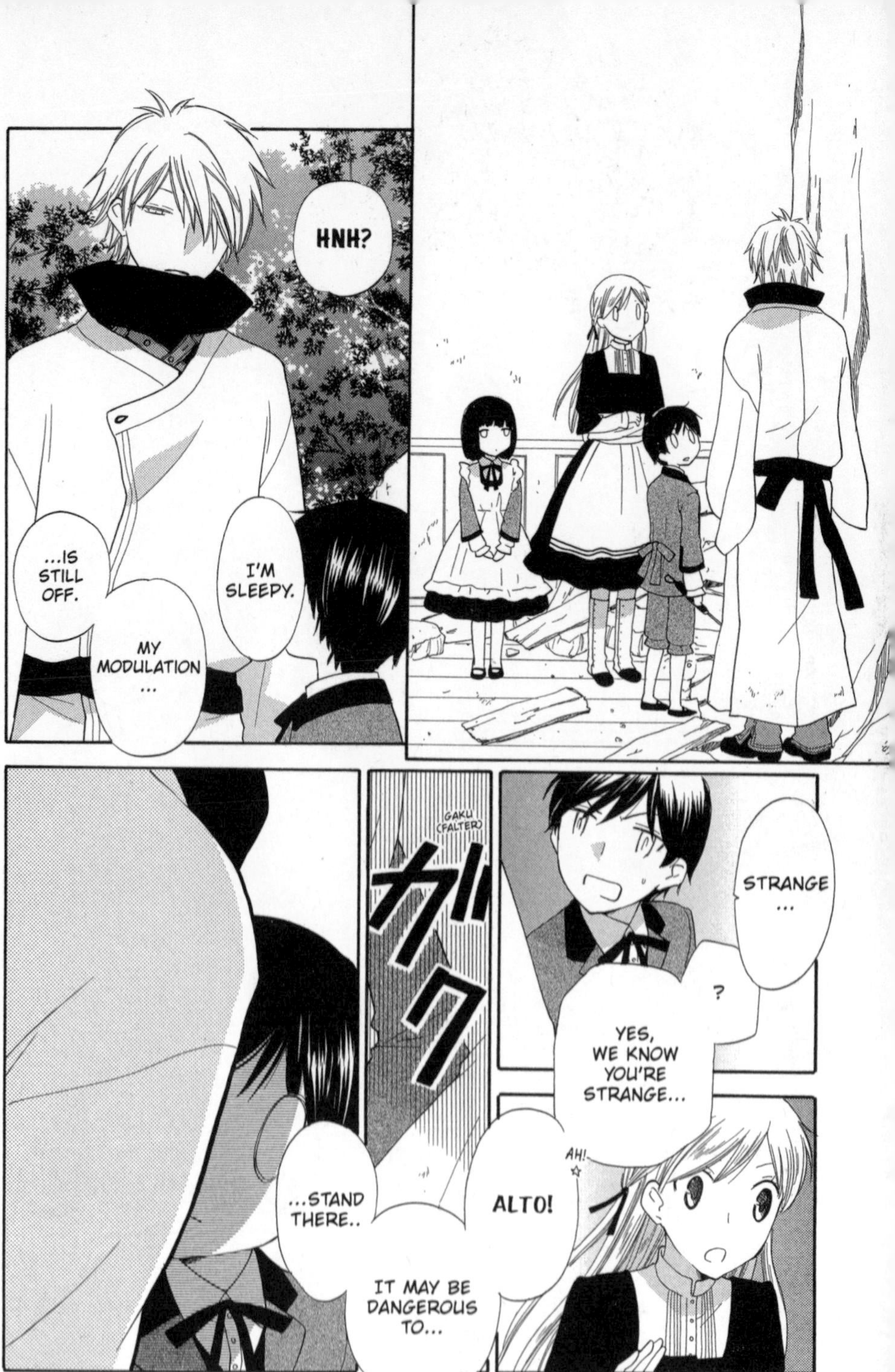
HNH?
I'M SLEEPY.
MY MODULATION ...
...IS STILL OFF.
STRANGE ...
?
YES, WE KNOW YOU'RE STRANGE...
AH!
ALTO!
IT MAY BE DANGEROUS TO...
...STAND THERE..
GAKU (FALTER)

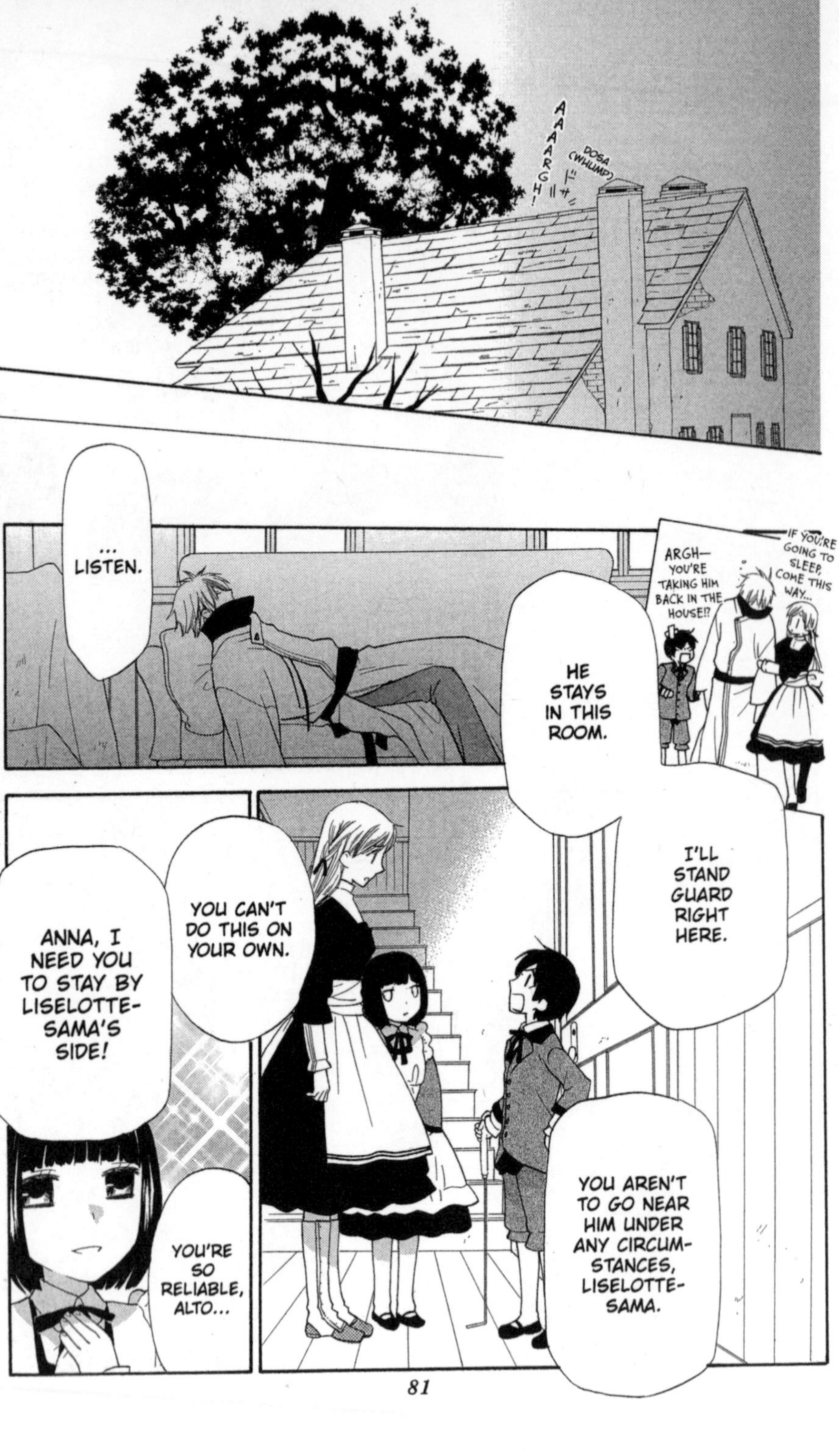
AAAARGH!
DOSA (WHUMP)
IF YOU'RE GOING TO SLEEP, COME THIS WAY...
ARGH— YOU'RE TAKING HIM BACK IN THE HOUSE!?
... LISTEN.
HE STAYS IN THIS ROOM.
I'LL STAND GUARD RIGHT HERE.
YOU AREN'T TO GO NEAR HIM UNDER ANY CIRCUM-STANCES, LISELOTTE-SAMA.
YOU CAN'T DO THIS ON YOUR OWN.
ANNA, I NEED YOU TO STAY BY LISELOTTE-SAMA'S SIDE!
YOU'RE SO RELIABLE, ALTO...

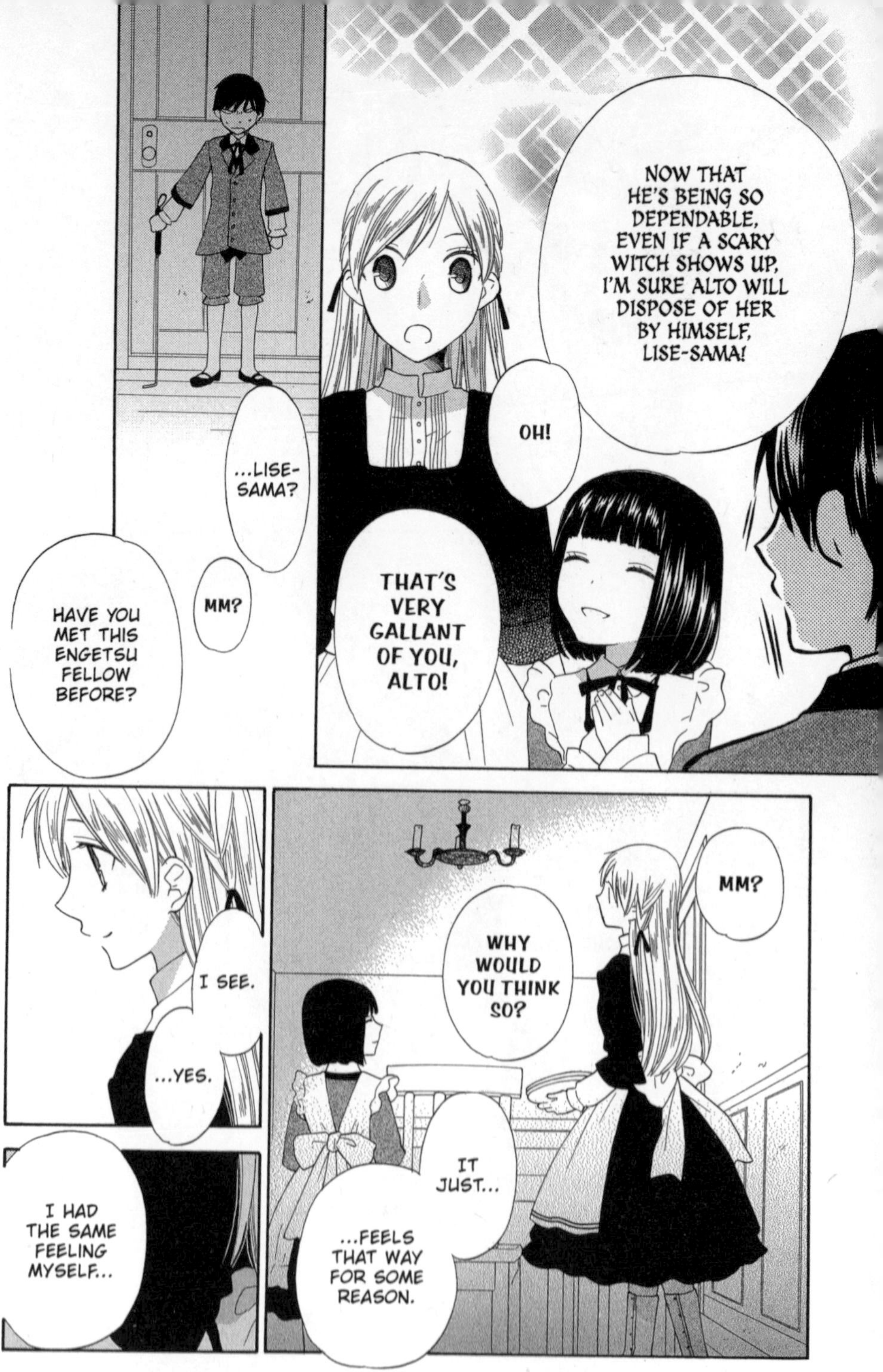
NOW THAT HE'S BEING SO DEPENDABLE, EVEN IF A SCARY WITCH SHOWS UP, I'M SURE ALTO WILL DISPOSE OF HER BY HIMSELF, LISE-SAMA!
OH!
THAT'S VERY GALLANT OF YOU, ALTO!
...LISE-SAMA?
MM?
HAVE YOU MET THIS ENGETSU FELLOW BEFORE?
MM?
WHY WOULD YOU THINK SO?
IT JUST...
...FEELS THAT WAY FOR SOME REASON.
I SEE.
...YES.
I HAD THE SAME FEELING MYSELF...

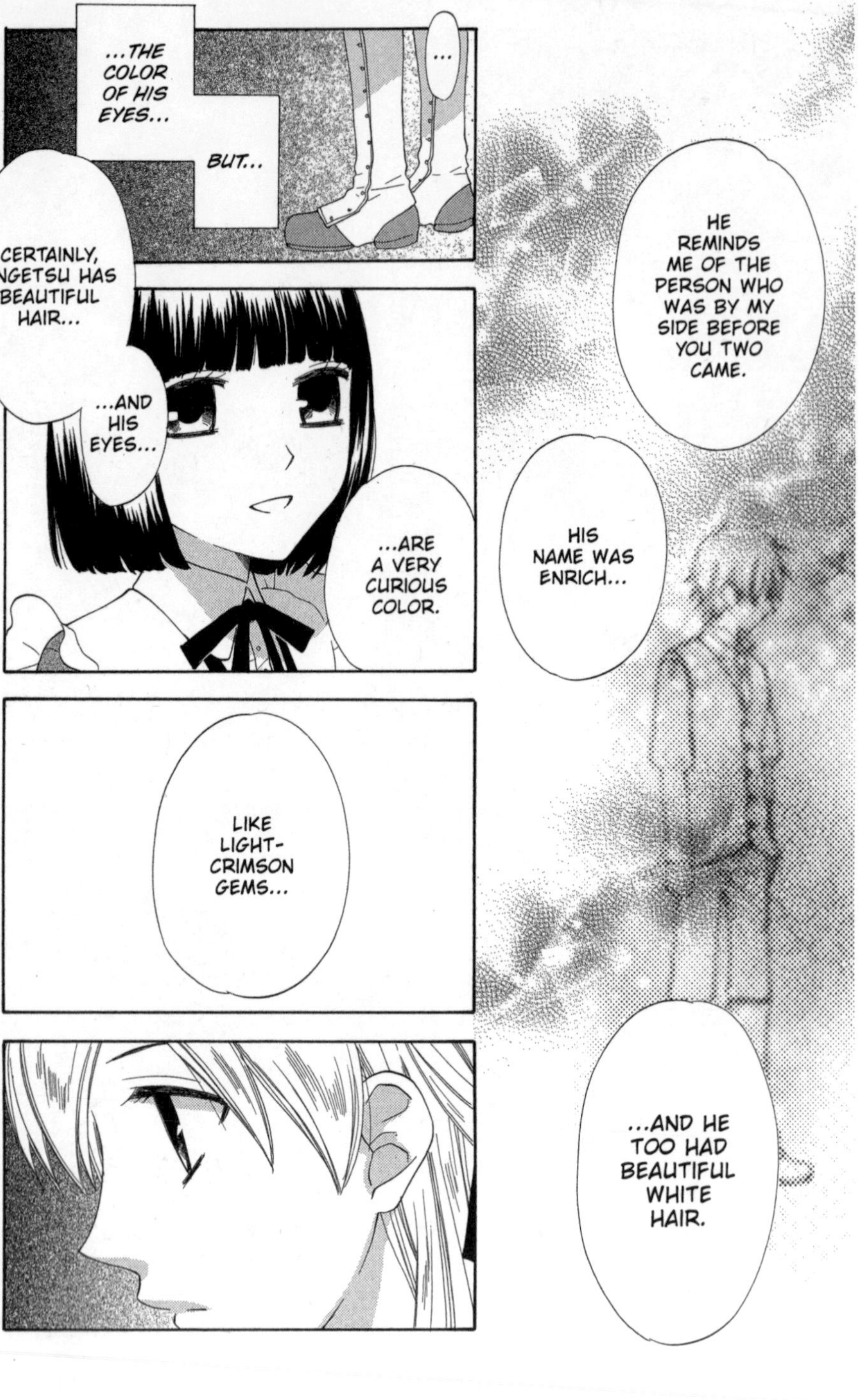
HE REMINDS ME OF THE PERSON WHO WAS BY MY SIDE BEFORE YOU TWO CAME.
HIS NAME WAS ENRICH...
...AND HE TOO HAD BEAUTIFUL WHITE HAIR.
...
...THE COLOR OF HIS EYES...
BUT...
CERTAINLY, ENGETSU HAS BEAUTIFUL HAIR...
...AND HIS EYES...
...ARE A VERY CURIOUS COLOR.
LIKE LIGHT-CRIMSON GEMS...

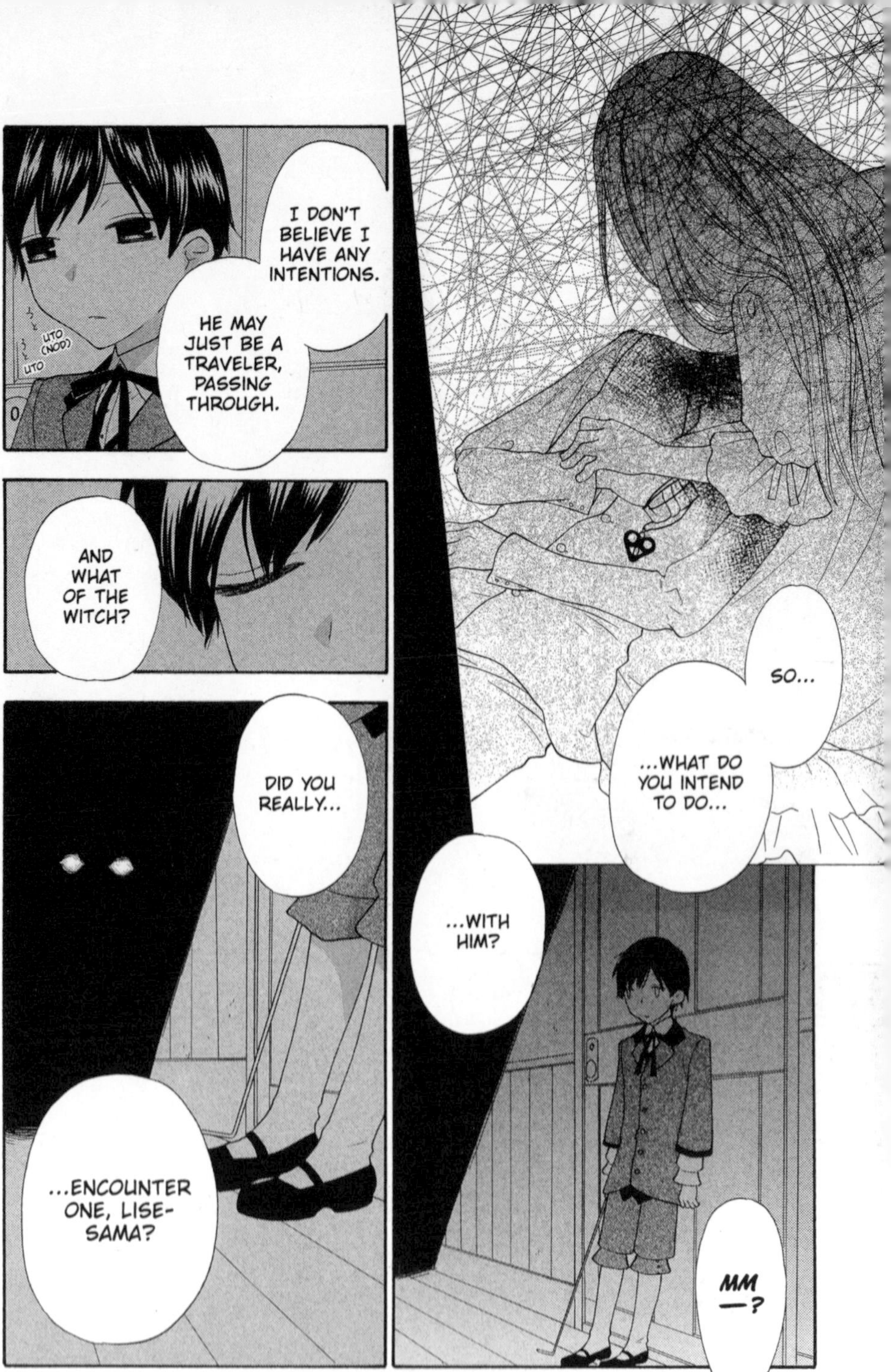
SO...
...WHAT DO YOU INTEND TO DO...
...WITH HIM?
MM—?
I DON'T BELIEVE I HAVE ANY INTENTIONS.
HE MAY JUST BE A TRAVELER, PASSING THROUGH.
UTO UTO (NOD)
AND WHAT OF THE WITCH?
DID YOU REALLY...
...ENCOUNTER ONE, LISE-SAMA?

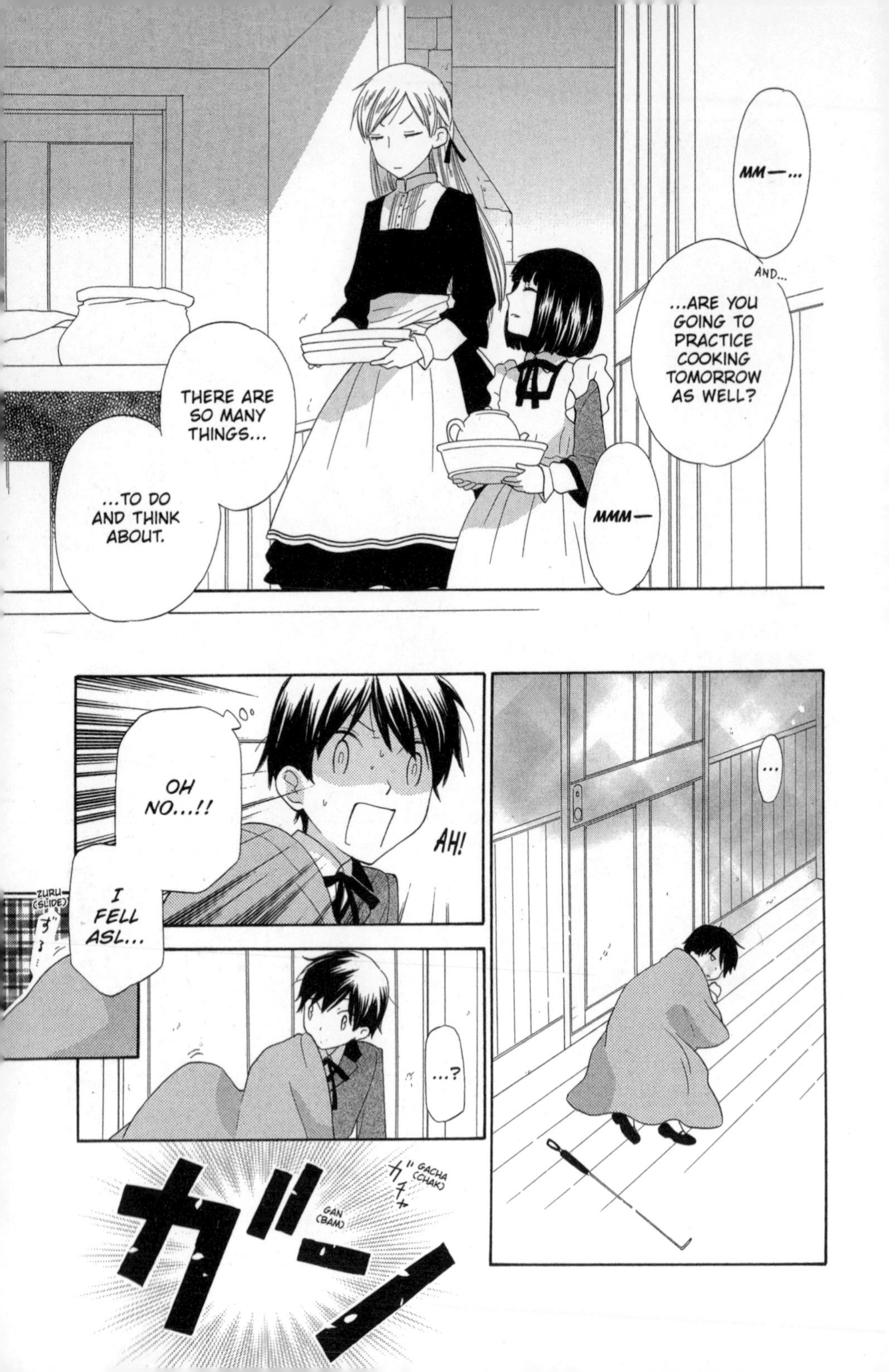
MM—...
AND...
...ARE YOU GOING TO PRACTICE COOKING TOMORROW AS WELL?
MMM—
THERE ARE SO MANY THINGS...
...TO DO AND THINK ABOUT.
...
AH!
OH NO...!!
I FELL ASL...
ZURU (SLIDE)
...?
GACHA (CHAK)
GAN (BAM)

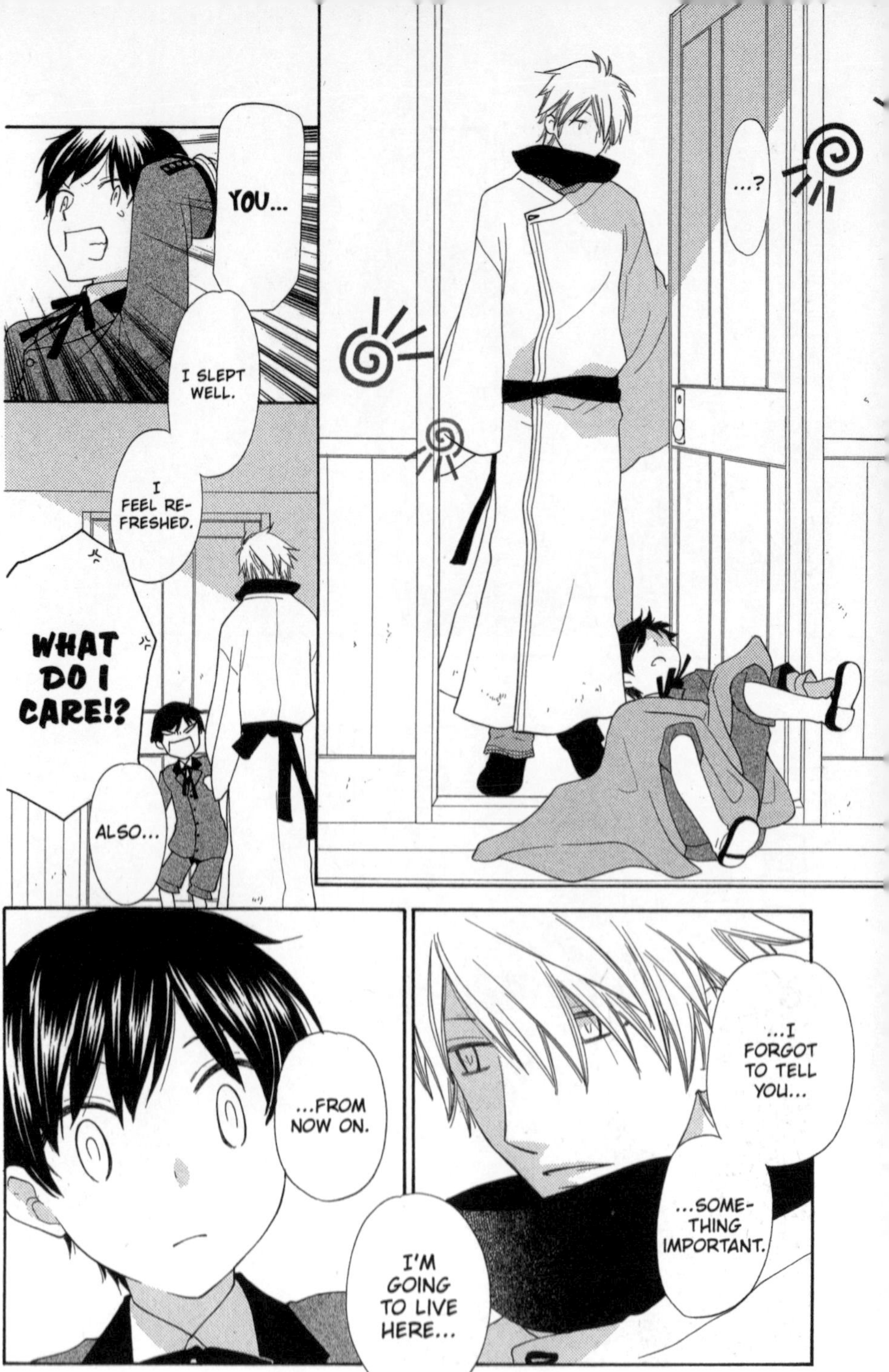
...?
YOU...
I SLEPT WELL.
I FEEL RE-FRESHED.
WHAT DO I CARE!?
ALSO...
...I FORGOT TO TELL YOU...
...SOME-THING IMPORTANT.
I'M GOING TO LIVE HERE...
...FROM NOW ON.

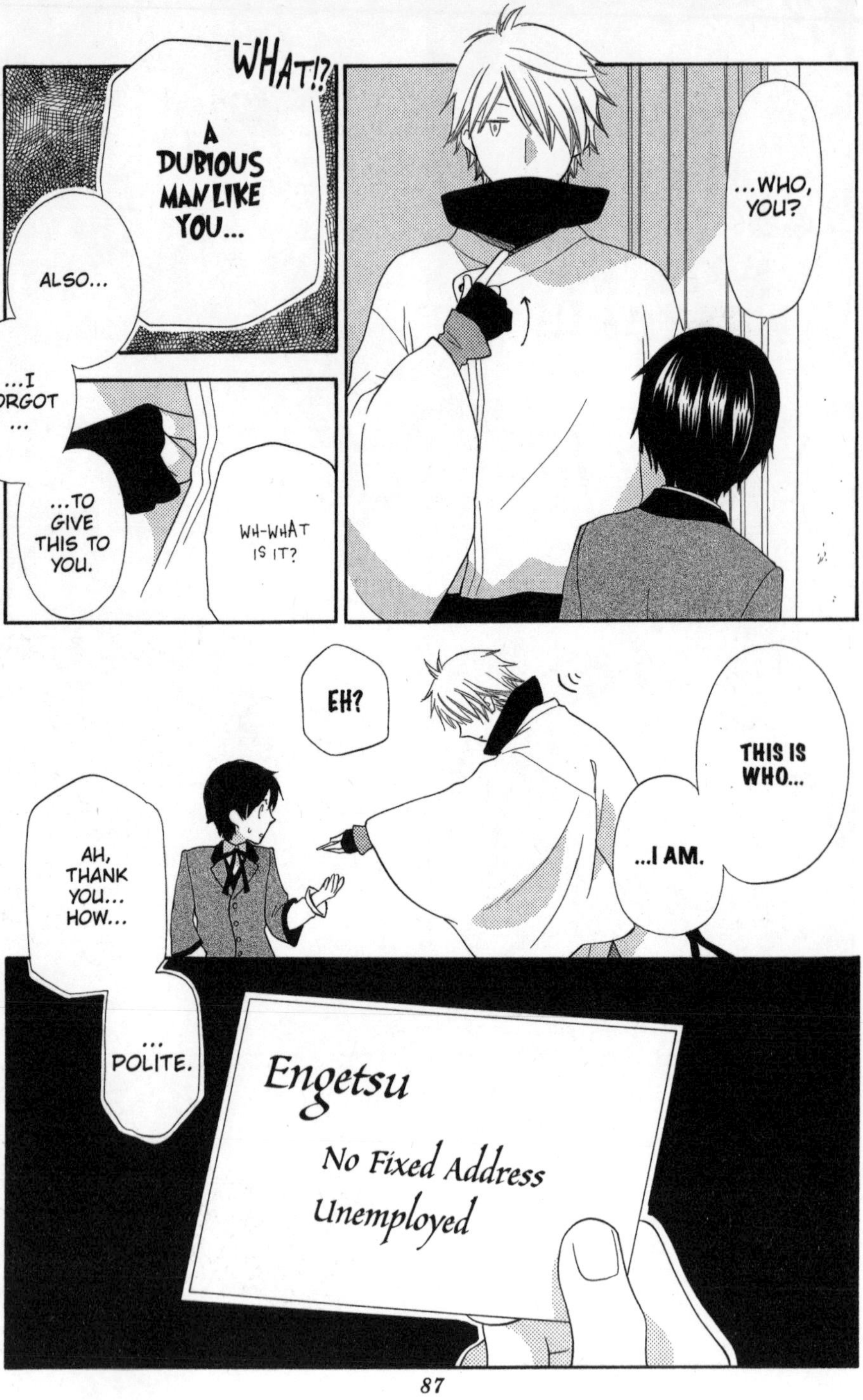
...WHO, YOU?
WHAT!?
A DUBIOUS MAN LIKE YOU...
ALSO...
...I FORGOT...
...TO GIVE THIS TO YOU.
WH-WHAT IS IT?
THIS IS WHO...
...I AM.
EH?
AH, THANK YOU... HOW...
... POLITE.
Engetsu
No Fixed Address
Unemployed

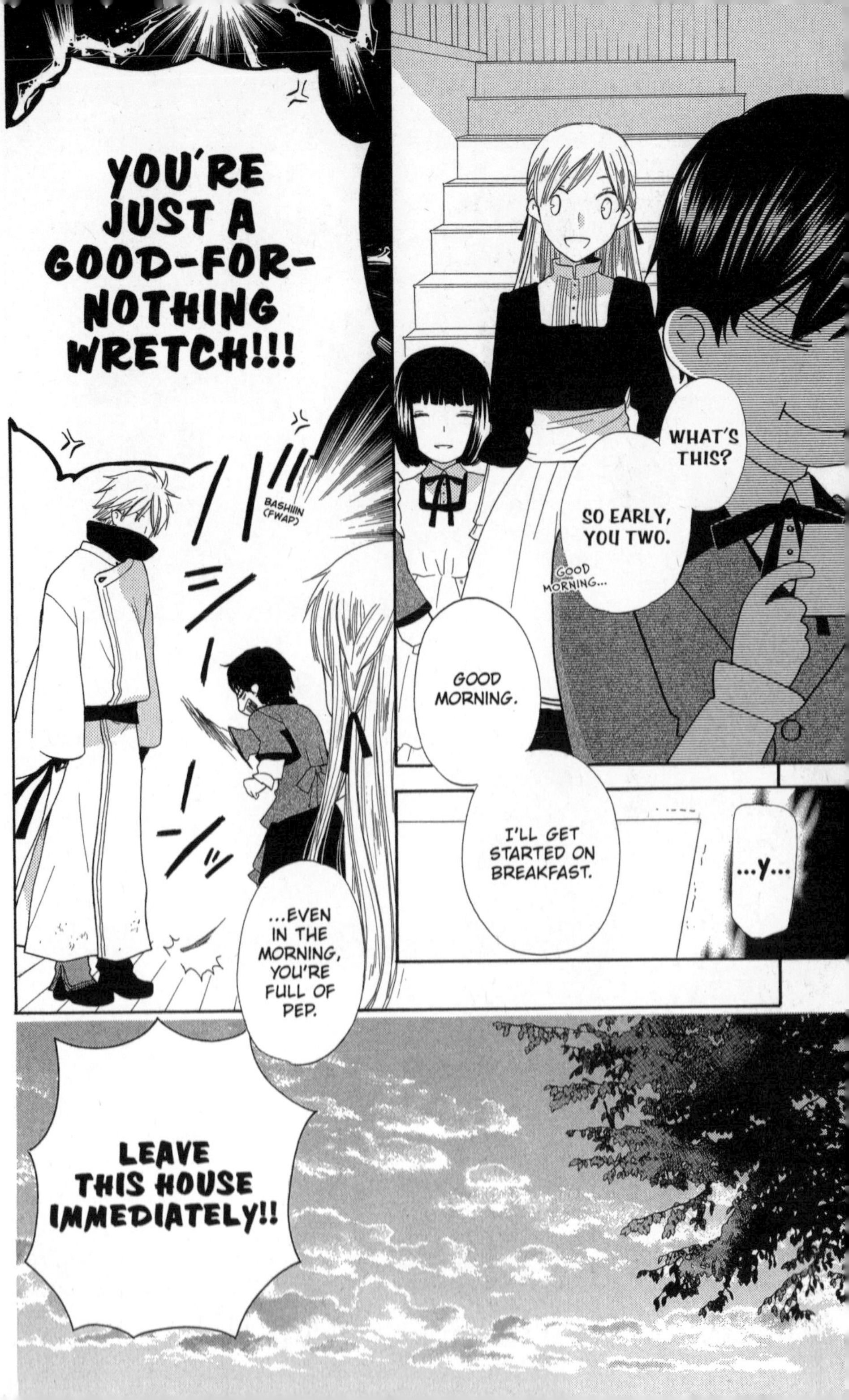
WHAT'S THIS?
SO EARLY, YOU TWO.
GOOD MORNING...
GOOD MORNING.
I'LL GET STARTED ON BREAKFAST.
...y...
YOU'RE JUST A GOOD-FOR-NOTHING WRETCH!!!
BASHIIN (FWAP)
...EVEN IN THE MORNING, YOU'RE FULL OF PEP.
LEAVE THIS HOUSE IMMEDIATELY!!

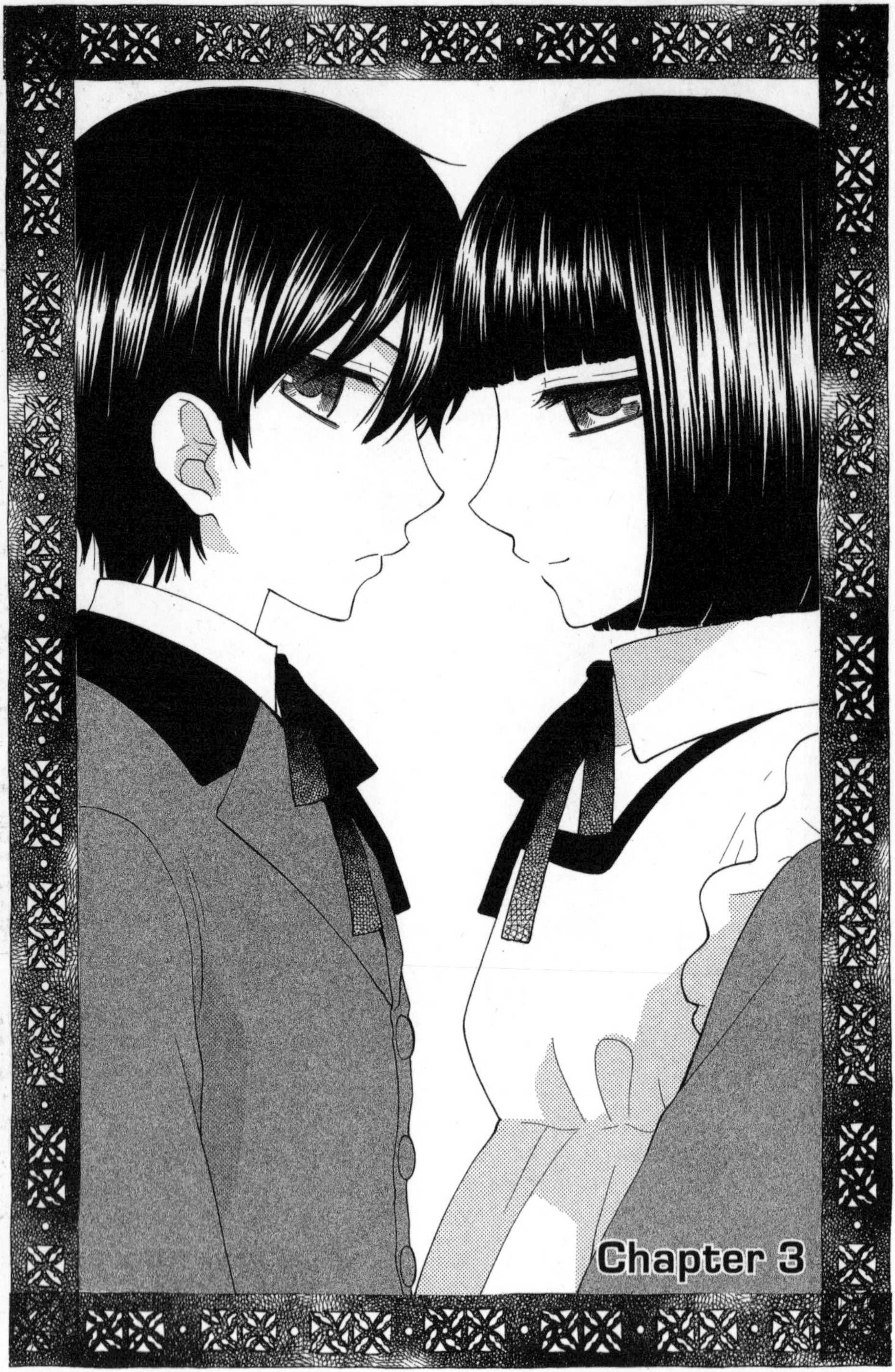
Chapter 3

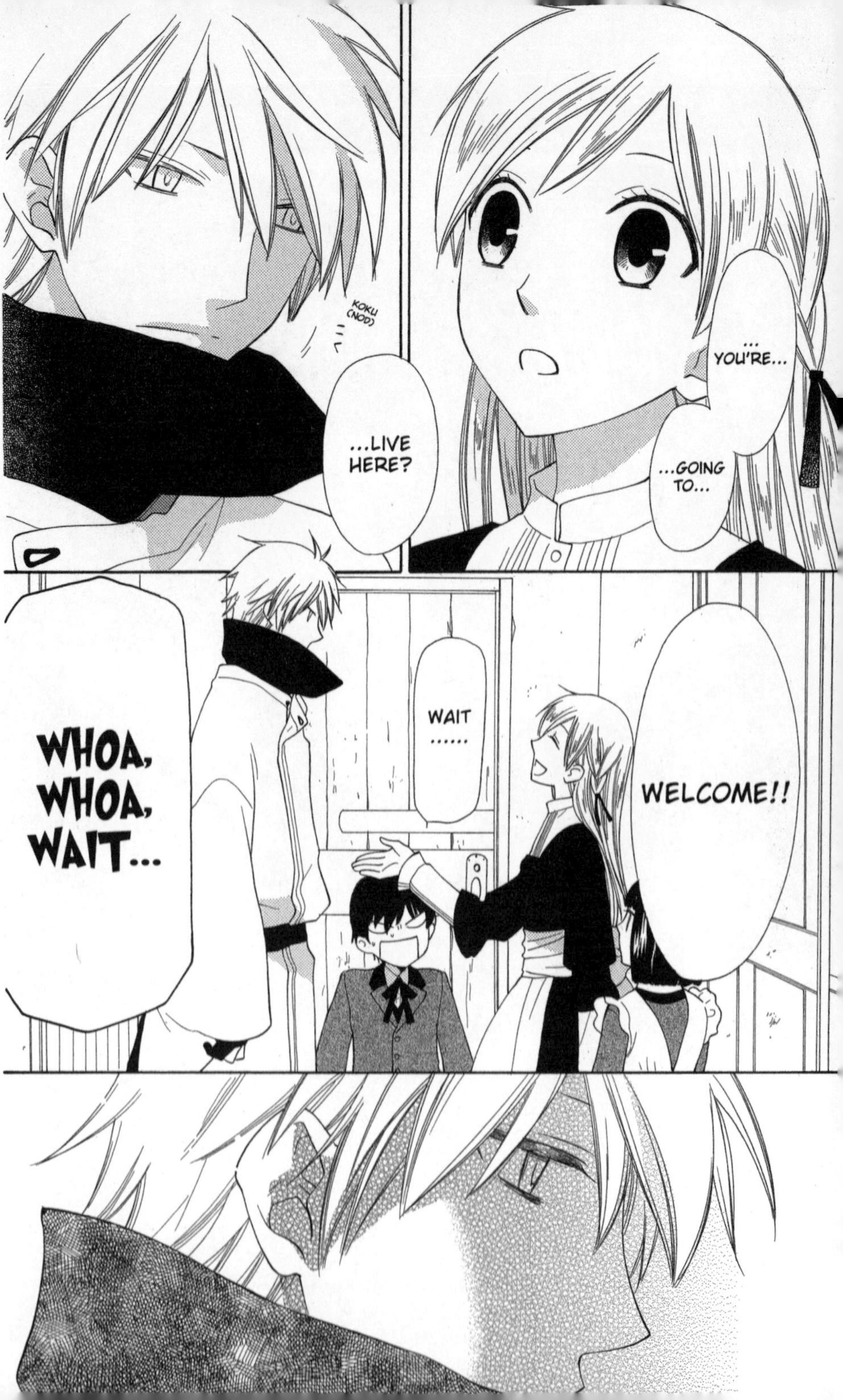
... YOU'RE...
...GOING TO...
...LIVE HERE?
KOKU (NOD)
WELCOME!!
WAIT ......
WHOA, WHOA, WAIT...

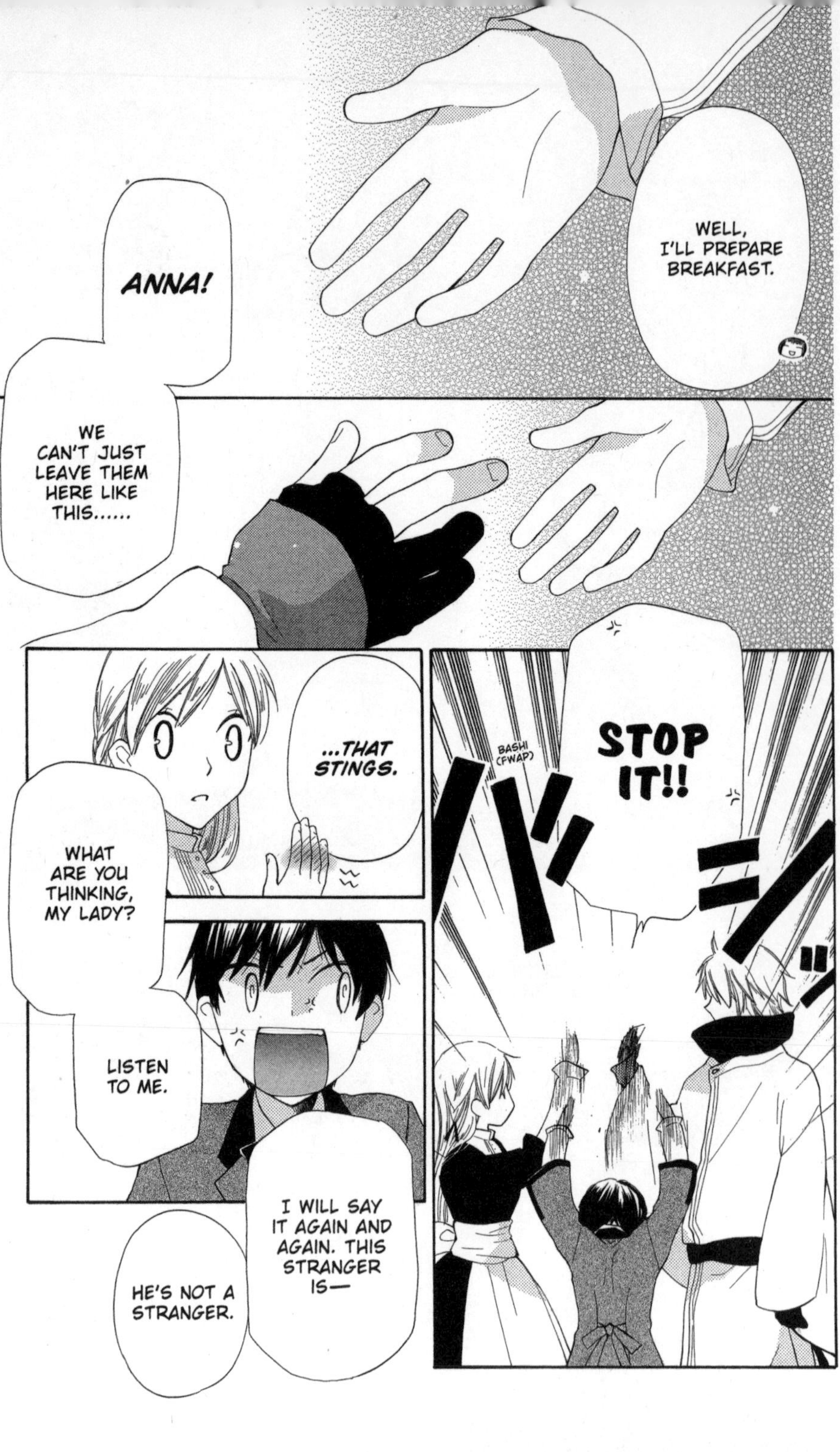
WELL, I'LL PREPARE BREAKFAST.
ANNA!
WE CAN'T JUST LEAVE THEM HERE LIKE THIS......
STOP IT!!
BASHI (FWAP)
...THAT STINGS.
WHAT ARE YOU THINKING, MY LADY?
LISTEN TO ME.
I WILL SAY IT AGAIN AND AGAIN. THIS STRANGER IS—
HE'S NOT A STRANGER.

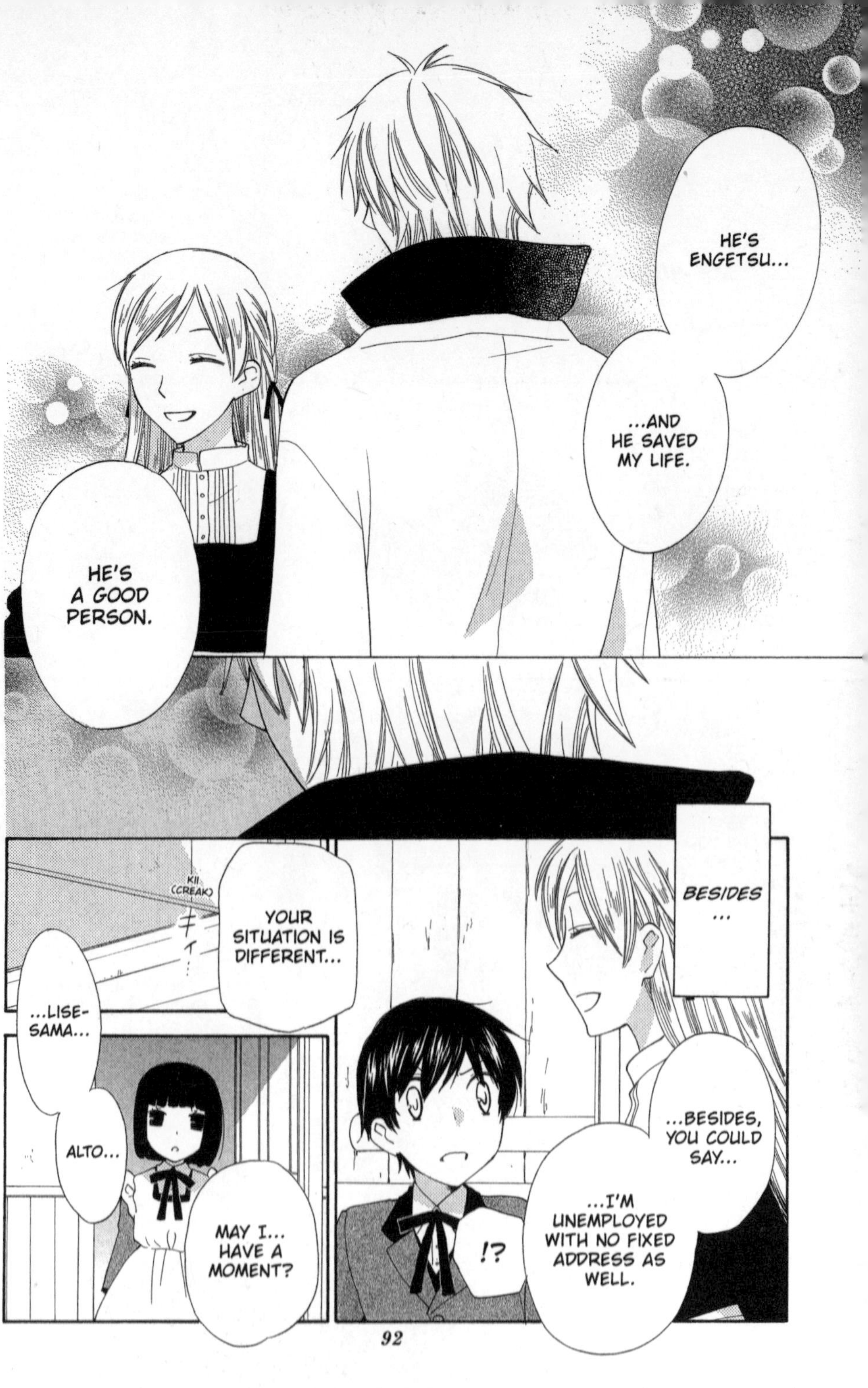
HE'S ENGETSU...
...AND HE SAVED MY LIFE.
HE'S A GOOD PERSON.
YOUR SITUATION IS DIFFERENT...
BESIDES...
...BESIDES, YOU COULD SAY...
...I'M UNEMPLOYED WITH NO FIXED ADDRESS AS WELL.
!?
KII (CREAK)
キィ…
...LISE-SAMA...
ALTO...
MAY I... HAVE A MOMENT?

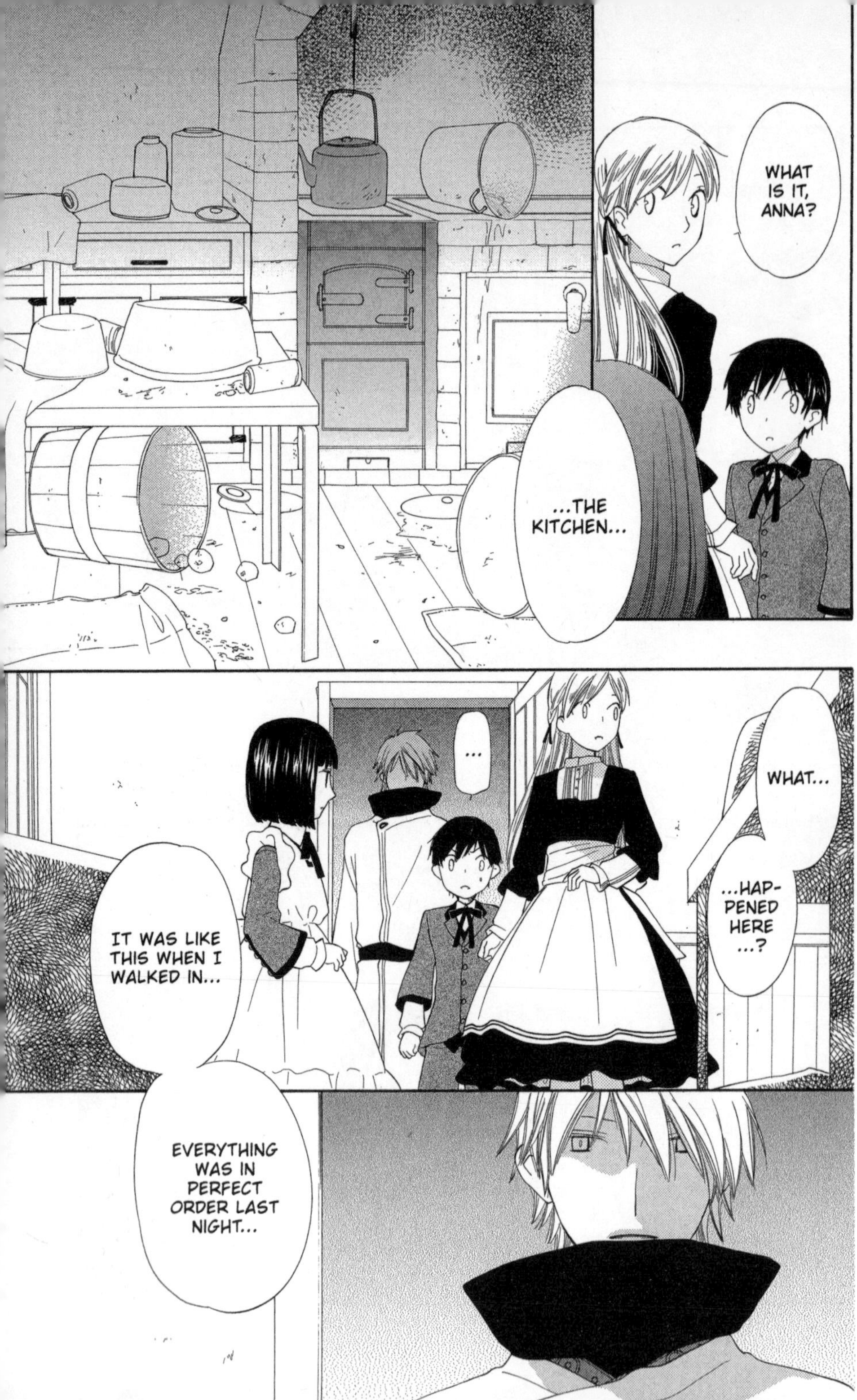
WHAT IS IT, ANNA?
...THE KITCHEN...
WHAT...
...HAP-PENED HERE ...?
...
IT WAS LIKE THIS WHEN I WALKED IN...
EVERYTHING WAS IN PERFECT ORDER LAST NIGHT...

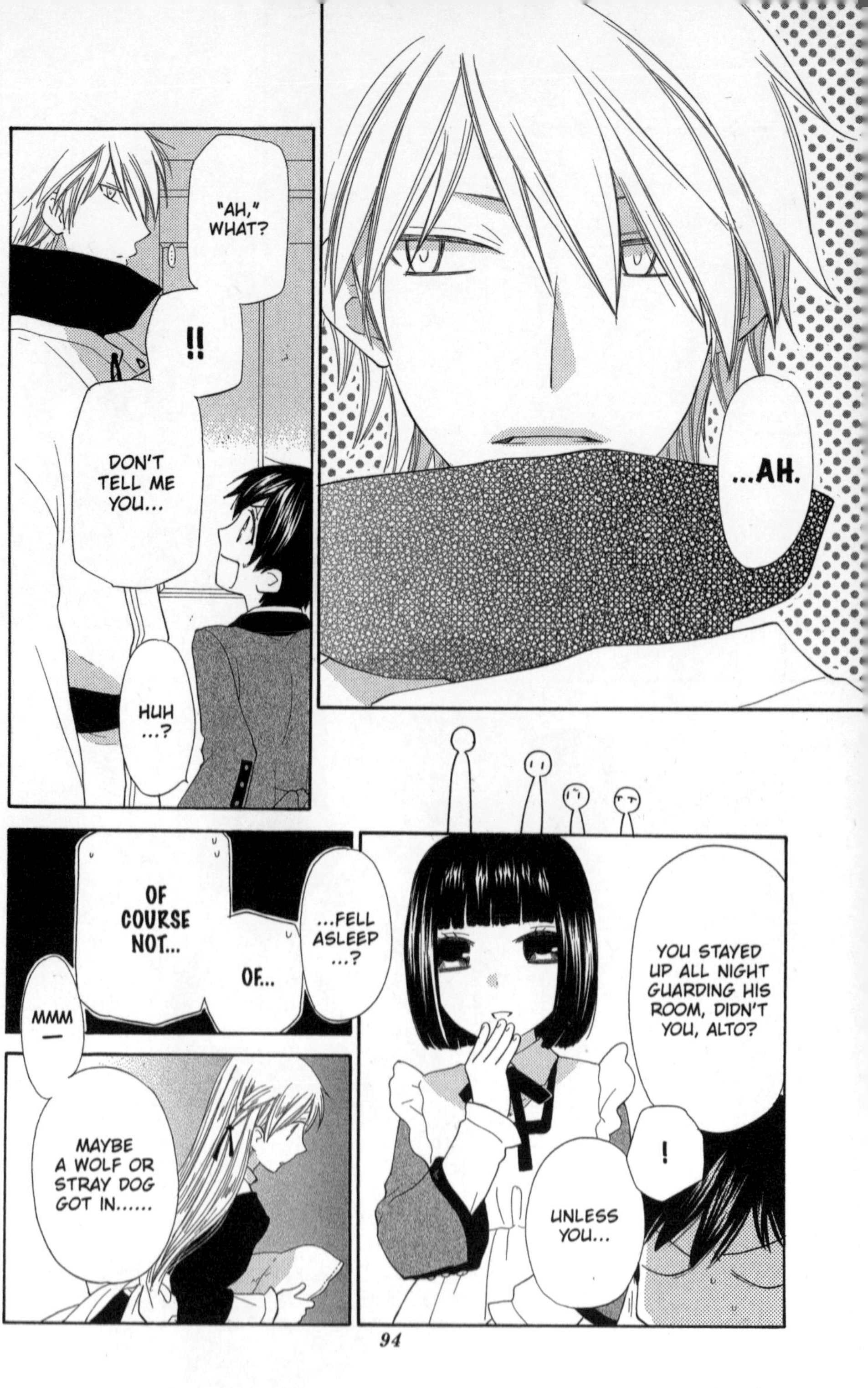

...AH.
"AH," WHAT?
!!
DON'T TELL ME YOU...
HUH ...?
YOU STAYED UP ALL NIGHT GUARDING HIS ROOM, DIDN'T YOU, ALTO?
!
UNLESS YOU...
...FELL ASLEEP ...?
OF COURSE NOT...
OF...
MMM—
MAYBE A WOLF OR STRAY DOG GOT IN......

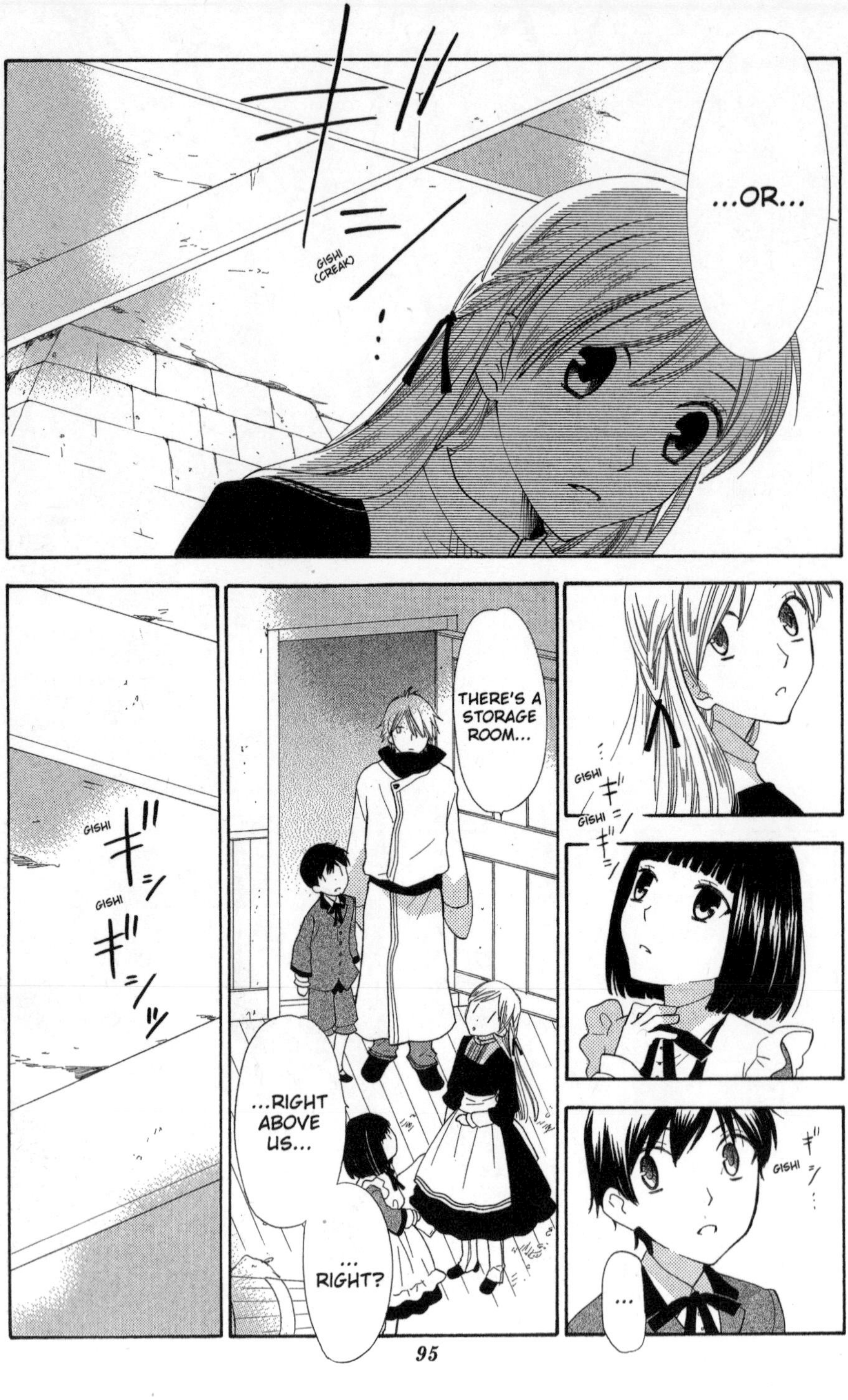
...OR...
GISHI (CREAK)
GISHI
GISHI
GISHI
...
THERE'S A STORAGE ROOM...
...RIGHT ABOVE US...
...RIGHT?
GISHI
GISHI

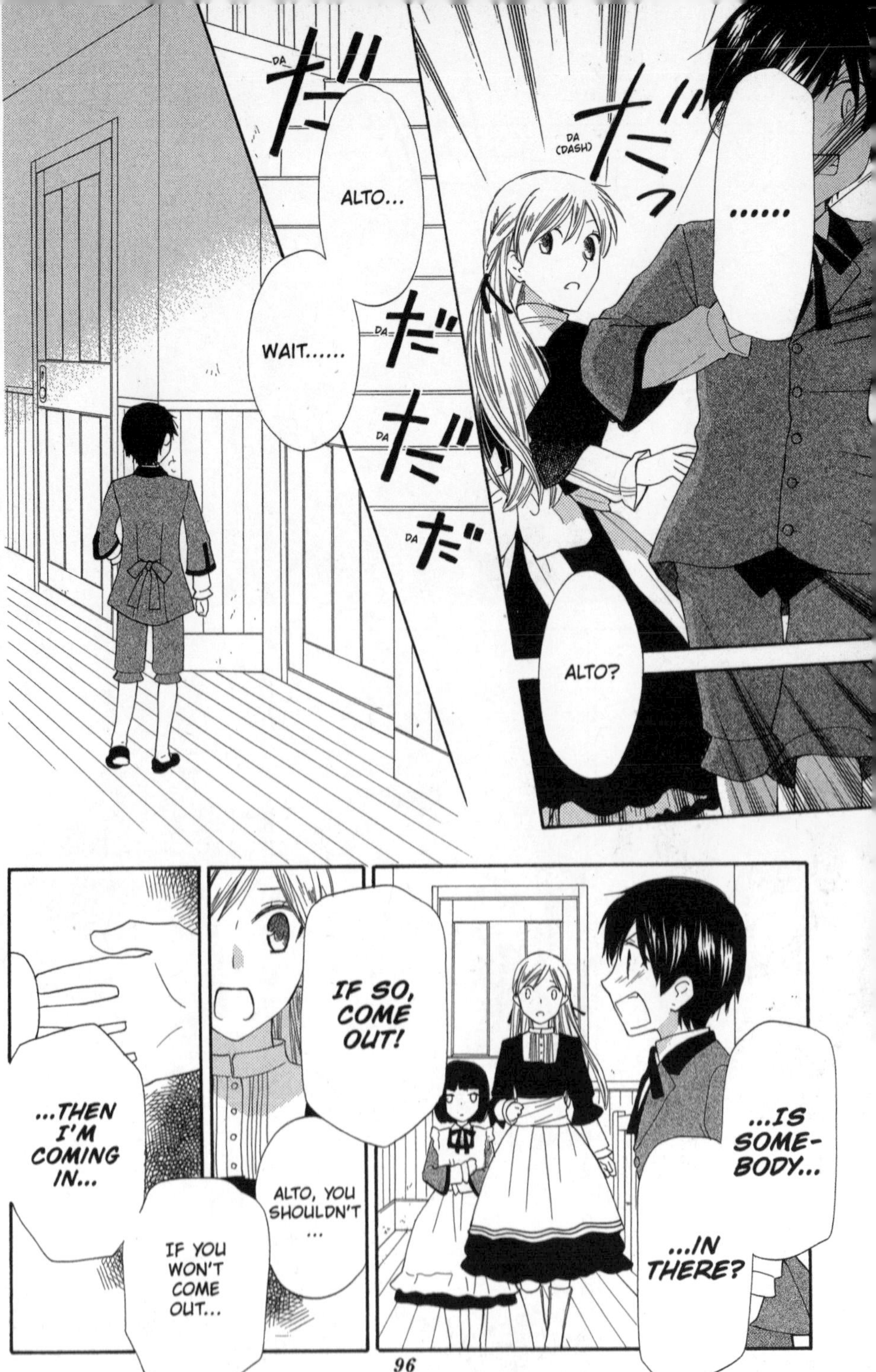

DA (DASH)
......
ALTO?
DA
ALTO...
WAIT......
DA
DA
DA
...IS SOMEBODY...
...IN THERE?
IF SO, COME OUT!
ALTO, YOU SHOULDN'T ...
IF YOU WON'T COME OUT...
...THEN I'M COMING IN...

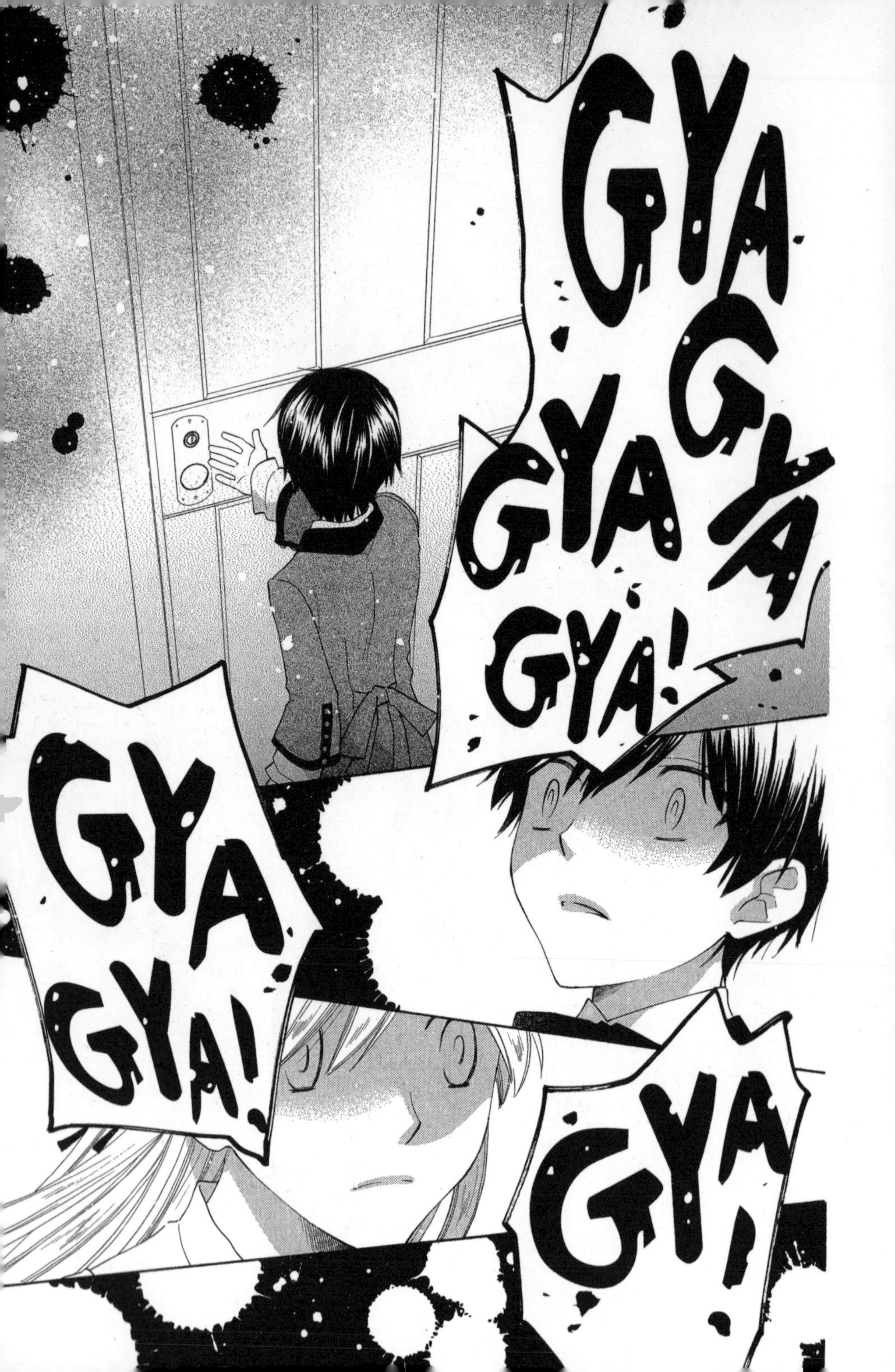
GYA GYA GYA GYA GYA!
GYA GYA GYA!
GYA GYA!

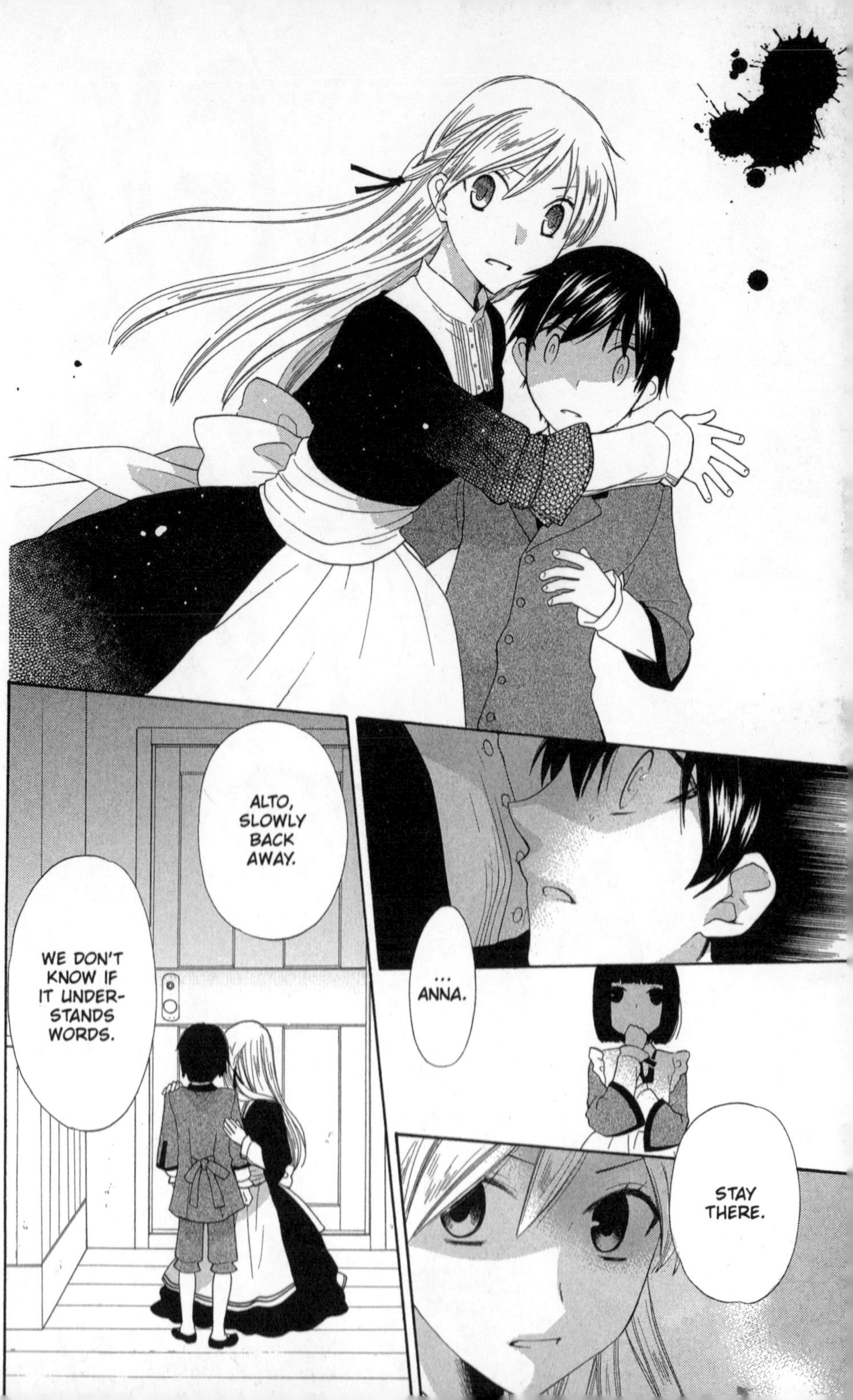
...
ANNA.
STAY THERE.
ALTO, SLOWLY BACK AWAY.
WE DON'T KNOW IF IT UNDER-STANDS WORDS.

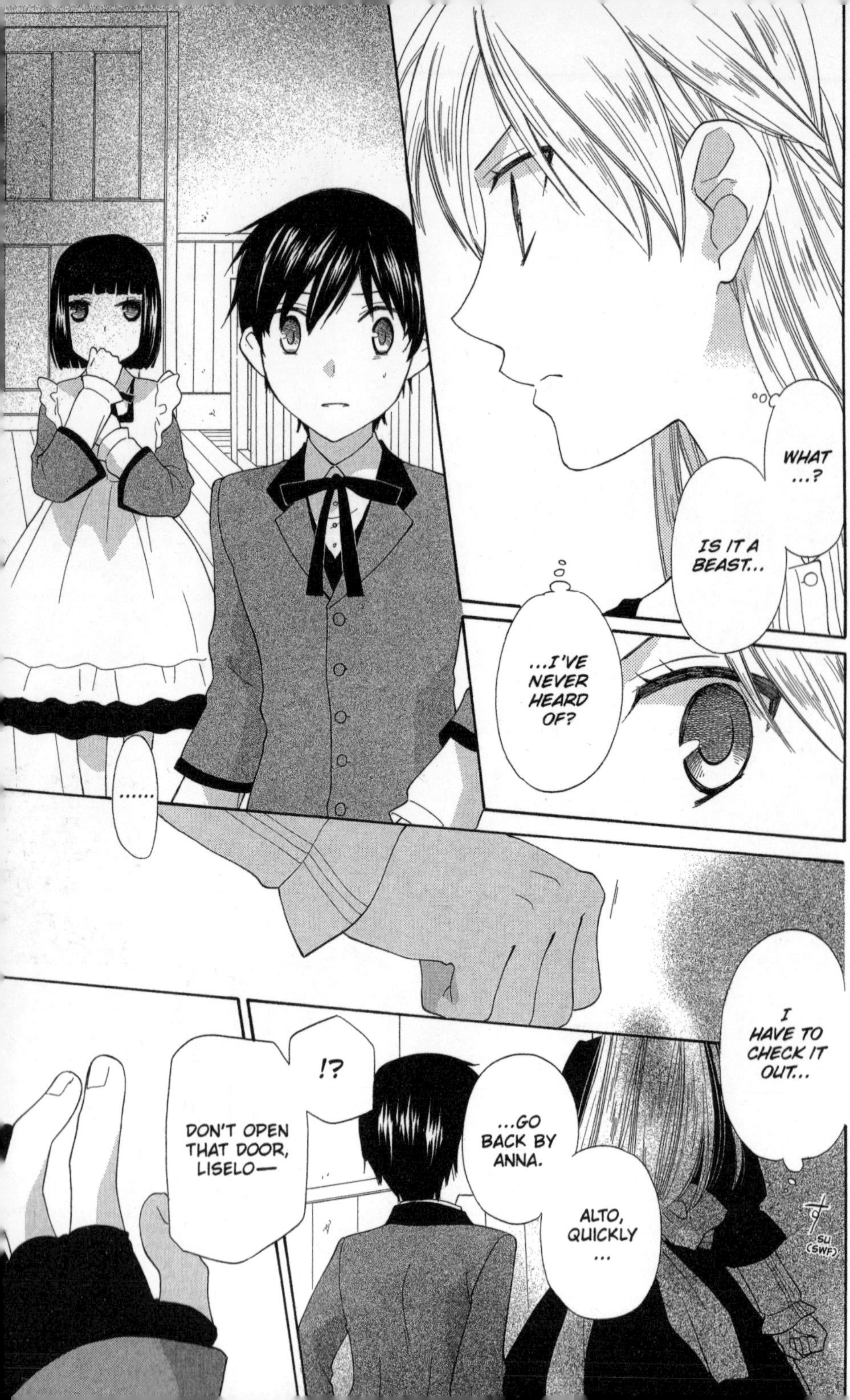
WHAT ...?
IS IT A BEAST...
...I'VE NEVER HEARD OF?
......
I HAVE TO CHECK IT OUT...
SU (SWF)
...GO BACK BY ANNA.
ALTO, QUICKLY ...
!?
DON'T OPEN THAT DOOR, LISELO—

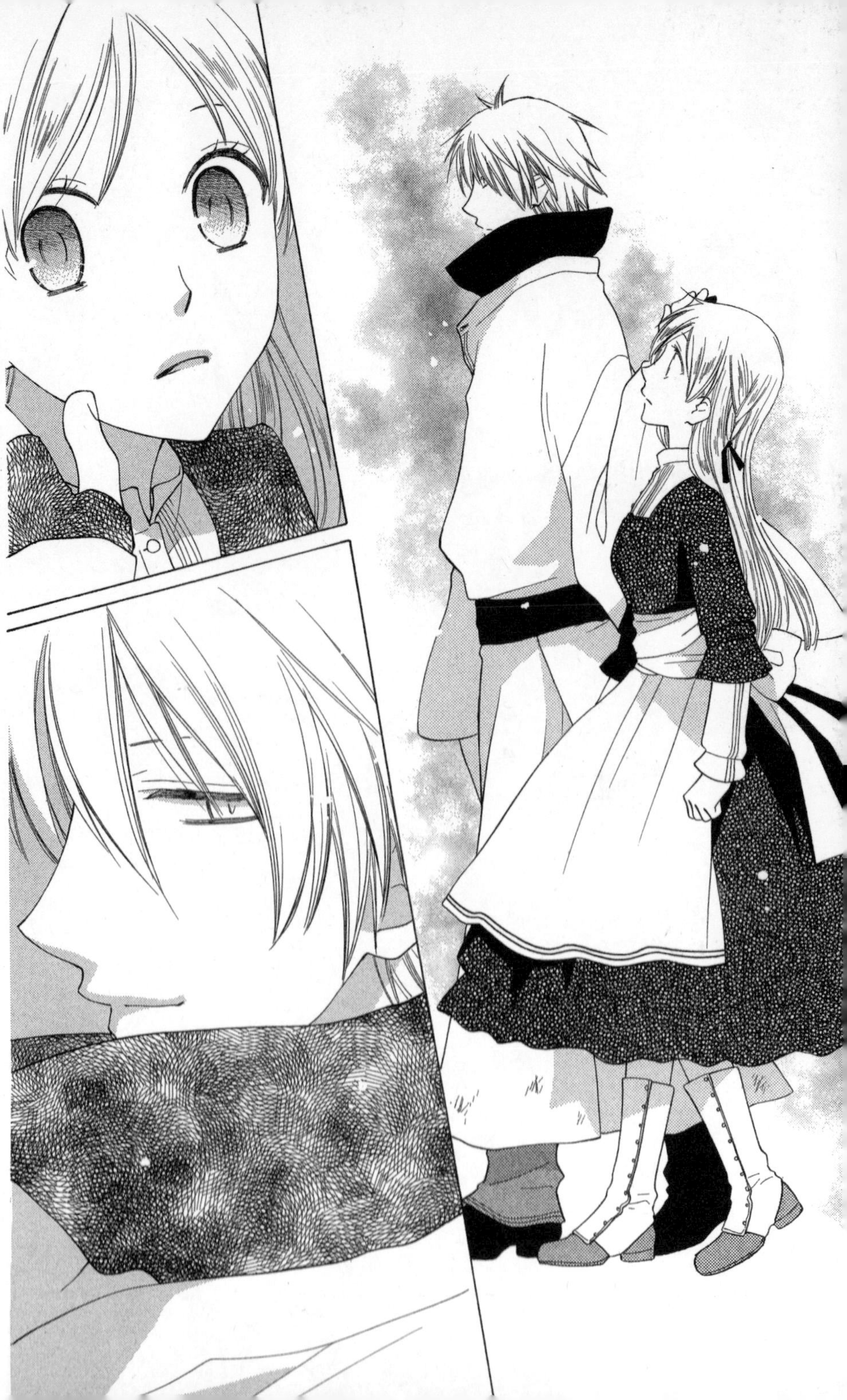

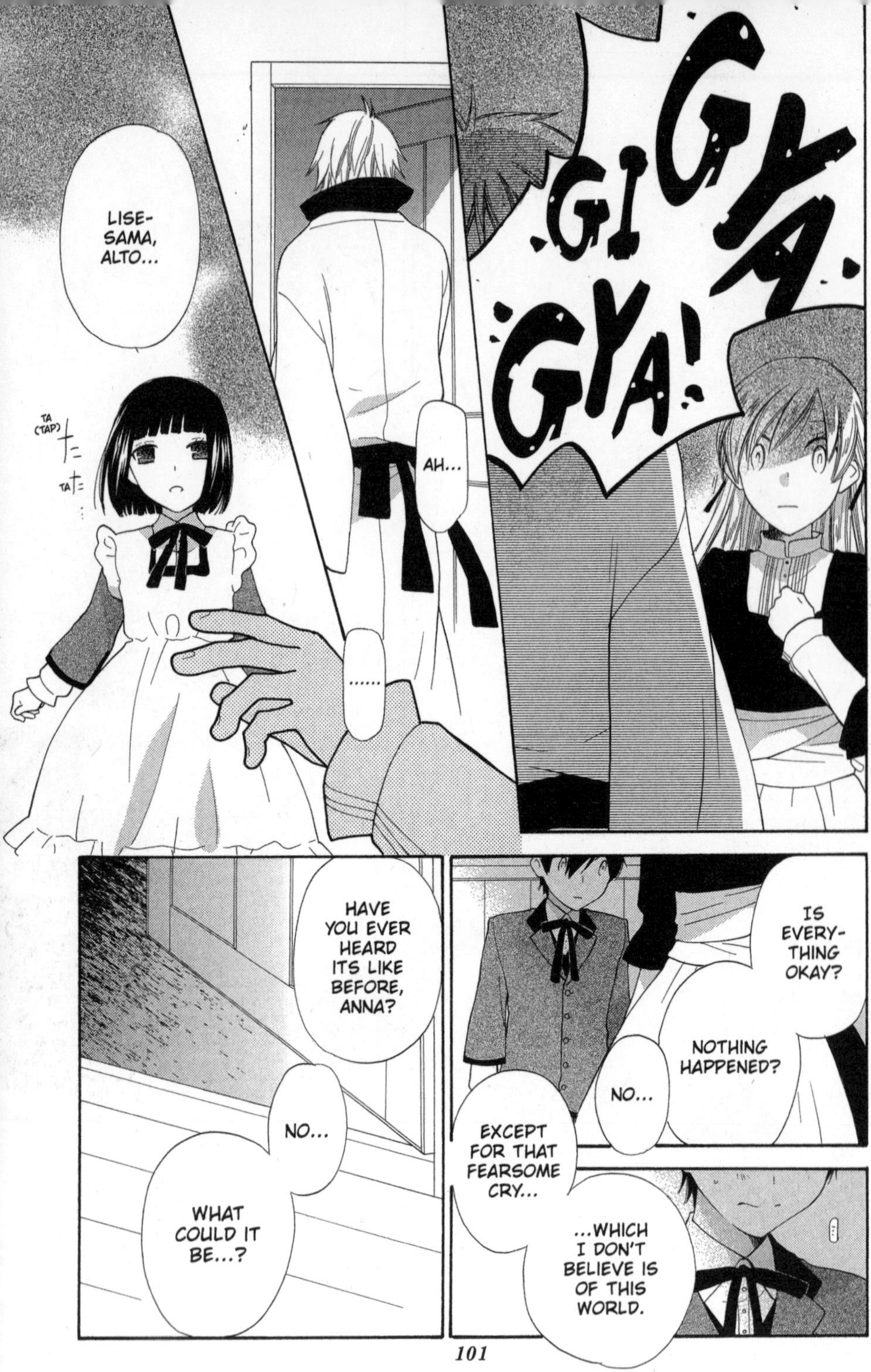
GYAA GI GYA!
LISE-SAMA, ALTO...
TA (TAP) TA
AH...
......
IS EVERYTHING OKAY?
NOTHING HAPPENED?
NO...
EXCEPT FOR THAT FEARSOME CRY...
...WHICH I DON'T BELIEVE IS OF THIS WORLD.
...
HAVE YOU EVER HEARD ITS LIKE BEFORE, ANNA?
NO...
WHAT COULD IT BE...?

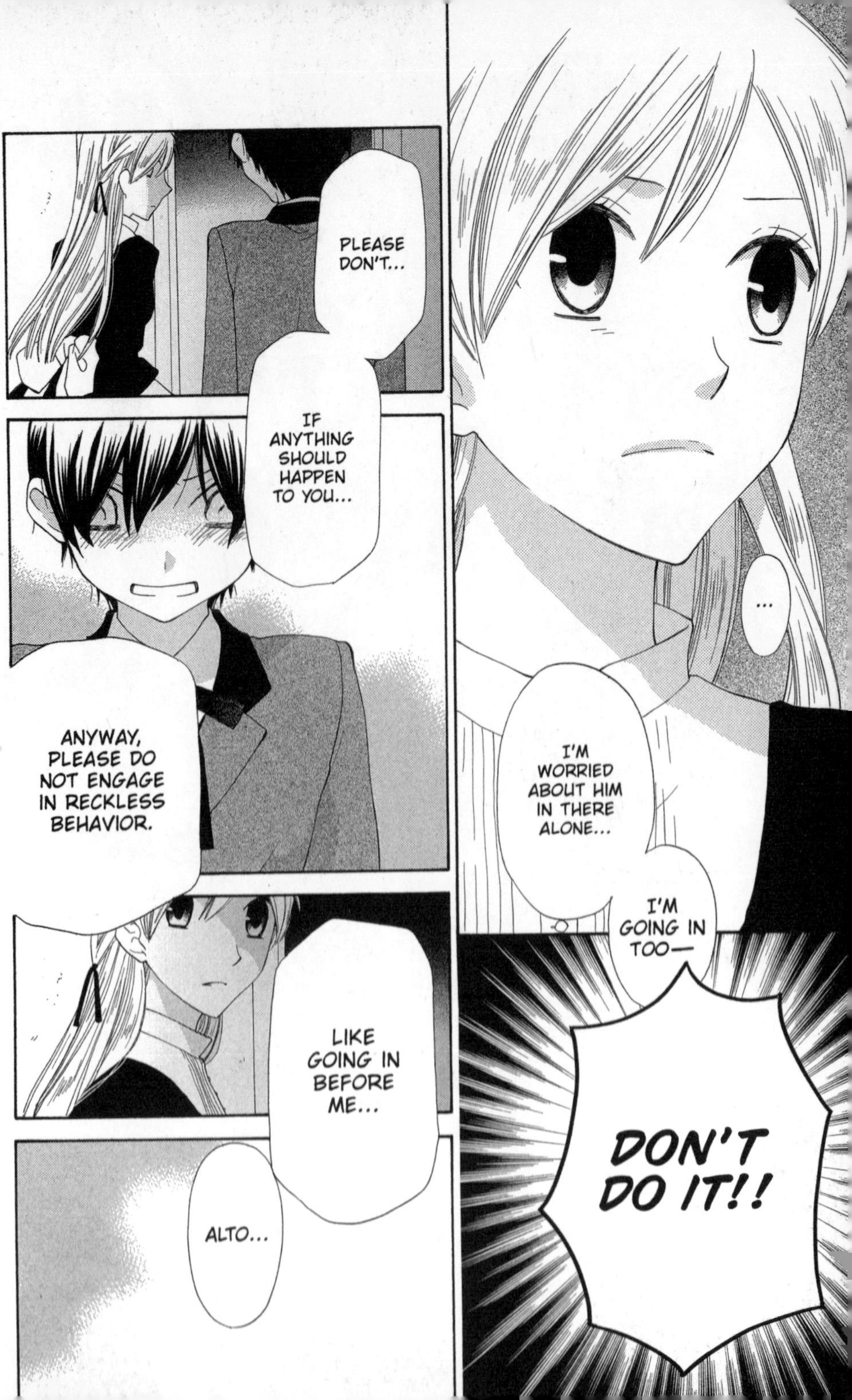
...
I'M WORRIED ABOUT HIM IN THERE ALONE...
I'M GOING IN TOO—
DON'T DO IT!!
PLEASE DON'T...
IF ANYTHING SHOULD HAPPEN TO YOU...
ANYWAY, PLEASE DO NOT ENGAGE IN RECKLESS BEHAVIOR.
LIKE GOING IN BEFORE ME...
ALTO...

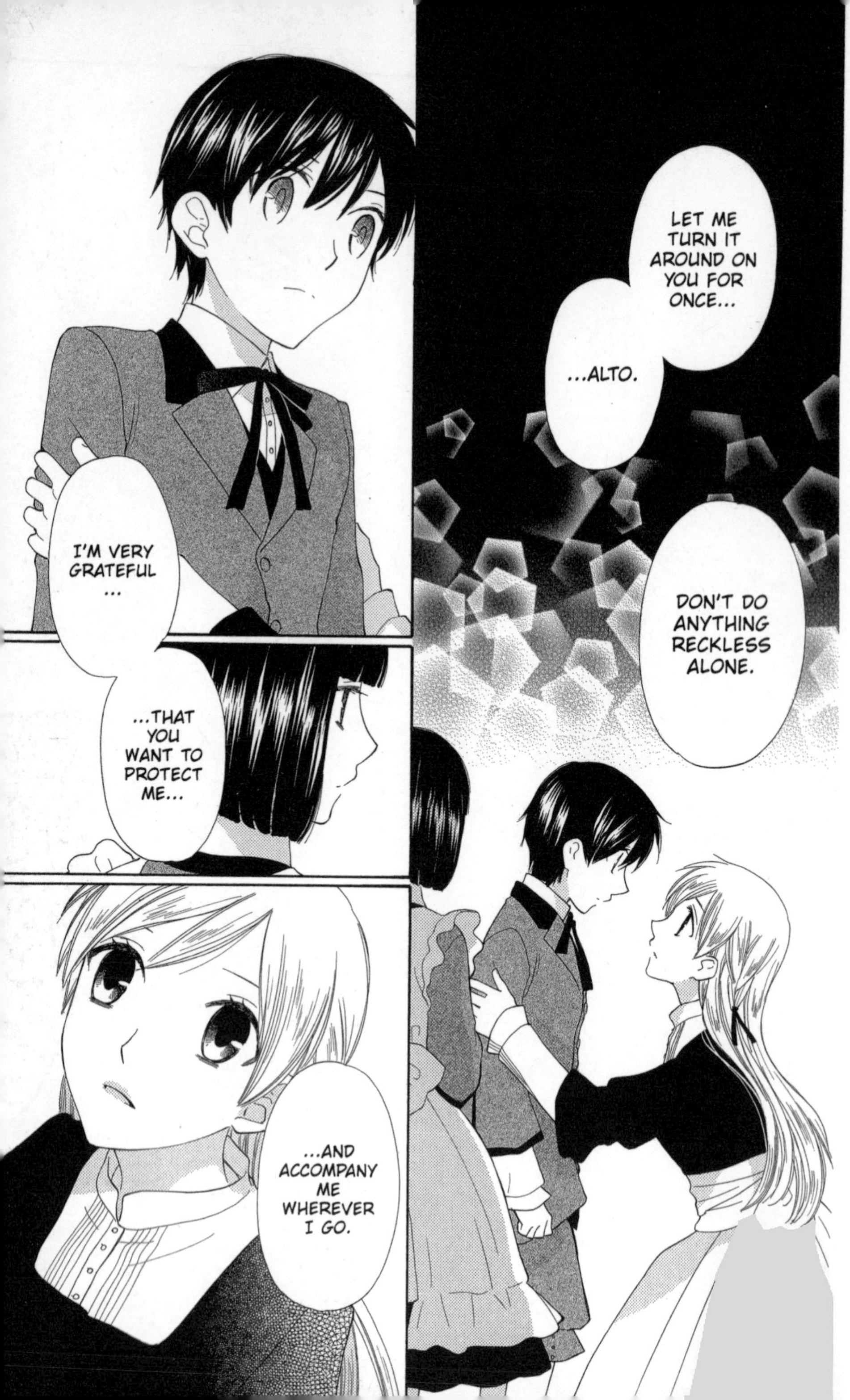
I'M VERY GRATEFUL ...
...THAT YOU WANT TO PROTECT ME...
LET ME TURN IT AROUND ON YOU FOR ONCE...
...ALTO.
DON'T DO ANYTHING RECKLESS ALONE.
...AND ACCOMPANY ME WHEREVER I GO.

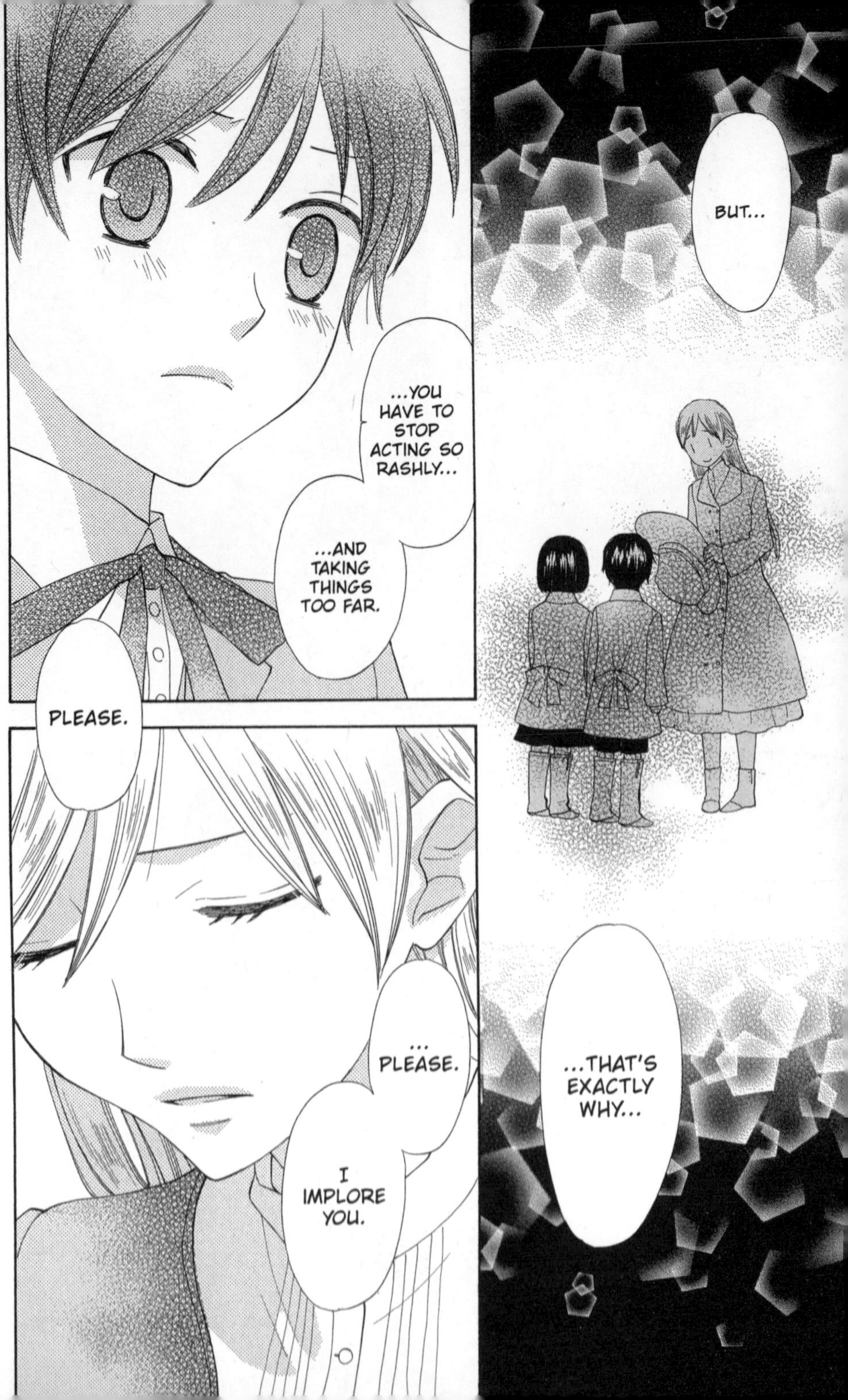
BUT...
...THAT'S EXACTLY WHY...
...YOU HAVE TO STOP ACTING SO RASHLY...
...AND TAKING THINGS TOO FAR.
PLEASE.
...PLEASE.
I IMPLORE YOU.

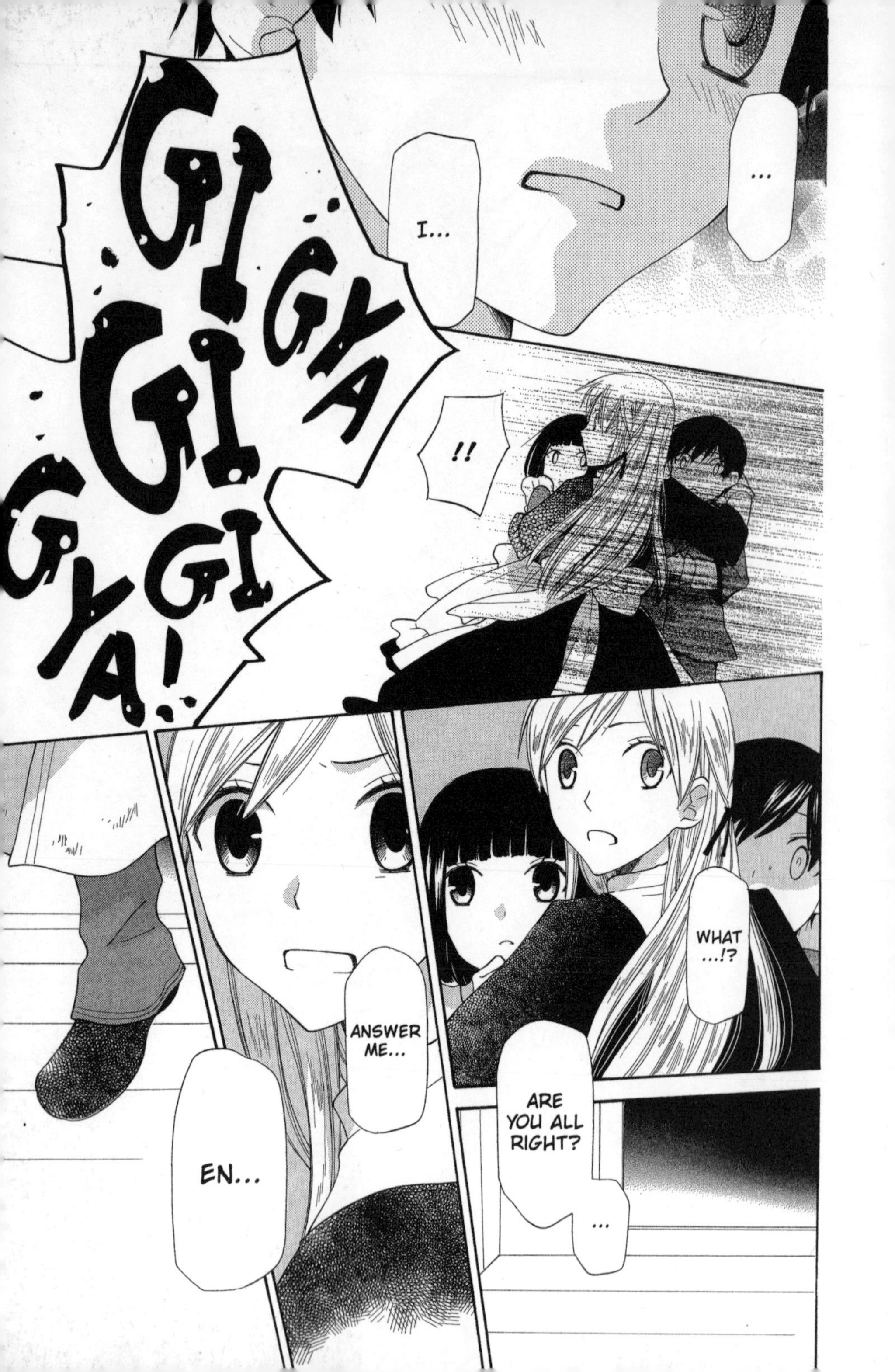
...
I...
GIGYA GIGI GYAGI GYA!
!!
WHAT ...!?
ARE YOU ALL RIGHT?
...
ANSWER ME...
EN...

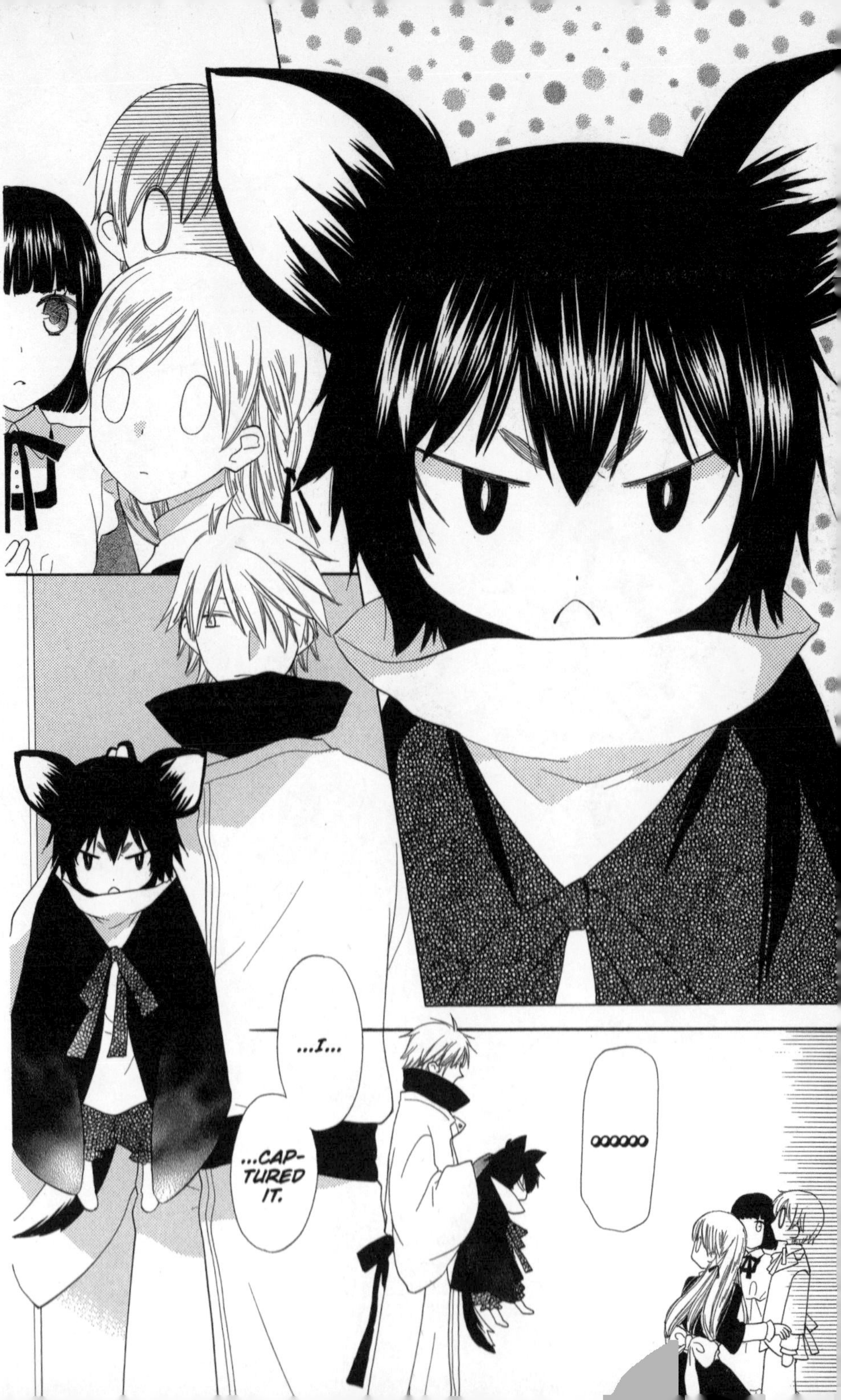
......
...I...
...CAP-TURED IT.

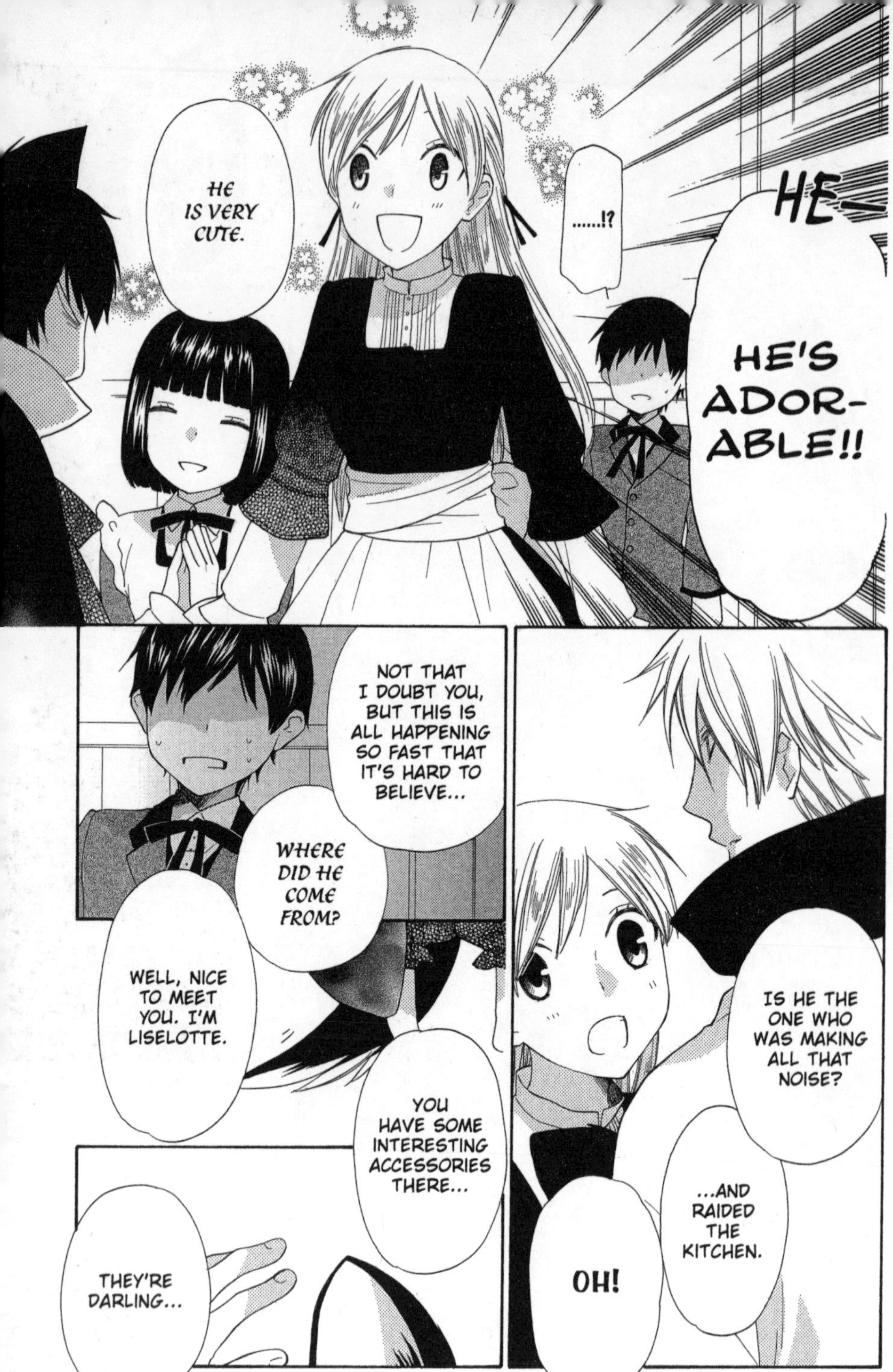
HE— HE'S ADORABLE!!
......!?
HE IS VERY CUTE.
IS HE THE ONE WHO WAS MAKING ALL THAT NOISE?
...AND RAIDED THE KITCHEN.
OH!
NOT THAT I DOUBT YOU, BUT THIS IS ALL HAPPENING SO FAST THAT IT'S HARD TO BELIEVE...
WHERE DID HE COME FROM?
WELL, NICE TO MEET YOU. I'M LISELOTTE.
YOU HAVE SOME INTERESTING ACCESSORIES THERE...
THEY'RE DARLING...

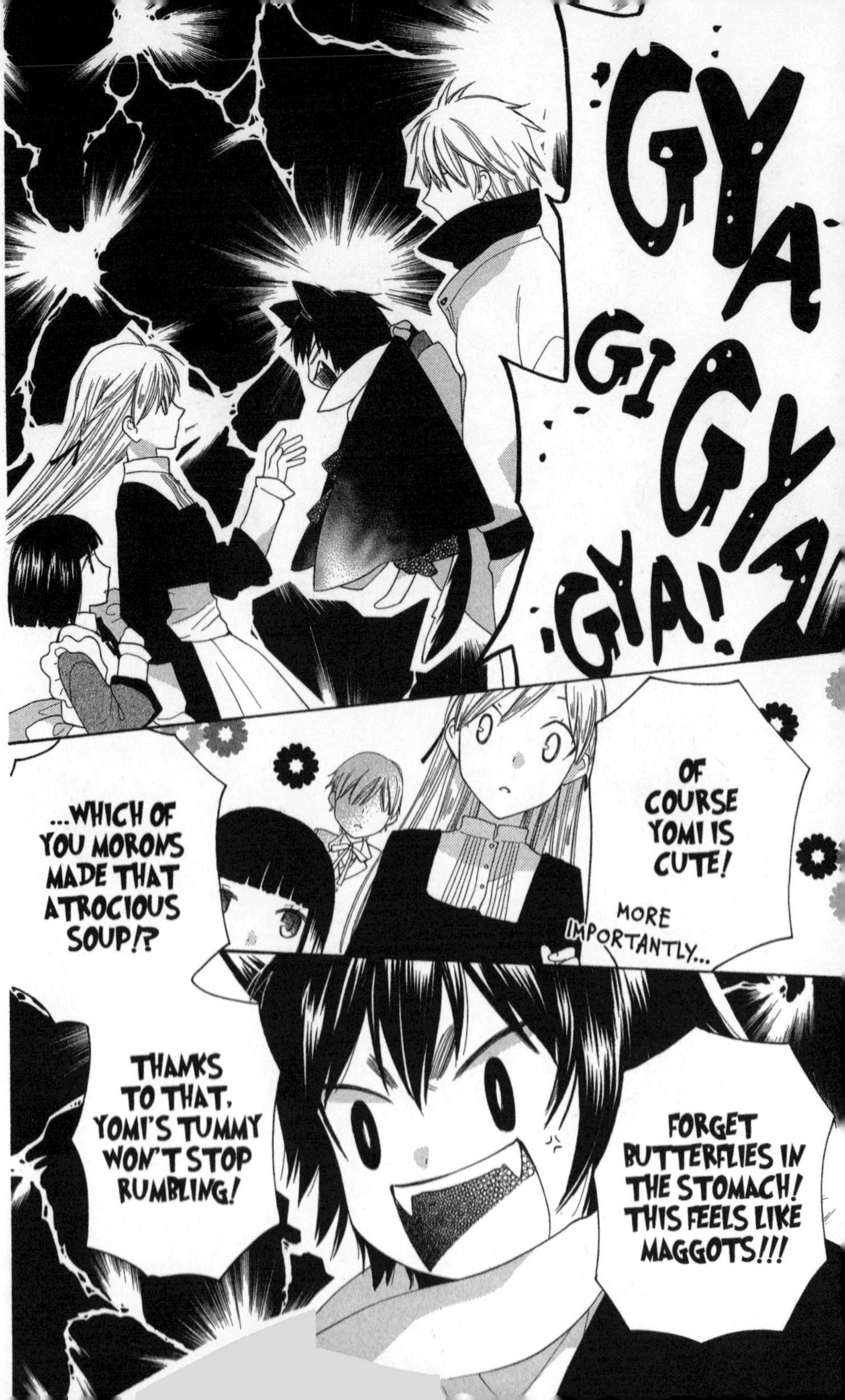
GYA GI GYAA GYA!
OF COURSE YOMI IS CUTE!
MORE IMPORTANTLY...
...WHICH OF YOU MORONS MADE THAT ATROCIOUS SOUP!?
FORGET BUTTERFLIES IN THE STOMACH! THIS FEELS LIKE MAGGOTS!!!
THANKS TO THAT, YOMI'S TUMMY WON'T STOP RUMBLING!

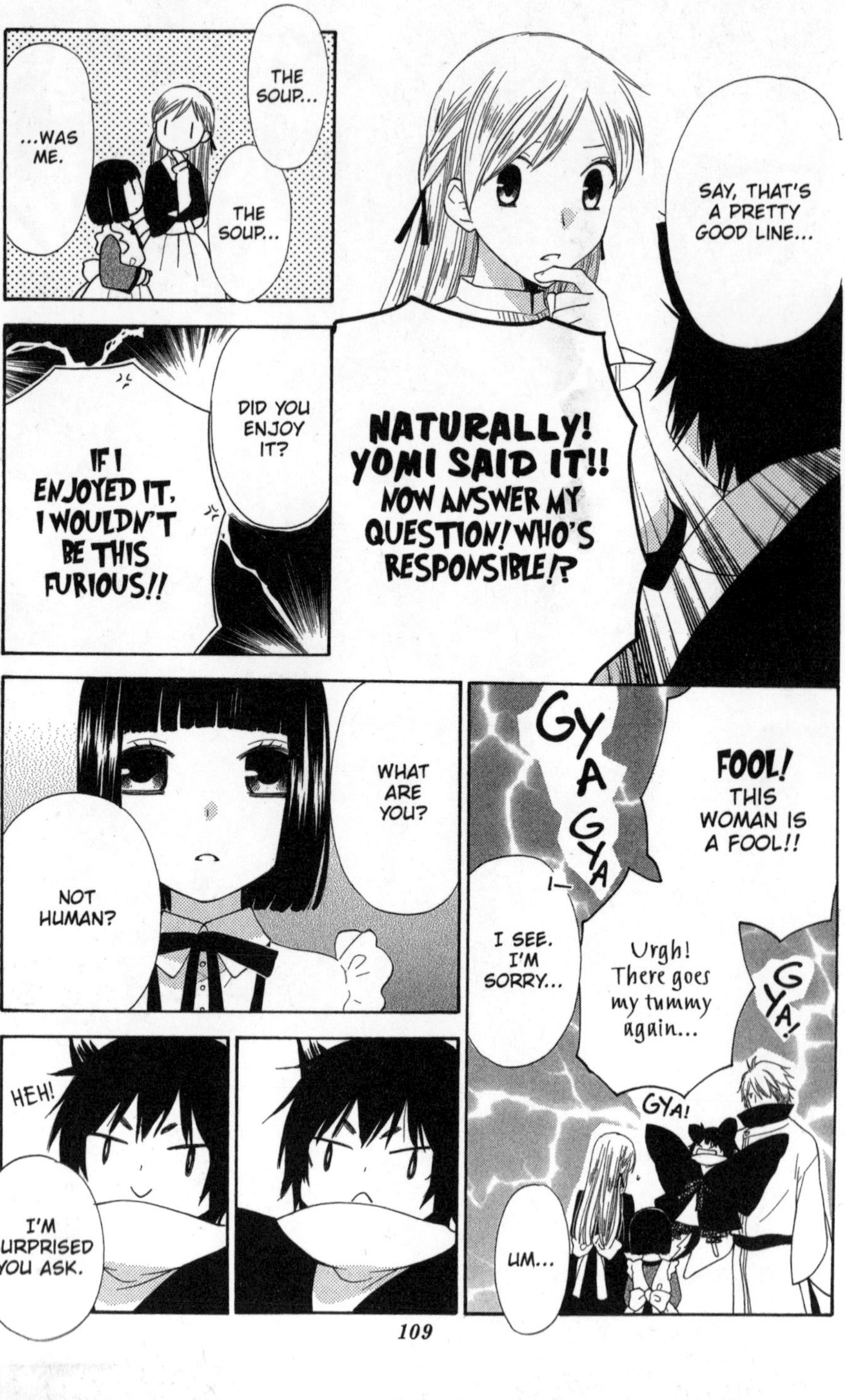
SAY, THAT'S A PRETTY GOOD LINE...
NATURALLY! YOMI SAID IT!! NOW ANSWER MY QUESTION! WHO'S RESPONSIBLE!?
THE SOUP...
THE SOUP...
...WAS ME.
DID YOU ENJOY IT?
IF I ENJOYED IT, I WOULDN'T BE THIS FURIOUS!!
FOOL! THIS WOMAN IS A FOOL!!
GYAGYA
I— I SEE. I'M SORRY...
Urgh! There goes my tummy again...
GYA!
GYA!
UM...
WHAT ARE YOU?
NOT HUMAN?
HEH!
I'M SURPRISED YOU ASK.

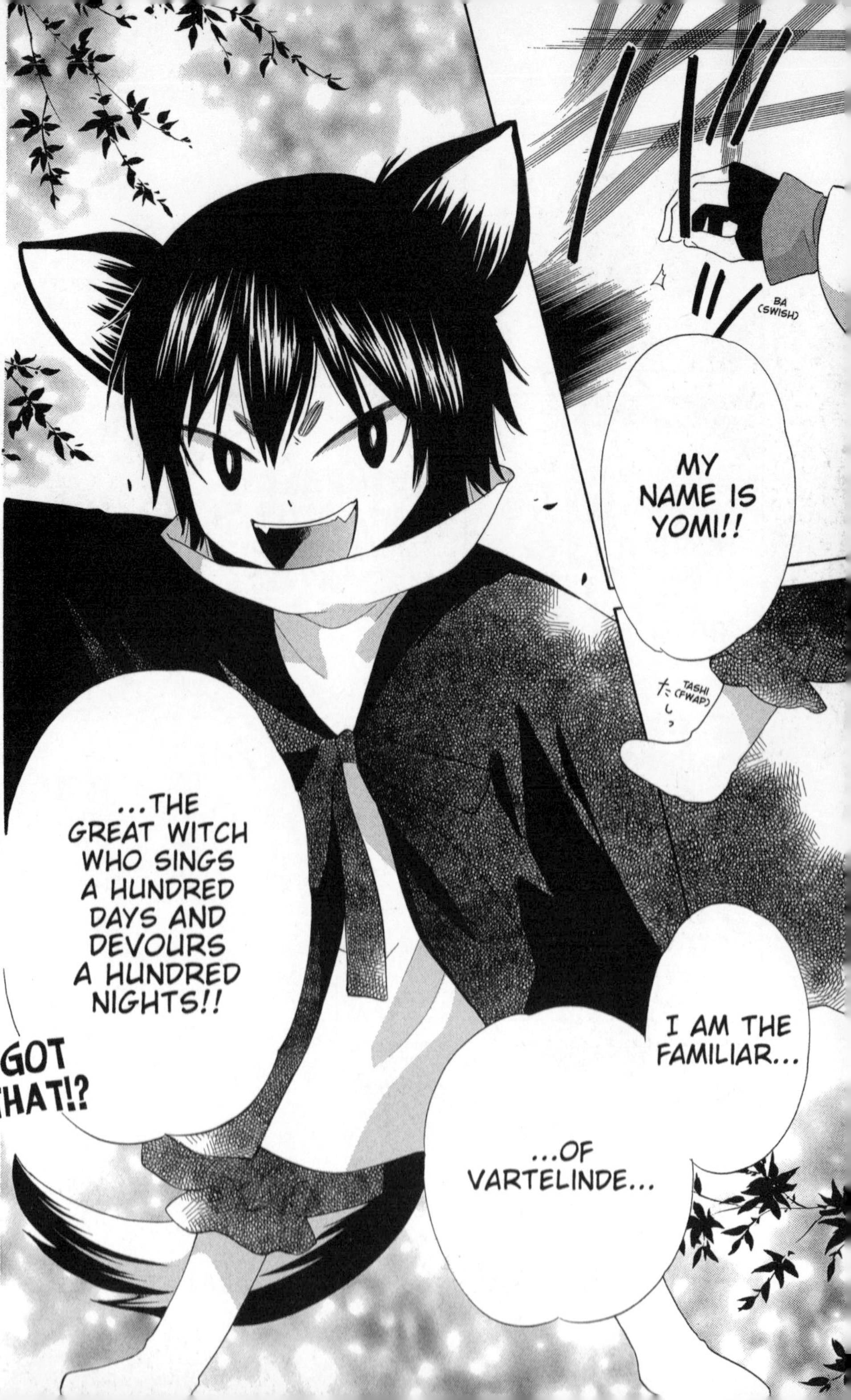
BA (SWISH)
MY NAME IS YOMI!!
たしっ TASHI (FWAP)
I AM THE FAMILIAR...
...OF VARTELINDE...
...THE GREAT WITCH WHO SINGS A HUNDRED DAYS AND DEVOURS A HUNDRED NIGHTS!!
GOT THAT!?

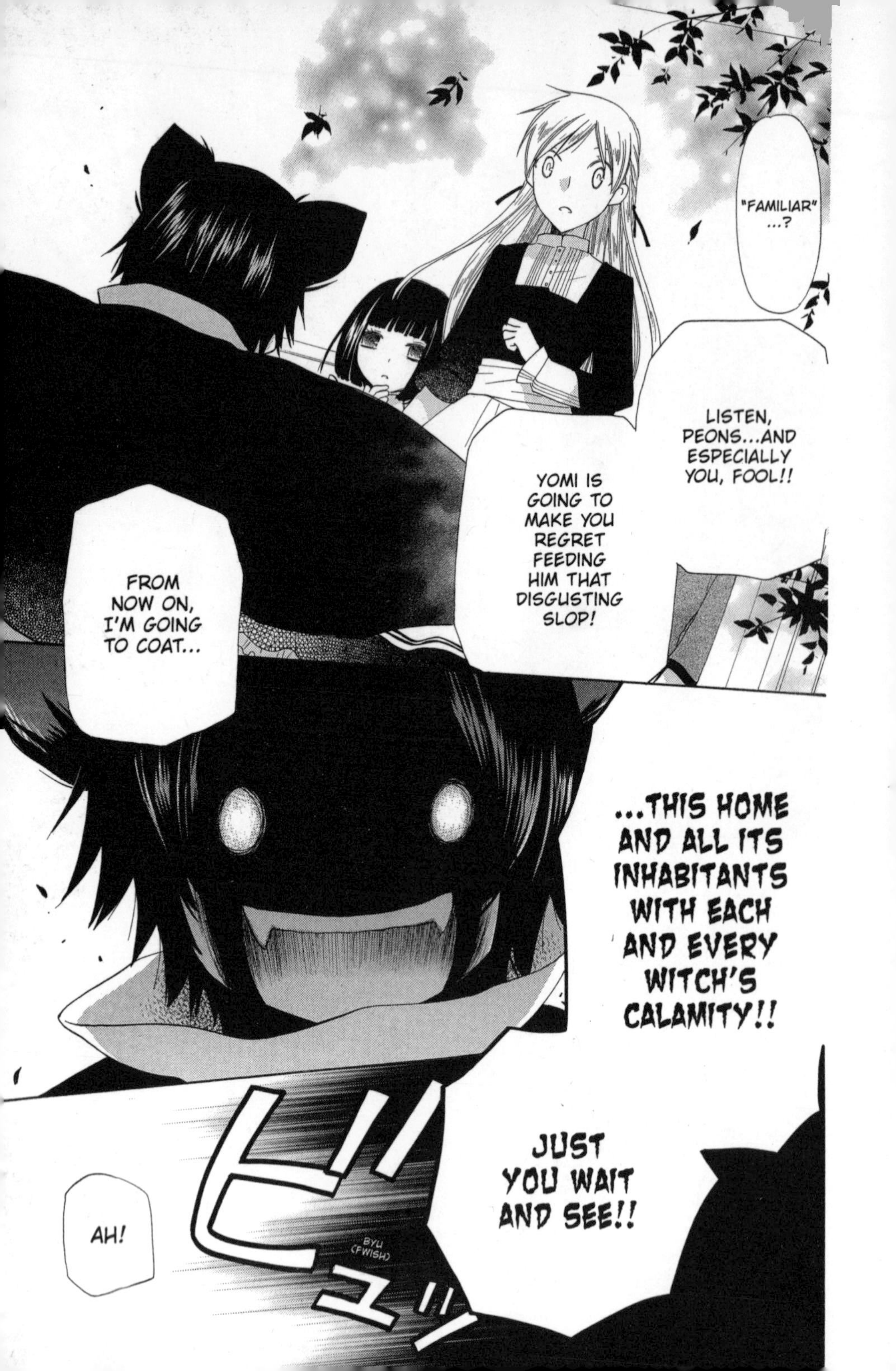
"FAMILIAR" ...?
LISTEN, PEONS...AND ESPECIALLY YOU, FOOL!!
YOMI IS GOING TO MAKE YOU REGRET FEEDING HIM THAT DISGUSTING SLOP!
FROM NOW ON, I'M GOING TO COAT...
...THIS HOME AND ALL ITS INHABITANTS WITH EACH AND EVERY WITCH'S CALAMITY!!
JUST YOU WAIT AND SEE!!
BYU (FWISH)
AH!

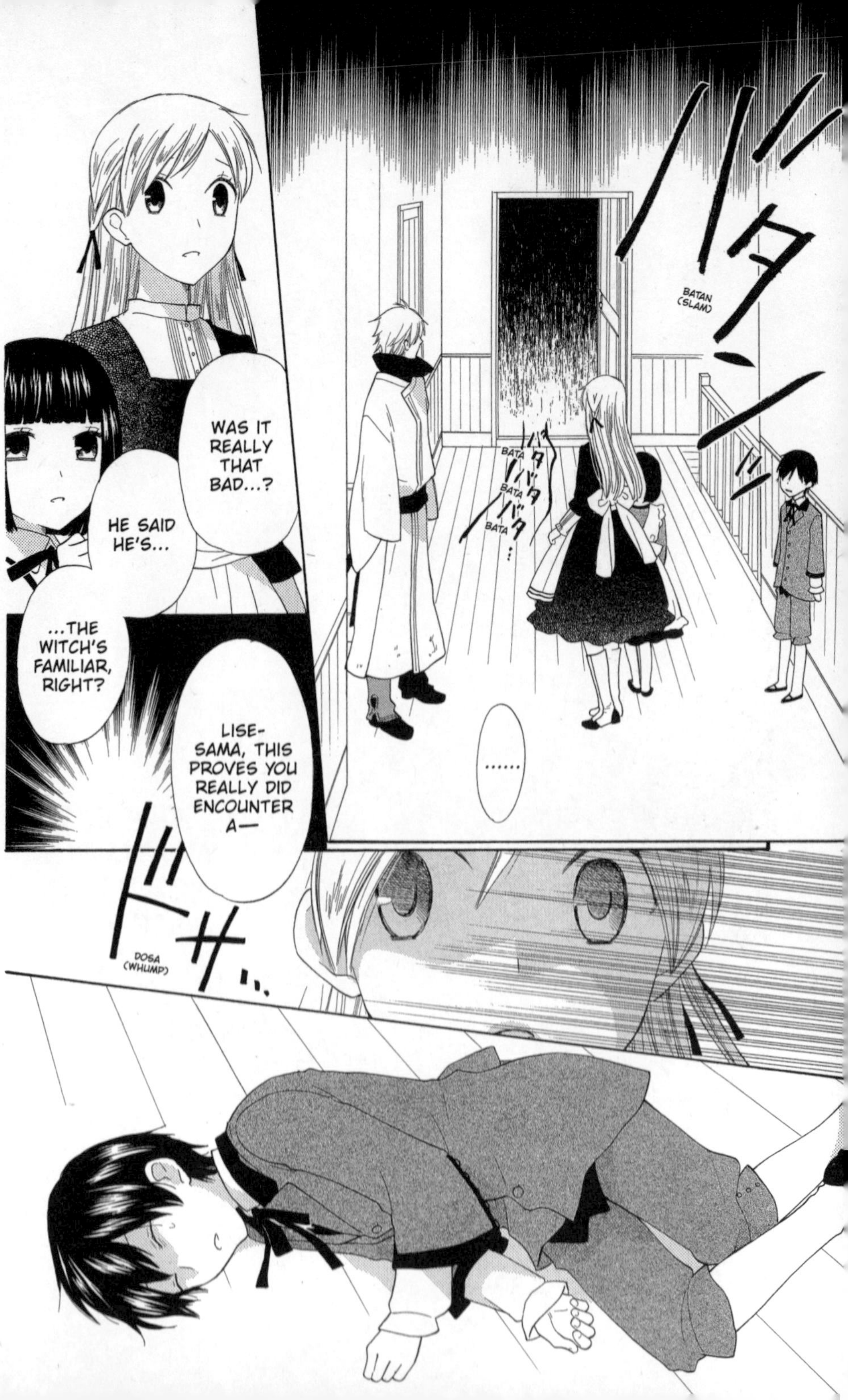
BATAN (SLAM)
BATA BATA BATA
......
WAS IT REALLY THAT BAD...?
HE SAID HE'S...
...THE WITCH'S FAMILIAR, RIGHT?
LISE-SAMA, THIS PROVES YOU REALLY DID ENCOUNTER A—
DOSA (WHUMP)

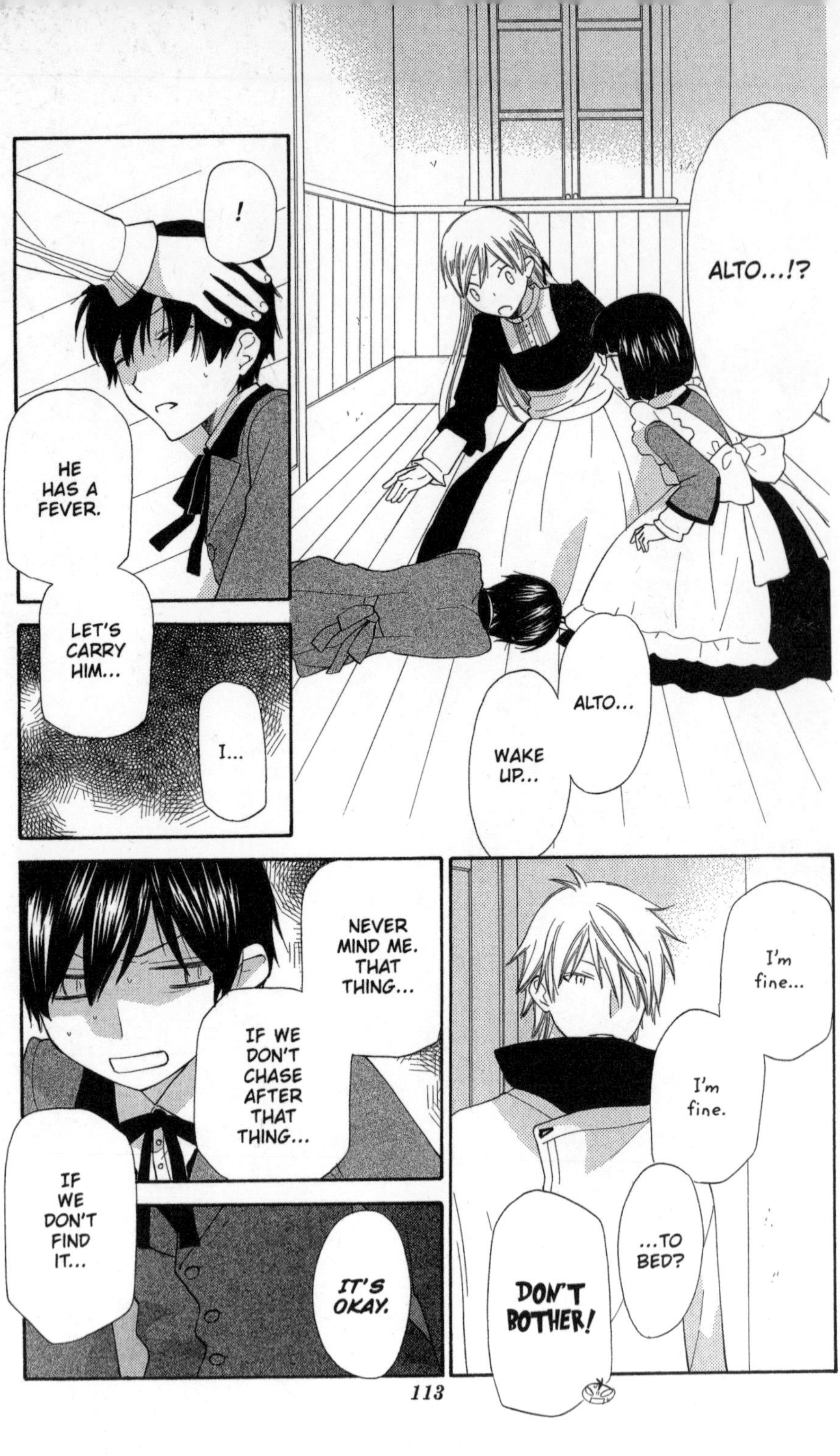
ALTO...!?
ALTO...
WAKE UP...
!
HE HAS A FEVER.
LET'S CARRY HIM...
I...
I'm fine...
I'm fine.
...TO BED?
DON'T BOTHER!
NEVER MIND ME. THAT THING...
IF WE DON'T CHASE AFTER THAT THING...
IF WE DON'T FIND IT...
IT'S OKAY.

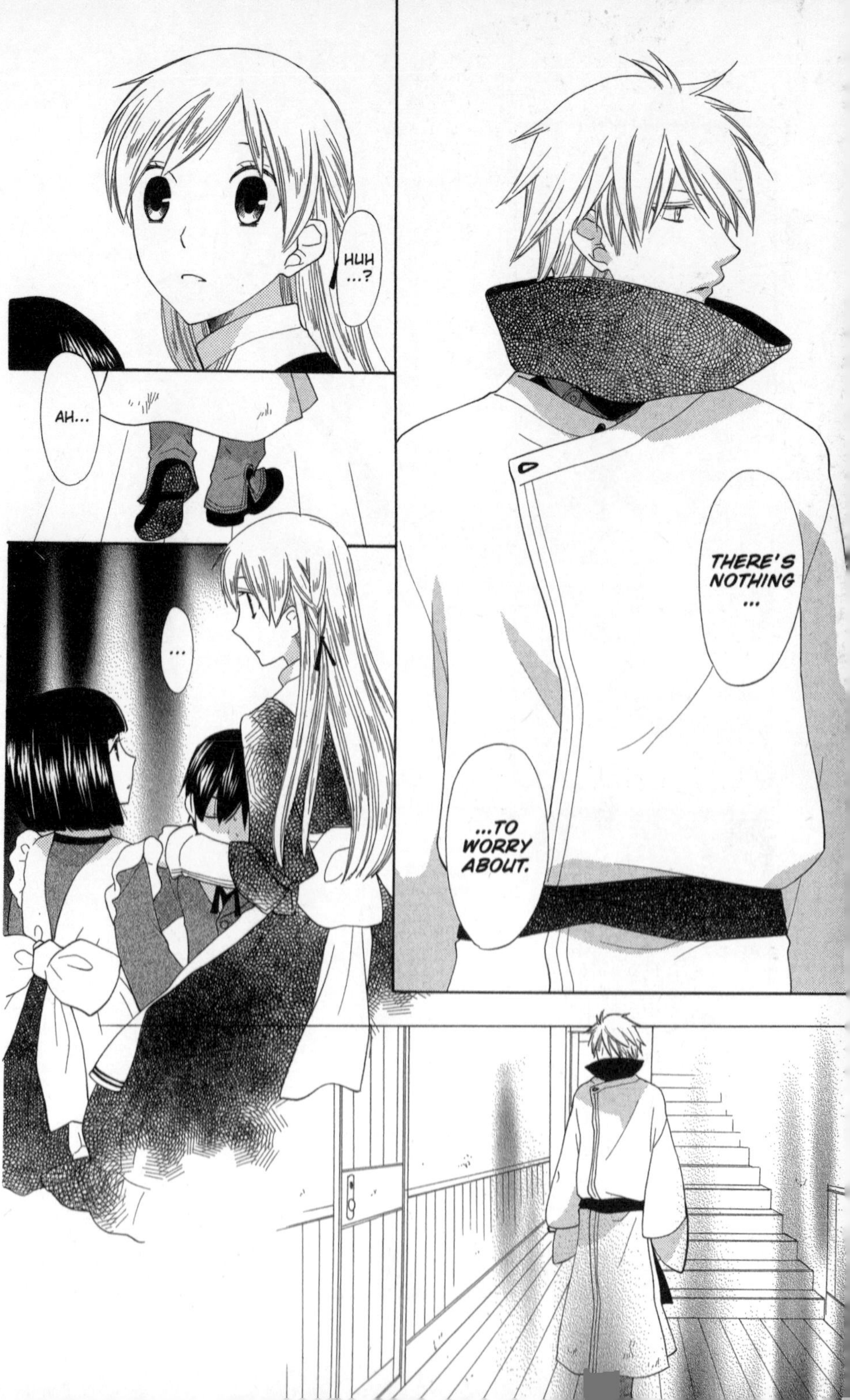
THERE'S NOTHING ...
...TO WORRY ABOUT.
HUH ...?
AH...
...

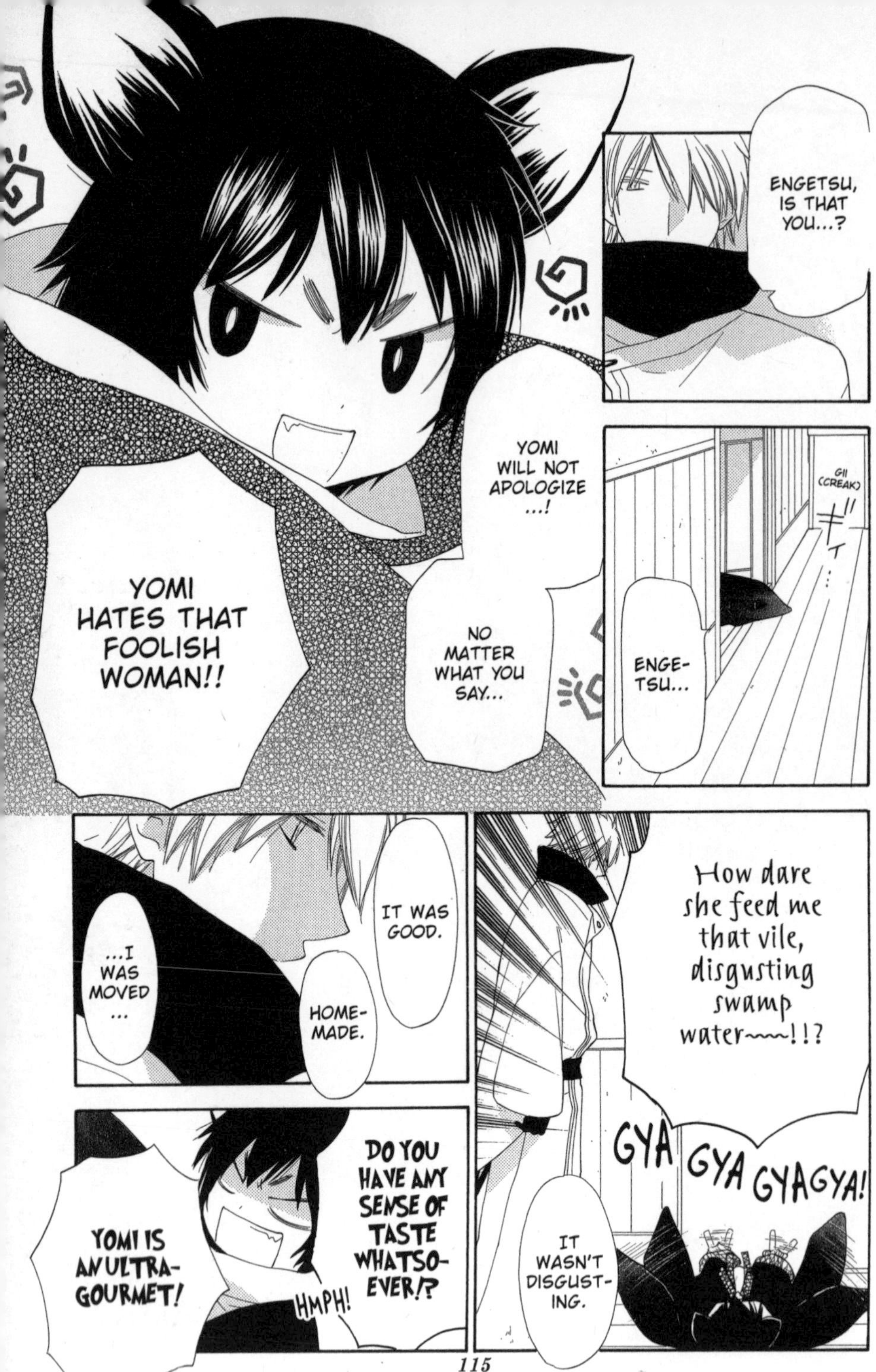
ENGETSU, IS THAT YOU...?
GII (CREAK)
ENGE-TSU...
YOMI WILL NOT APOLOGIZE...!
NO MATTER WHAT YOU SAY...
YOMI HATES THAT FOOLISH WOMAN!!
How dare she feed me that vile, disgusting swamp water~~~!!?
GYA GYA GYAGYA!
IT WASN'T DISGUST-ING.
IT WAS GOOD.
HOME-MADE.
...I WAS MOVED...
DO YOU HAVE ANY SENSE OF TASTE WHATSO-EVER!?
HMPH!
YOMI IS AN ULTRA-GOURMET!

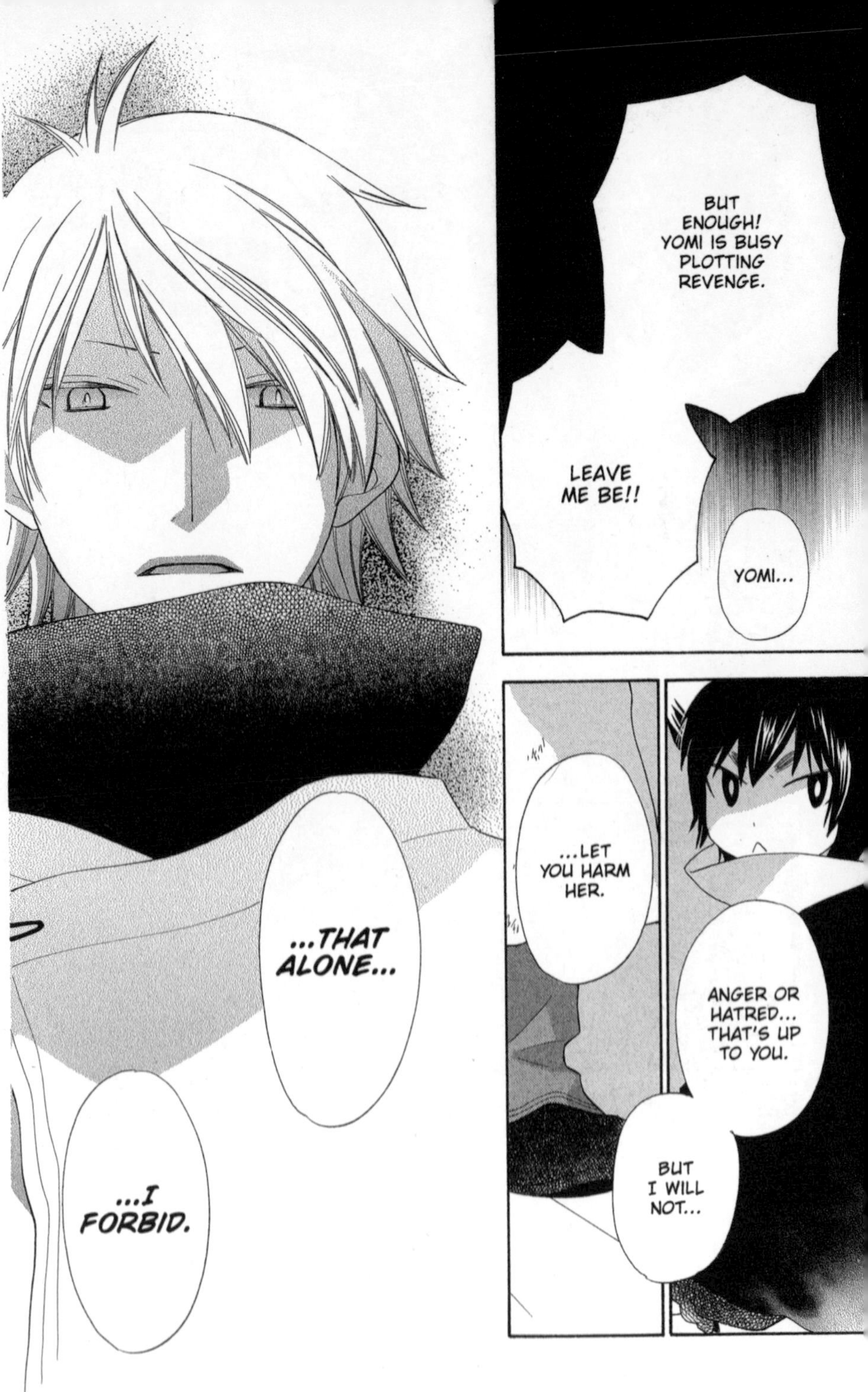
BUT ENOUGH! YOMI IS BUSY PLOTTING REVENGE.
LEAVE ME BE!!
YOMI...
ANGER OR HATRED... THAT'S UP TO YOU.
BUT I WILL NOT...
...LET YOU HARM HER.
...THAT ALONE...
...I FORBID.

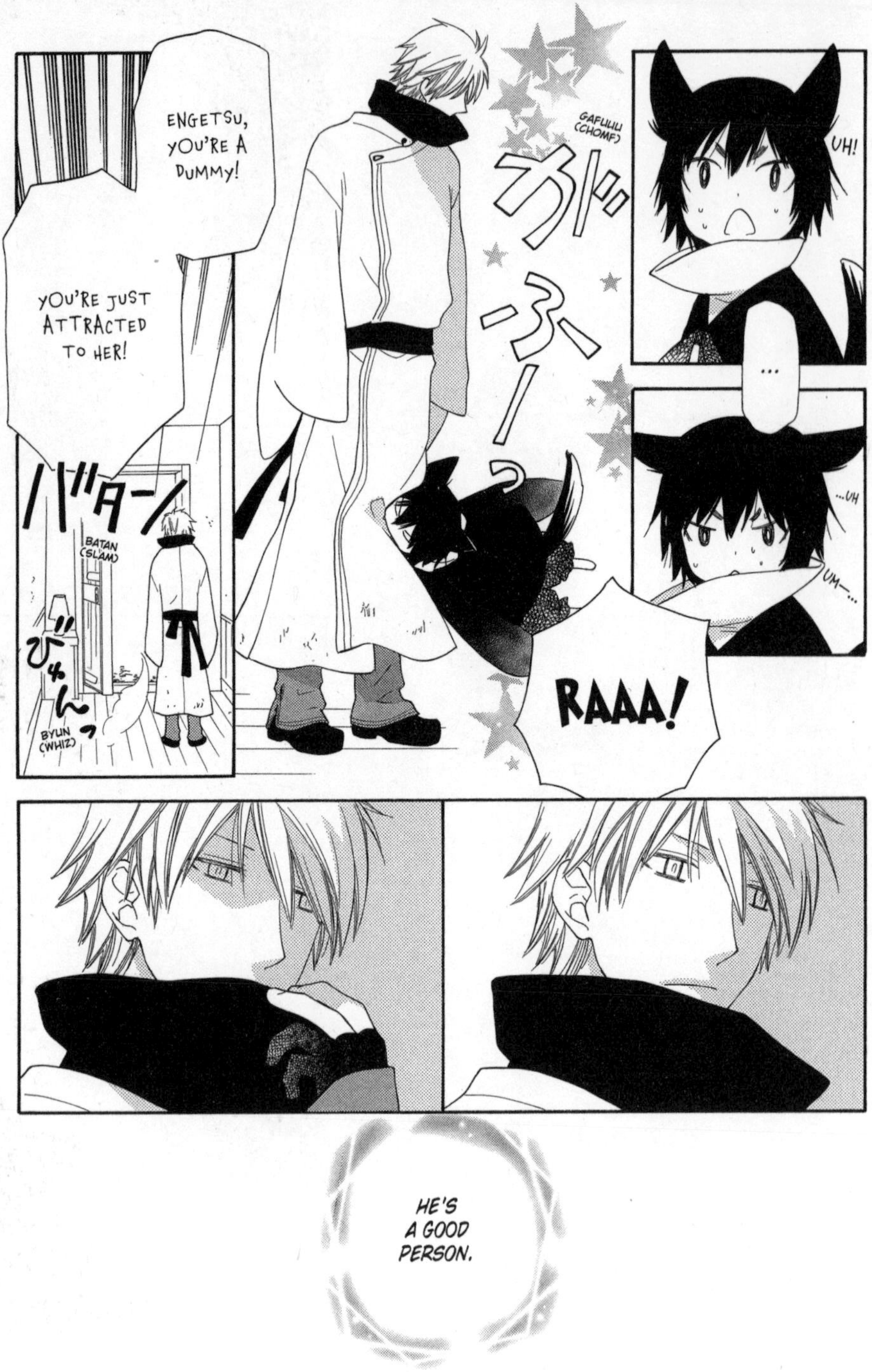

UH!
GAFUUU (CHOMF)
...
...UH
UM—...
RAAA!
ENGETSU, YOU'RE A DUMMY!
YOU'RE JUST ATTRACTED TO HER!
バターン
BATAN (SLAM)
びゅんっ
BYUN (WHIZ)
HE'S A GOOD PERSON.

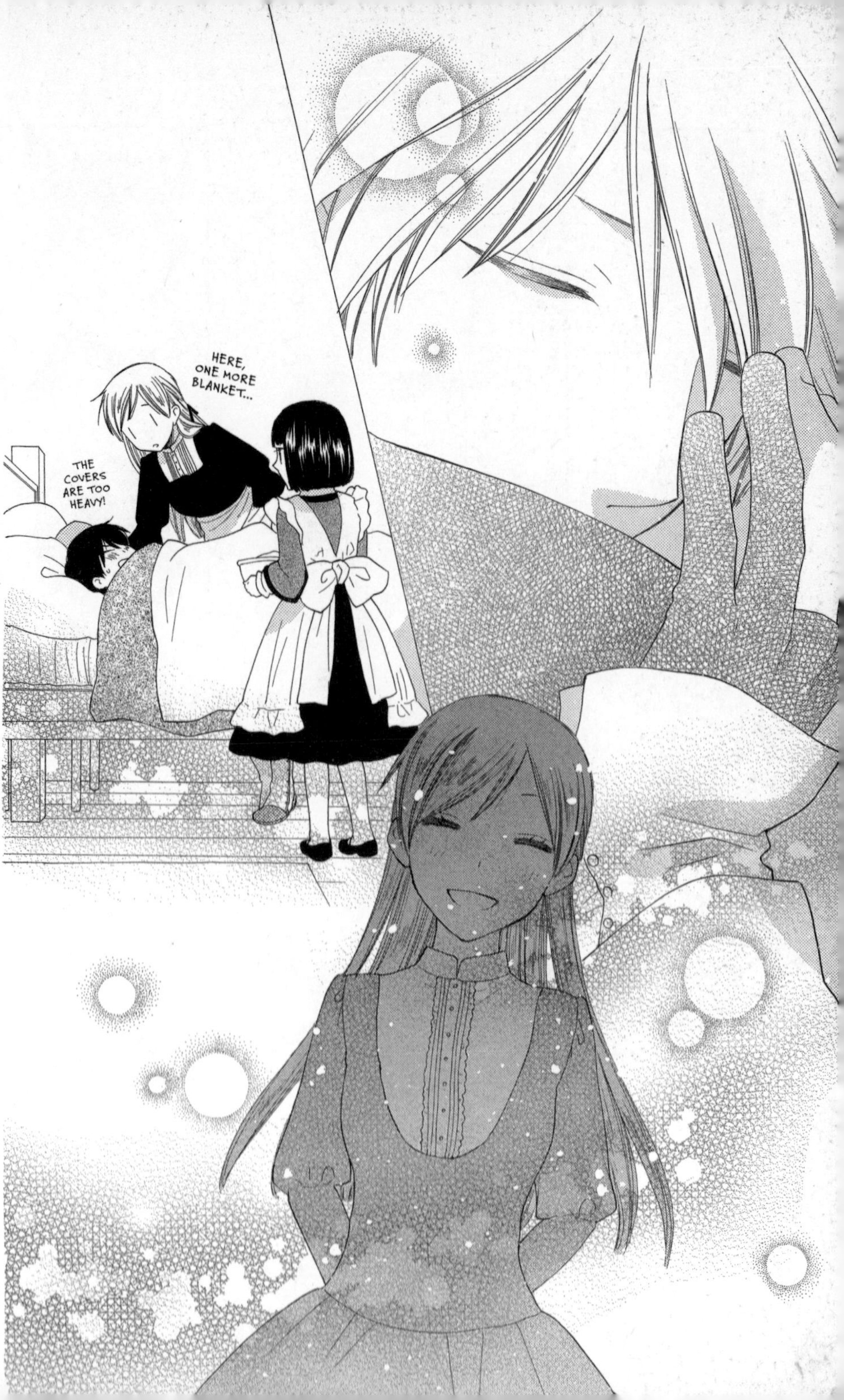
HERE, ONE MORE BLANKET...
THE COVERS ARE TOO HEAVY!

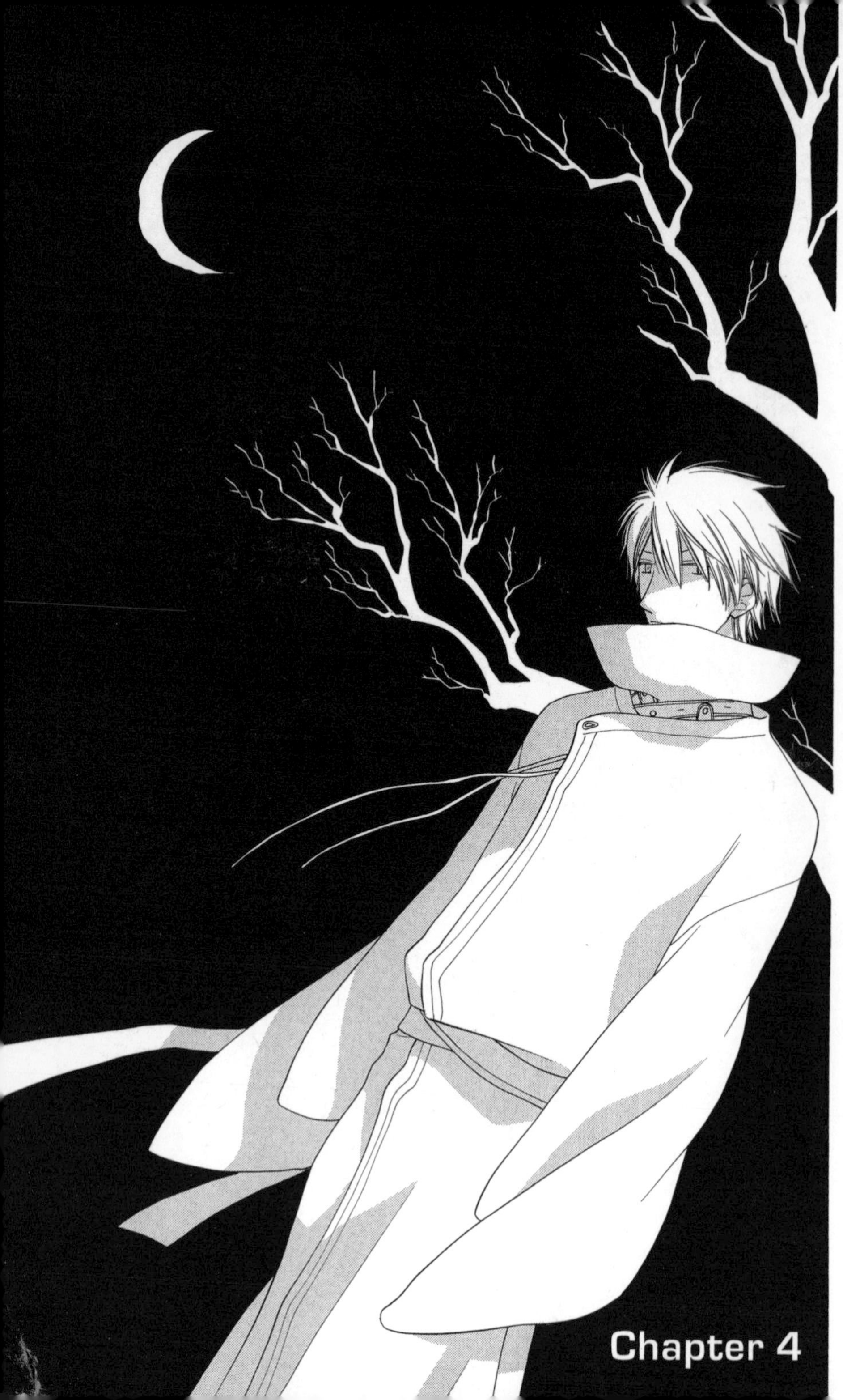

Chapter 4

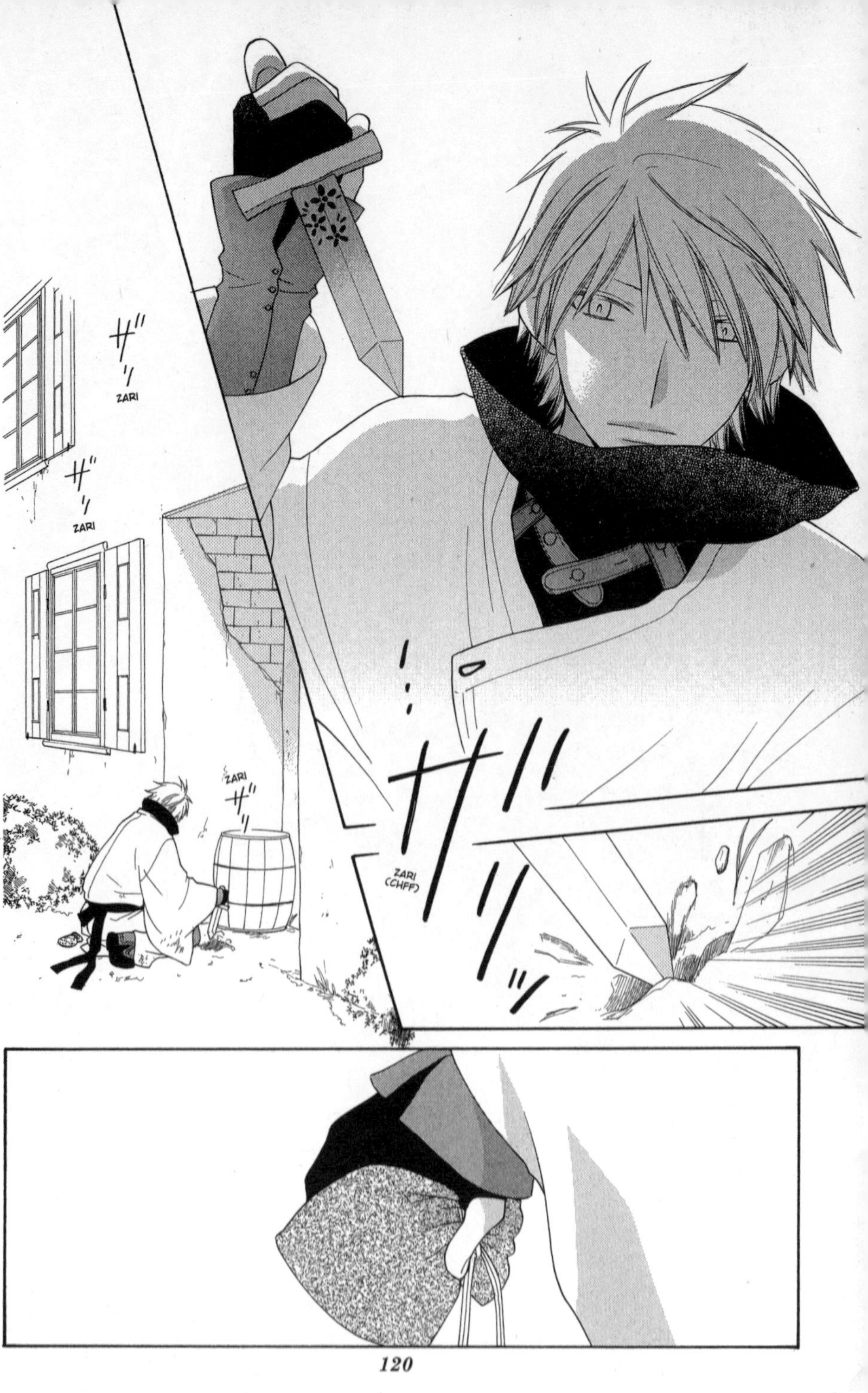
ザリ
ZARI (CHFF)
ザリ
ZARI
ザリ
ZARI
ZARI
ザリ

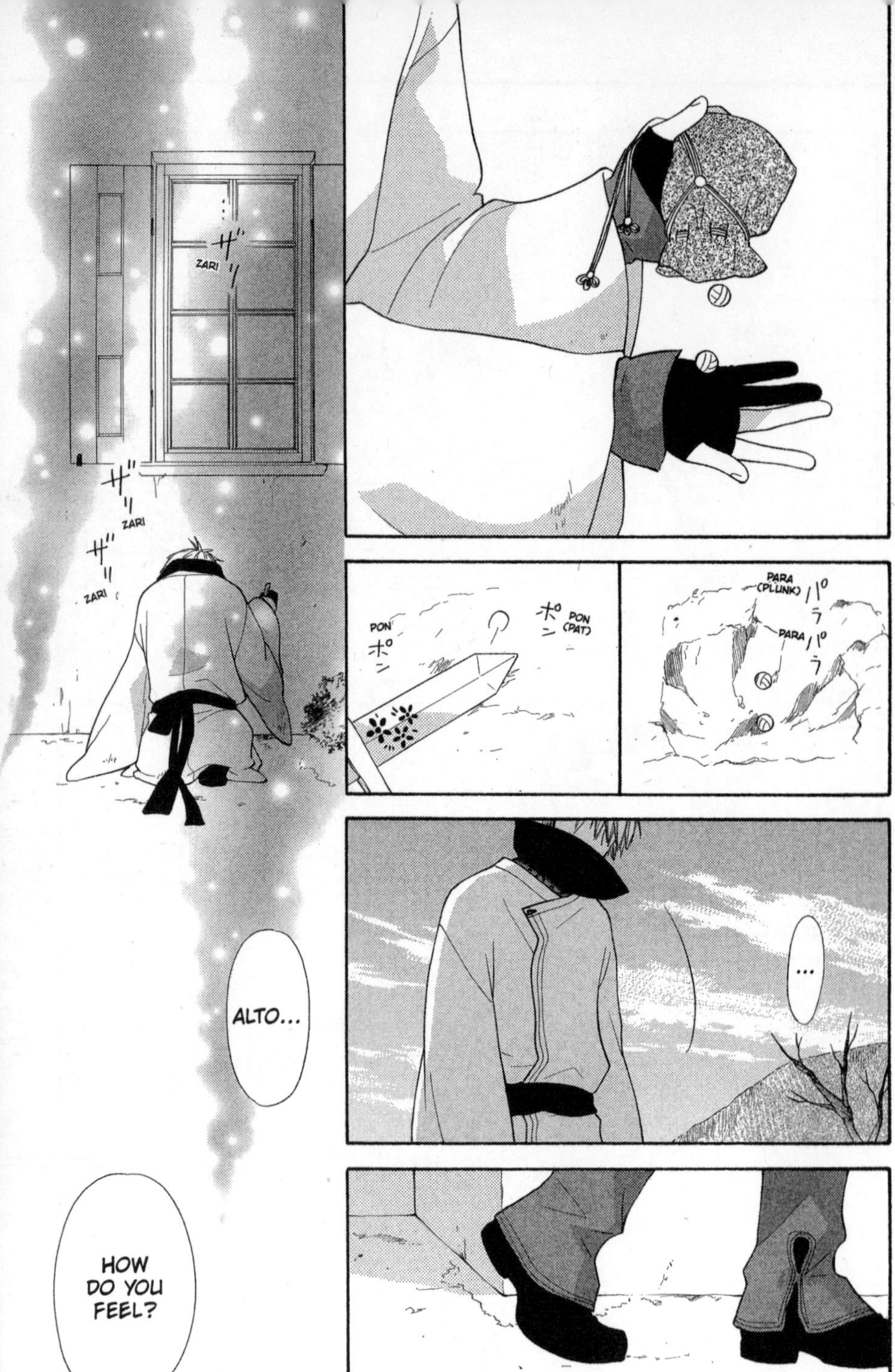

パラ PARA (PLUNK)
パラ PARA
ポン PON (PAT)
ポン PON
...
ザリ ZARI
ザリ ZARI
ザリ ZARI
ALTO...
HOW DO YOU FEEL?

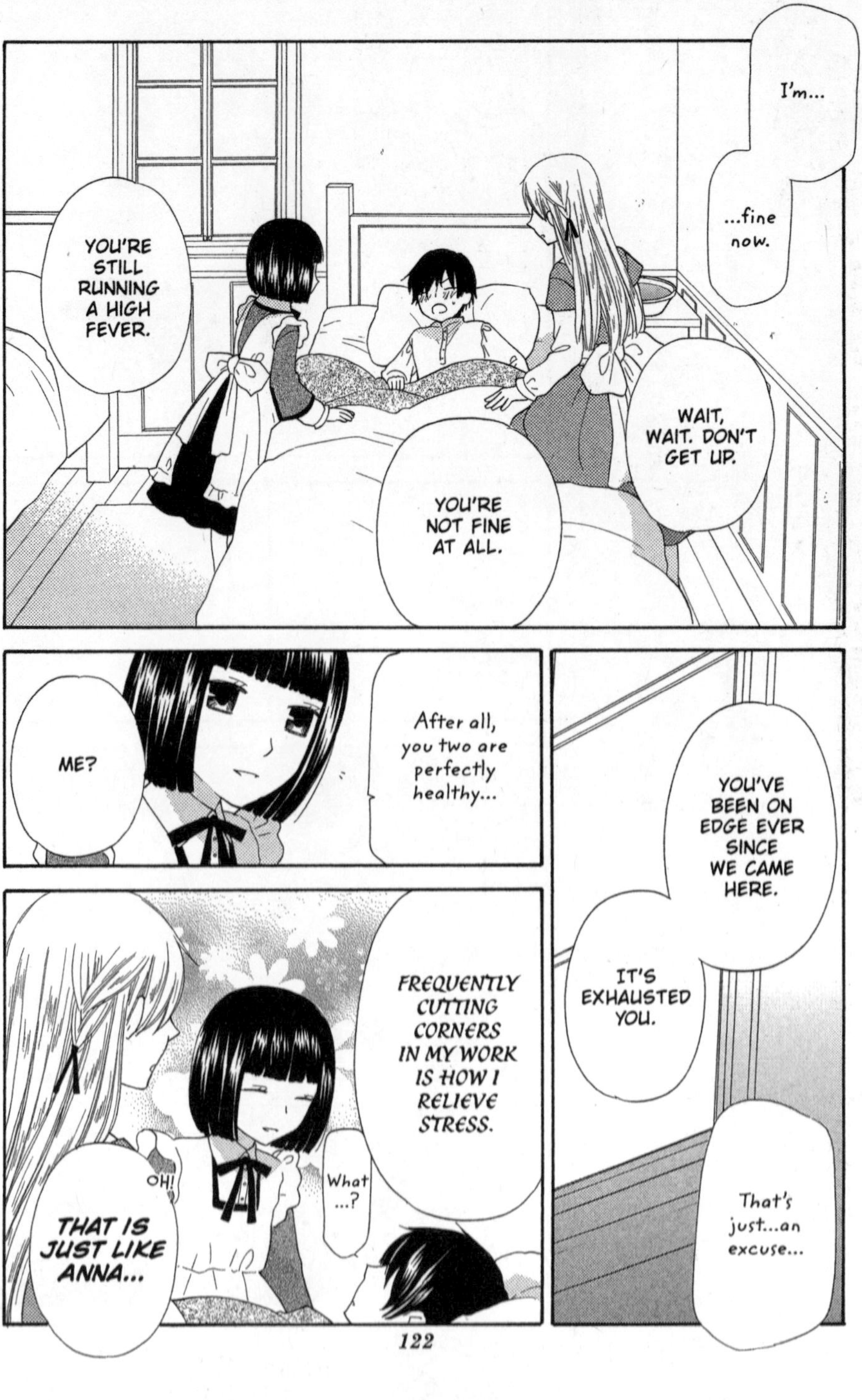
I'm...
...fine now.
WAIT, WAIT. DON'T GET UP.
YOU'RE NOT FINE AT ALL.
YOU'RE STILL RUNNING A HIGH FEVER.
YOU'VE BEEN ON EDGE EVER SINCE WE CAME HERE.
IT'S EXHAUSTED YOU.
That's just...an excuse...
After all, you two are perfectly healthy...
ME?
FREQUENTLY CUTTING CORNERS IN MY WORK IS HOW I RELIEVE STRESS.
What...?
OH!
THAT IS JUST LIKE ANNA...

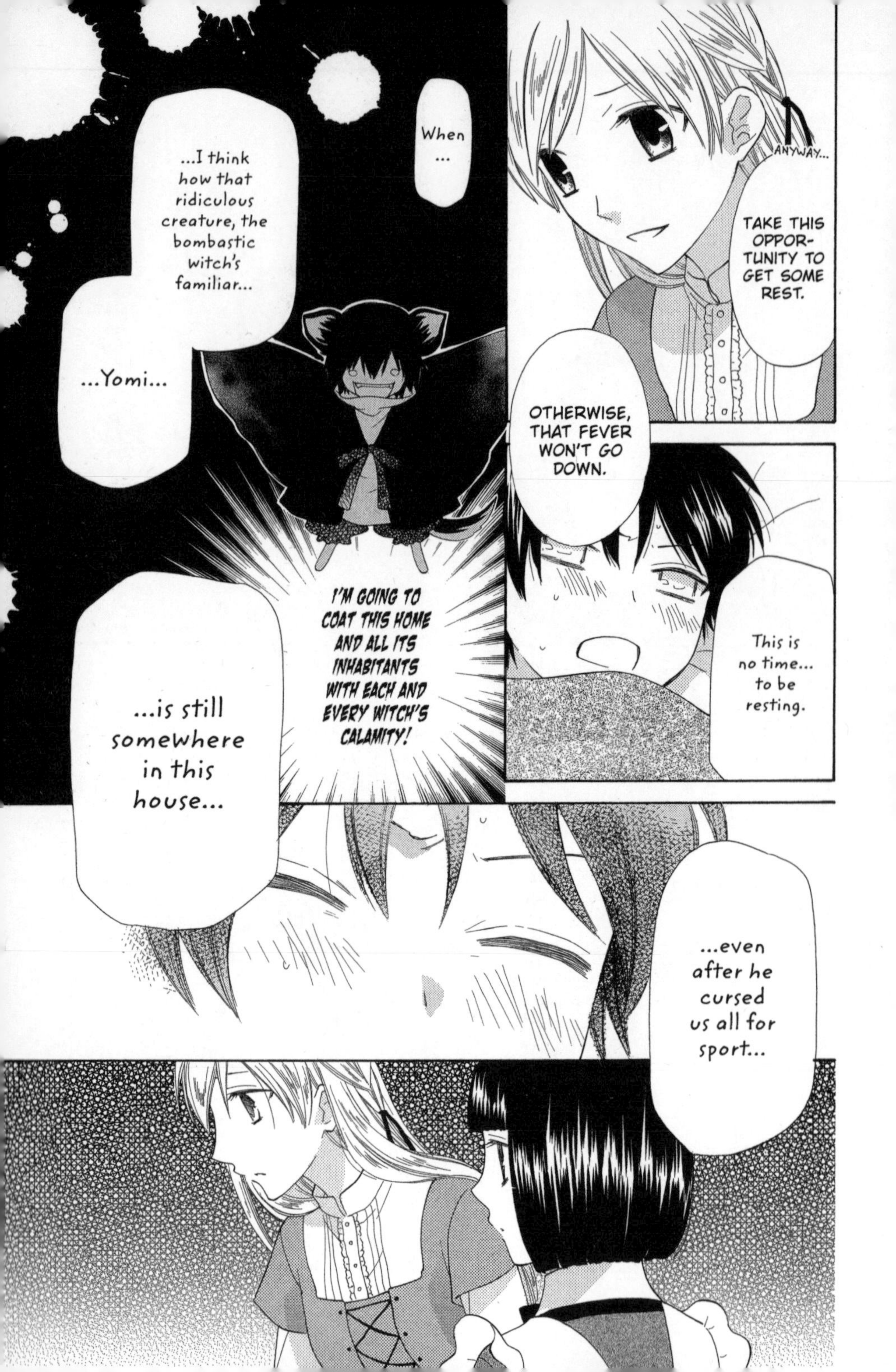
ANYWAY...
TAKE THIS OPPORTUNITY TO GET SOME REST.
OTHERWISE, THAT FEVER WON'T GO DOWN.
This is no time... to be resting.
When...
...I think how that ridiculous creature, the bombastic witch's familiar...
...Yomi...
I'M GOING TO COAT THIS HOME AND ALL ITS INHABITANTS WITH EACH AND EVERY WITCH'S CALAMITY!
...is still somewhere in this house...
...even after he cursed us all for sport...

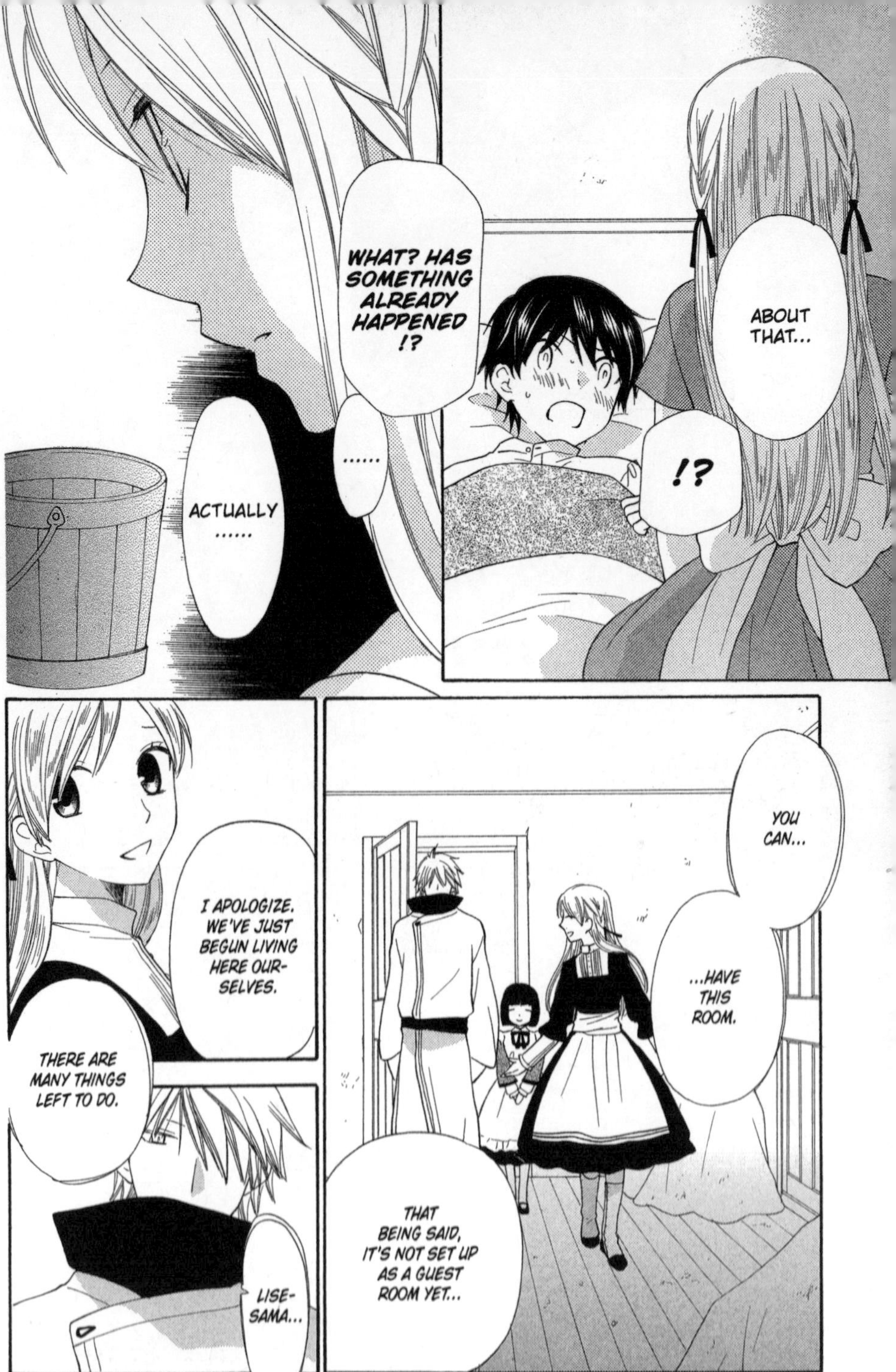
ABOUT THAT...
!?
WHAT? HAS SOMETHING ALREADY HAPPENED !?
......
ACTUALLY ......
YOU CAN...
...HAVE THIS ROOM.
THAT BEING SAID, IT'S NOT SET UP AS A GUEST ROOM YET...
I APOLOGIZE. WE'VE JUST BEGUN LIVING HERE OUR-SELVES.
THERE ARE MANY THINGS LEFT TO DO.
LISE-SAMA...

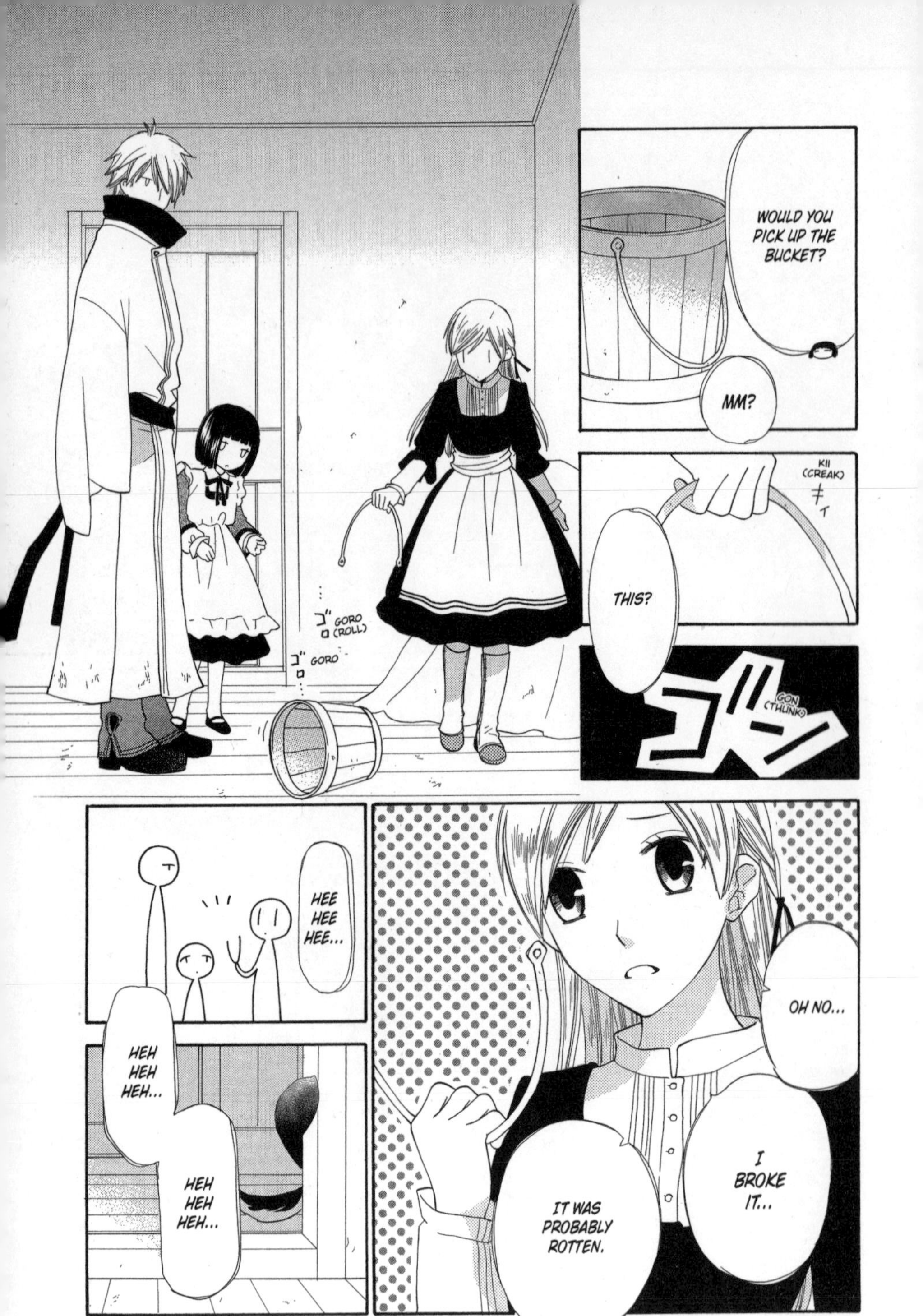
WOULD YOU PICK UP THE BUCKET?
MM?
キイ
KII (CREAK)
THIS?
ゴーン
GON (THUNK)
ゴロ
GORO (ROLL)
ゴロ
GORO
OH NO...
I BROKE IT...
IT WAS PROBABLY ROTTEN.
HEE HEE HEE...
HEH HEH HEH...
HEH HEH HEH...

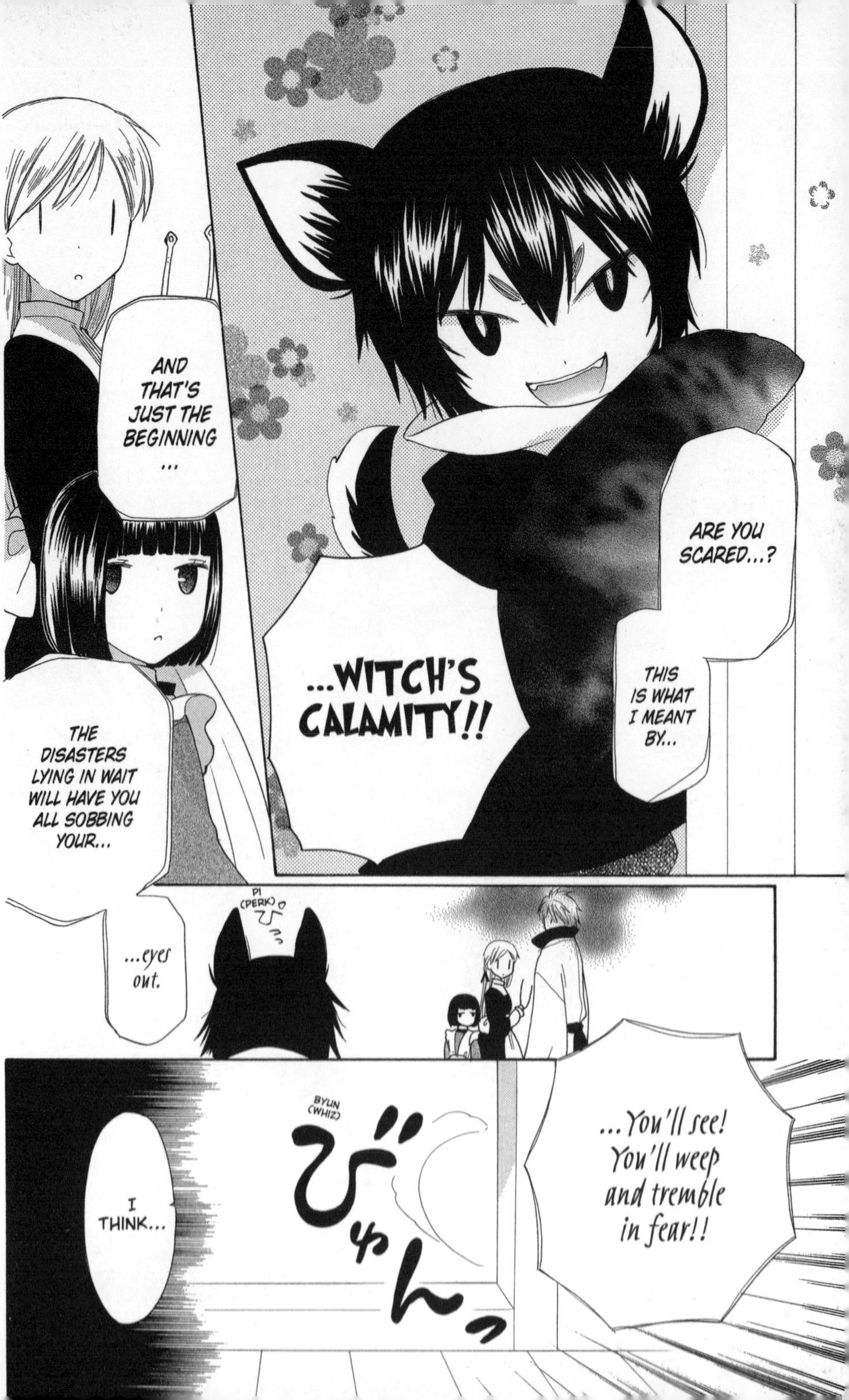
ARE YOU SCARED...?
THIS IS WHAT I MEANT BY...
...WITCH'S CALAMITY!!
AND THAT'S JUST THE BEGINNING...
THE DISASTERS LYING IN WAIT WILL HAVE YOU ALL SOBBING YOUR...
PI (PERK)
...eyes out.
...You'll see! You'll weep and tremble in fear!!
BYUN (WHIZ)
I THINK...

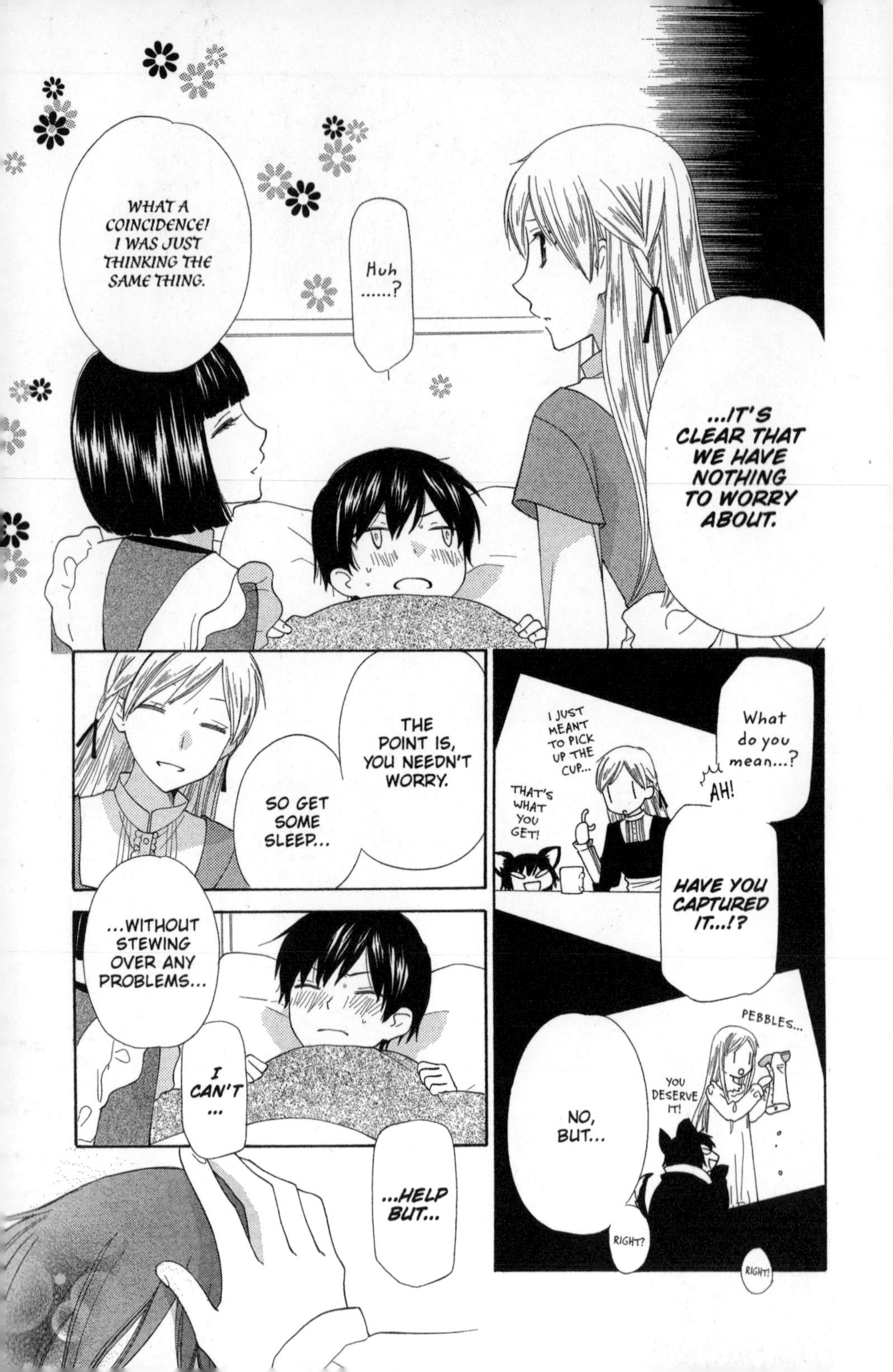
...IT'S CLEAR THAT WE HAVE NOTHING TO WORRY ABOUT.
Huh ......?
WHAT A COINCIDENCE! I WAS JUST THINKING THE SAME THING.
What do you mean...?
AH!
I JUST MEANT TO PICK UP THE CUP...
THAT'S WHAT YOU GET!
HAVE YOU CAPTURED IT...!?
PEBBLES...
YOU DESERVE IT!
NO, BUT...
RIGHT?
RIGHT!
THE POINT IS, YOU NEEDN'T WORRY.
SO GET SOME SLEEP...
...WITHOUT STEWING OVER ANY PROBLEMS...
I CAN'T ...
...HELP BUT...

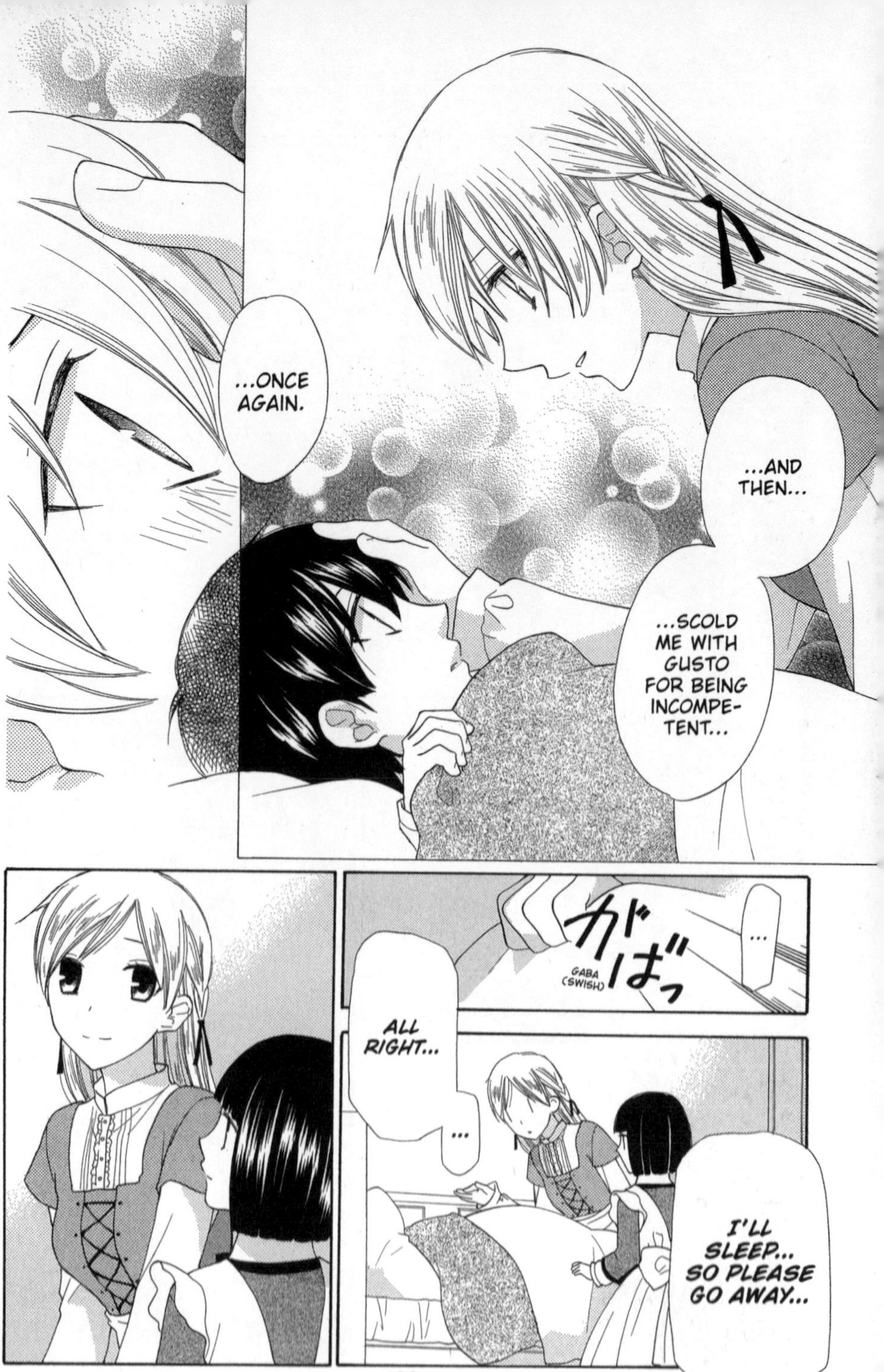
...AND THEN...
...SCOLD ME WITH GUSTO FOR BEING INCOMPETENT...
...ONCE AGAIN.
...
がばっ
GABA (SWISH)
ALL RIGHT...
...
I'LL SLEEP... SO PLEASE GO AWAY...

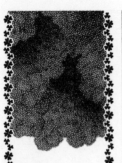

WITH ANNA-SAN, I'M TRYING FOR A BOB WITH STRAIGHT-CUT BANGS, BUT IN THE FIRST CHAPTER, I THINK MAYBE IT WAS TOO LOOSE AND DISHEVELED, SO I'VE BEEN MAKING MINOR ADJUSTMENTS EACH TIME.

AS FOR YOMI-SAN, I HAVE A FEELING HE'S BEEN GETTING MORE COMPACT WITH EACH CHAPTER, BUT I'VE TOLD MYSELF THAT I DON'T CARE. (LOL)

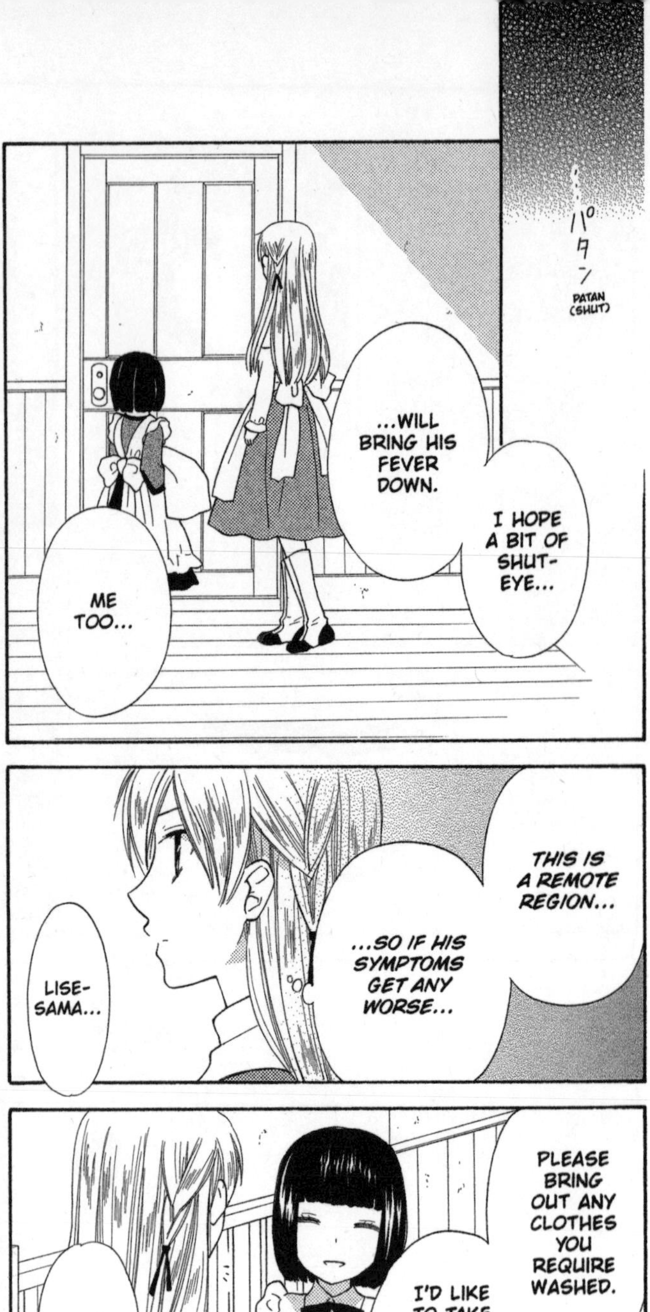
パタン
PATAN (SHUT)
I HOPE A BIT OF SHUT-EYE...
...WILL BRING HIS FEVER DOWN.
ME TOO...
THIS IS A REMOTE REGION...
...SO IF HIS SYMPTOMS GET ANY WORSE...
LISE-SAMA...
PLEASE BRING OUT ANY CLOTHES YOU REQUIRE WASHED.
I'D LIKE TO TAKE CARE OF LAUNDRY BEFORE IT STARTS PILING UP.
I'LL HELP YOU.

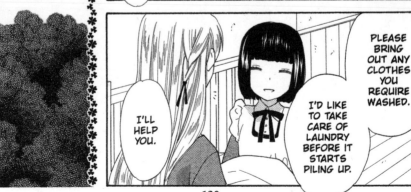

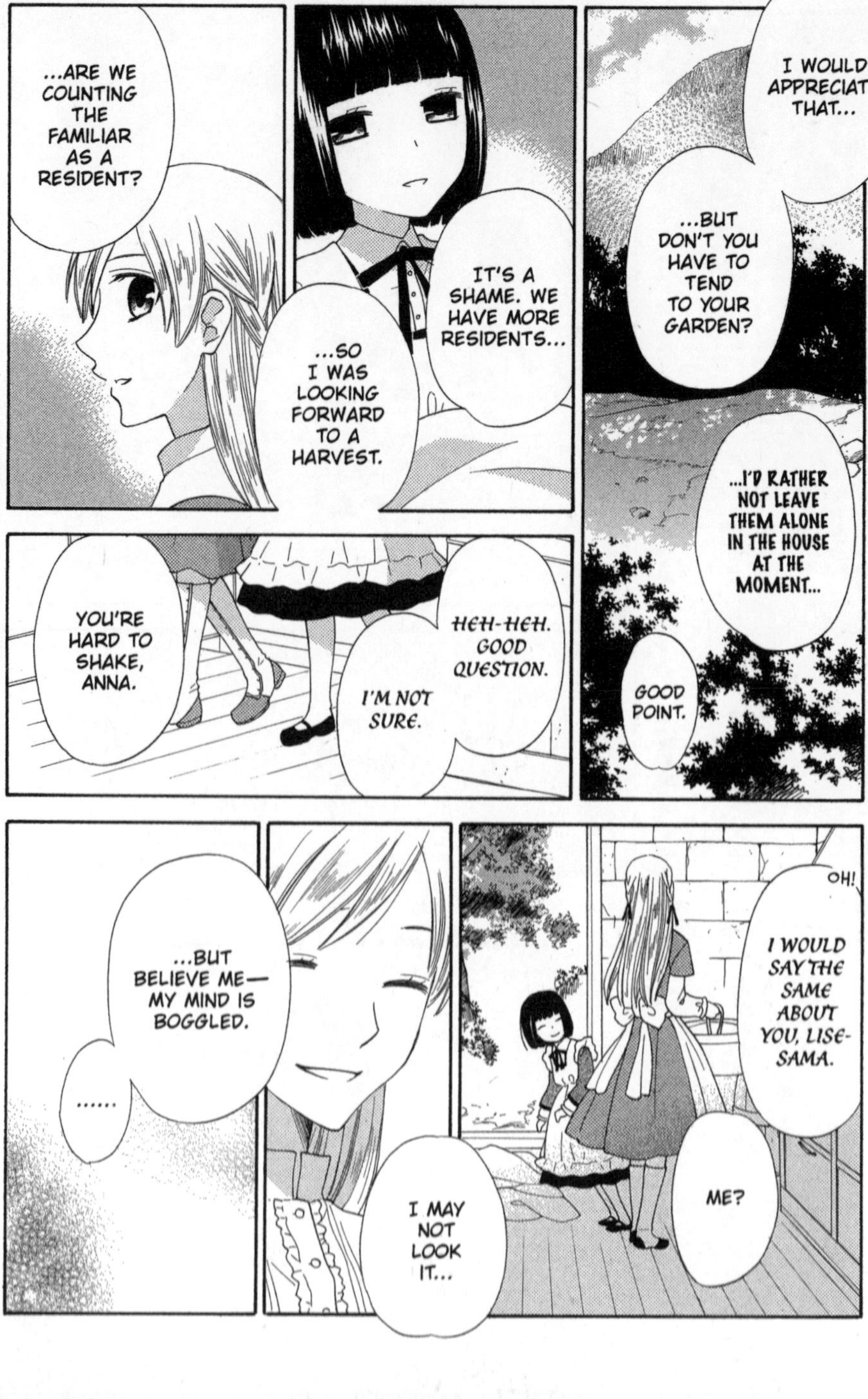
I WOULD APPRECIATE THAT...
...BUT DON'T YOU HAVE TO TEND TO YOUR GARDEN?
...I'D RATHER NOT LEAVE THEM ALONE IN THE HOUSE AT THE MOMENT...
GOOD POINT.
IT'S A SHAME. WE HAVE MORE RESIDENTS...
...SO I WAS LOOKING FORWARD TO A HARVEST.
...ARE WE COUNTING THE FAMILIAR AS A RESIDENT?
HEH-HEH. GOOD QUESTION.
I'M NOT SURE.
YOU'RE HARD TO SHAKE, ANNA.
OH!
I WOULD SAY THE SAME ABOUT YOU, LISE-SAMA.
ME?
I MAY NOT LOOK IT...
...BUT BELIEVE ME— MY MIND IS BOGGLED.
......

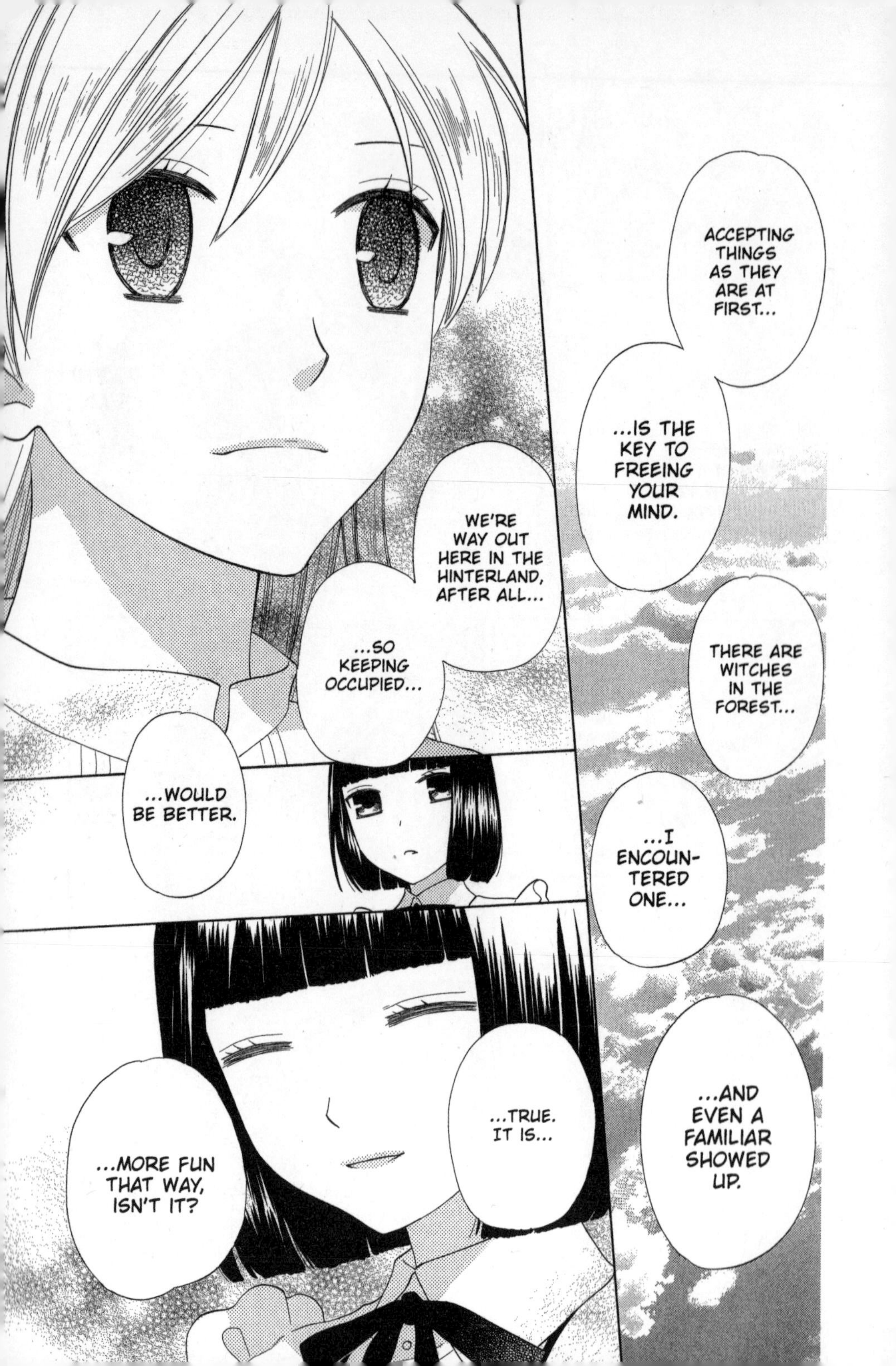
ACCEPTING THINGS AS THEY ARE AT FIRST...
...IS THE KEY TO FREEING YOUR MIND.
THERE ARE WITCHES IN THE FOREST...
...I ENCOUN-TERED ONE...
...AND EVEN A FAMILIAR SHOWED UP.
WE'RE WAY OUT HERE IN THE HINTERLAND, AFTER ALL...
...SO KEEPING OCCUPIED...
...WOULD BE BETTER.
...TRUE. IT IS...
...MORE FUN THAT WAY, ISN'T IT?

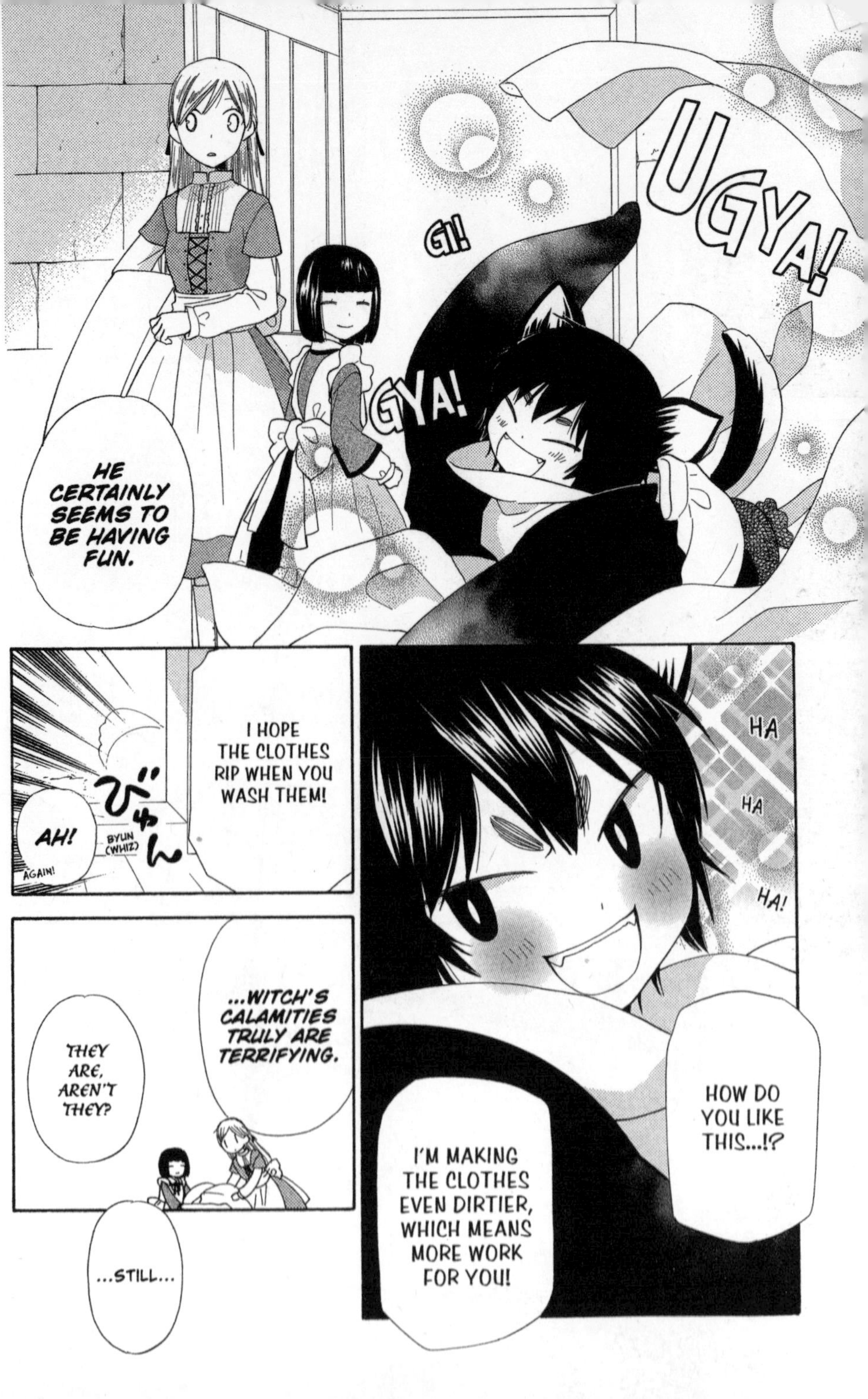
UGYA!
GI!
UGYA!
HE CERTAINLY SEEMS TO BE HAVING FUN.
HA
HA
HA!
HOW DO YOU LIKE THIS...!?
I'M MAKING THE CLOTHES EVEN DIRTIER, WHICH MEANS MORE WORK FOR YOU!
I HOPE THE CLOTHES RIP WHEN YOU WASH THEM!
びゅん
BYUN (WHIZ)
AH!
AGAIN!
...WITCH'S CALAMITIES TRULY ARE TERRIFYING.
THEY ARE, AREN'T THEY?
...STILL...

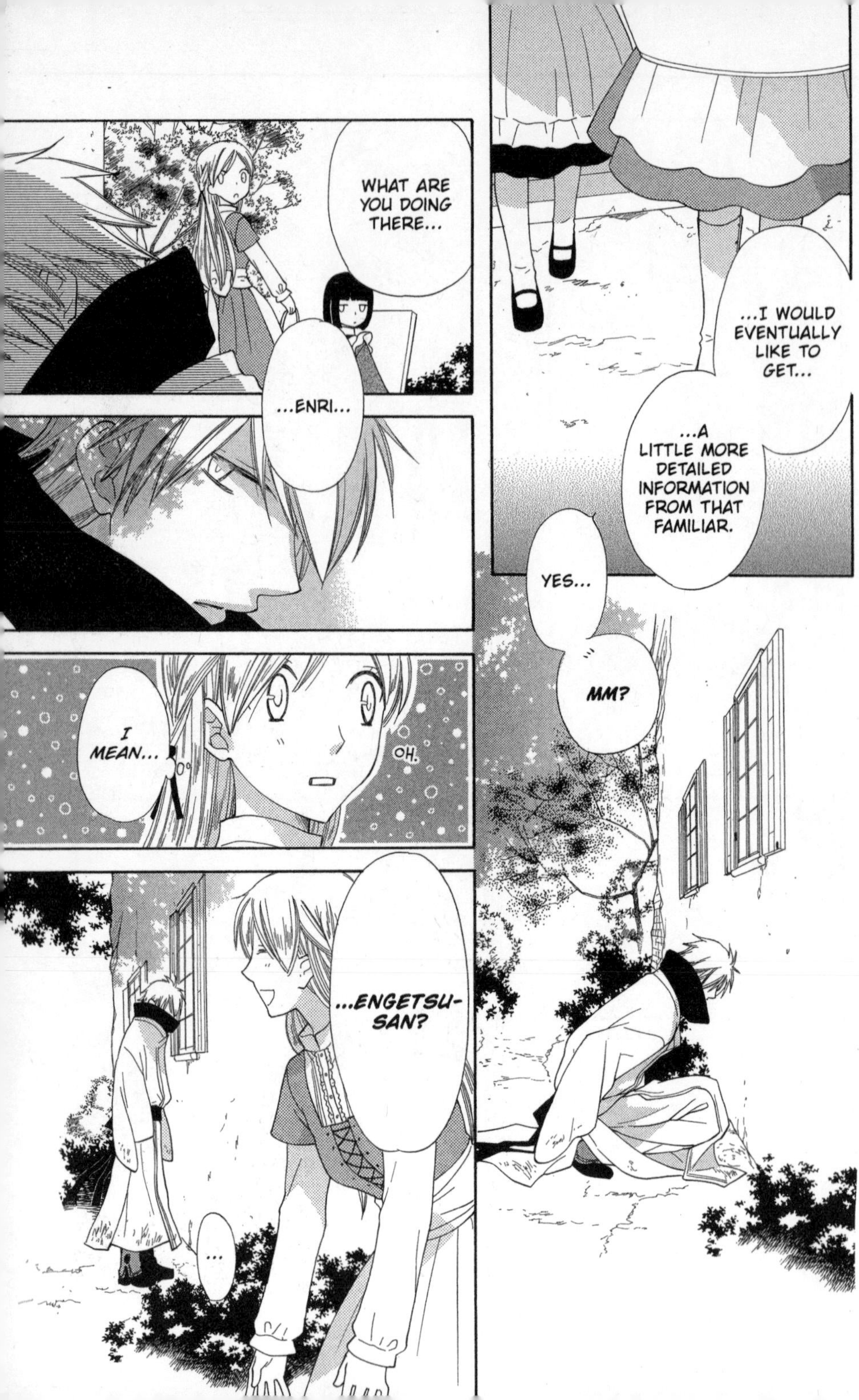
...I WOULD EVENTUALLY LIKE TO GET...
...A LITTLE MORE DETAILED INFORMATION FROM THAT FAMILIAR.
YES...
MM?
WHAT ARE YOU DOING THERE...
...ENRI...
OH.
I MEAN...
...ENGETSU-SAN?
...

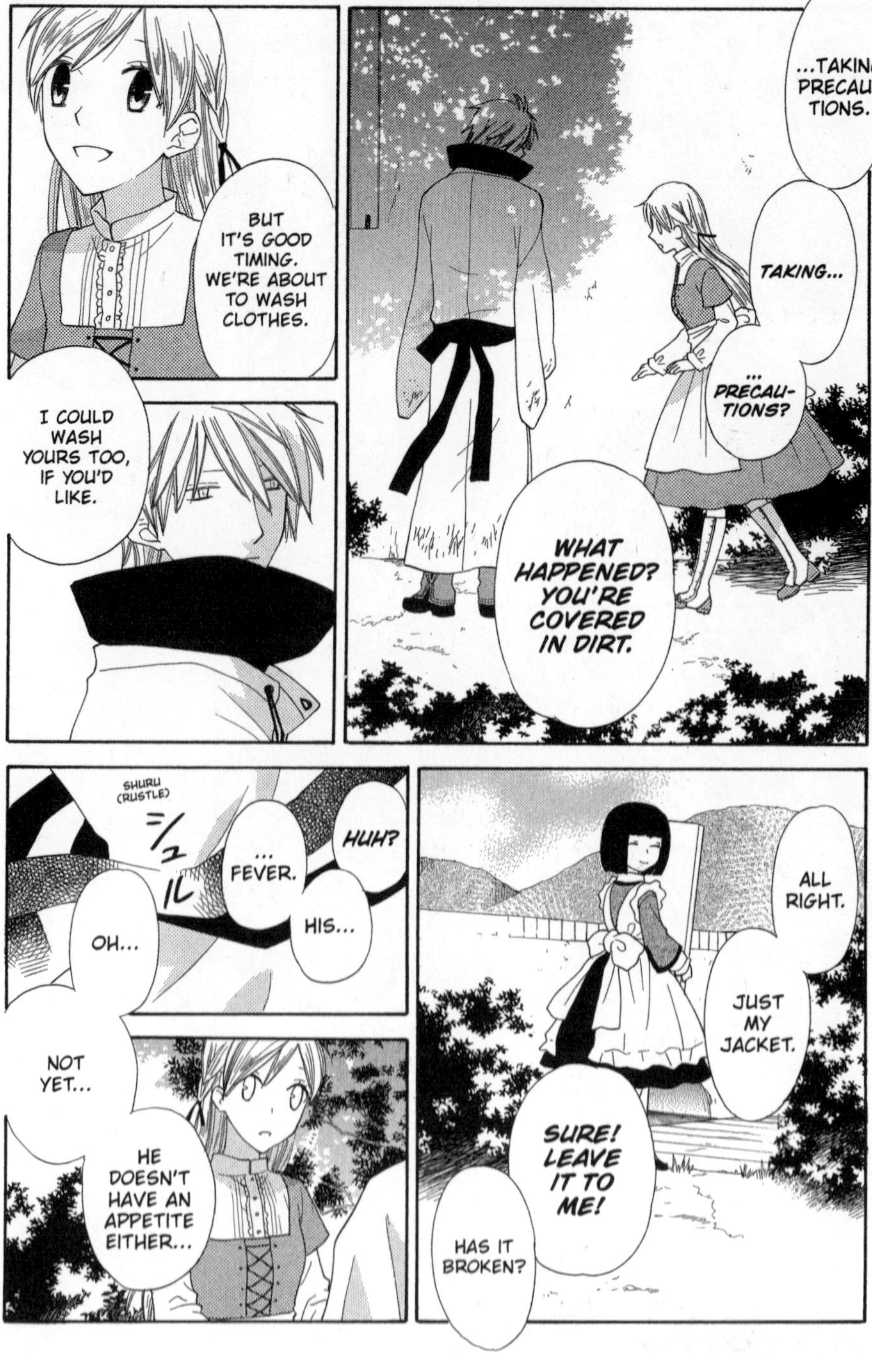
...TAKING PRECAU- TIONS.
TAKING...
... PRECAU- TIONS?
WHAT HAPPENED? YOU'RE COVERED IN DIRT.
BUT IT'S GOOD TIMING. WE'RE ABOUT TO WASH CLOTHES.
I COULD WASH YOURS TOO, IF YOU'D LIKE.
ALL RIGHT.
JUST MY JACKET.
SURE! LEAVE IT TO ME!
HAS IT BROKEN?
HUH?
... FEVER.
HIS...
SHURU (RUSTLE)
シュル
OH...
NOT YET...
HE DOESN'T HAVE AN APPETITE EITHER...

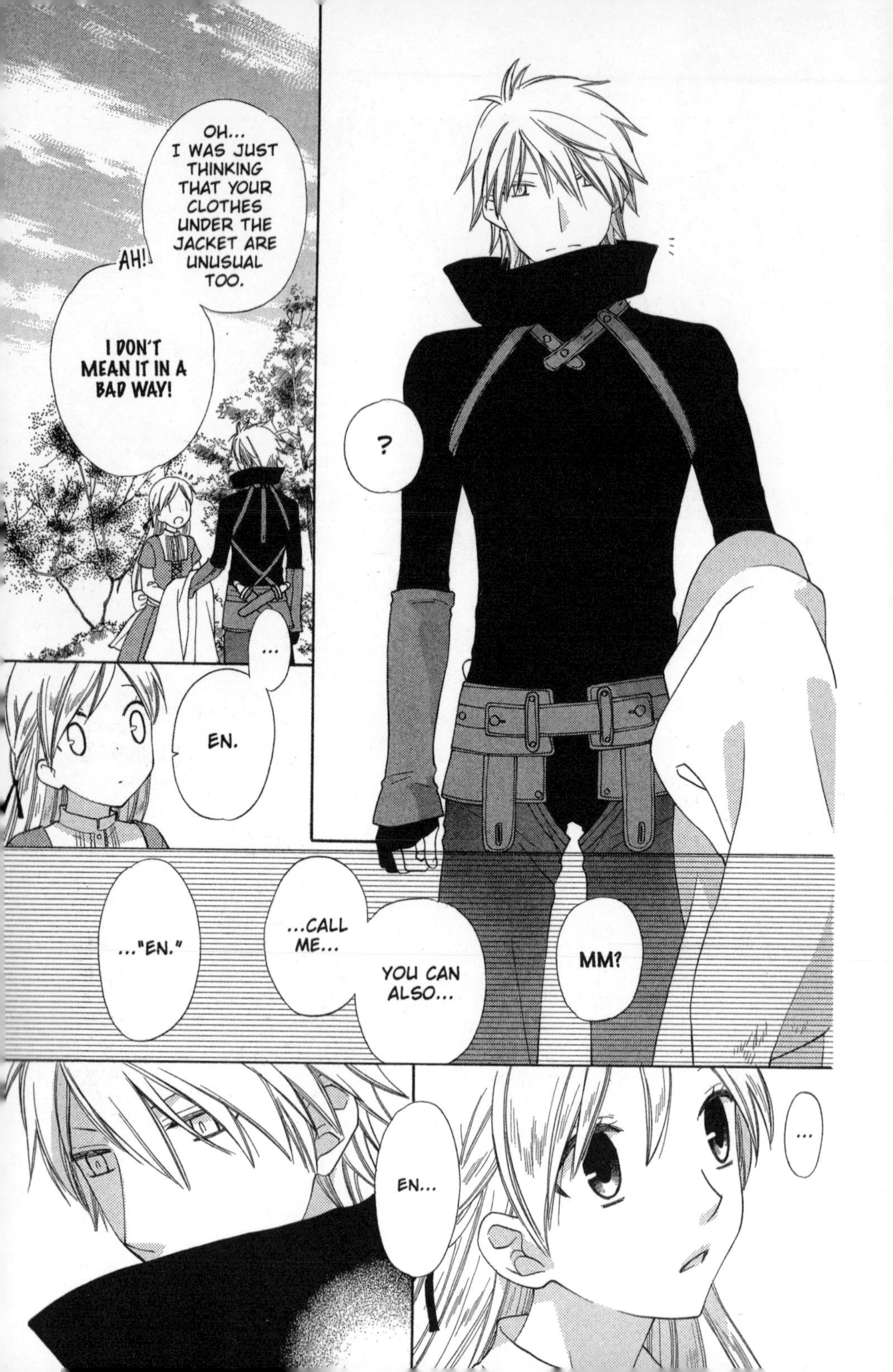
?
OH... I WAS JUST THINKING THAT YOUR CLOTHES UNDER THE JACKET ARE UNUSUAL TOO.
AH!
I DON'T MEAN IT IN A BAD WAY!
...
EN.
MM?
YOU CAN ALSO...
...CALL ME...
..."EN."
...
EN...

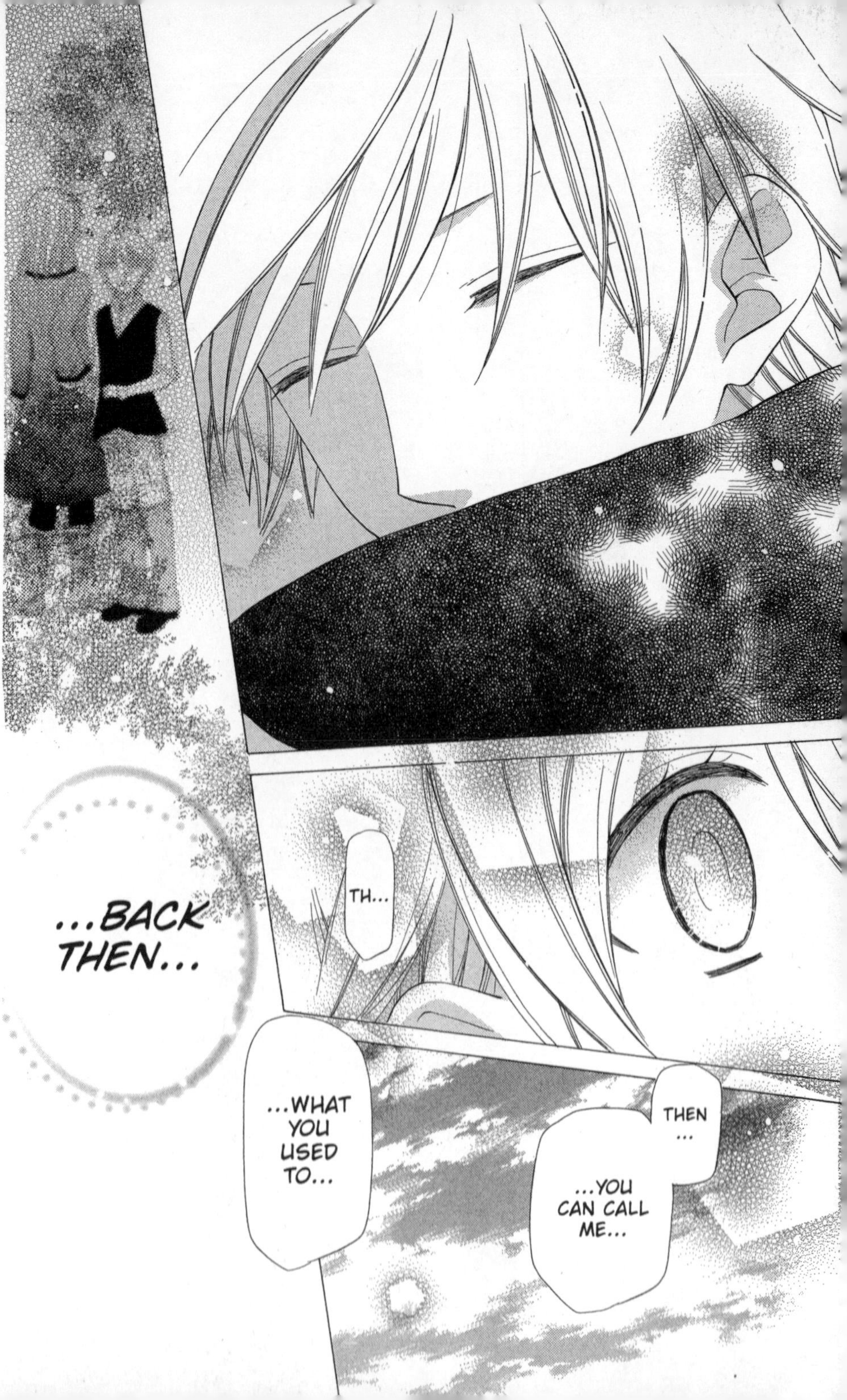
TH...
THEN...
...YOU CAN CALL ME...
...WHAT YOU USED TO...
...BACK THEN...

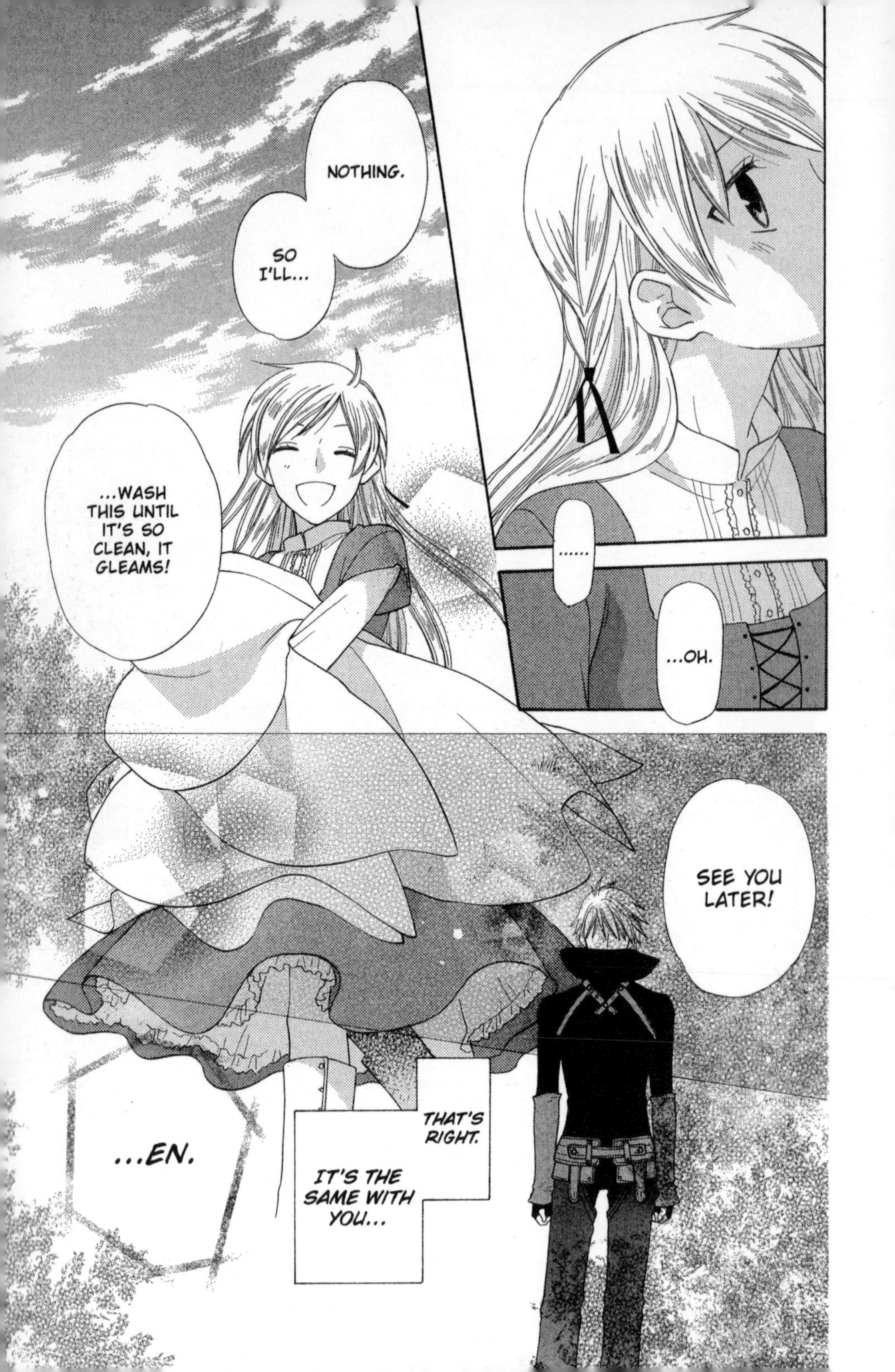
......
...OH.
NOTHING.
SO I'LL...
...WASH THIS UNTIL IT'S SO CLEAN, IT GLEAMS!
SEE YOU LATER!
THAT'S RIGHT.
IT'S THE SAME WITH YOU...
...EN.

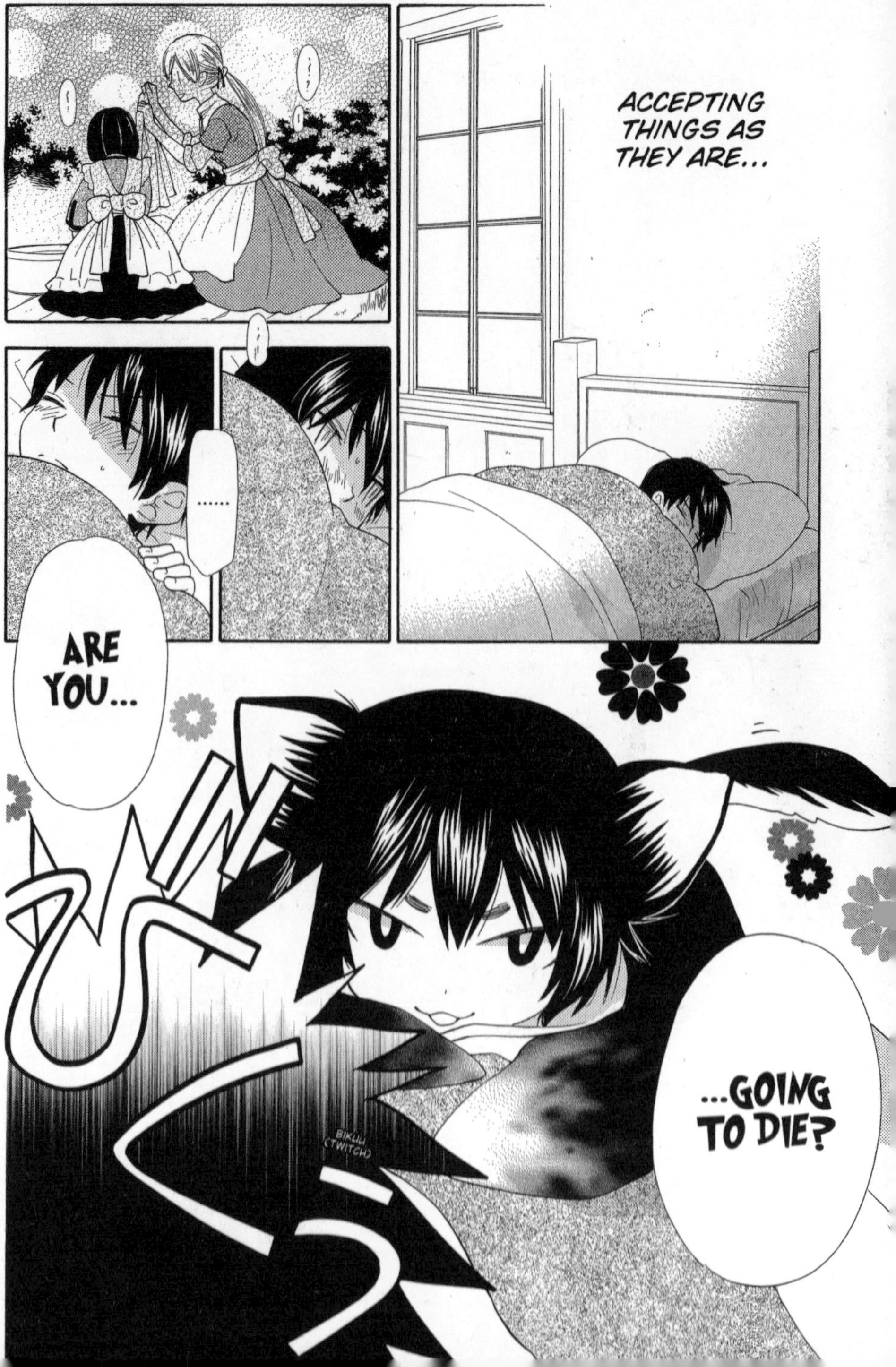
ACCEPTING THINGS AS THEY ARE...
......
ARE YOU...
BIKUU (TWITCH)
...GOING TO DIE?

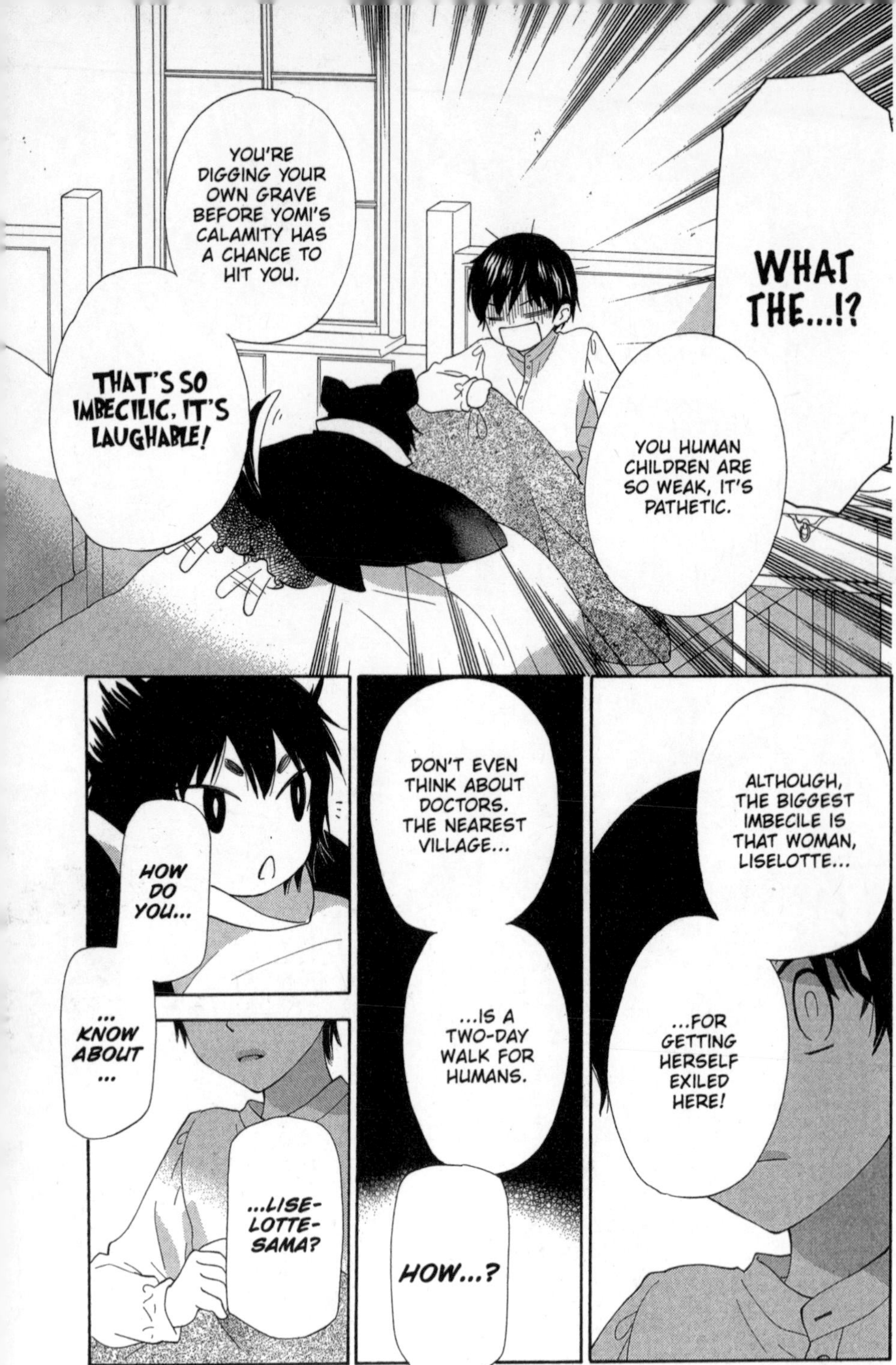

WHAT THE...!?
YOU HUMAN CHILDREN ARE SO WEAK, IT'S PATHETIC.
YOU'RE DIGGING YOUR OWN GRAVE BEFORE YOMI'S CALAMITY HAS A CHANCE TO HIT YOU.
THAT'S SO IMBECILIC, IT'S LAUGHABLE!
ALTHOUGH, THE BIGGEST IMBECILE IS THAT WOMAN, LISELOTTE...
...FOR GETTING HERSELF EXILED HERE!
DON'T EVEN THINK ABOUT DOCTORS. THE NEAREST VILLAGE...
...IS A TWO-DAY WALK FOR HUMANS.
HOW...?
HOW DO YOU...
...KNOW ABOUT...
...LISE-LOTTE-SAMA?

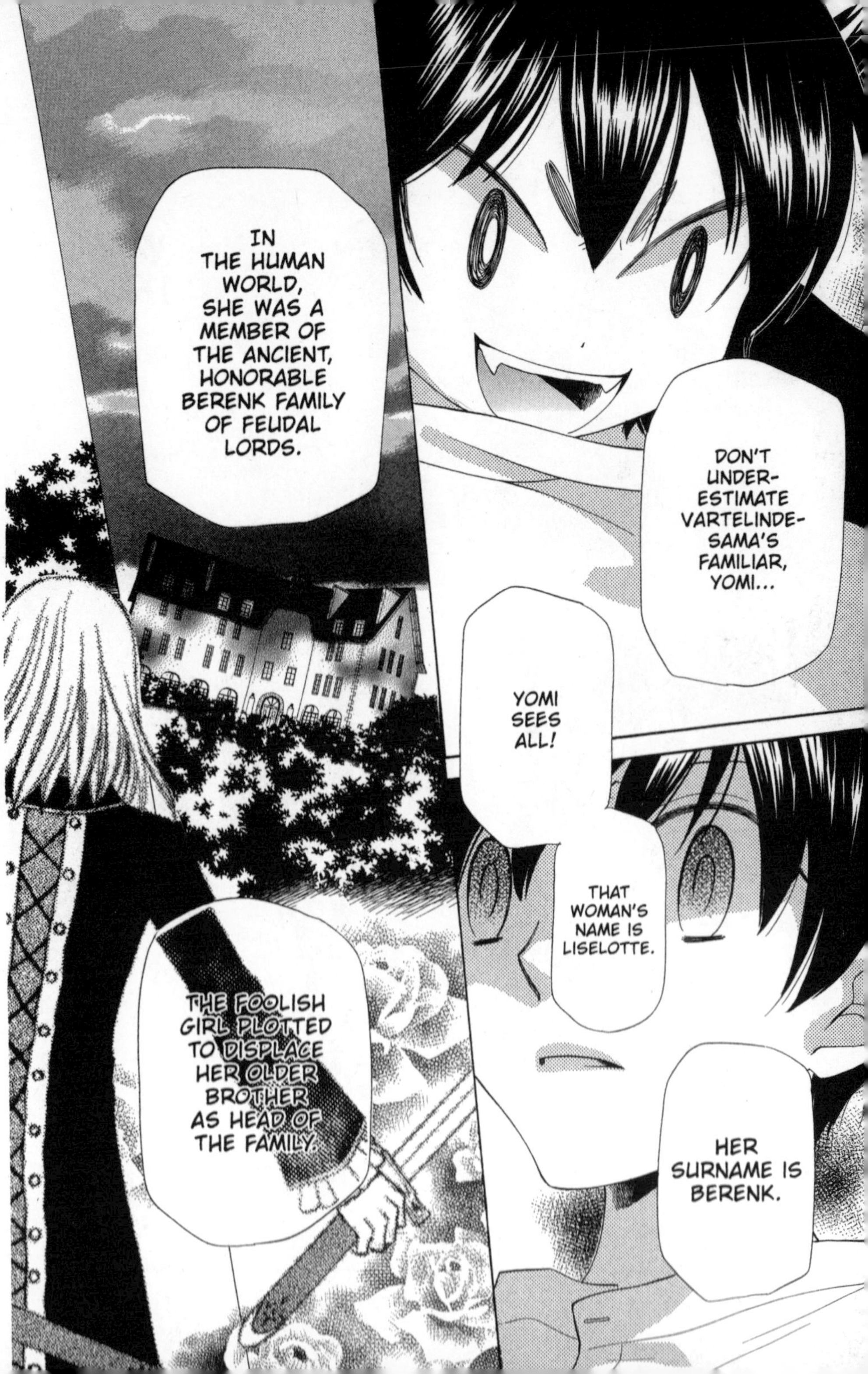
DON'T UNDER-ESTIMATE VARTELINDE-SAMA'S FAMILIAR, YOMI...
YOMI SEES ALL!
THAT WOMAN'S NAME IS LISELOTTE.
HER SURNAME IS BERENK.
IN THE HUMAN WORLD, SHE WAS A MEMBER OF THE ANCIENT, HONORABLE BERENK FAMILY OF FEUDAL LORDS.
THE FOOLISH GIRL PLOTTED TO DISPLACE HER OLDER BROTHER AS HEAD OF THE FAMILY.

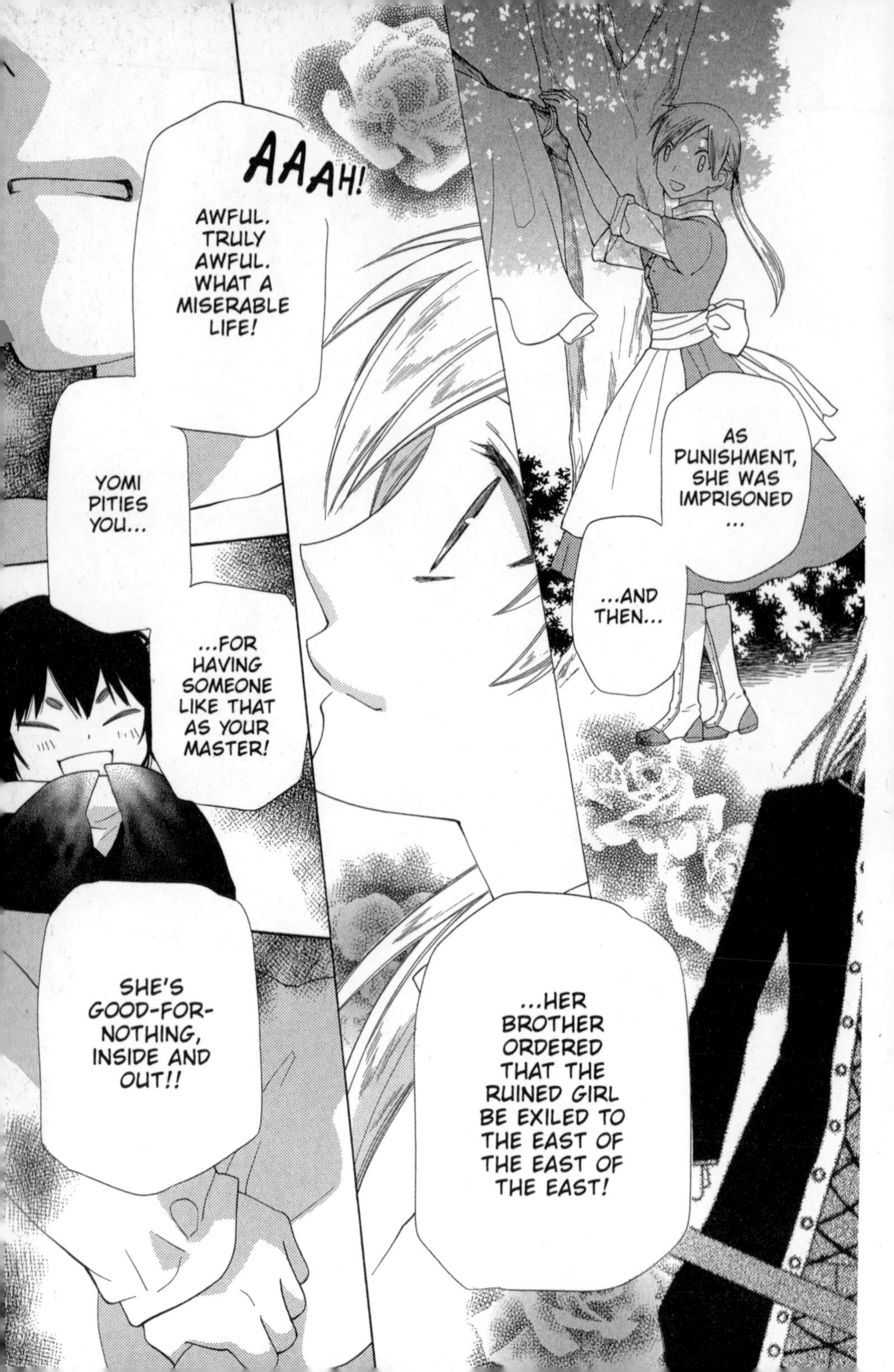
AS PUNISHMENT, SHE WAS IMPRISONED ...
...AND THEN...
...HER BROTHER ORDERED THAT THE RUINED GIRL BE EXILED TO THE EAST OF THE EAST OF THE EAST!
AAAH!
AWFUL. TRULY AWFUL. WHAT A MISERABLE LIFE!
YOMI PITIES YOU...
...FOR HAVING SOMEONE LIKE THAT AS YOUR MASTER!
SHE'S GOOD-FOR-NOTHING, INSIDE AND OUT!!

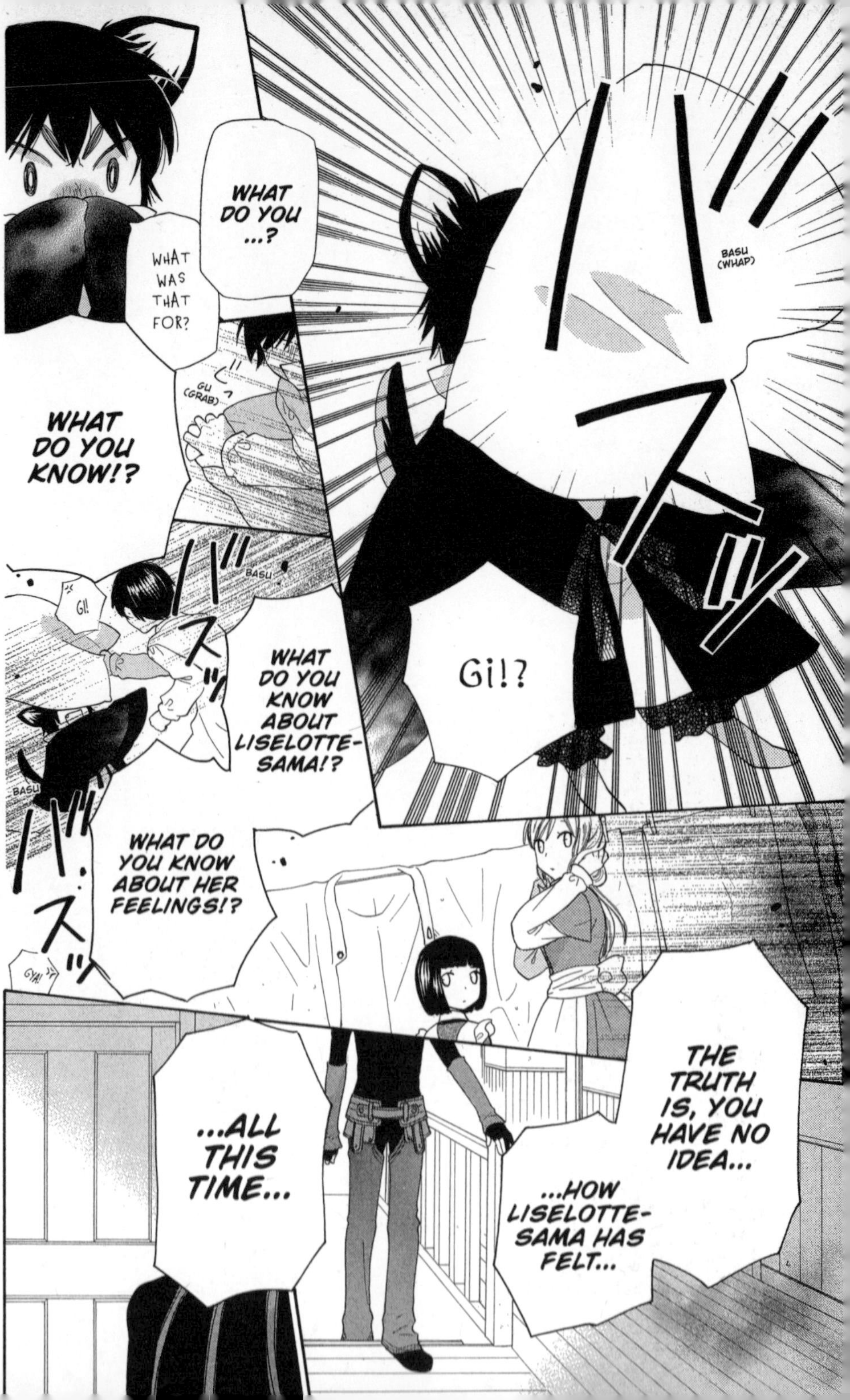
BASU (WHAP)
Gi!?
WHAT DO YOU ...?
WHAT WAS THAT FOR?
GU (GRAB)
WHAT DO YOU KNOW!?
BASU
Gi!
WHAT DO YOU KNOW ABOUT LISELOTTE-SAMA!?
BASU
WHAT DO YOU KNOW ABOUT HER FEELINGS!?
GYA!
THE TRUTH IS, YOU HAVE NO IDEA...
...HOW LISELOTTE-SAMA HAS FELT...
...ALL THIS TIME...

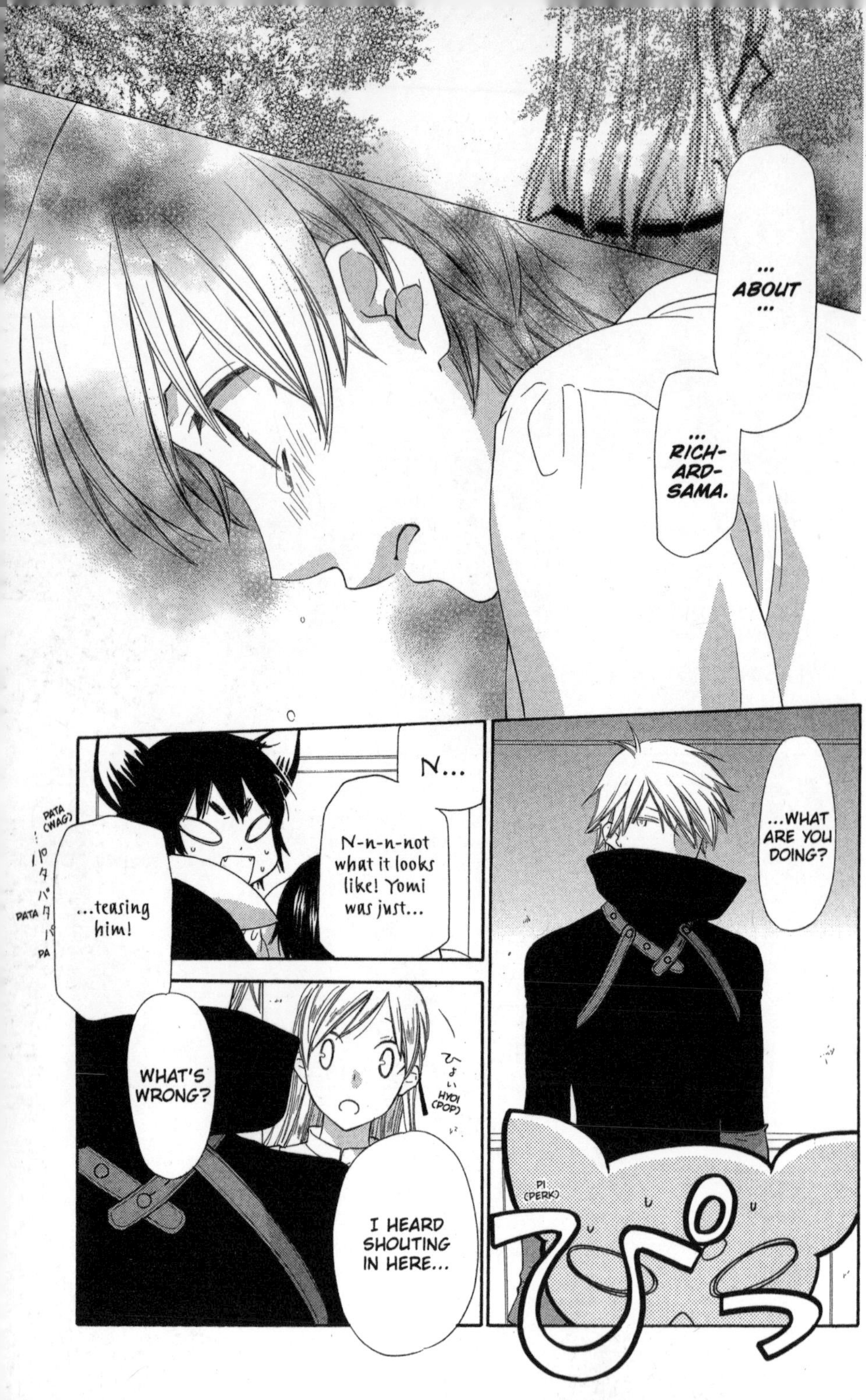
...ABOUT...
...RICHARD-SAMA.
...WHAT ARE YOU DOING?
PI (PERK)
N...
N-n-n-not what it looks like! Yomi was just...
...teasing him!
PATA (WAG) パタパタ PATA PA
WHAT'S WRONG?
ひょい HYOI (POP)
I HEARD SHOUTING IN HERE...

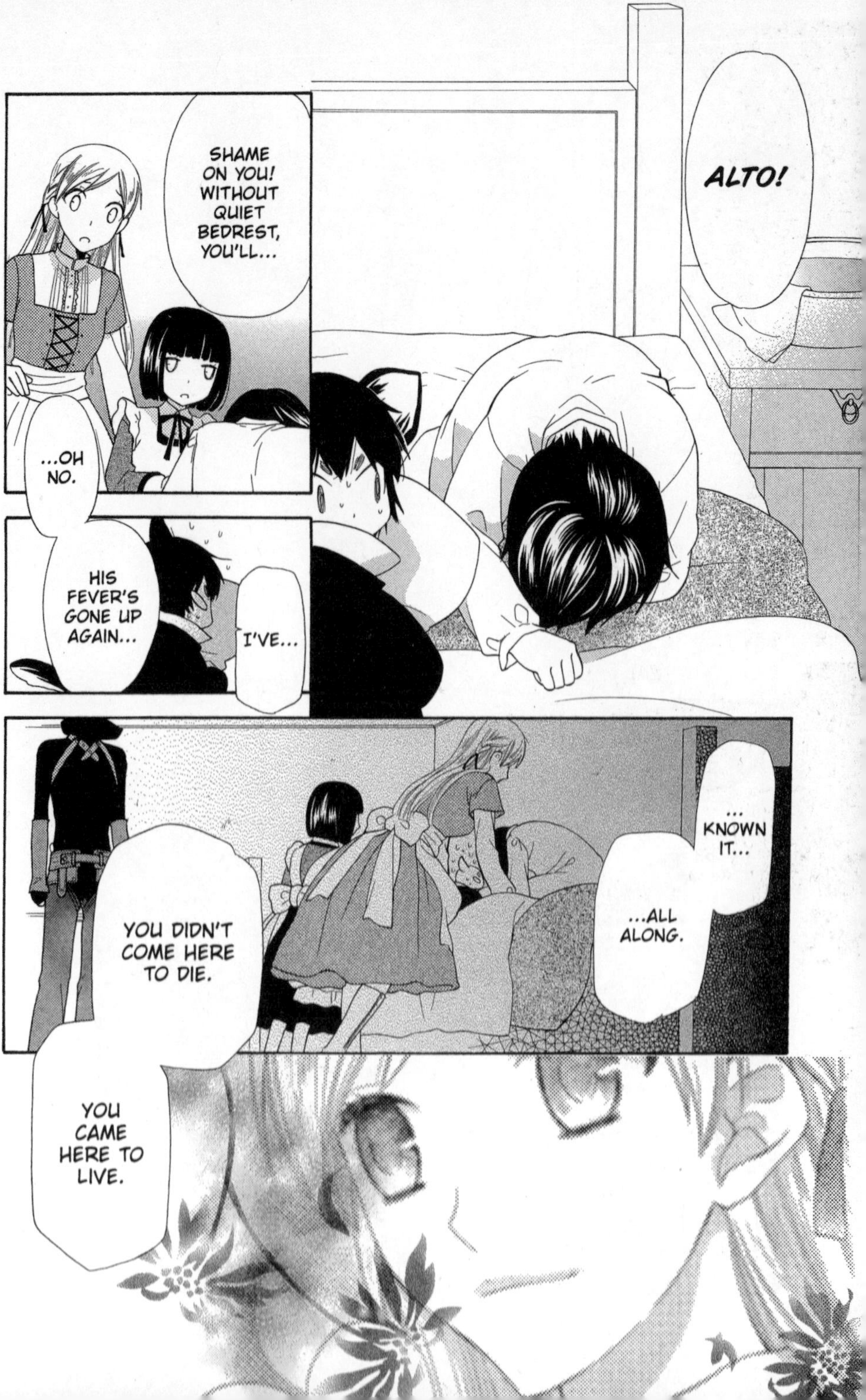
ALTO!
SHAME ON YOU! WITHOUT QUIET BEDREST, YOU'LL...
...OH NO.
HIS FEVER'S GONE UP AGAIN...
I'VE...
...KNOWN IT...
...ALL ALONG.
YOU DIDN'T COME HERE TO DIE.
YOU CAME HERE TO LIVE.

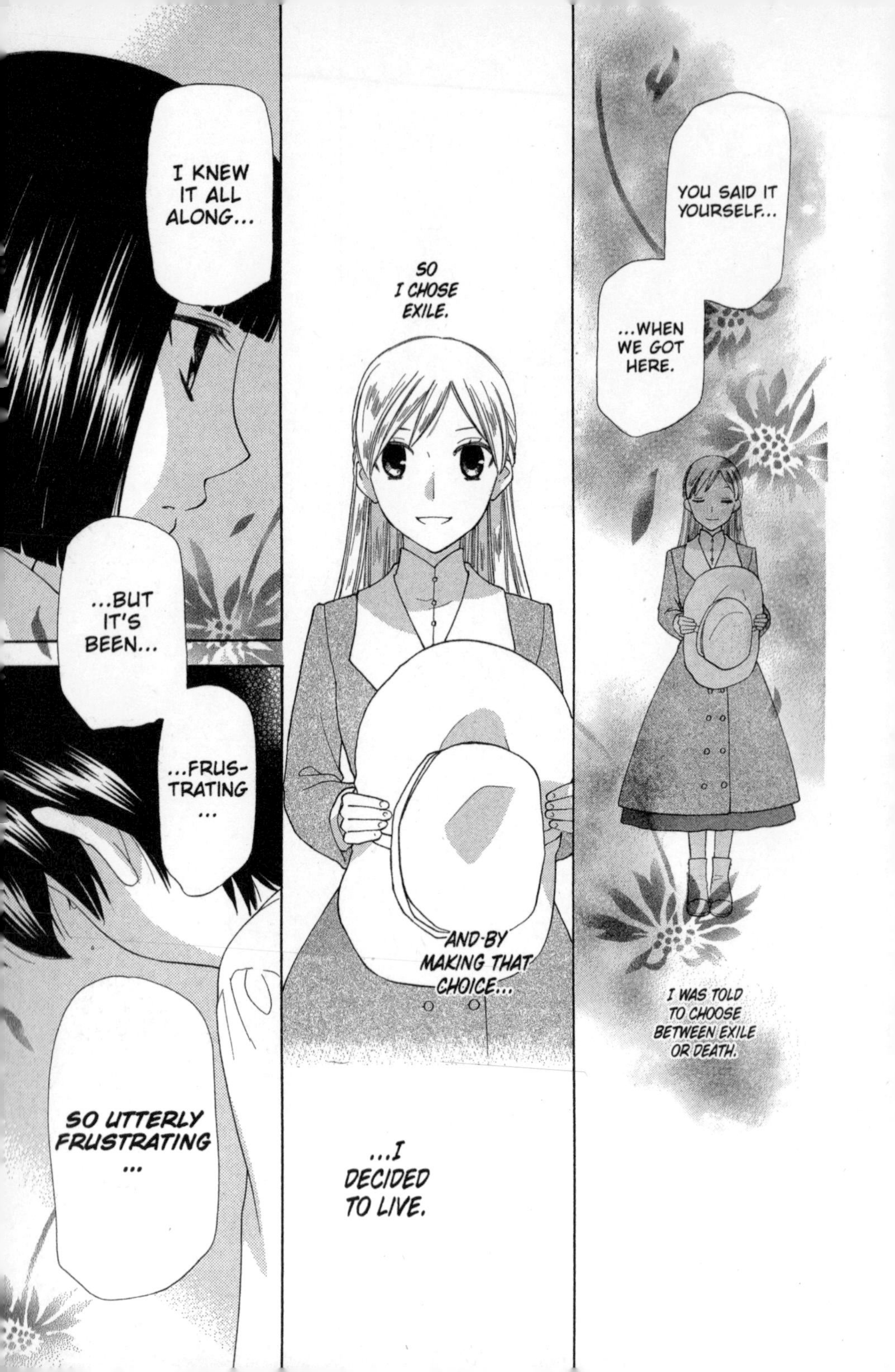
YOU SAID IT YOURSELF...
...WHEN WE GOT HERE.
I WAS TOLD TO CHOOSE BETWEEN EXILE OR DEATH.
SO I CHOSE EXILE.
AND BY MAKING THAT CHOICE...
...I DECIDED TO LIVE.
I KNEW IT ALL ALONG...
...BUT IT'S BEEN...
...FRUS-TRATING...
SO UTTERLY FRUSTRATING...

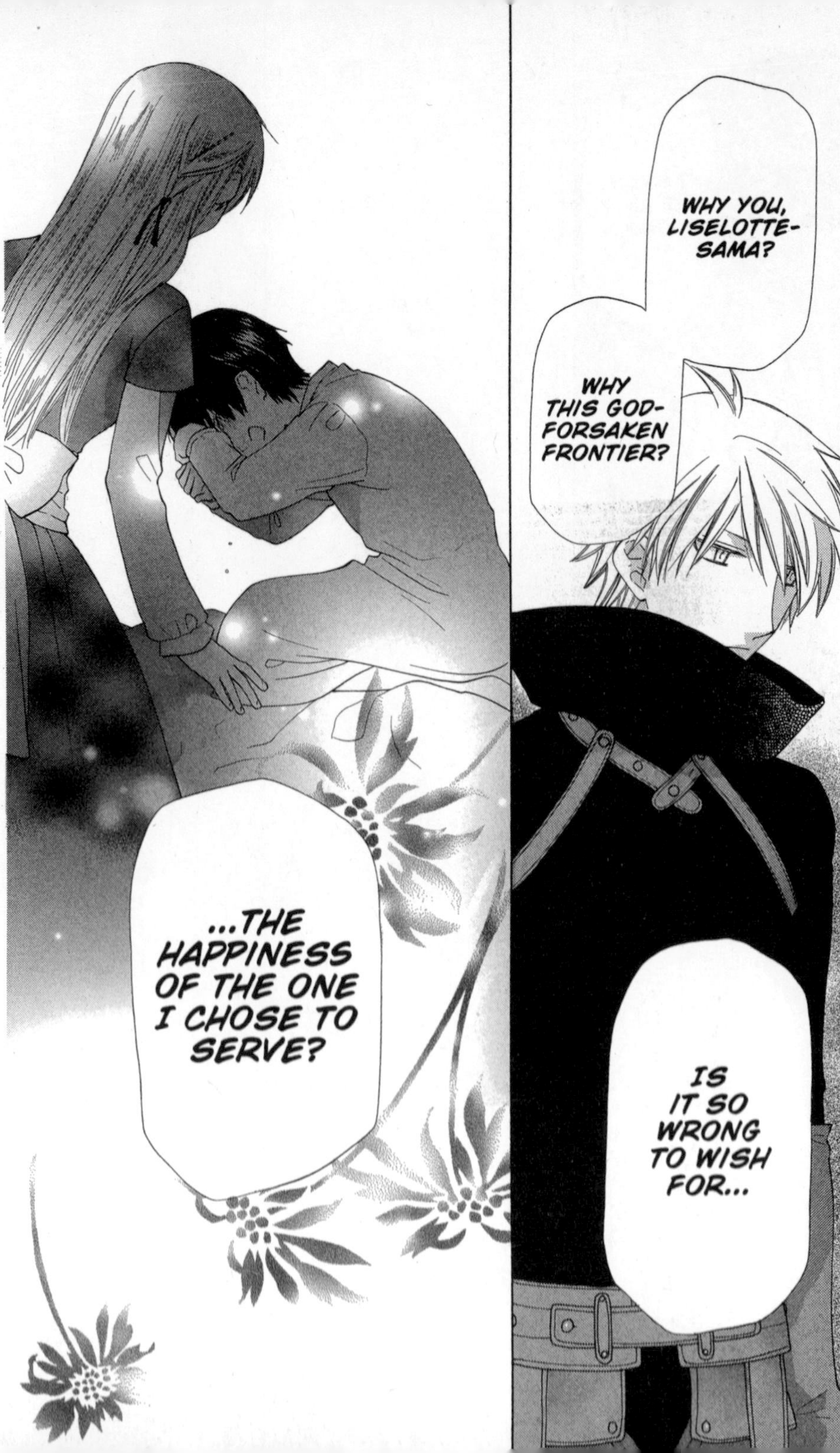
WHY YOU, LISELOTTE-SAMA?
WHY THIS GOD-FORSAKEN FRONTIER?
IS IT SO WRONG TO WISH FOR...
...THE HAPPINESS OF THE ONE I CHOSE TO SERVE?

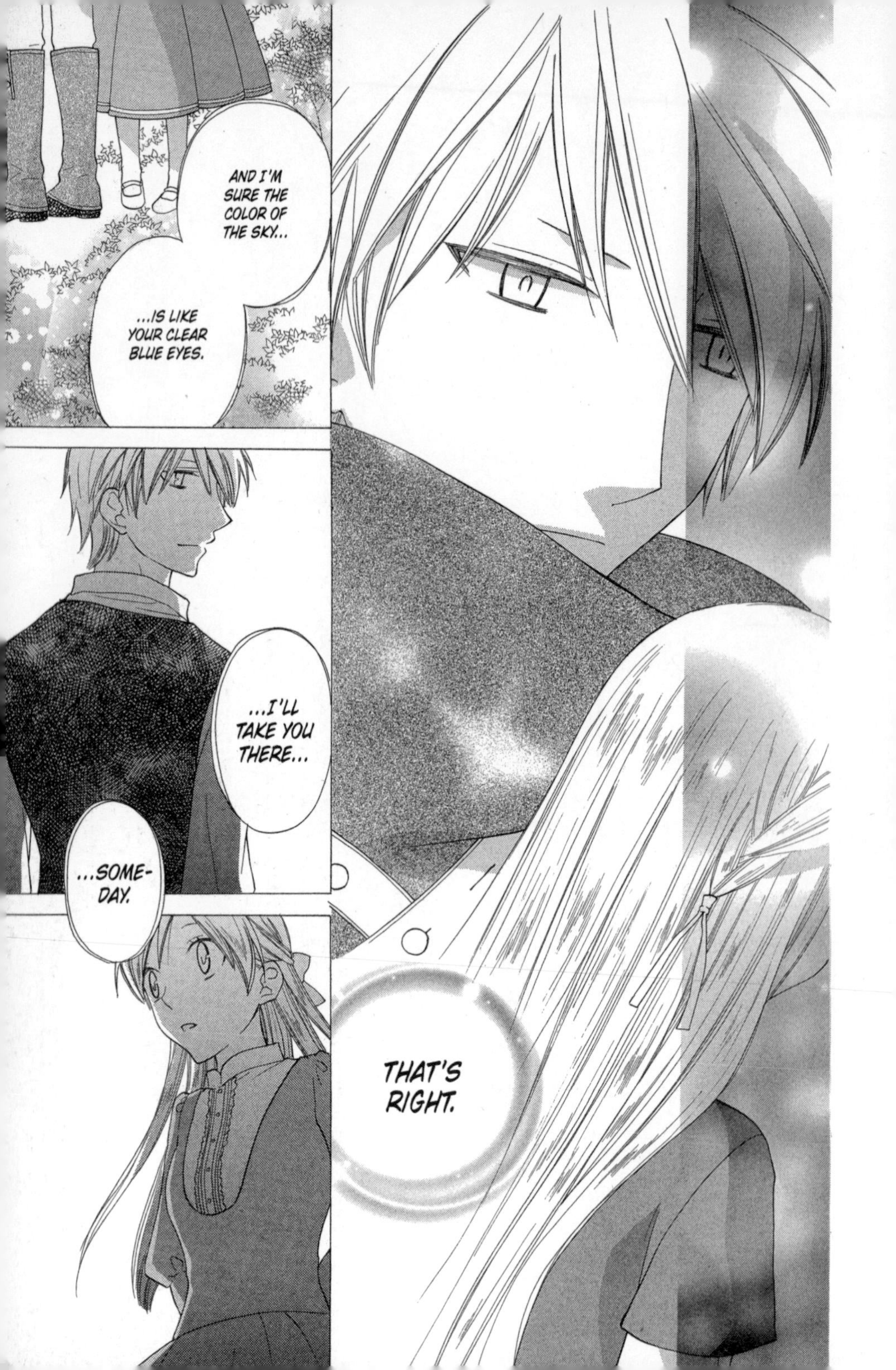
THAT'S RIGHT.
AND I'M SURE THE COLOR OF THE SKY...
...IS LIKE YOUR CLEAR BLUE EYES.
...I'LL TAKE YOU THERE...
...SOME-DAY.

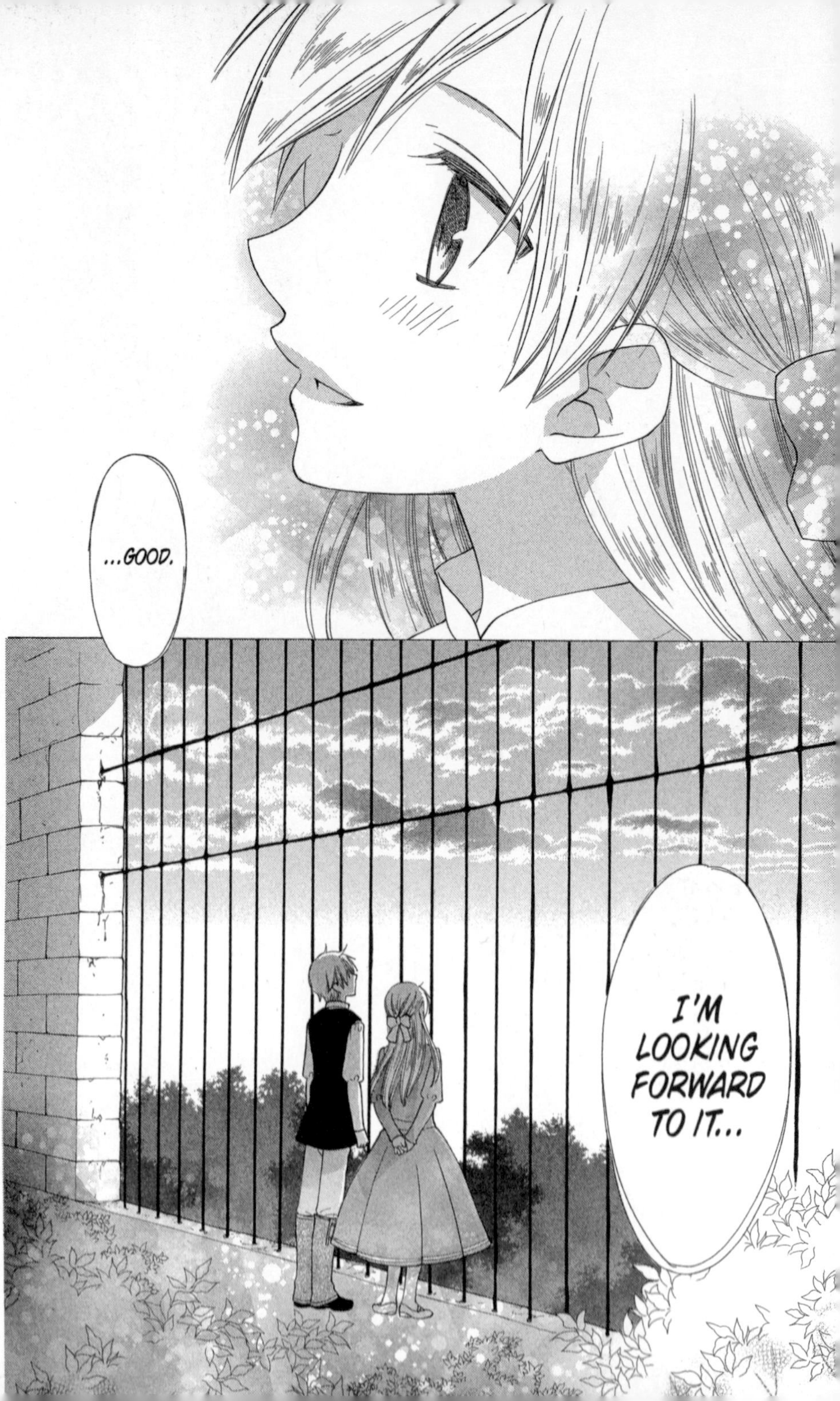
...GOOD.
I'M LOOKING FORWARD TO IT...

Chapter 5

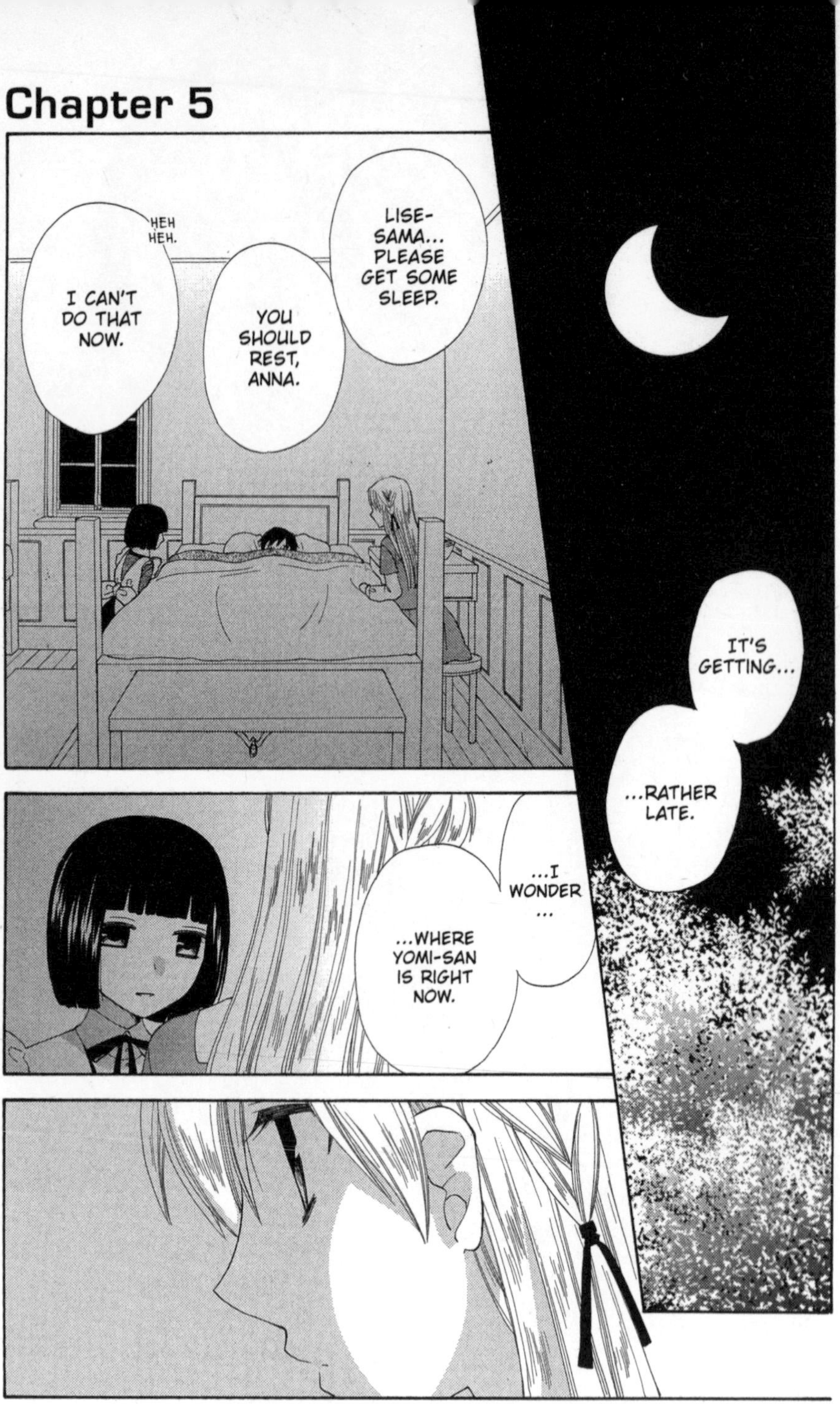
IT'S GETTING...
...RATHER LATE.
LISE-SAMA... PLEASE GET SOME SLEEP.
YOU SHOULD REST, ANNA.
HEH HEH.
I CAN'T DO THAT NOW.
...I WONDER...
...WHERE YOMI-SAN IS RIGHT NOW.

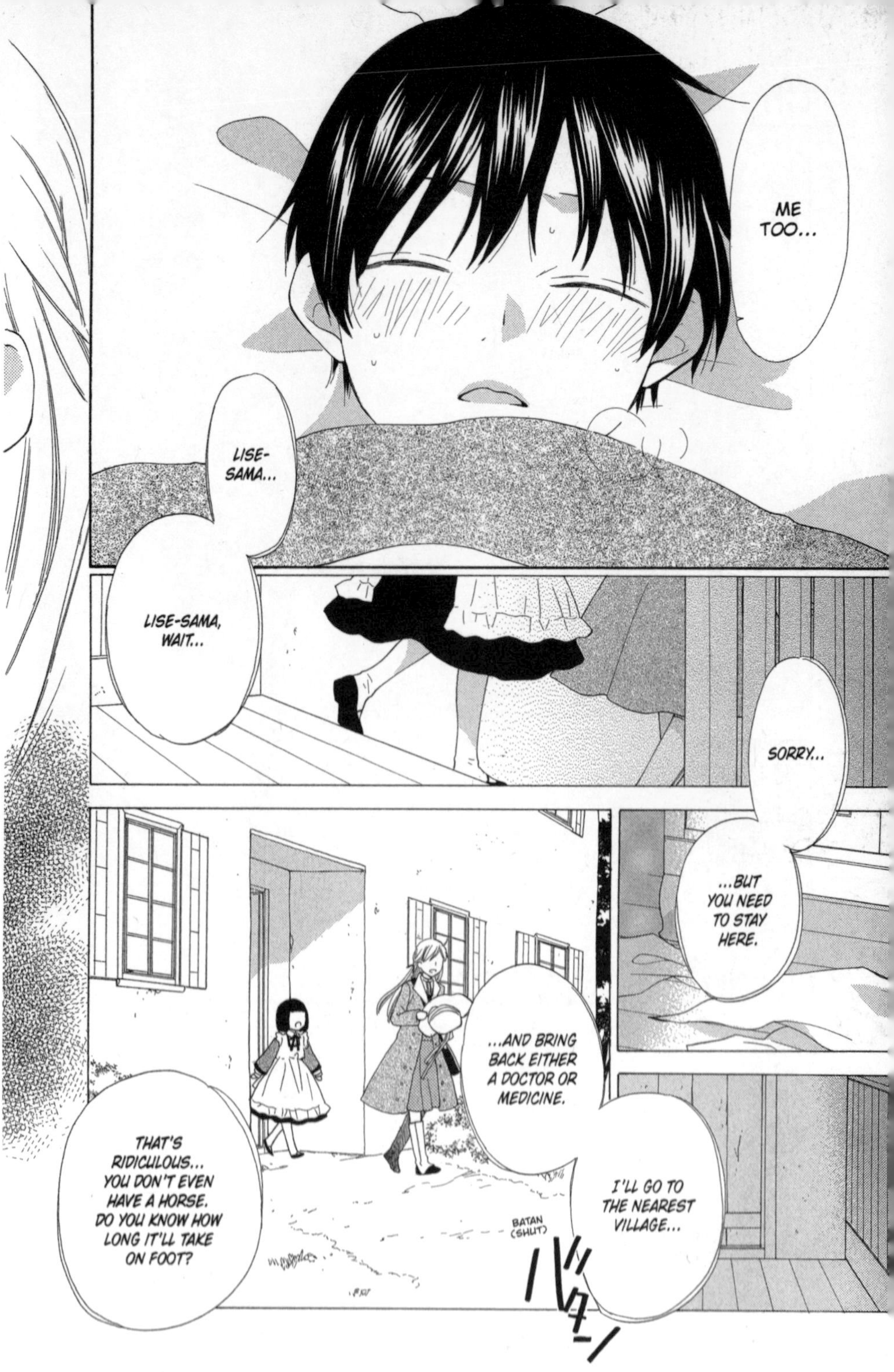
ME TOO...
LISE-SAMA...
LISE-SAMA, WAIT...
SORRY...
...BUT YOU NEED TO STAY HERE.
I'LL GO TO THE NEAREST VILLAGE...
...AND BRING BACK EITHER A DOCTOR OR MEDICINE.
BATAN (SHUT)
THAT'S RIDICULOUS... YOU DON'T EVEN HAVE A HORSE. DO YOU KNOW HOW LONG IT'LL TAKE ON FOOT?

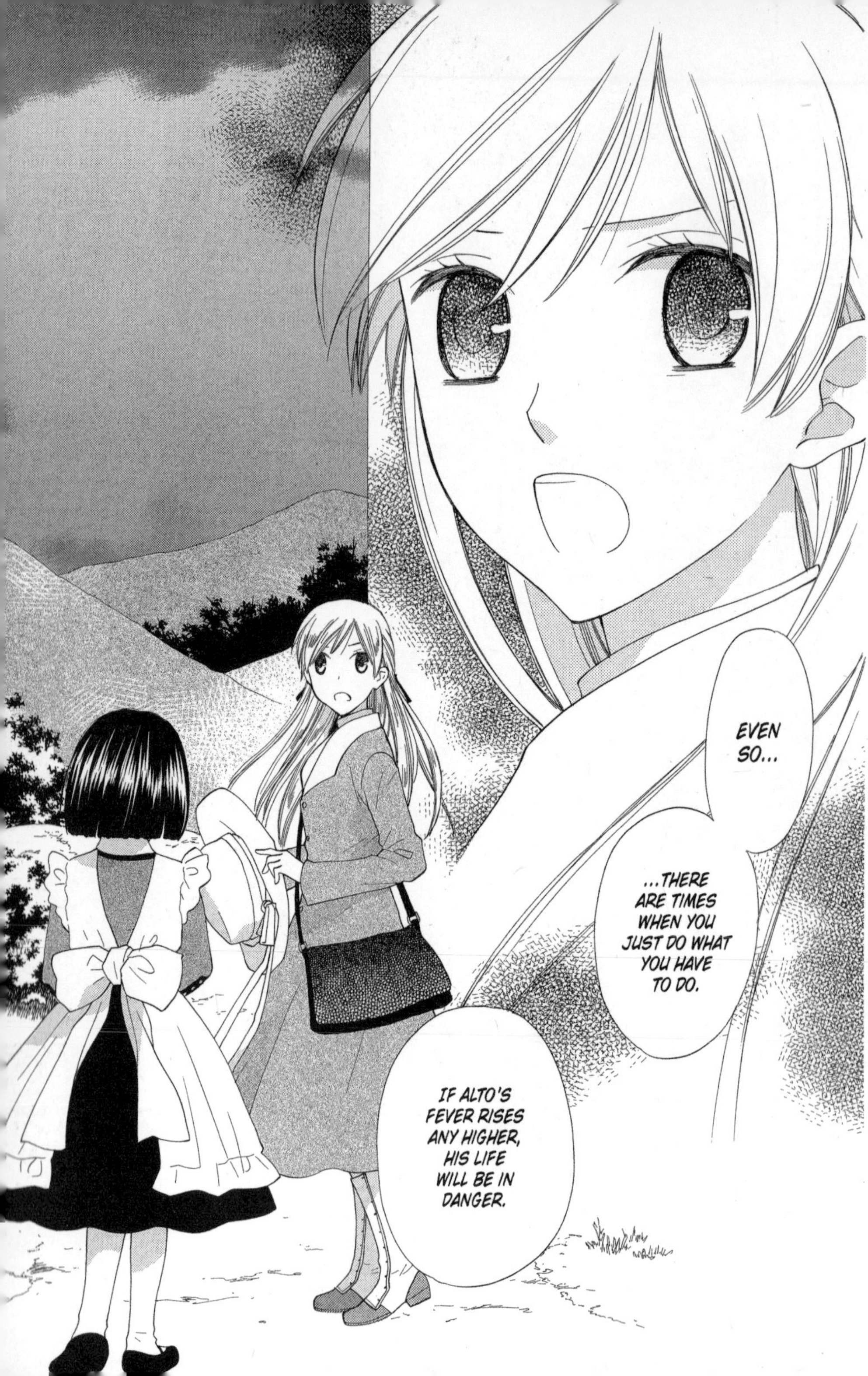
EVEN SO...
...THERE ARE TIMES WHEN YOU JUST DO WHAT YOU HAVE TO DO.
IF ALTO'S FEVER RISES ANY HIGHER, HIS LIFE WILL BE IN DANGER.

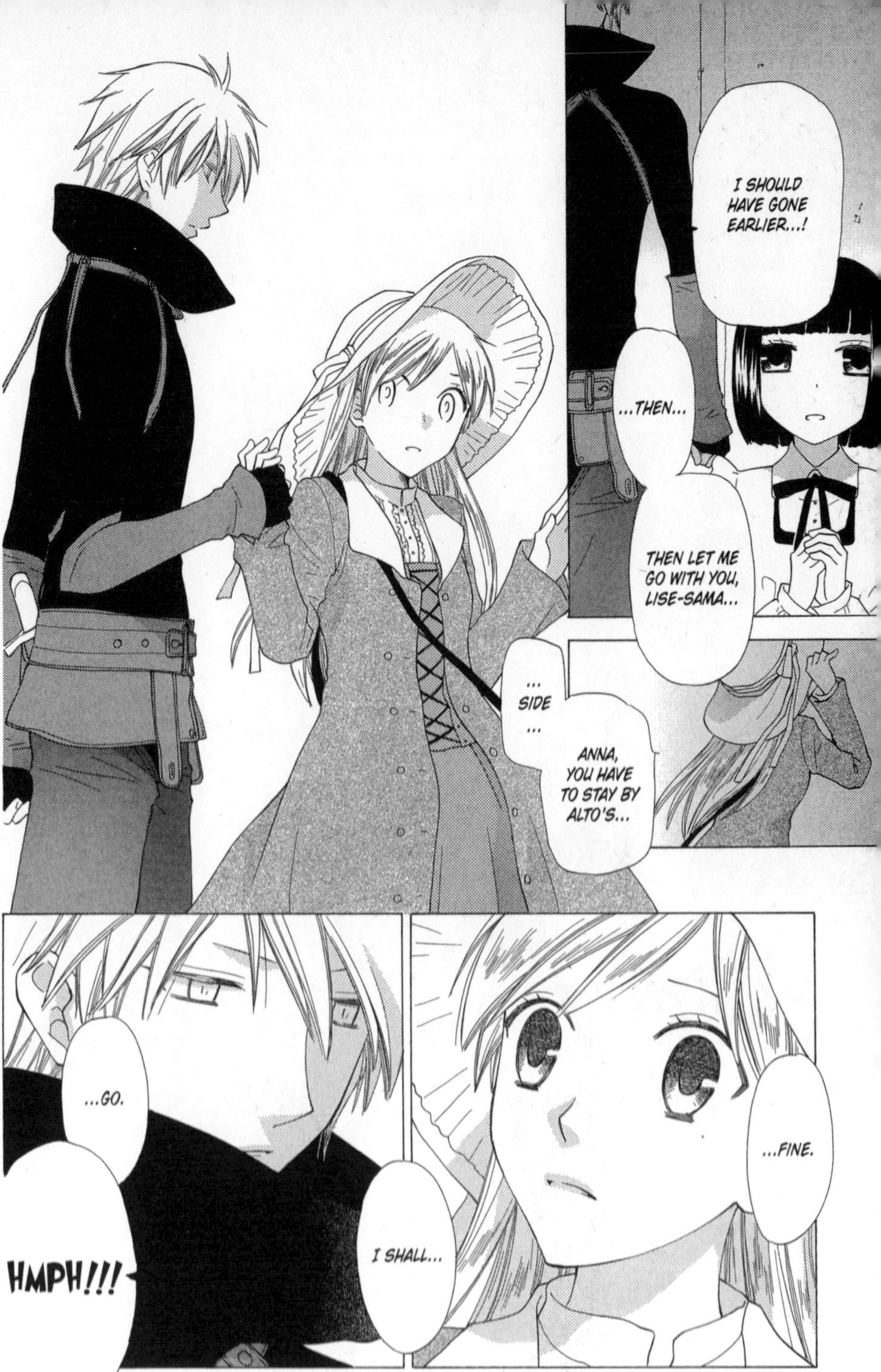
I SHOULD HAVE GONE EARLIER...!
...THEN...
THEN LET ME GO WITH YOU, LISE-SAMA...
ANNA, YOU HAVE TO STAY BY ALTO'S...
... SIDE ...
...FINE.
I SHALL...
...GO.
HMPH!!!

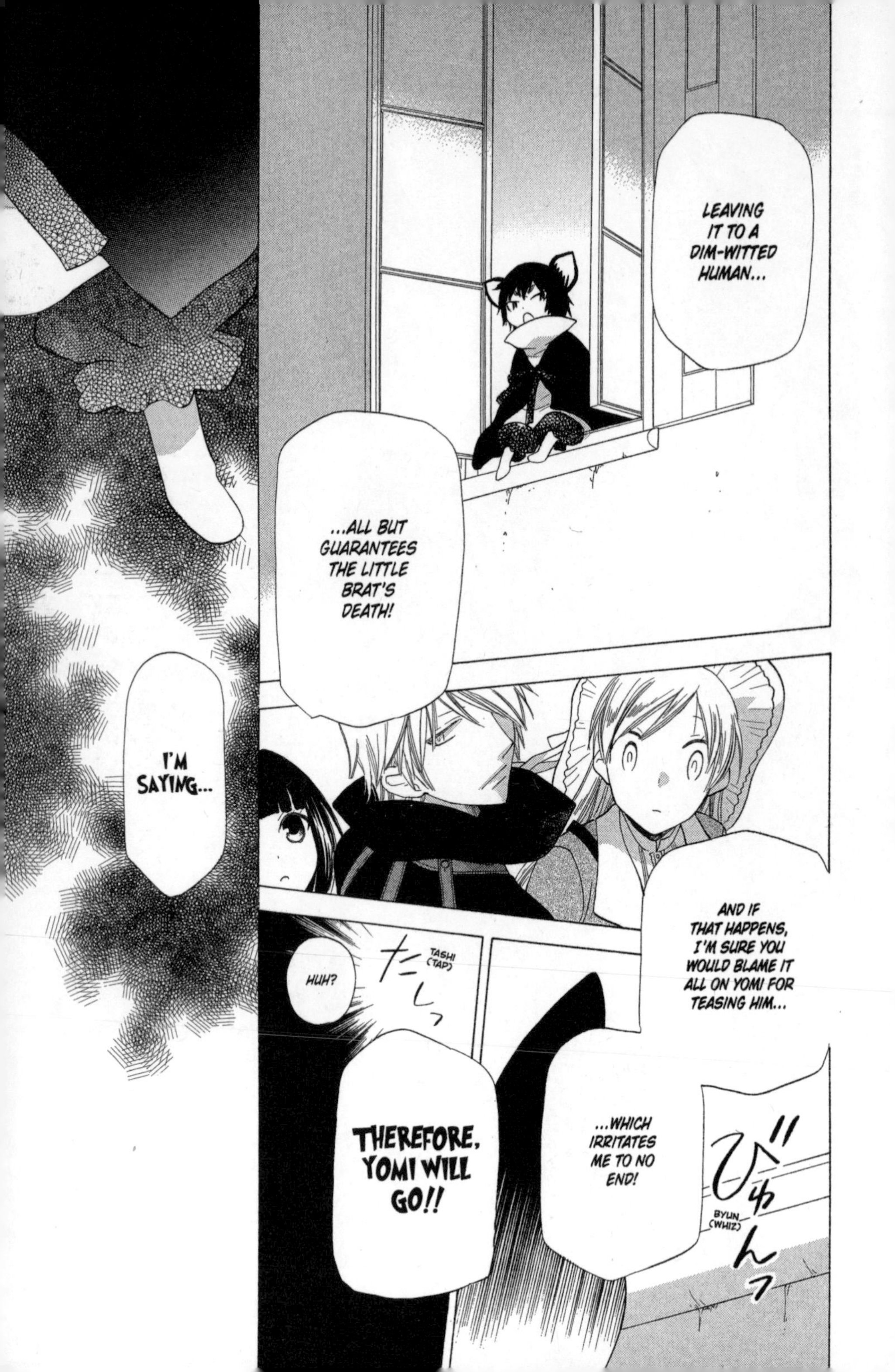
LEAVING IT TO A DIM-WITTED HUMAN...
...ALL BUT GUARANTEES THE LITTLE BRAT'S DEATH!
AND IF THAT HAPPENS, I'M SURE YOU WOULD BLAME IT ALL ON YOMI FOR TEASING HIM...
BYUN (WHIZ)
...WHICH IRRITATES ME TO NO END!
THEREFORE, YOMI WILL GO!!
TASHI (TAP)
HUH?
I'M SAYING...

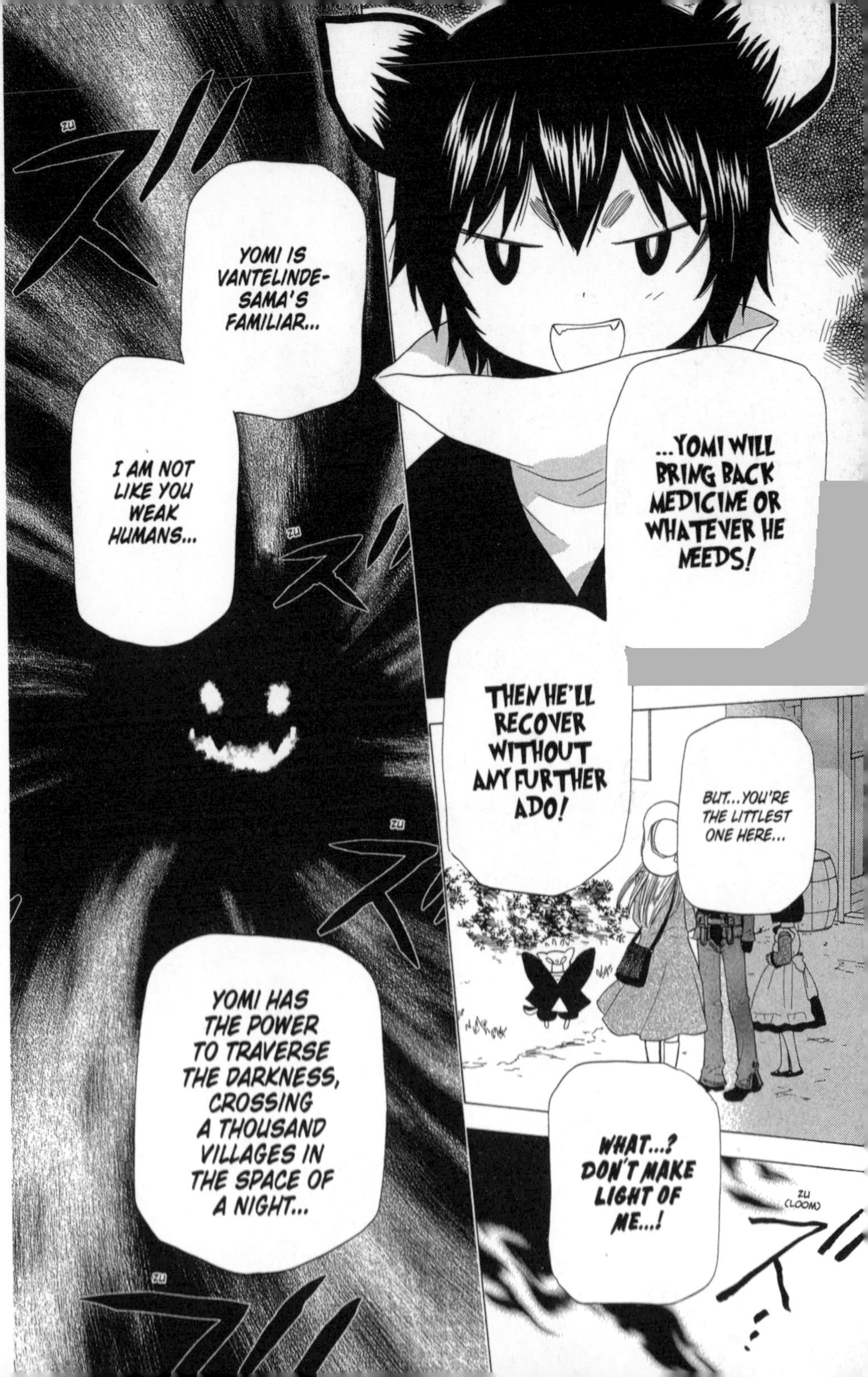
ZU
YOMI IS VANTELINDE-SAMA'S FAMILIAR...
I AM NOT LIKE YOU WEAK HUMANS...
ZU
ZU
YOMI HAS THE POWER TO TRAVERSE THE DARKNESS, CROSSING A THOUSAND VILLAGES IN THE SPACE OF A NIGHT...
ZU
...YOMI WILL BRING BACK MEDICINE OR WHATEVER HE NEEDS!
THEN HE'LL RECOVER WITHOUT ANY FURTHER ADO!
BUT...YOU'RE THE LITTLEST ONE HERE...
WHAT...? DON'T MAKE LIGHT OF ME...!
ZU (LOOM)

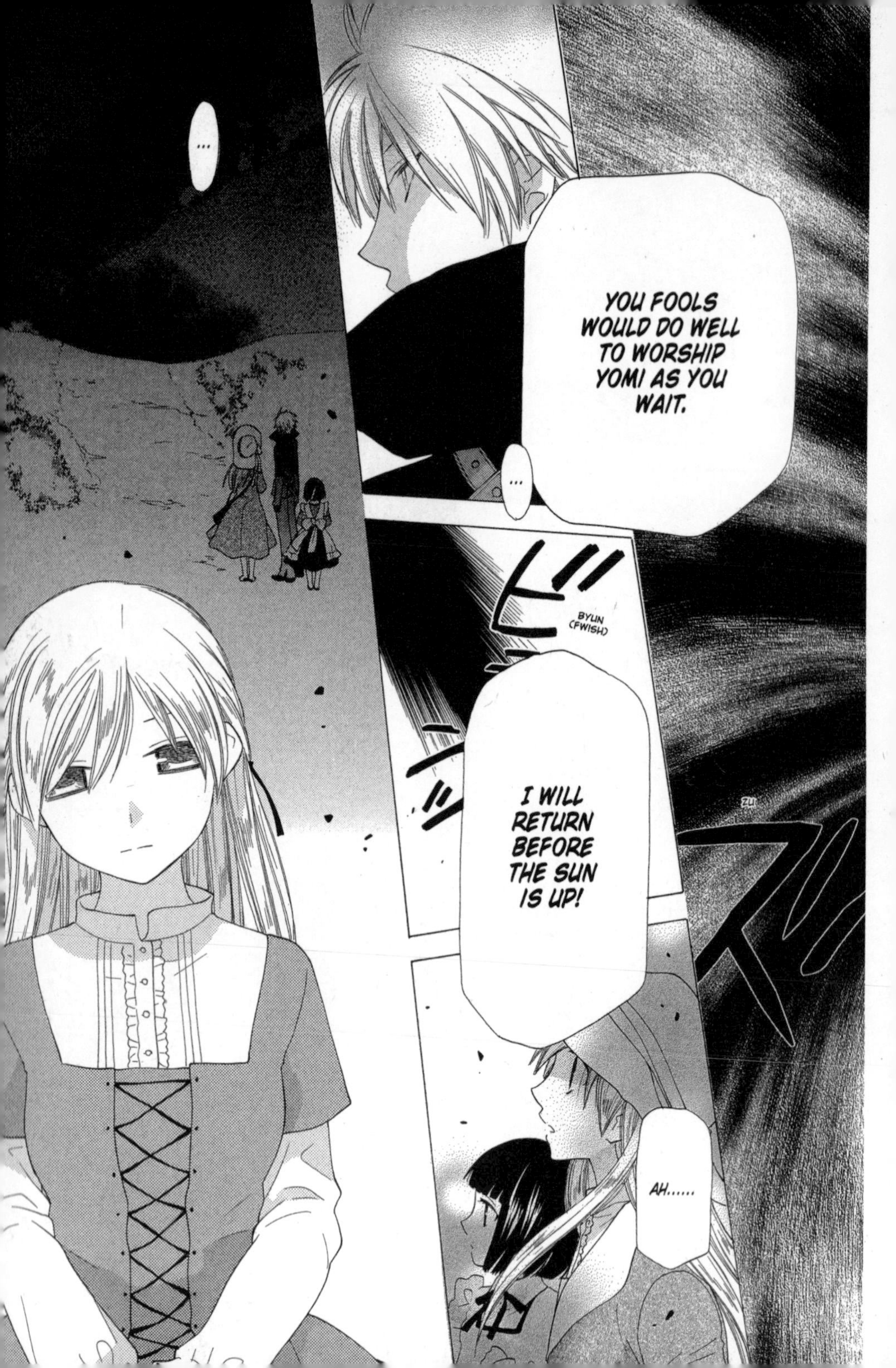
YOU FOOLS WOULD DO WELL TO WORSHIP YOMI AS YOU WAIT.
...
ZU
BYUN (FWISH)
I WILL RETURN BEFORE THE SUN IS UP!
AH......
...

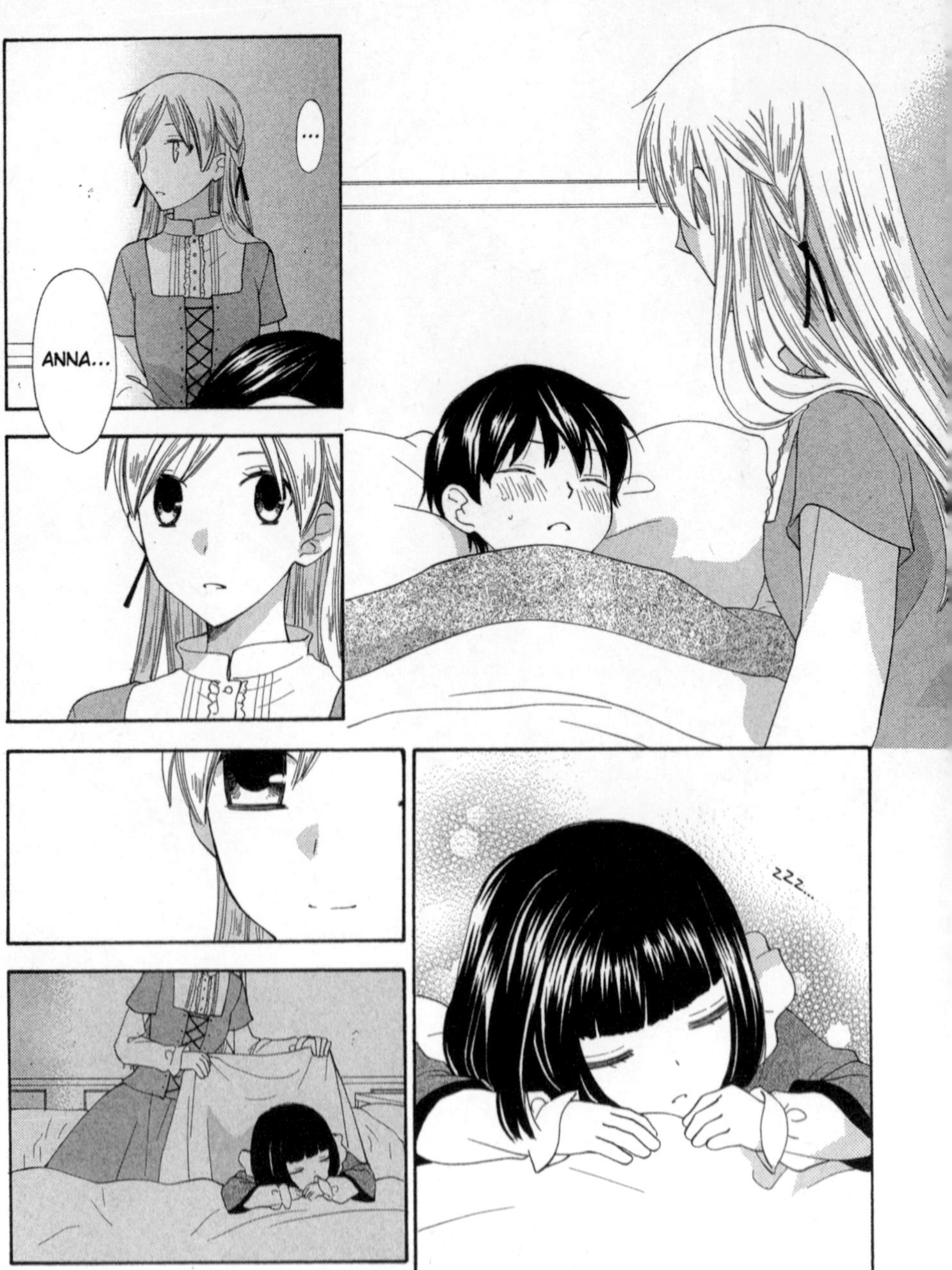
...
ANNA...
ZZZ...

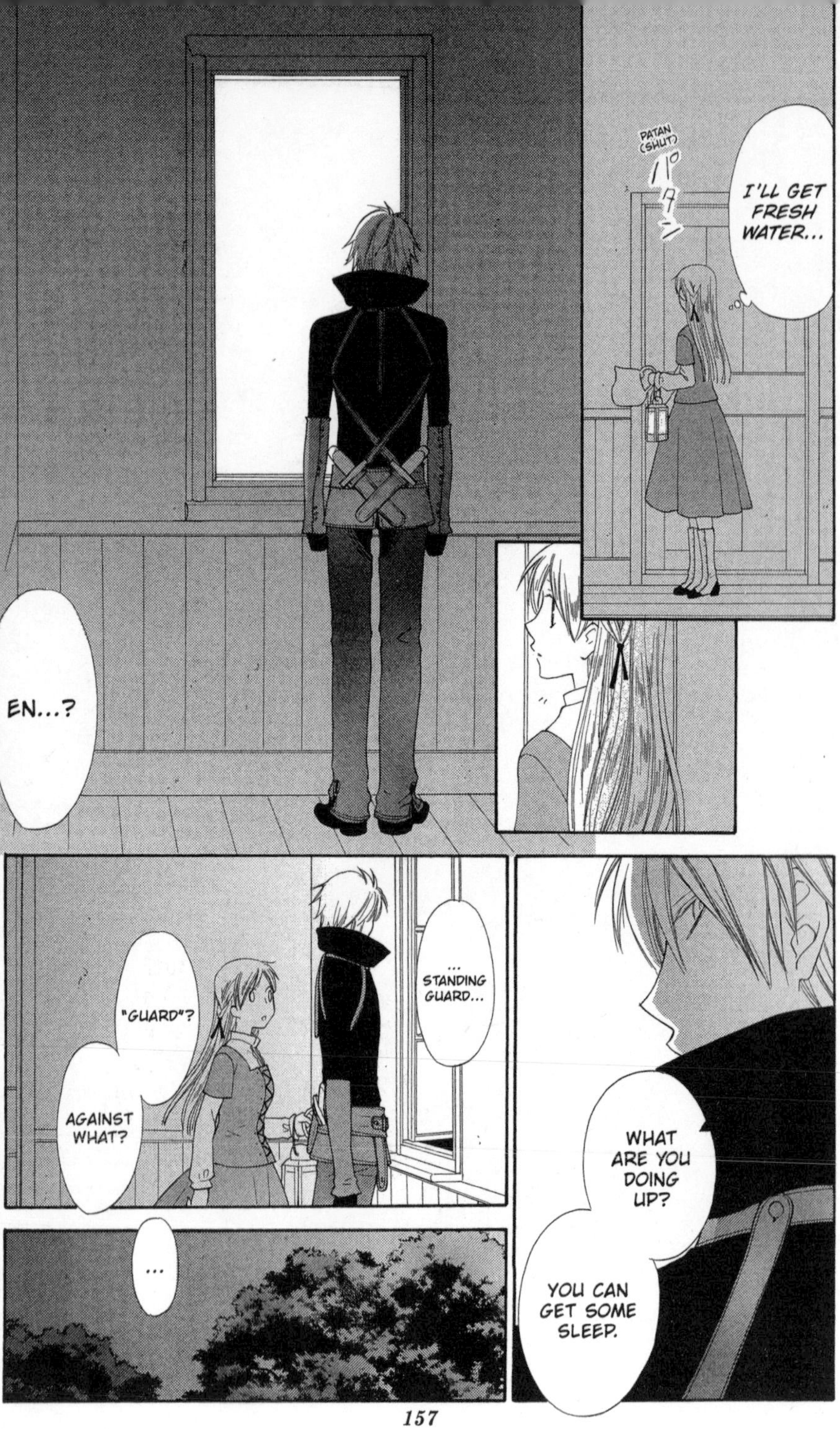
PATAN (SHUT)
パタン
I'LL GET FRESH WATER...
EN...?
WHAT ARE YOU DOING UP?
YOU CAN GET SOME SLEEP.
... STANDING GUARD...
"GUARD"?
AGAINST WHAT?
...

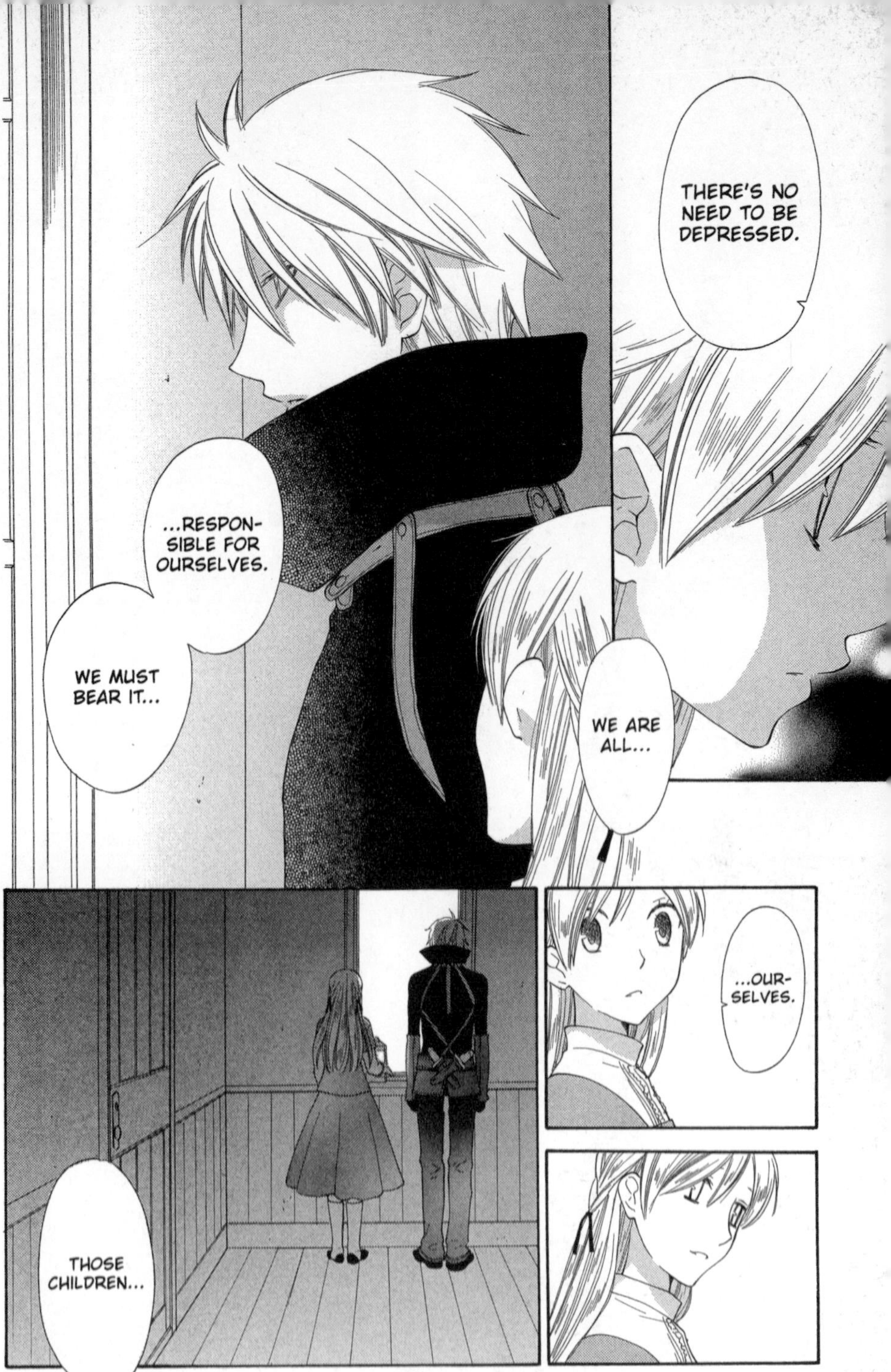
THERE'S NO NEED TO BE DEPRESSED.
WE ARE ALL...
...RESPON-SIBLE FOR OURSELVES.
WE MUST BEAR IT...
...OUR-SELVES.
THOSE CHILDREN...

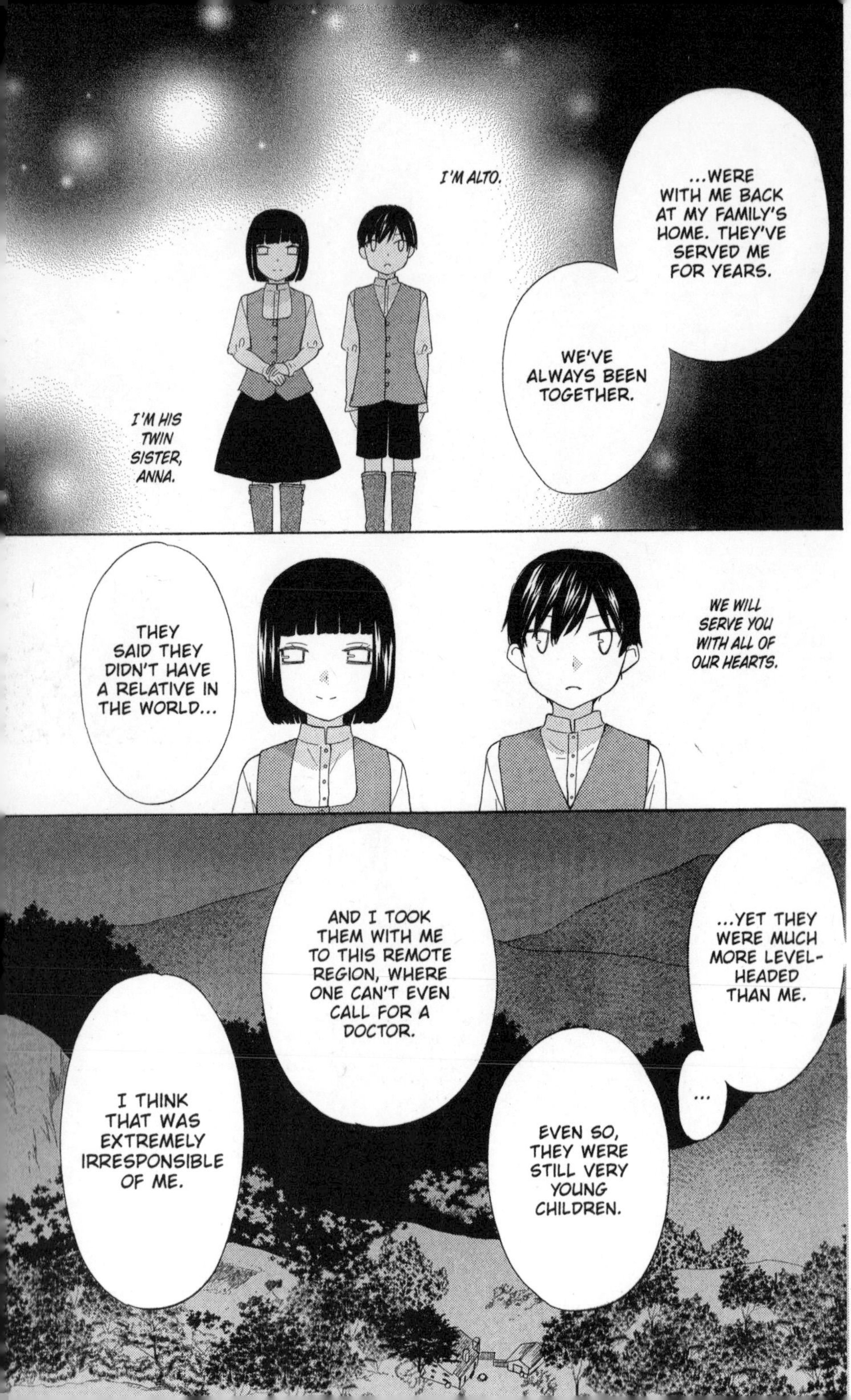
...WERE WITH ME BACK AT MY FAMILY'S HOME. THEY'VE SERVED ME FOR YEARS.
WE'VE ALWAYS BEEN TOGETHER.
I'M ALTO.
I'M HIS TWIN SISTER, ANNA.
WE WILL SERVE YOU WITH ALL OF OUR HEARTS.
THEY SAID THEY DIDN'T HAVE A RELATIVE IN THE WORLD...
...YET THEY WERE MUCH MORE LEVEL-HEADED THAN ME.
AND I TOOK THEM WITH ME TO THIS REMOTE REGION, WHERE ONE CAN'T EVEN CALL FOR A DOCTOR.
...
EVEN SO, THEY WERE STILL VERY YOUNG CHILDREN.
I THINK THAT WAS EXTREMELY IRRESPONSIBLE OF ME.

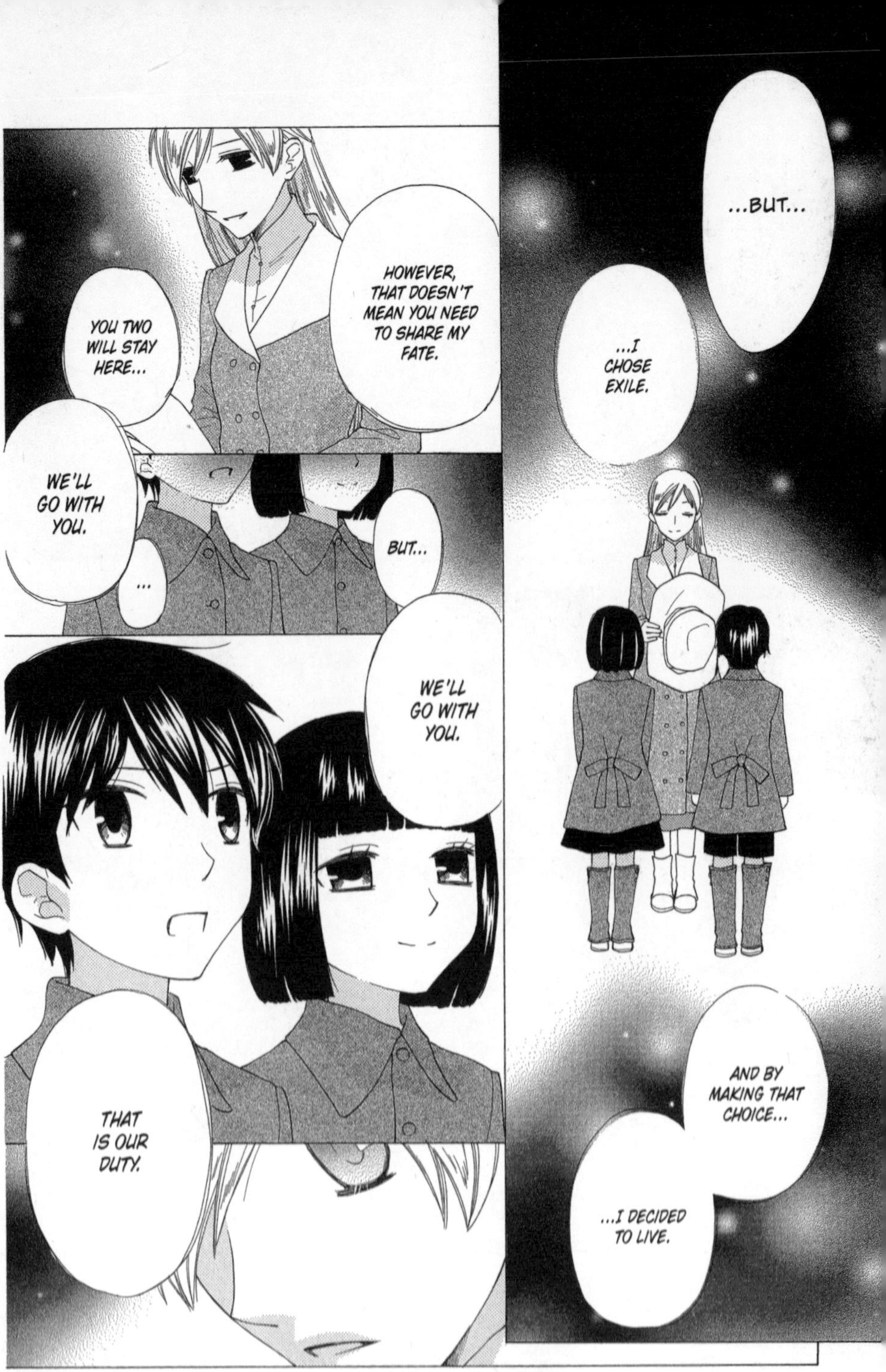
...BUT...
...I CHOSE EXILE.
AND BY MAKING THAT CHOICE...
...I DECIDED TO LIVE.
HOWEVER, THAT DOESN'T MEAN YOU NEED TO SHARE MY FATE.
YOU TWO WILL STAY HERE...
BUT...
...
WE'LL GO WITH YOU.
WE'LL GO WITH YOU.
THAT IS OUR DUTY.

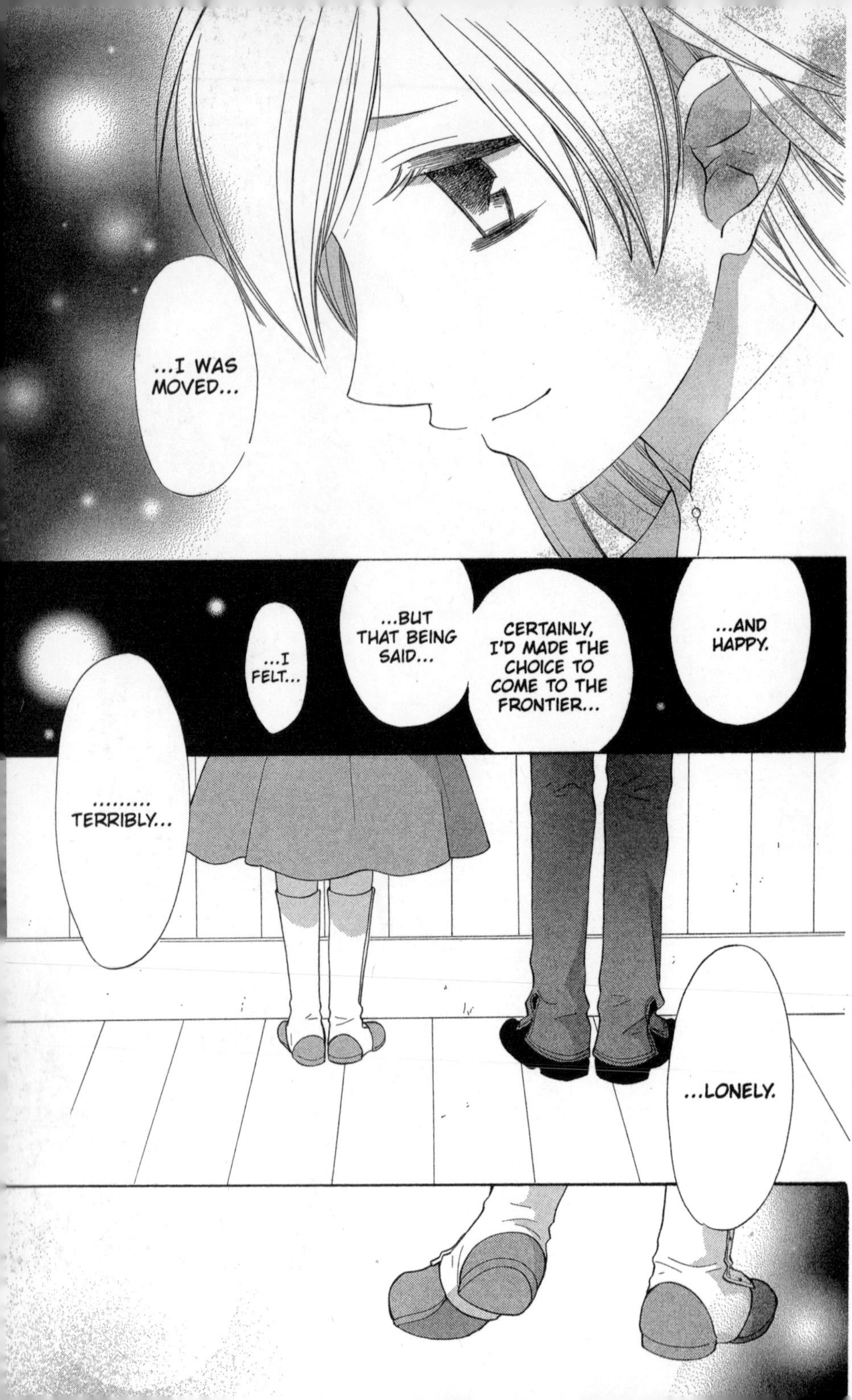
...I WAS MOVED...
...AND HAPPY.
CERTAINLY, I'D MADE THE CHOICE TO COME TO THE FRONTIER...
...BUT THAT BEING SAID...
...I FELT...
.... TERRIBLY...
...LONELY.

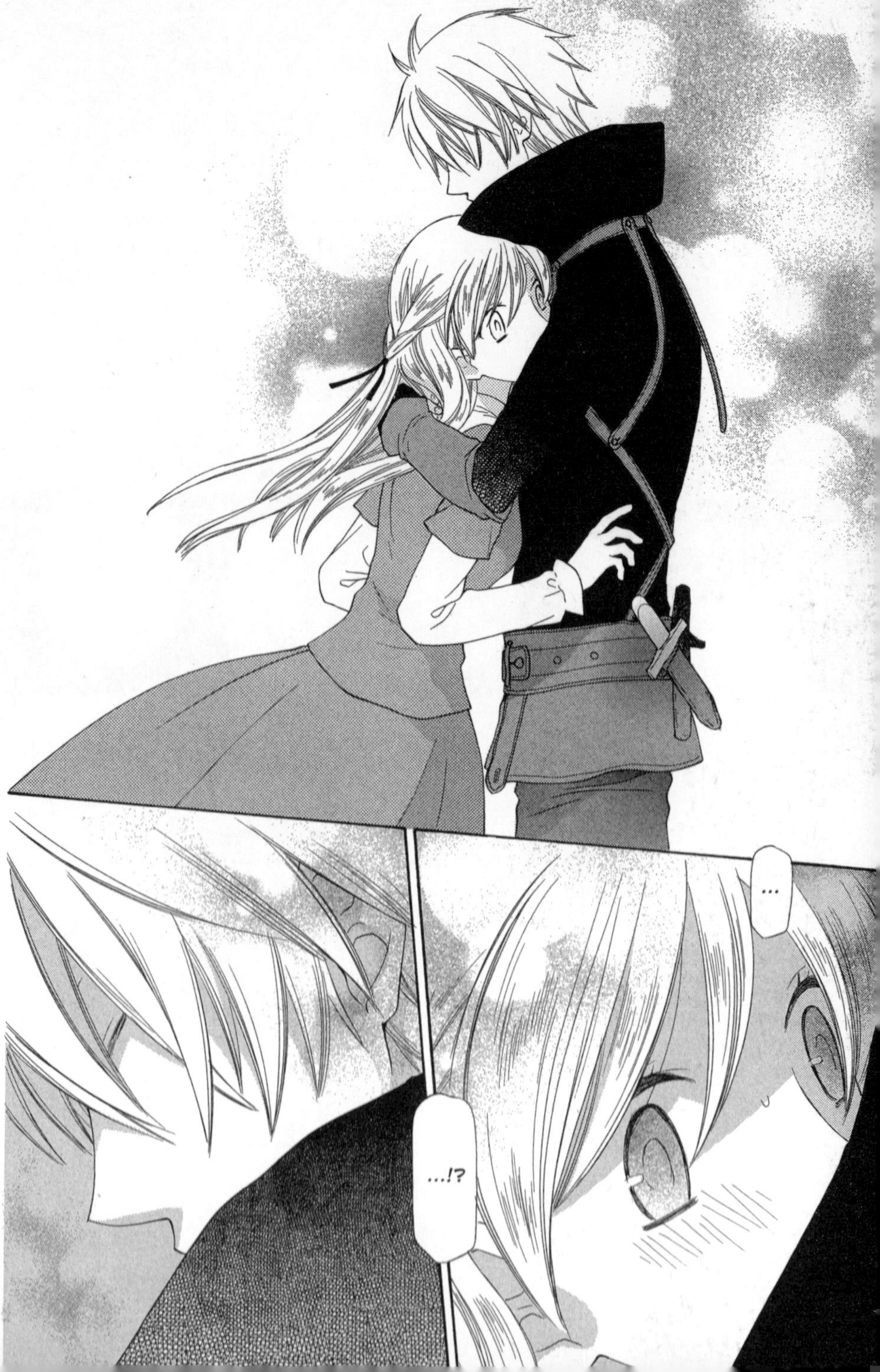
...
...!?

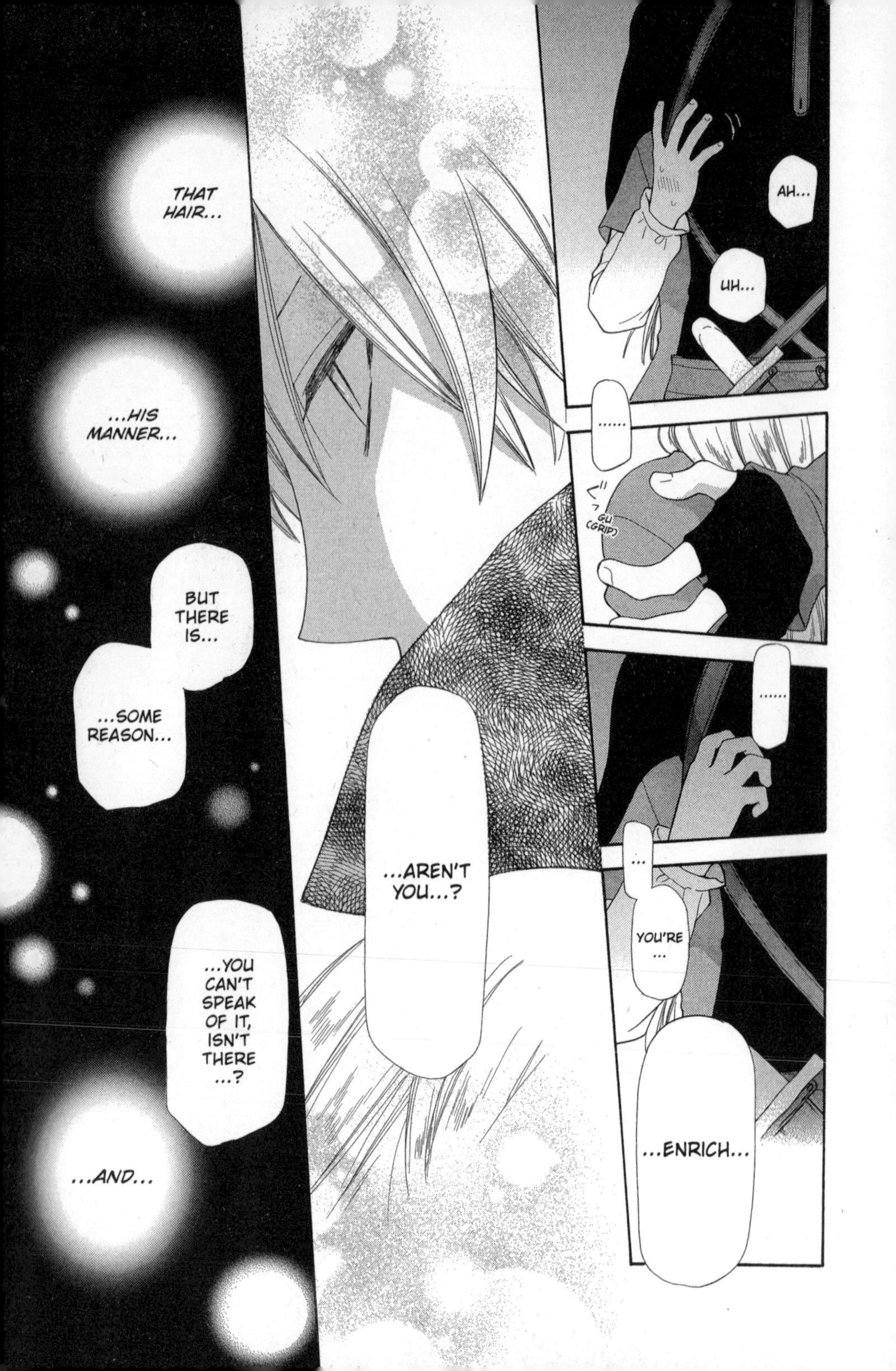
AH...
UH...
......
GU (GRIP)
......
...
YOU'RE...
...ENRICH...
...AREN'T YOU...?
THAT HAIR...
...HIS MANNER...
BUT THERE IS...
...SOME REASON...
...YOU CAN'T SPEAK OF IT, ISN'T THERE...?
...AND...

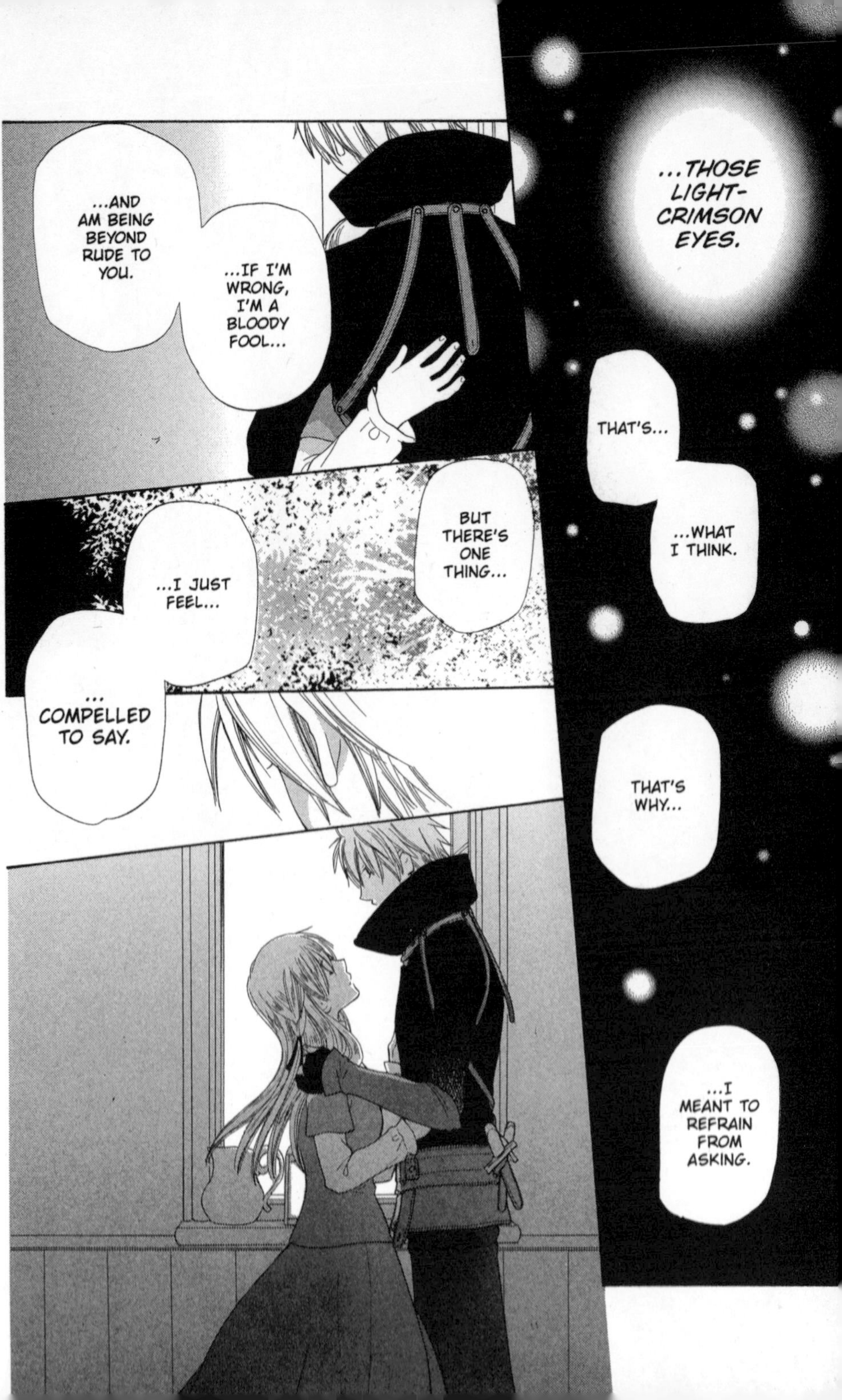
...THOSE LIGHT-CRIMSON EYES.
THAT'S...
...WHAT I THINK.
THAT'S WHY...
...I MEANT TO REFRAIN FROM ASKING.
...IF I'M WRONG, I'M A BLOODY FOOL...
...AND AM BEING BEYOND RUDE TO YOU.
BUT THERE'S ONE THING...
...I JUST FEEL...
...COMPELLED TO SAY.

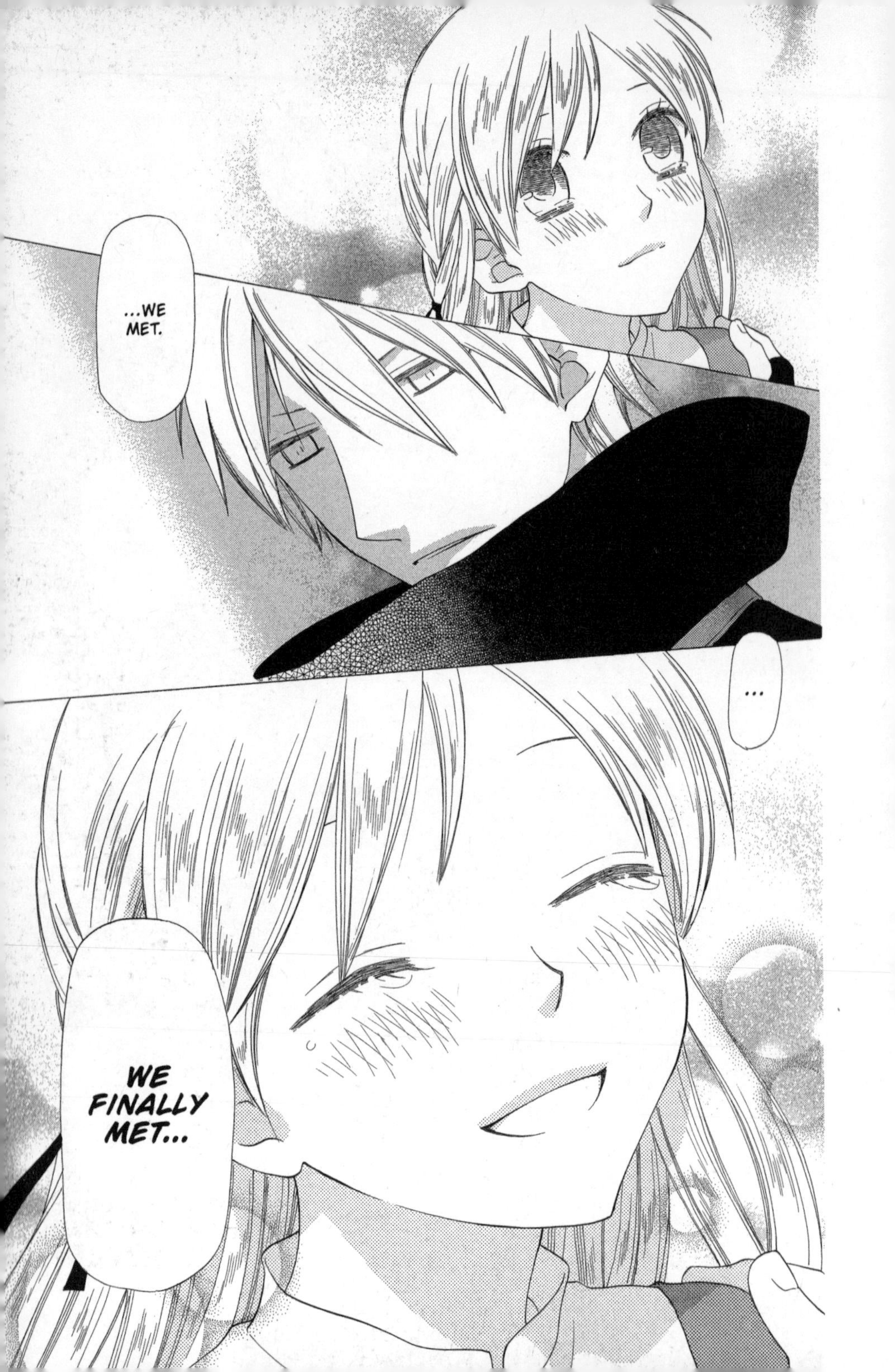
...WE MET.
...
WE FINALLY MET...

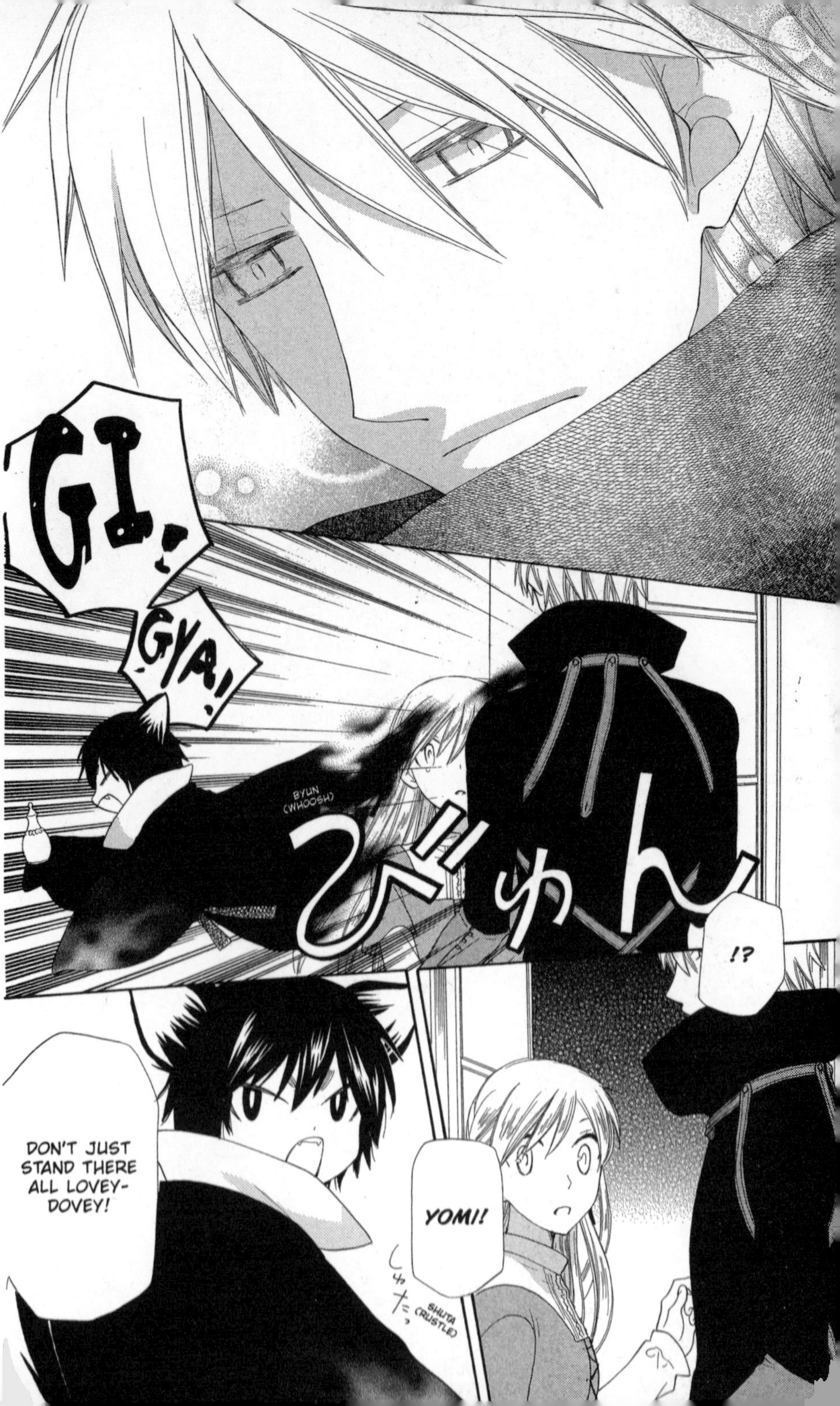
GI!
GYA!
びゅん
BYUN (WHOOSH)
!?
YOMI!
しゅたっ
SHUTA (RUSTLE)
DON'T JUST STAND THERE ALL LOVEY-DOVEY!

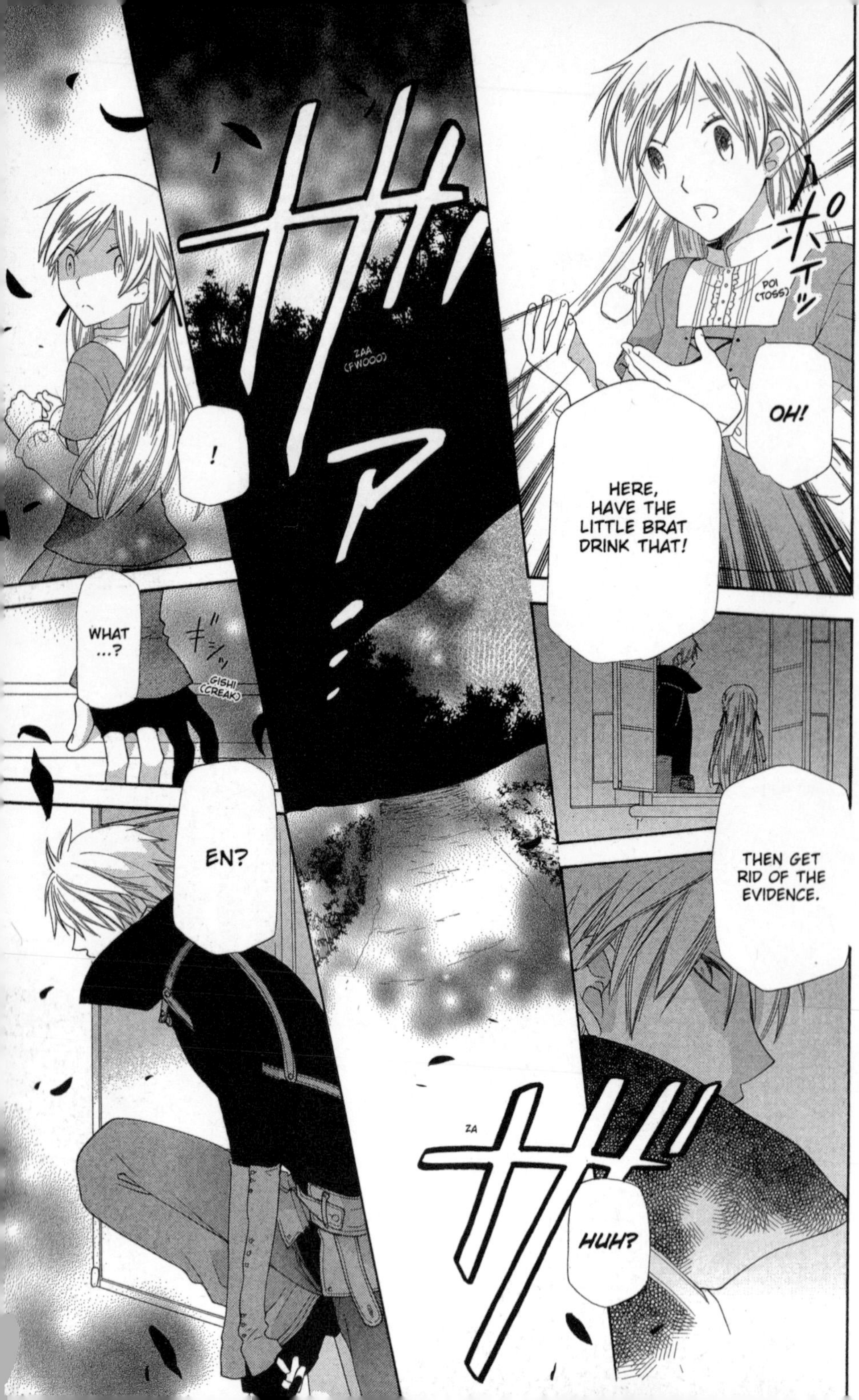

POI (TOSS)
OH!
HERE, HAVE THE LITTLE BRAT DRINK THAT!
THEN GET RID OF THE EVIDENCE.
ZA
HUH?
ZAA (FWOOO)
!
WHAT ...?
GISHI (CREAK)
EN?

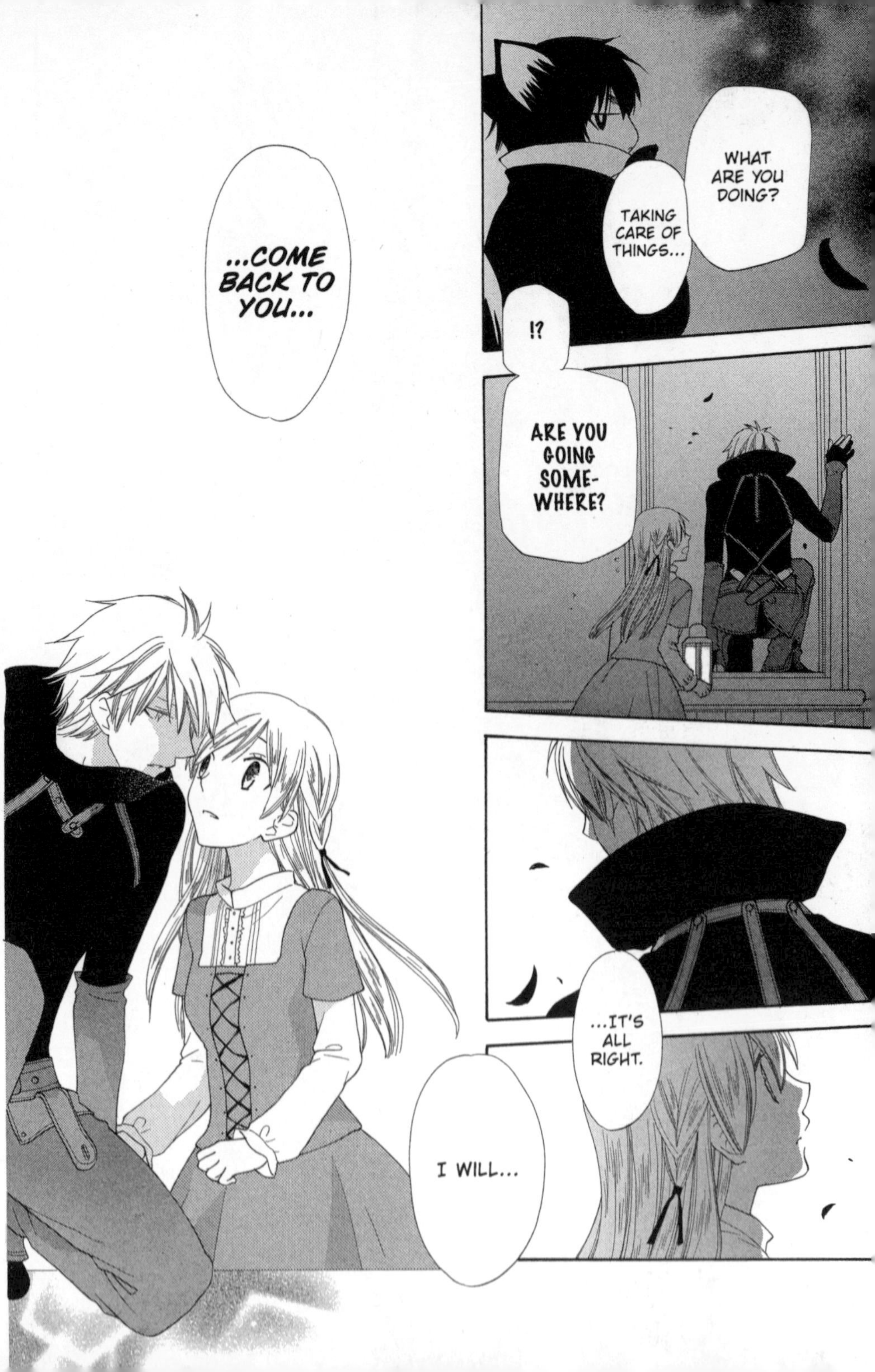

WHAT ARE YOU DOING?
TAKING CARE OF THINGS...
!?
ARE YOU GOING SOME-WHERE?
...IT'S ALL RIGHT.
I WILL...
...COME BACK TO YOU...

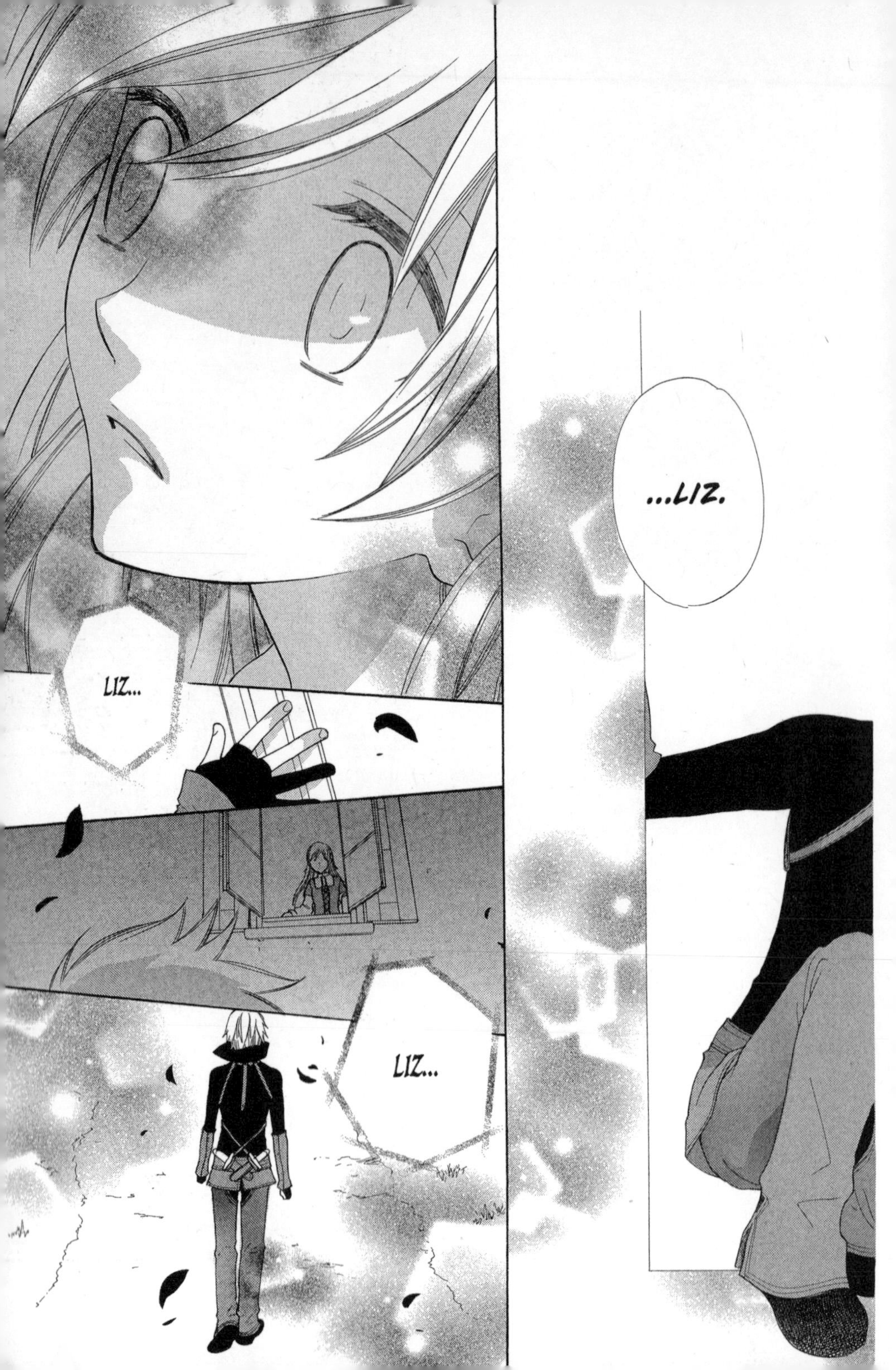

...LIZ.
LIZ...
LIZ...

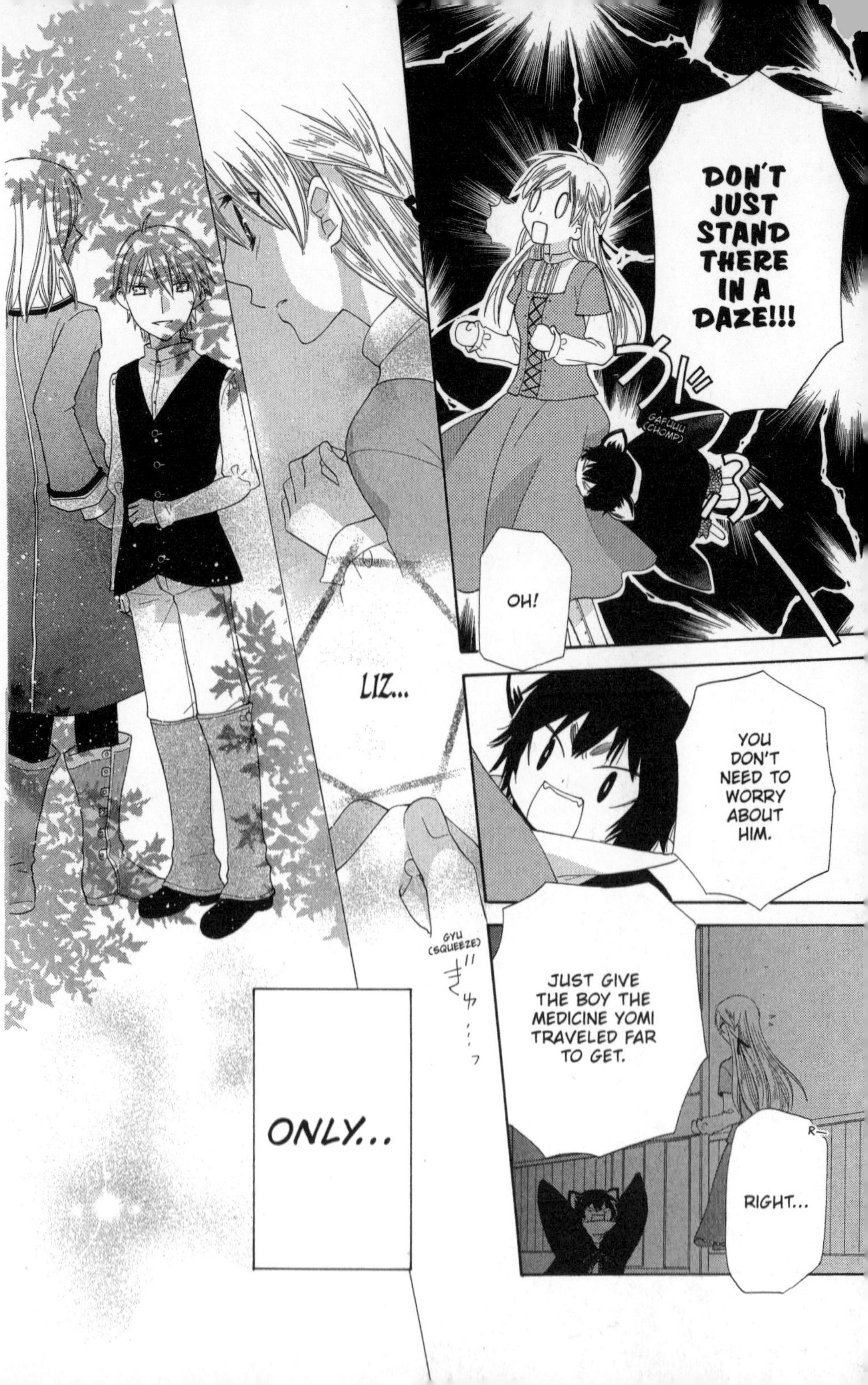
DON'T JUST STAND THERE IN A DAZE!!!
GAFUUU (CHOMP)
OH!
YOU DON'T NEED TO WORRY ABOUT HIM.
JUST GIVE THE BOY THE MEDICINE YOMI TRAVELED FAR TO GET.
RIGHT...
LIZ...
GYU (SQUEEZE)
ONLY...

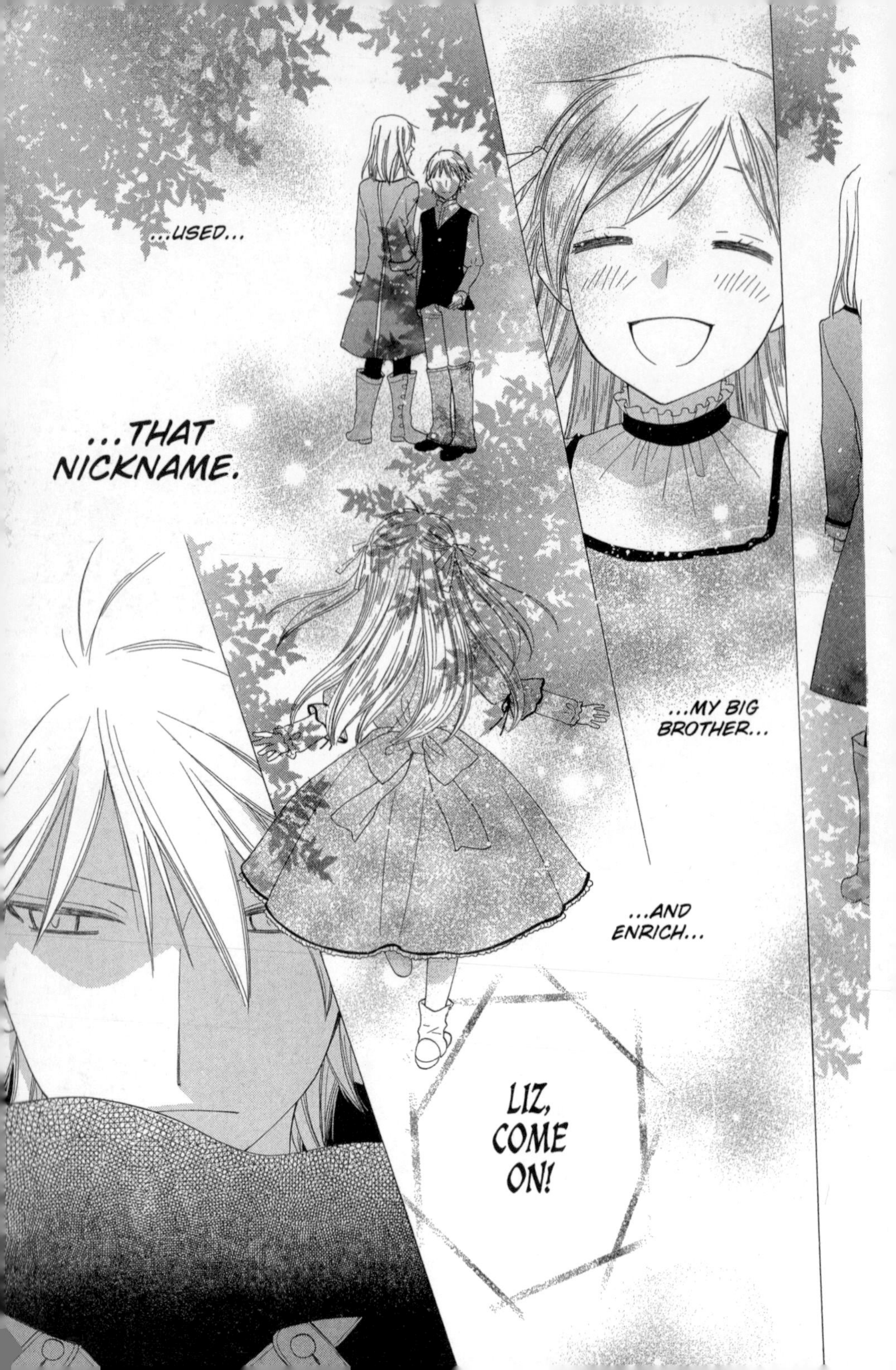
...MY BIG BROTHER...
...AND ENRICH...
LIZ, COME ON!
...USED...
...THAT NICKNAME.

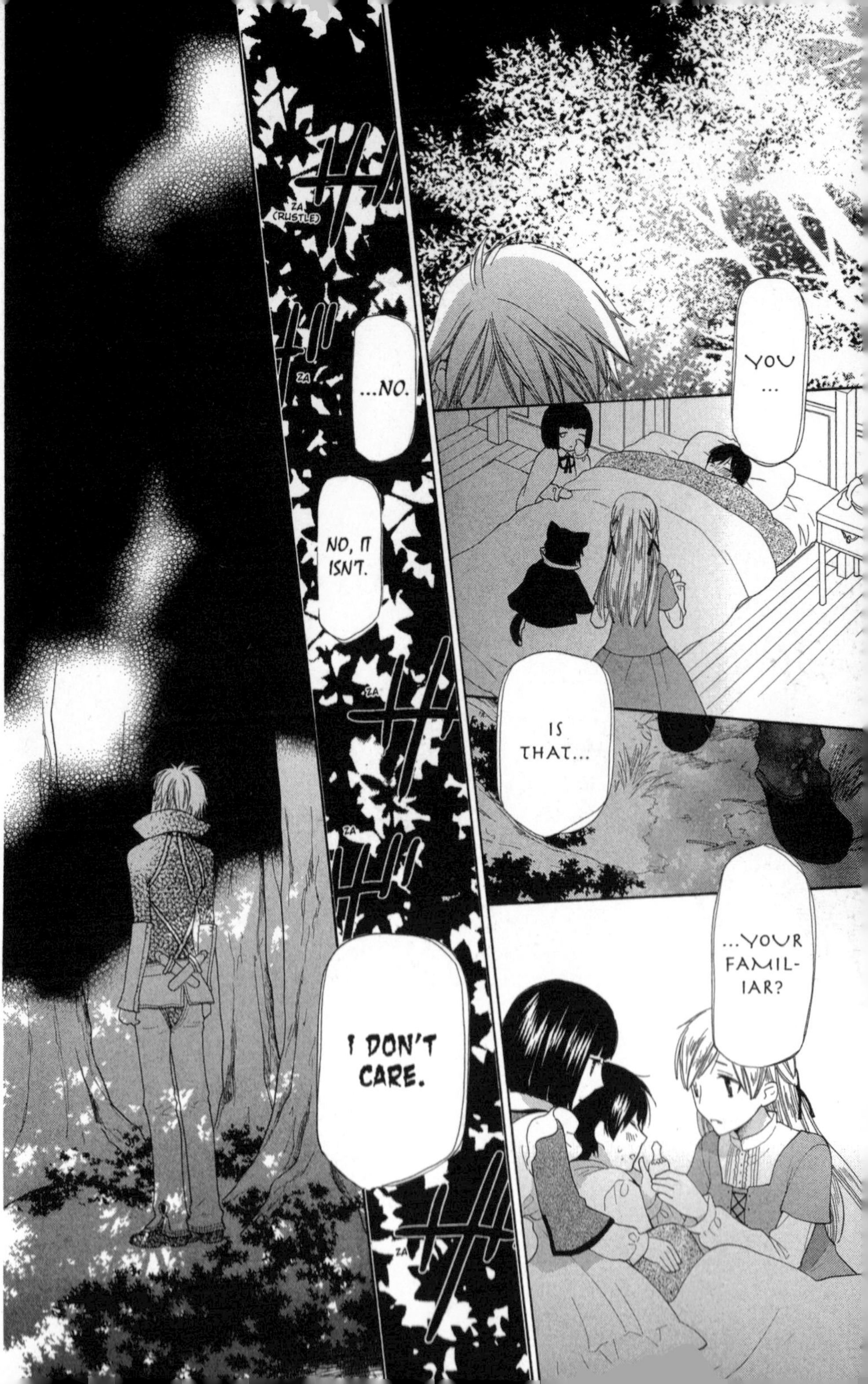
YOU ...
IS THAT...
...YOUR FAMIL-IAR?
ZA (RUSTLE)
ZA
...NO.
NO, IT ISN'T.
ZA
ZA
I DON'T CARE.
ZA

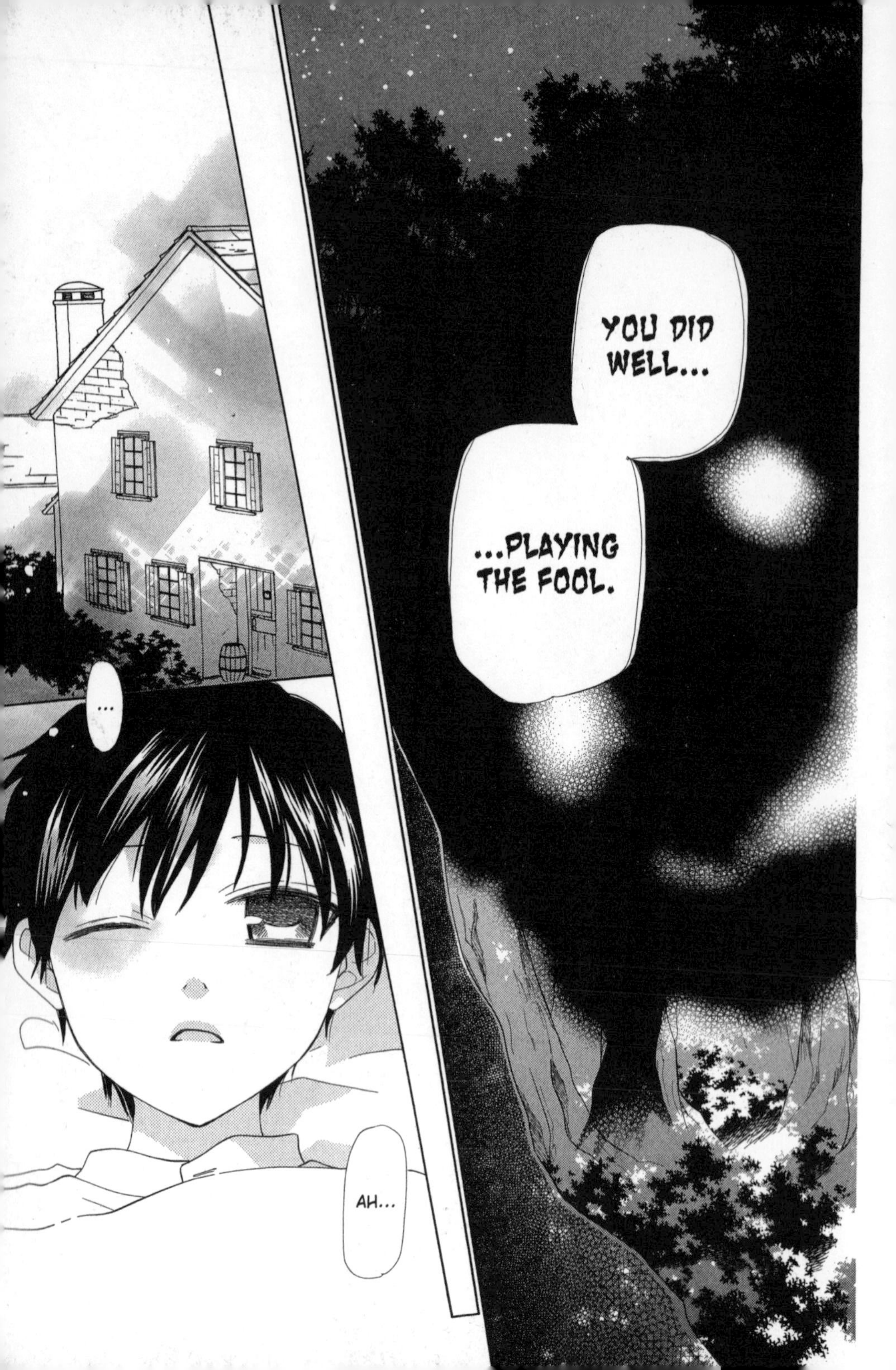
YOU DID WELL...
...PLAYING THE FOOL.
...
AH...

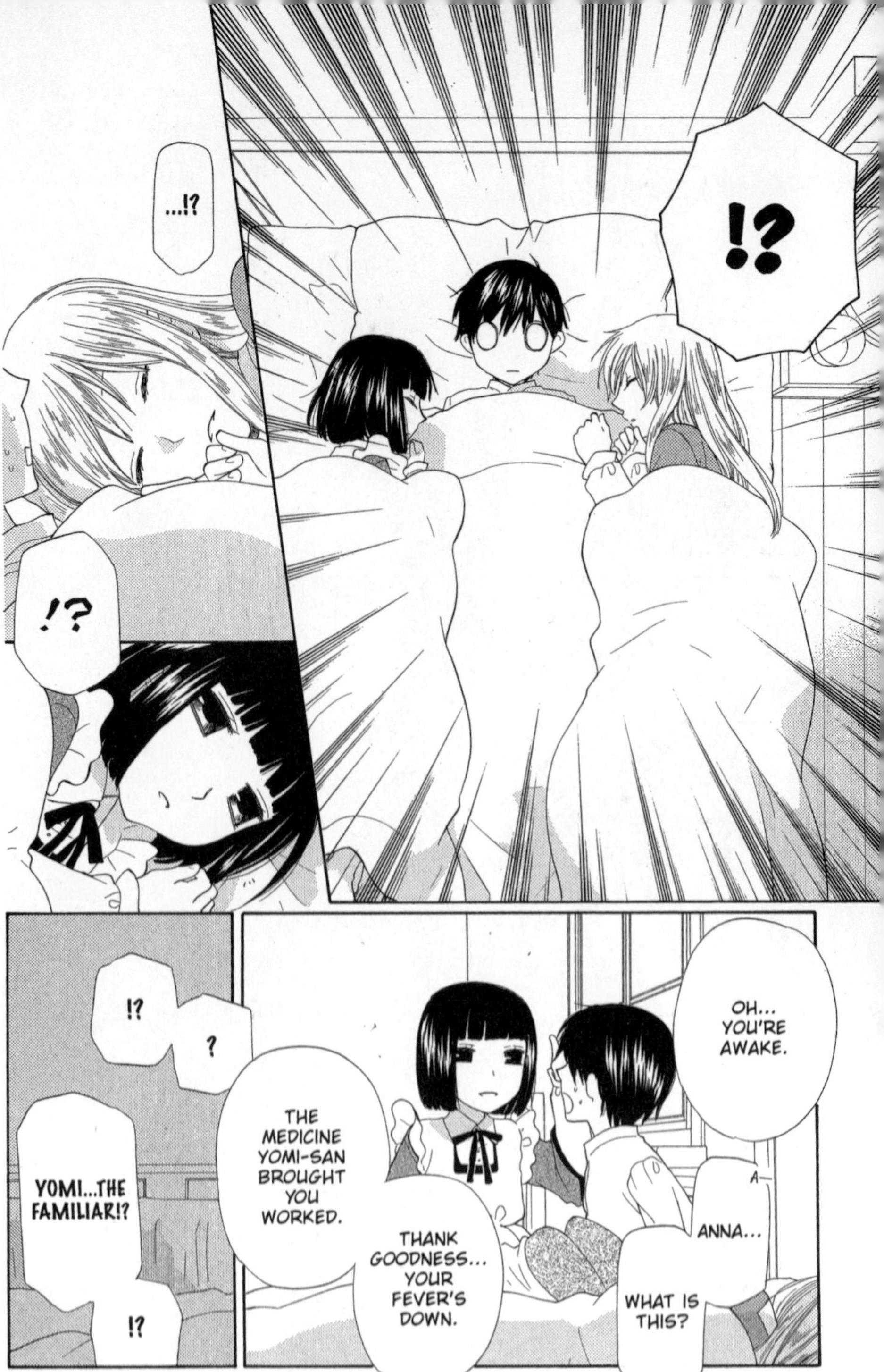
!?
...!?
!?
OH... YOU'RE AWAKE.
A— ANNA...
THE MEDICINE YOMI-SAN BROUGHT YOU WORKED.
WHAT IS THIS?
THANK GOODNESS... YOUR FEVER'S DOWN.
!?
?
YOMI...THE FAMILIAR!?
!?

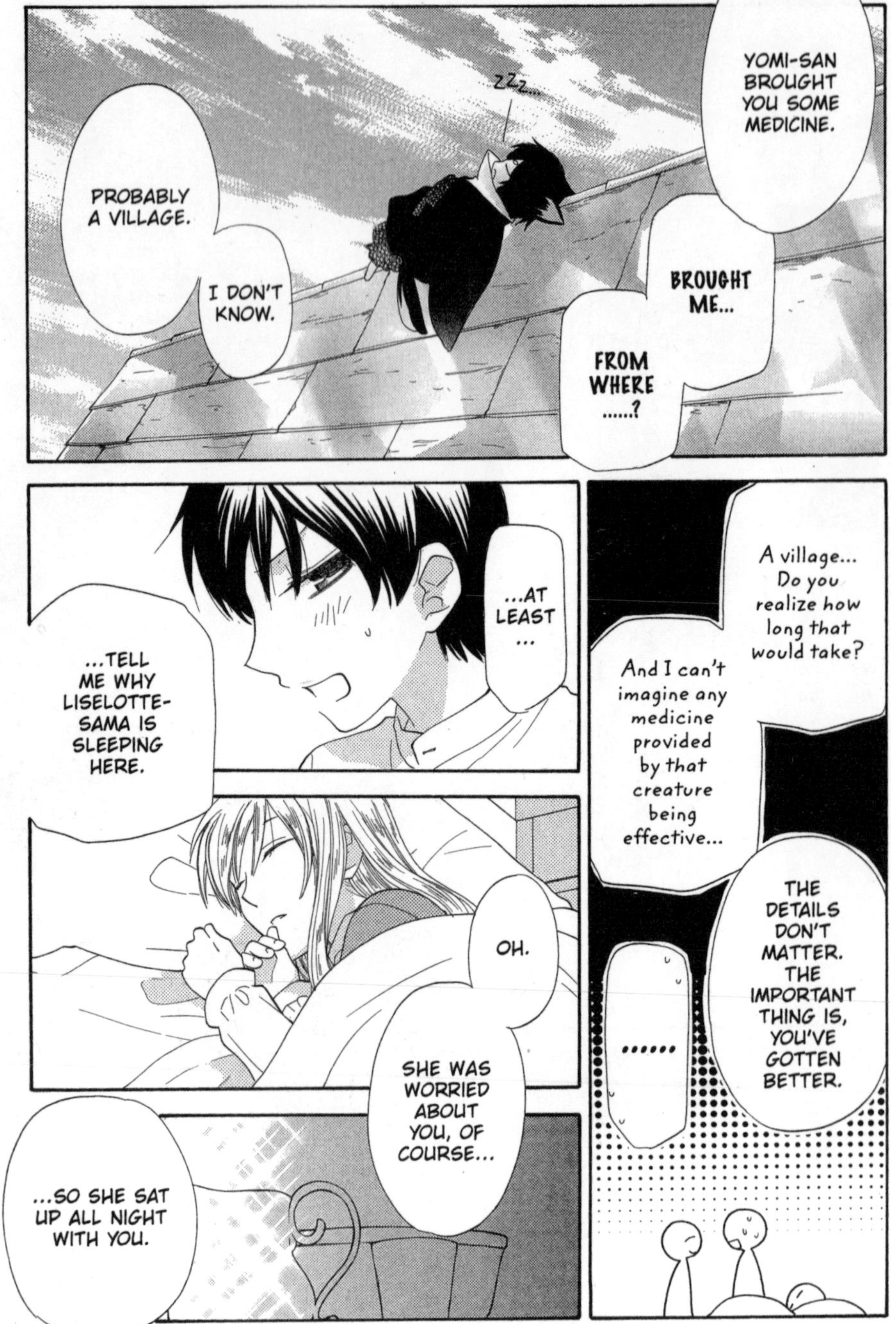
YOMI-SAN BROUGHT YOU SOME MEDICINE.
BROUGHT ME...
FROM WHERE ......?
zzz...
I DON'T KNOW.
PROBABLY A VILLAGE.
A village... Do you realize how long that would take?
And I can't imagine any medicine provided by that creature being effective...
THE DETAILS DON'T MATTER. THE IMPORTANT THING IS, YOU'VE GOTTEN BETTER.
......
...AT LEAST...
...TELL ME WHY LISELOTTE-SAMA IS SLEEPING HERE.
OH.
SHE WAS WORRIED ABOUT YOU, OF COURSE...
...SO SHE SAT UP ALL NIGHT WITH YOU.

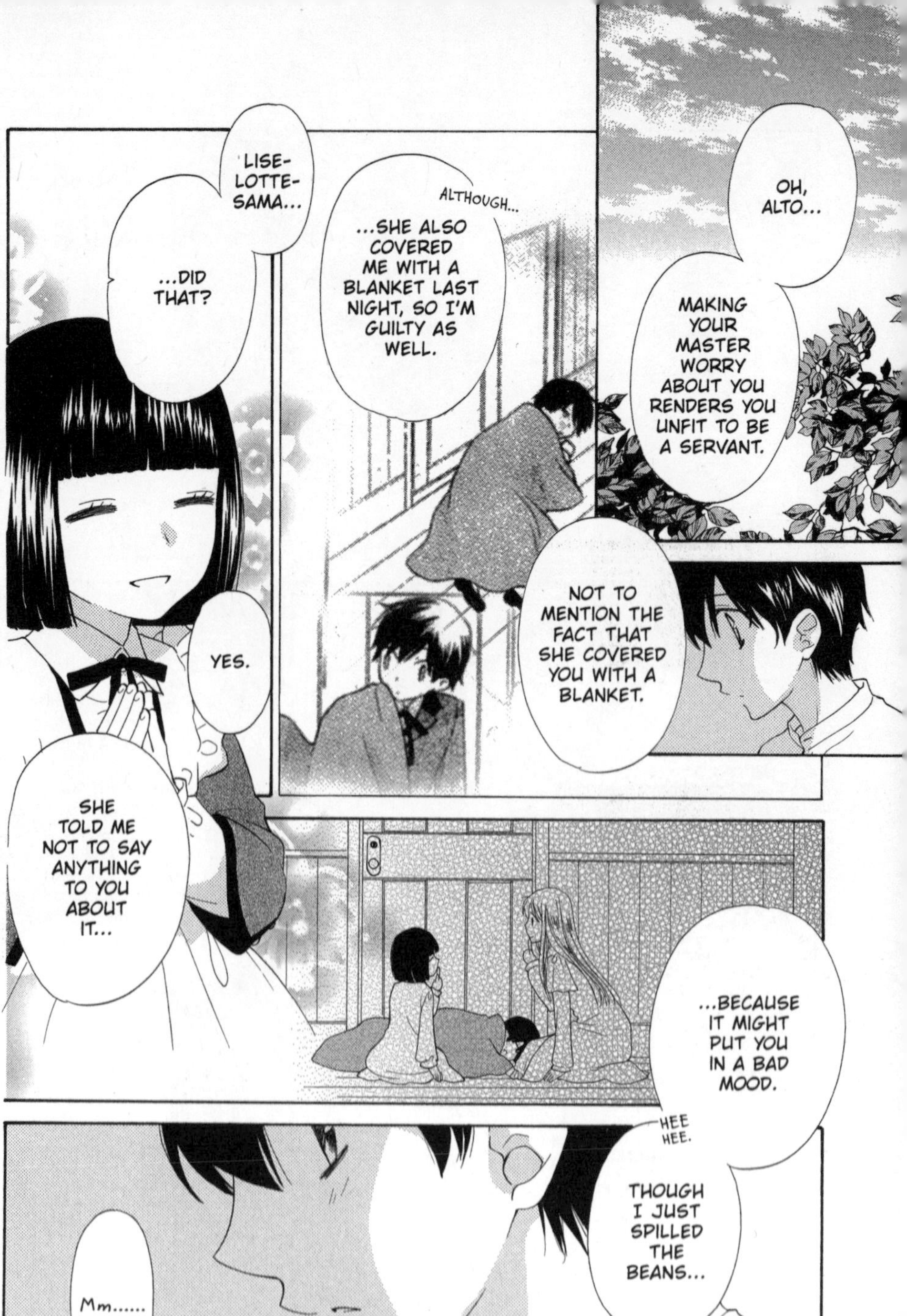
OH, ALTO...
MAKING YOUR MASTER WORRY ABOUT YOU RENDERS YOU UNFIT TO BE A SERVANT.
NOT TO MENTION THE FACT THAT SHE COVERED YOU WITH A BLANKET.
ALTHOUGH...
...SHE ALSO COVERED ME WITH A BLANKET LAST NIGHT, SO I'M GUILTY AS WELL.
LISE-LOTTE-SAMA...
...DID THAT?
YES.
SHE TOLD ME NOT TO SAY ANYTHING TO YOU ABOUT IT...
...BECAUSE IT MIGHT PUT YOU IN A BAD MOOD.
HEE HEE.
THOUGH I JUST SPILLED THE BEANS...
Mm......

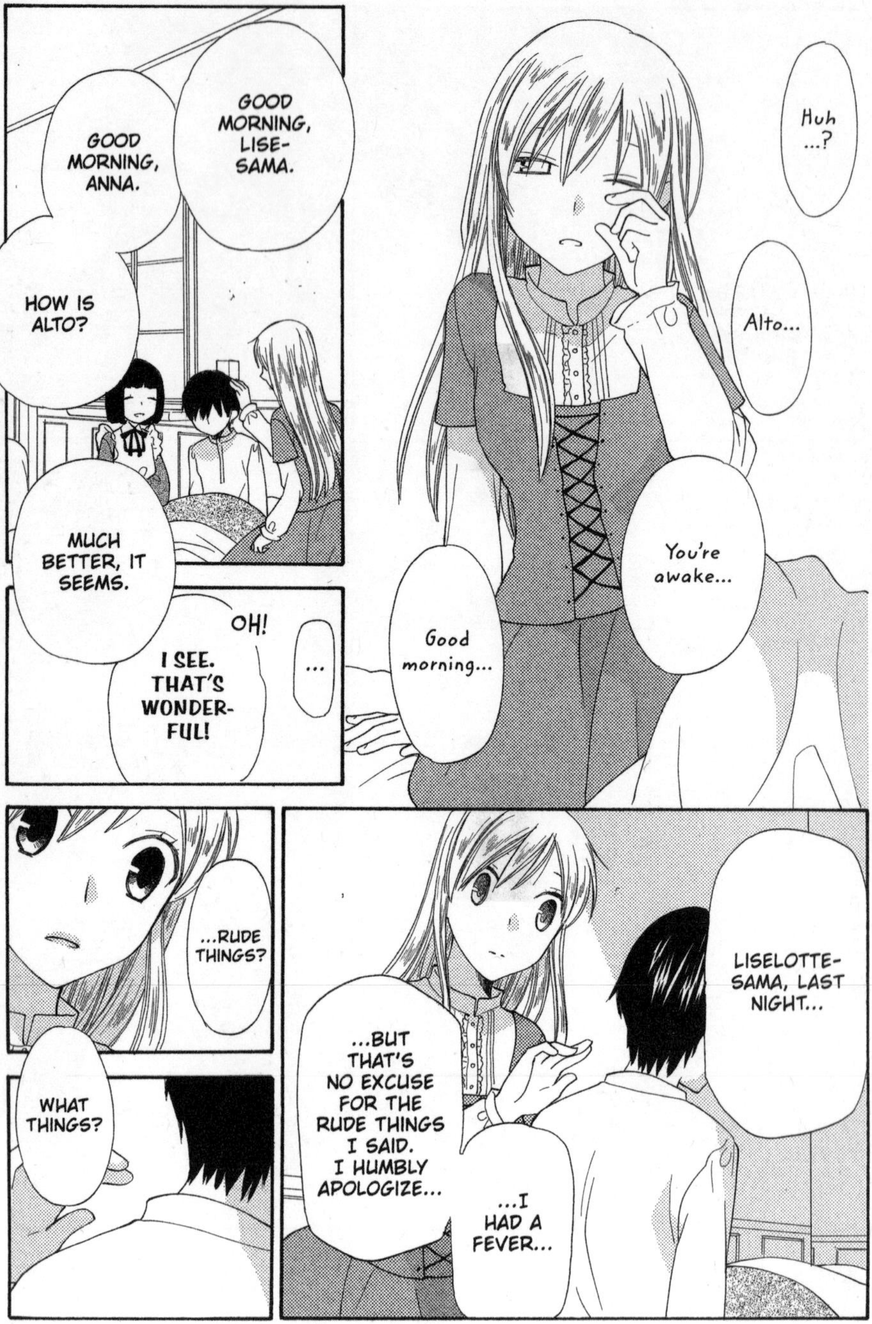

Huh ...?
Alto...
You're awake...
Good morning...
GOOD MORNING, LISE-SAMA.
GOOD MORNING, ANNA.
HOW IS ALTO?
MUCH BETTER, IT SEEMS.
OH!
I SEE. THAT'S WONDERFUL!
...
LISELOTTE-SAMA, LAST NIGHT...
...I HAD A FEVER...
...BUT THAT'S NO EXCUSE FOR THE RUDE THINGS I SAID. I HUMBLY APOLOGIZE...
...RUDE THINGS?
WHAT THINGS?

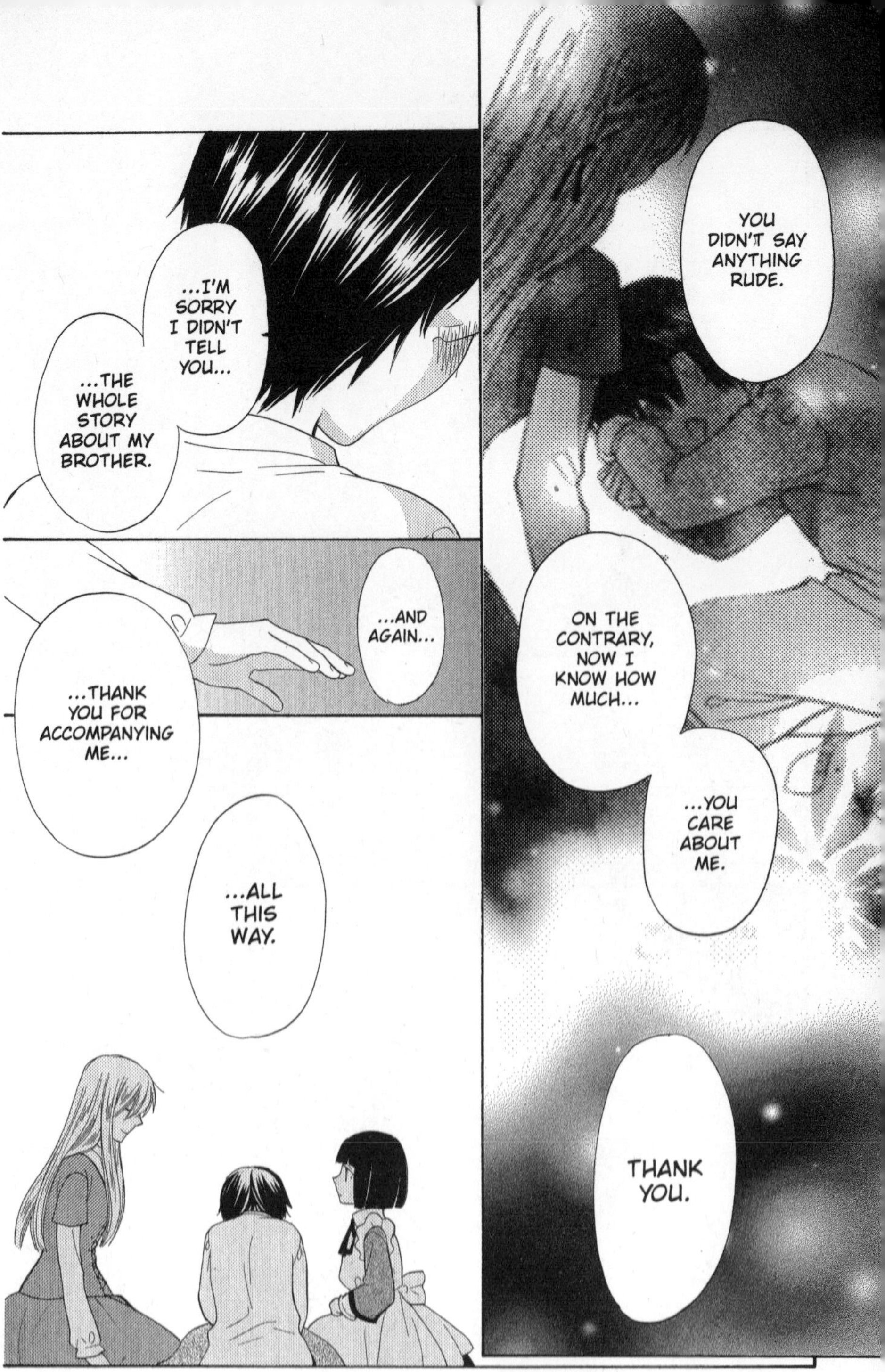
YOU DIDN'T SAY ANYTHING RUDE.
ON THE CONTRARY, NOW I KNOW HOW MUCH...
...YOU CARE ABOUT ME.
THANK YOU.
...I'M SORRY I DIDN'T TELL YOU...
...THE WHOLE STORY ABOUT MY BROTHER.
...AND AGAIN...
...THANK YOU FOR ACCOMPANYING ME...
...ALL THIS WAY.

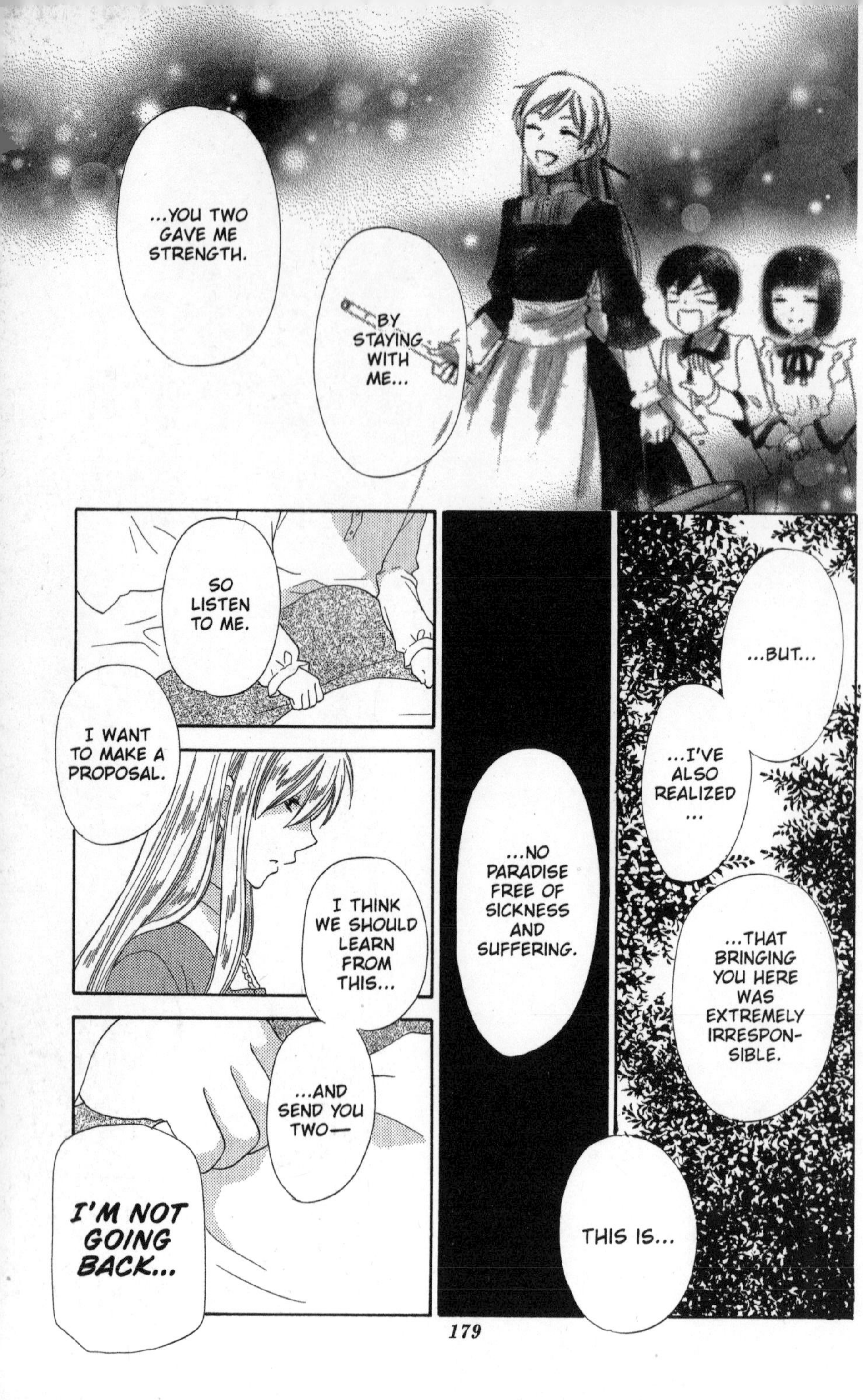
BY STAYING WITH ME...
...YOU TWO GAVE ME STRENGTH.
...BUT...
...I'VE ALSO REALIZED...
...THAT BRINGING YOU HERE WAS EXTREMELY IRRESPONSIBLE.
THIS IS...
...NO PARADISE FREE OF SICKNESS AND SUFFERING.
SO LISTEN TO ME.
I WANT TO MAKE A PROPOSAL.
I THINK WE SHOULD LEARN FROM THIS...
...AND SEND YOU TWO—
I'M NOT GOING BACK...

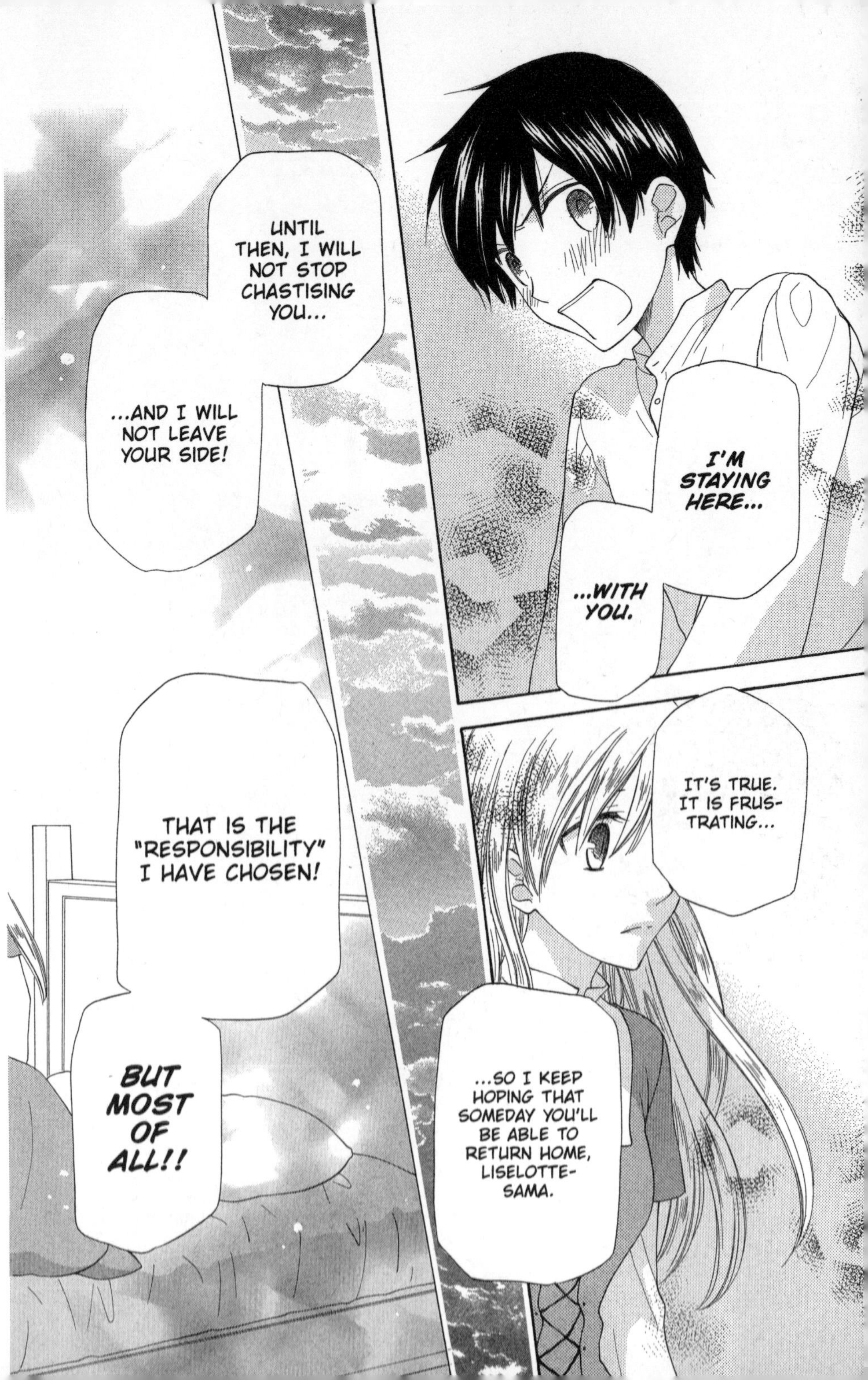
I'M STAYING HERE...
...WITH YOU.
IT'S TRUE. IT IS FRUS-TRATING...
...SO I KEEP HOPING THAT SOMEDAY YOU'LL BE ABLE TO RETURN HOME, LISELOTTE-SAMA.
UNTIL THEN, I WILL NOT STOP CHASTISING YOU...
...AND I WILL NOT LEAVE YOUR SIDE!
THAT IS THE "RESPONSIBILITY" I HAVE CHOSEN!
BUT MOST OF ALL!!

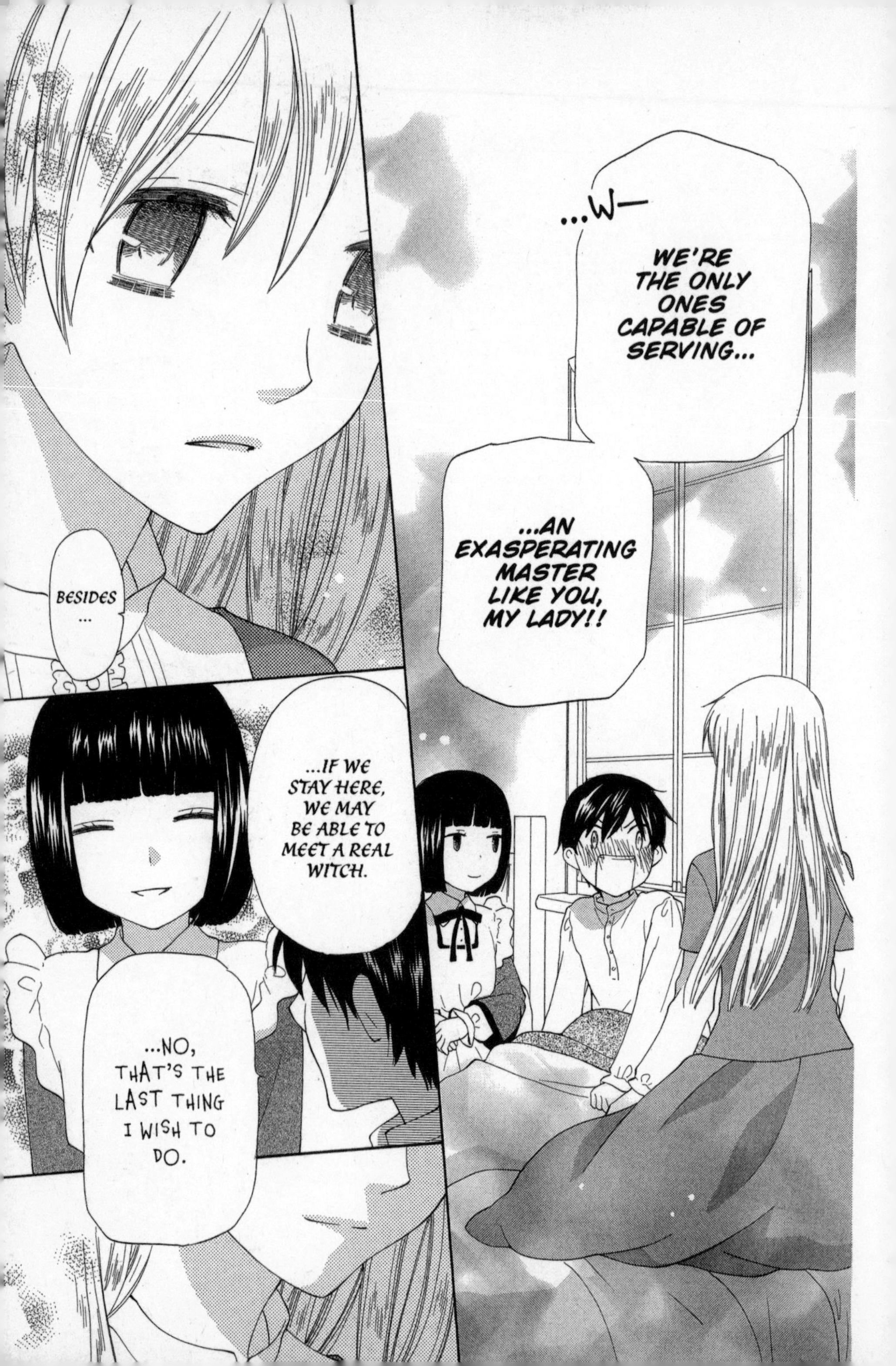
...W—
WE'RE THE ONLY ONES CAPABLE OF SERVING...
...AN EXASPERATING MASTER LIKE YOU, MY LADY!!
BESIDES ...
...IF WE STAY HERE, WE MAY BE ABLE TO MEET A REAL WITCH.
...NO, THAT'S THE LAST THING I WISH TO DO.

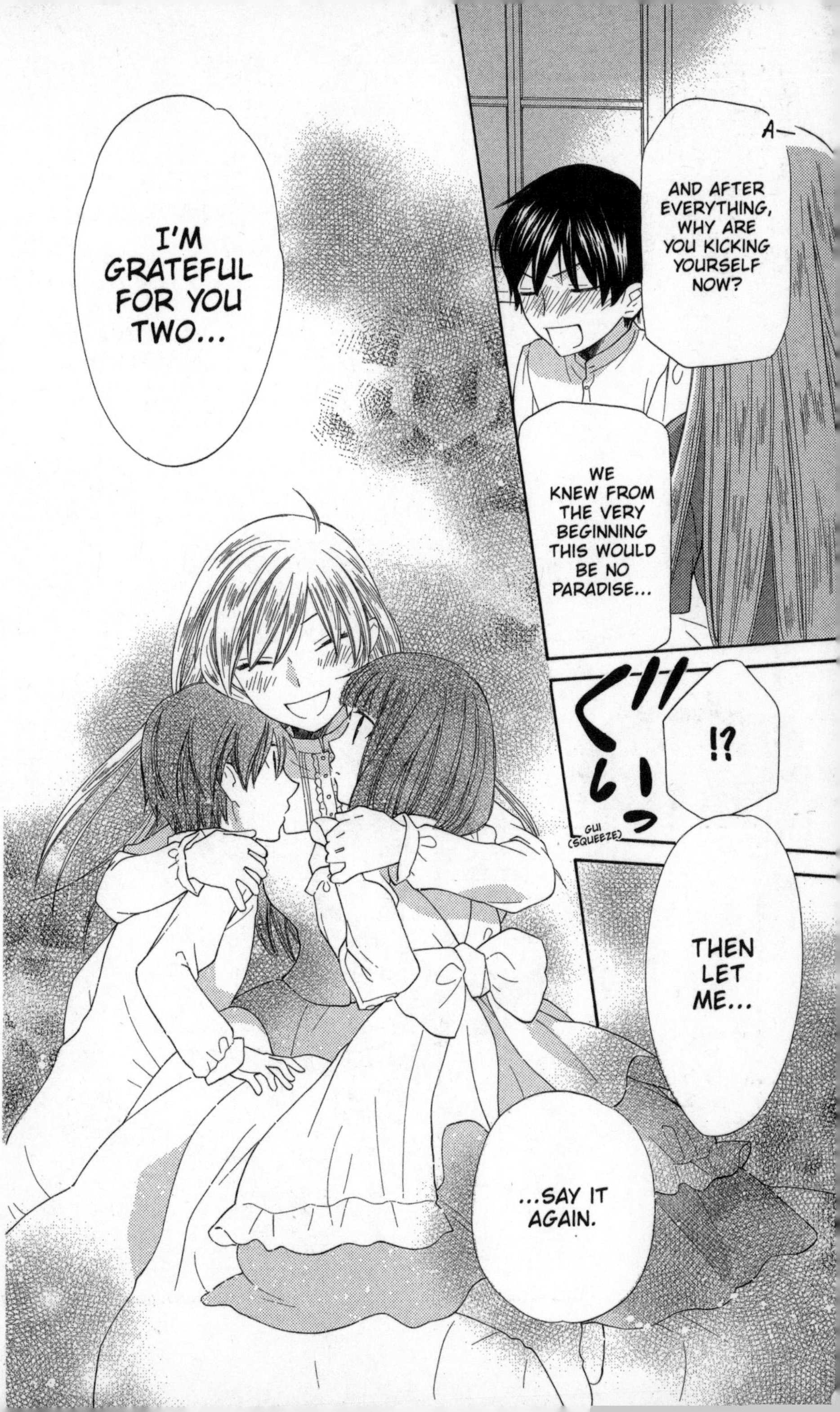
A—
AND AFTER EVERYTHING, WHY ARE YOU KICKING YOURSELF NOW?
WE KNEW FROM THE VERY BEGINNING THIS WOULD BE NO PARADISE...
GUI (SQUEEZE)
!?
THEN LET ME...
...SAY IT AGAIN.
I'M GRATEFUL FOR YOU TWO...

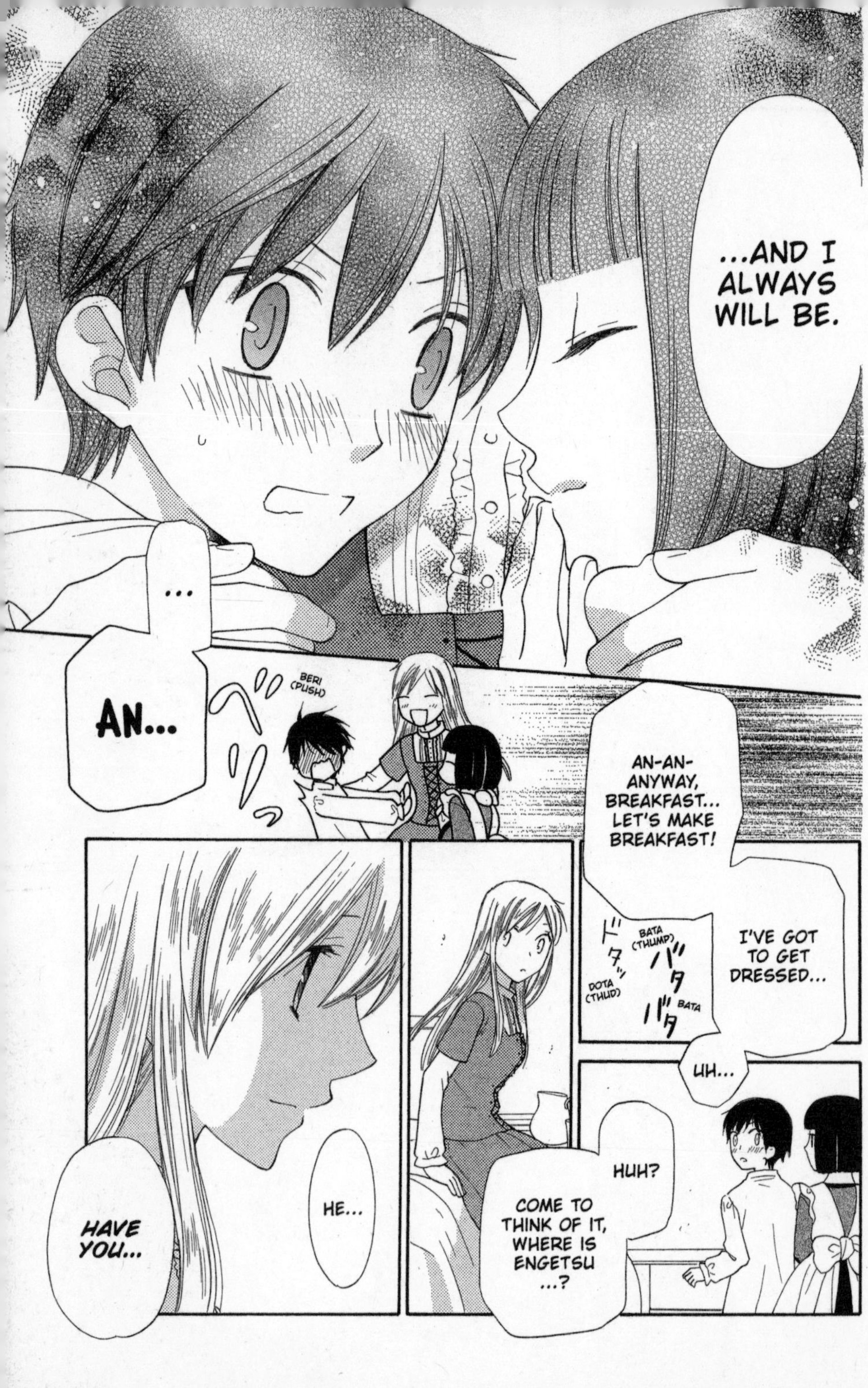
...AND I ALWAYS WILL BE.
...
AN...
BERI (PUSH)
AN-AN- ANYWAY, BREAKFAST... LET'S MAKE BREAKFAST!
BATA (THUMP)
バタバタ
BATA
ドタッ
DOTA (THUD)
I'VE GOT TO GET DRESSED...
UH...
HUH?
COME TO THINK OF IT, WHERE IS ENGETSU ...?
HE...
HAVE YOU...

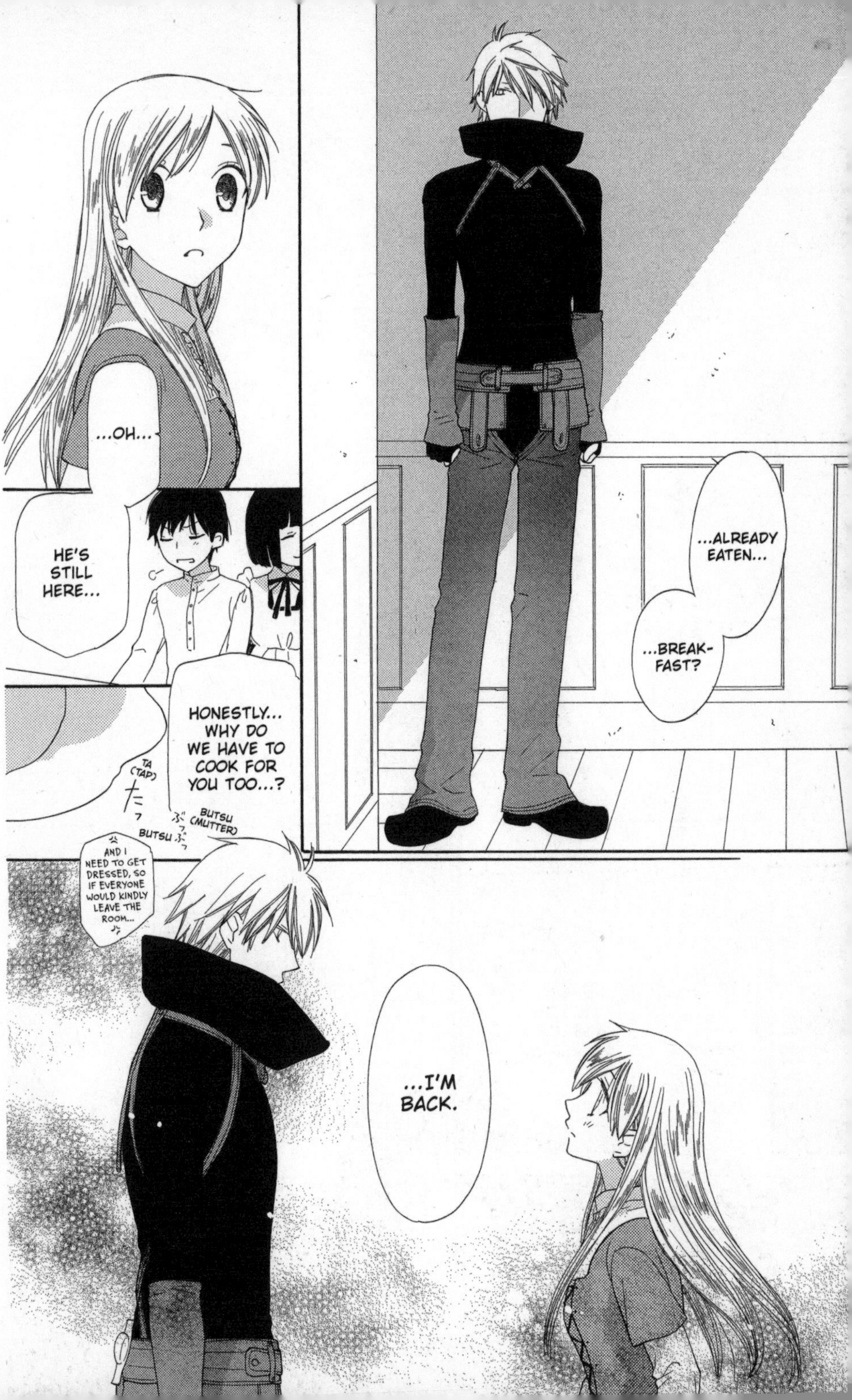
...ALREADY EATEN...
...BREAK-FAST?
...OH...
HE'S STILL HERE...
HONESTLY... WHY DO WE HAVE TO COOK FOR YOU TOO...?
TA (TAP)
BUTSU (MUTTER)
BUTSU
AND I NEED TO GET DRESSED, SO IF EVERYONE WOULD KINDLY LEAVE THE ROOM...
...I'M BACK.

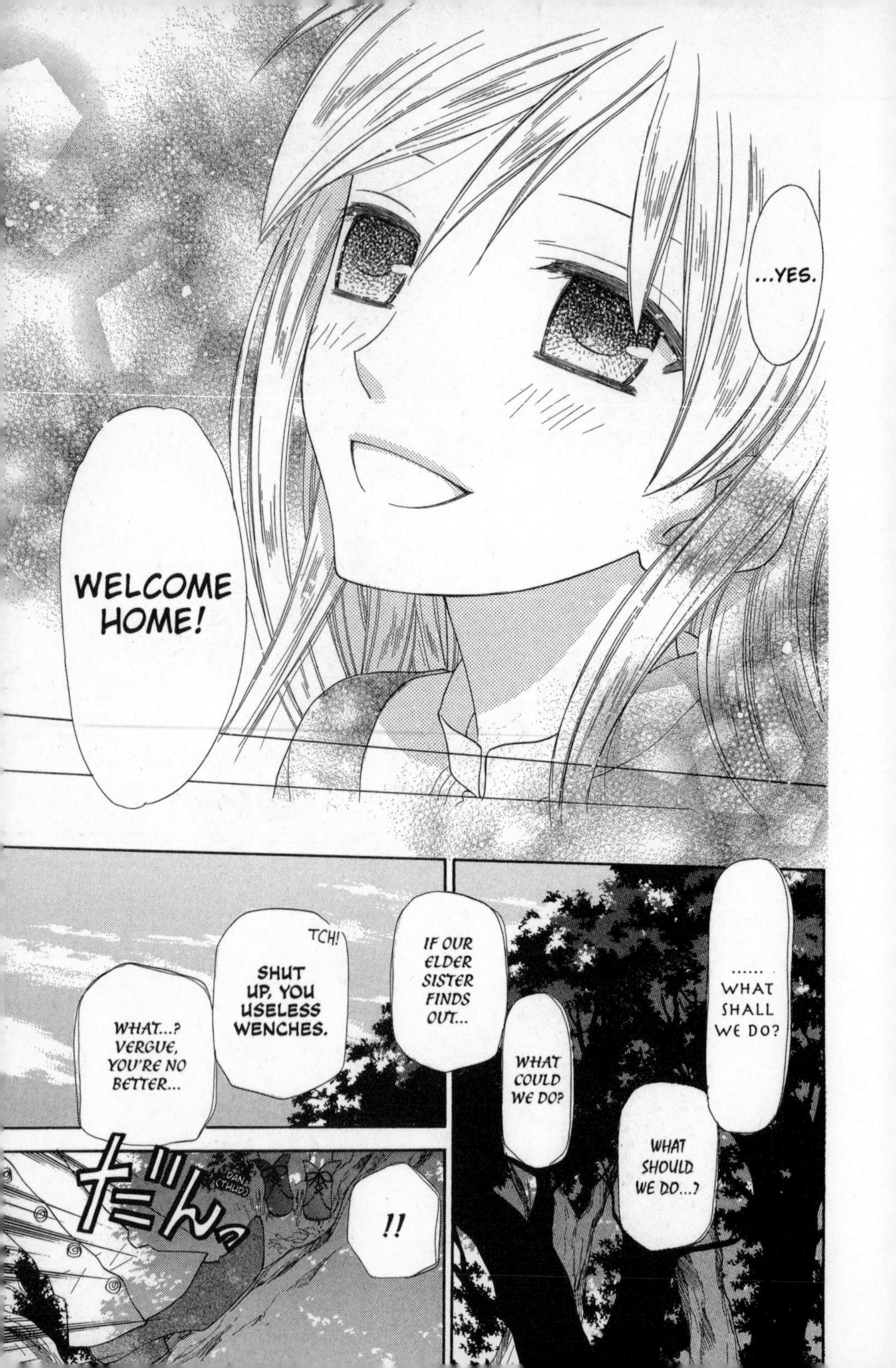
...YES.
WELCOME HOME!
...... WHAT SHALL WE DO?
IF OUR ELDER SISTER FINDS OUT...
WHAT COULD WE DO?
WHAT SHOULD WE DO...?
TCH!
SHUT UP, YOU USELESS WENCHES.
WHAT...? VERGUE, YOU'RE NO BETTER...
!!
だんっ
DAN (THUD)

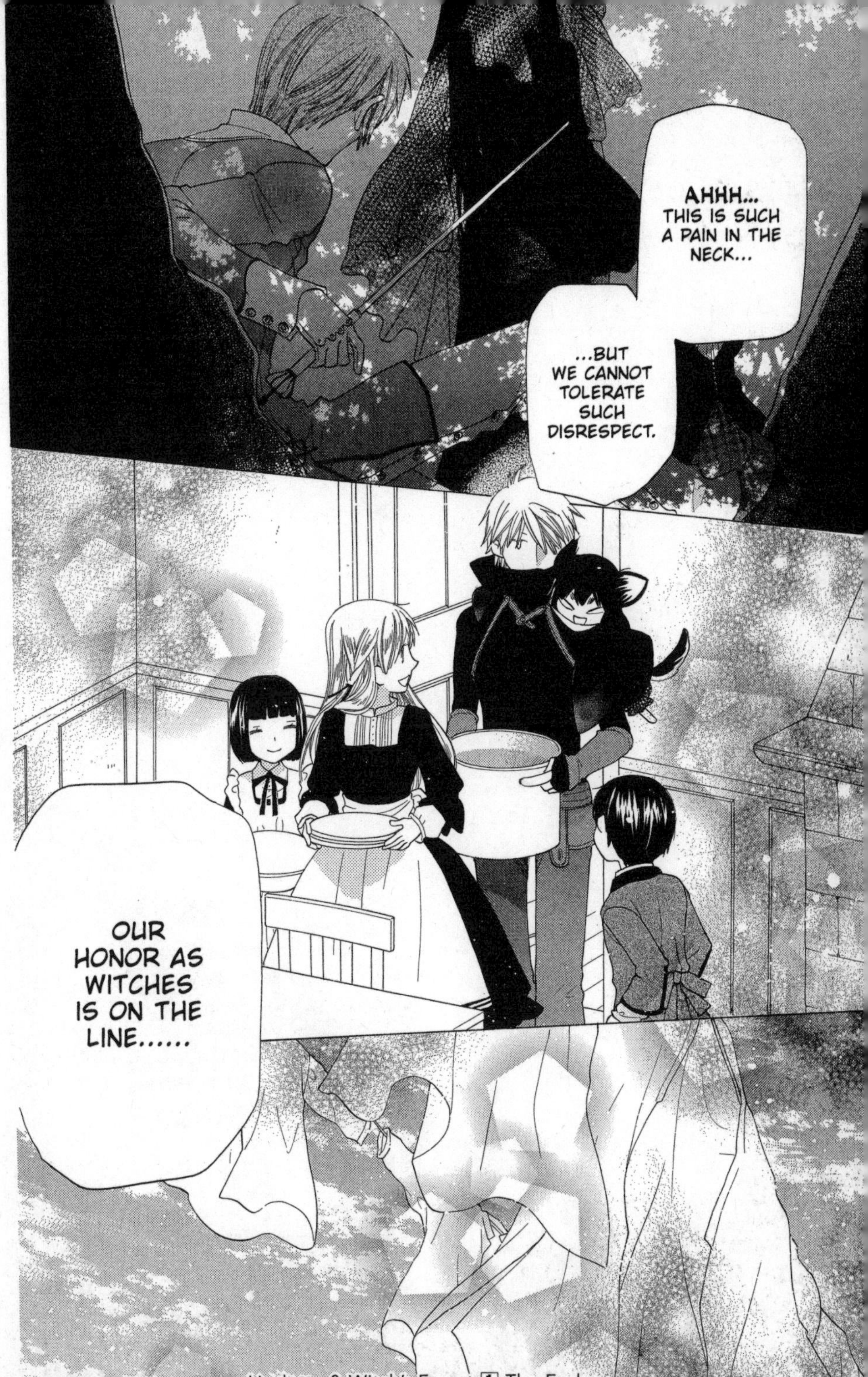
AHHH... THIS IS SUCH A PAIN IN THE NECK...
...BUT WE CANNOT TOLERATE SUCH DISRESPECT.
OUR HONOR AS WITCHES IS ON THE LINE......

Liselotte & Witch's Forest 1 The End

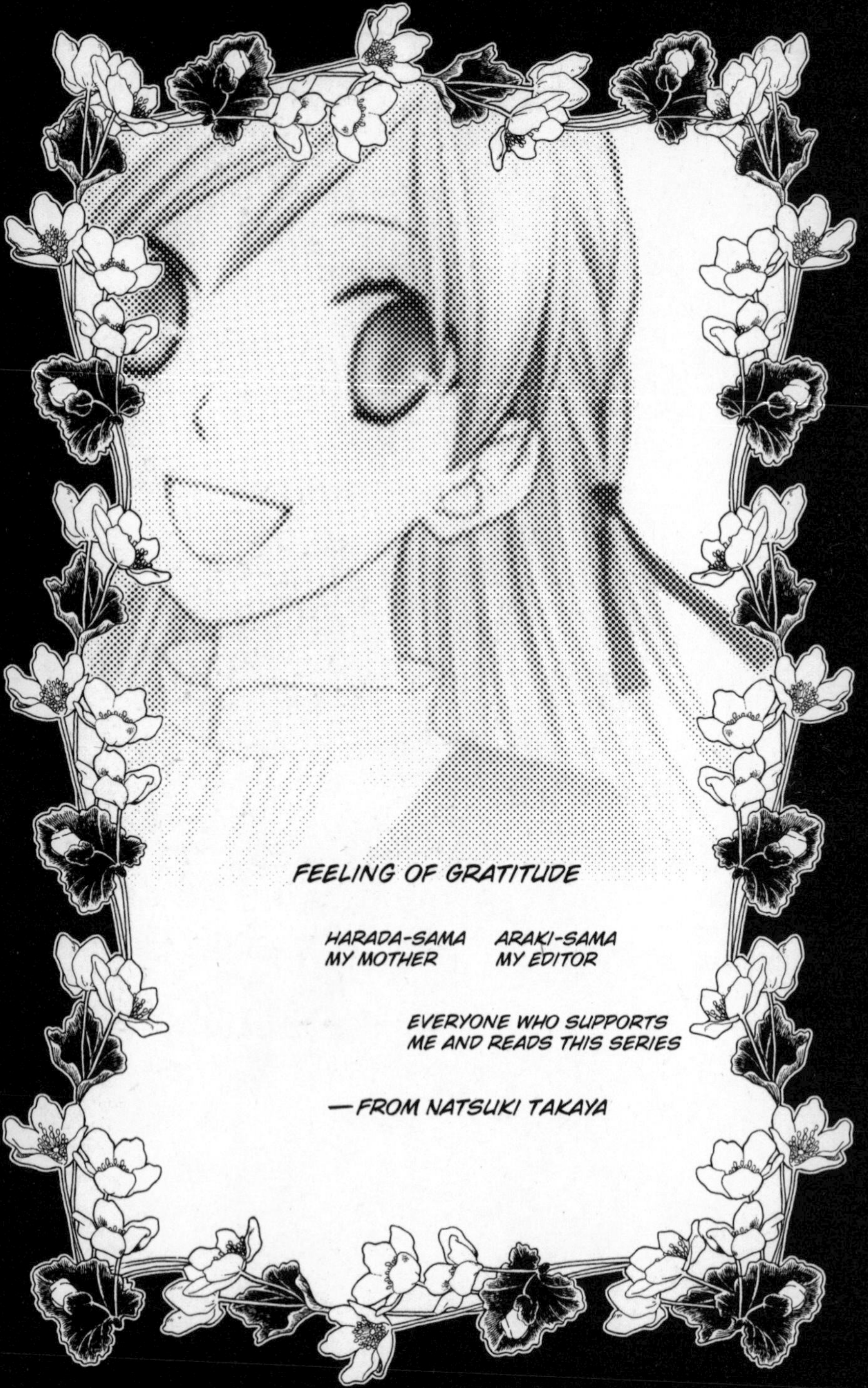
FEELING OF GRATITUDE
HARADA-SAMA
MY MOTHER
ARAKI-SAMA
MY EDITOR
EVERYONE WHO SUPPORTS ME AND READS THIS SERIES
—FROM NATSUKI TAKAYA

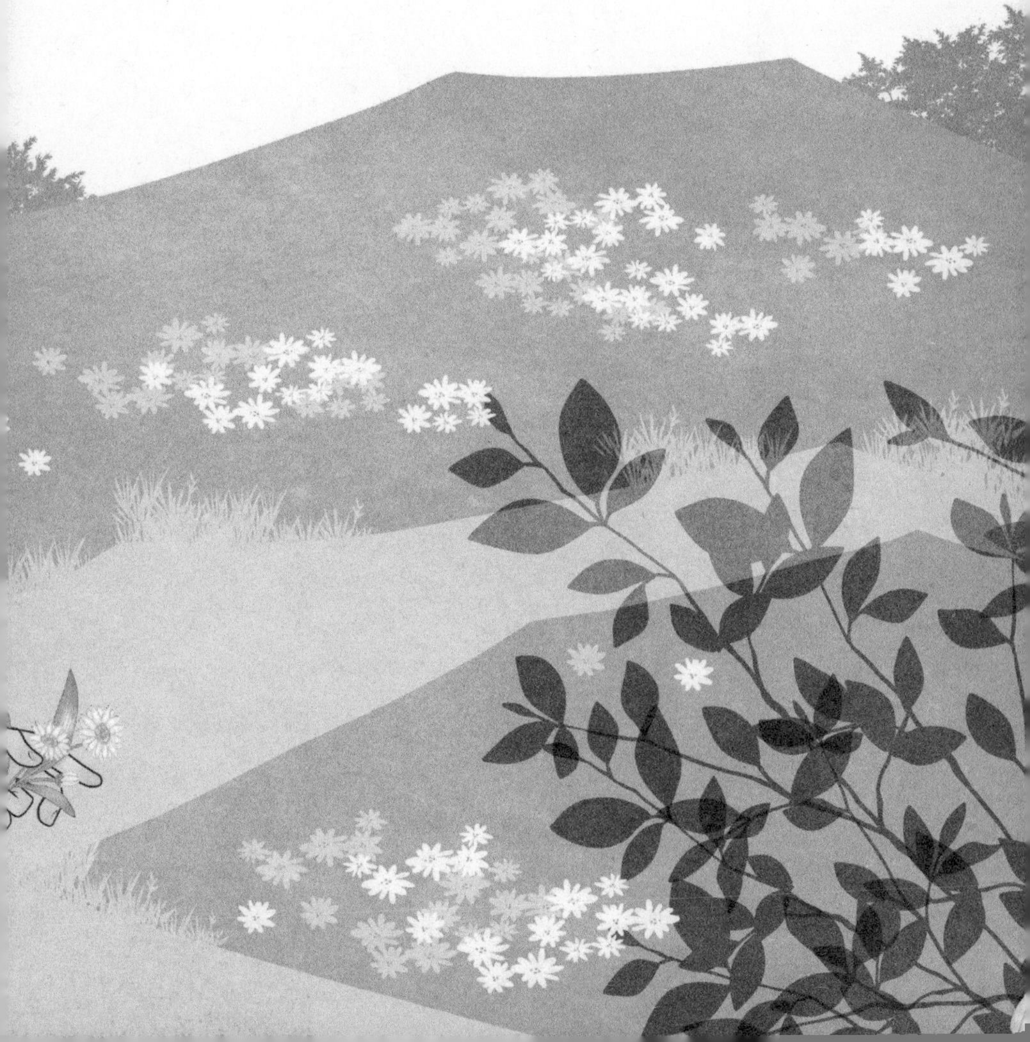

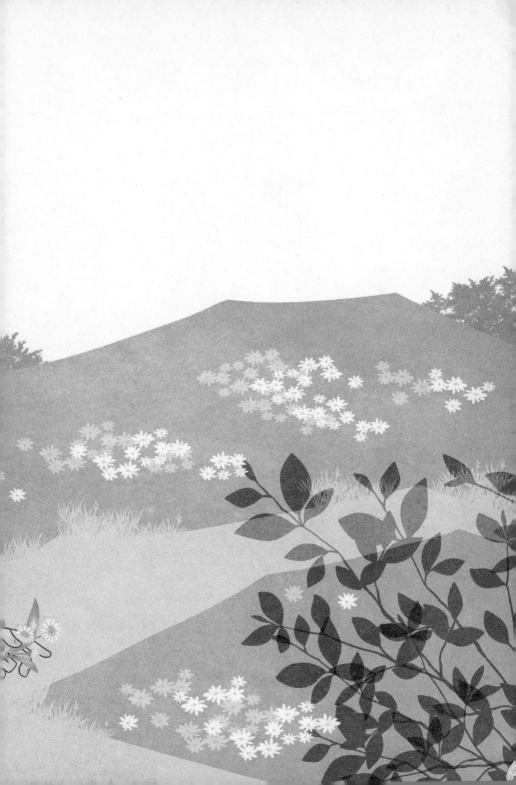

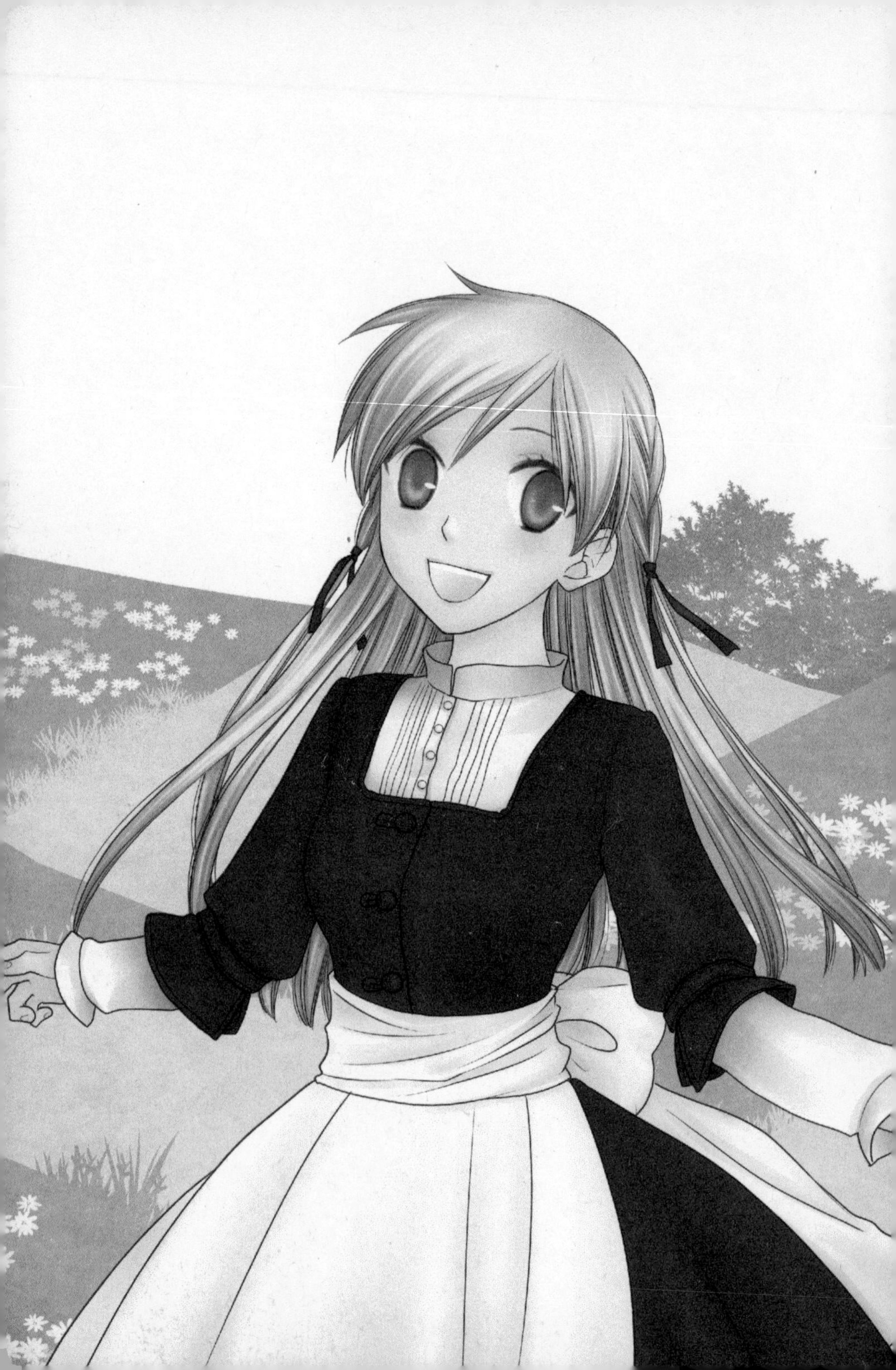

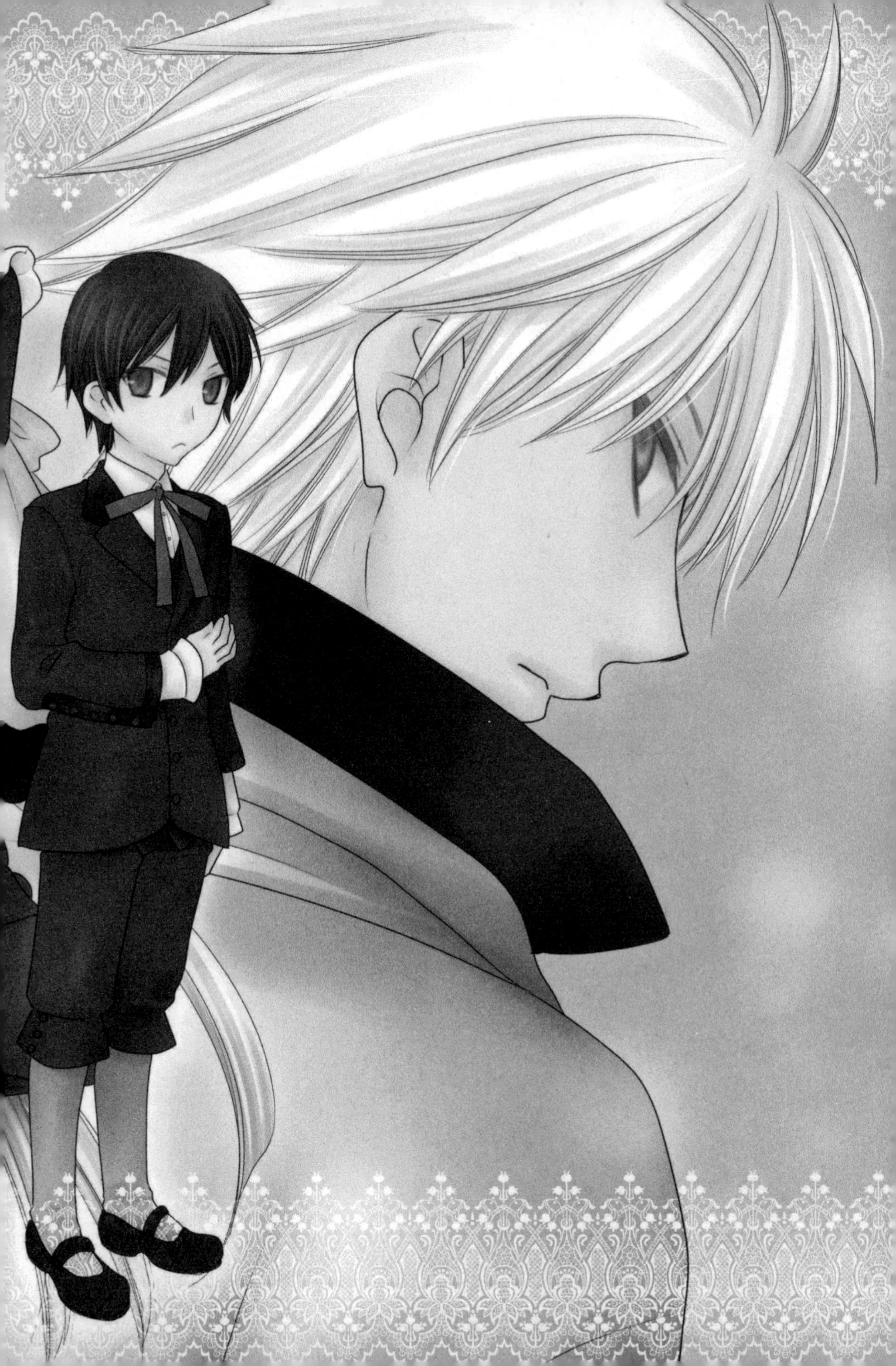

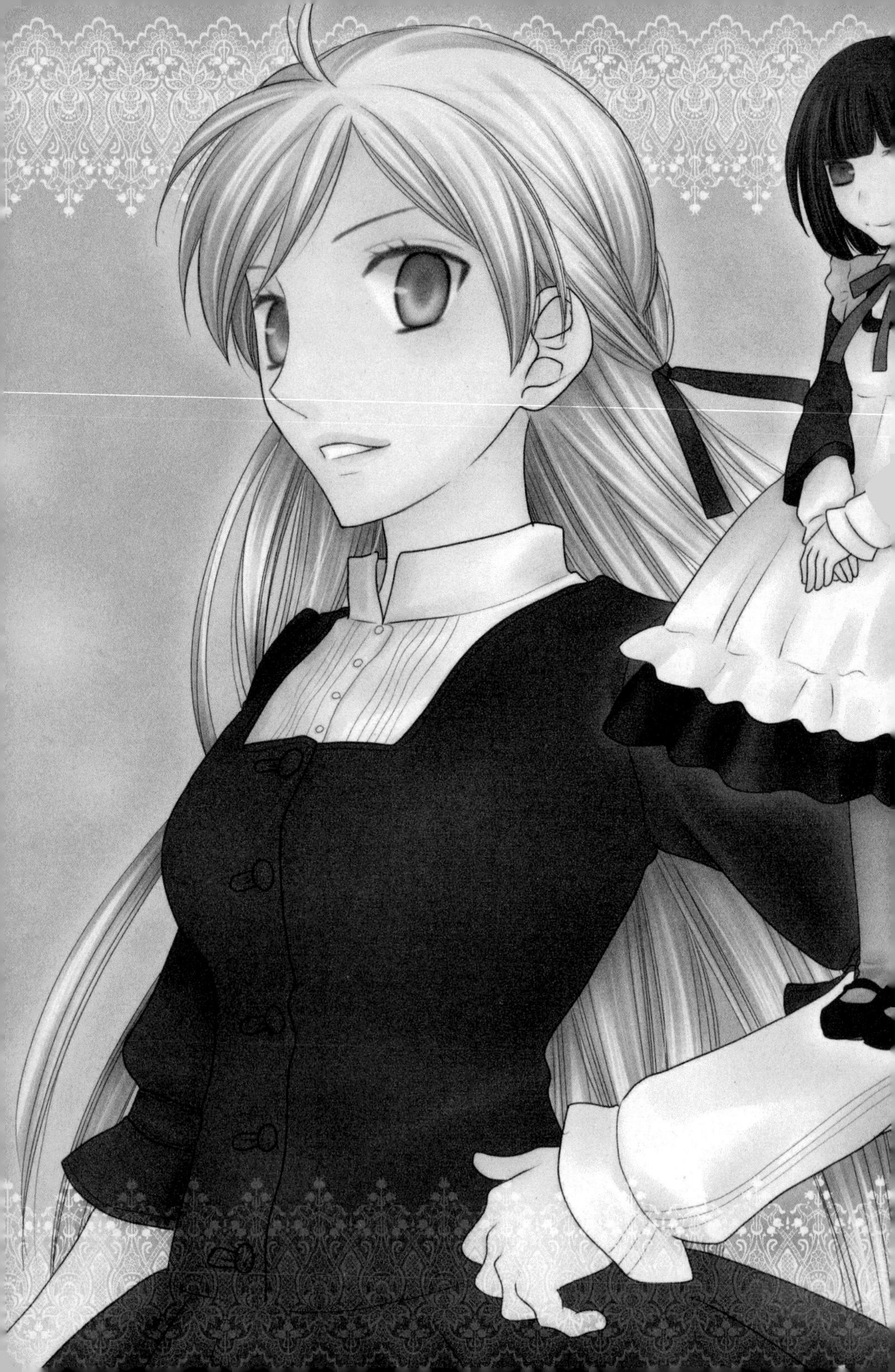

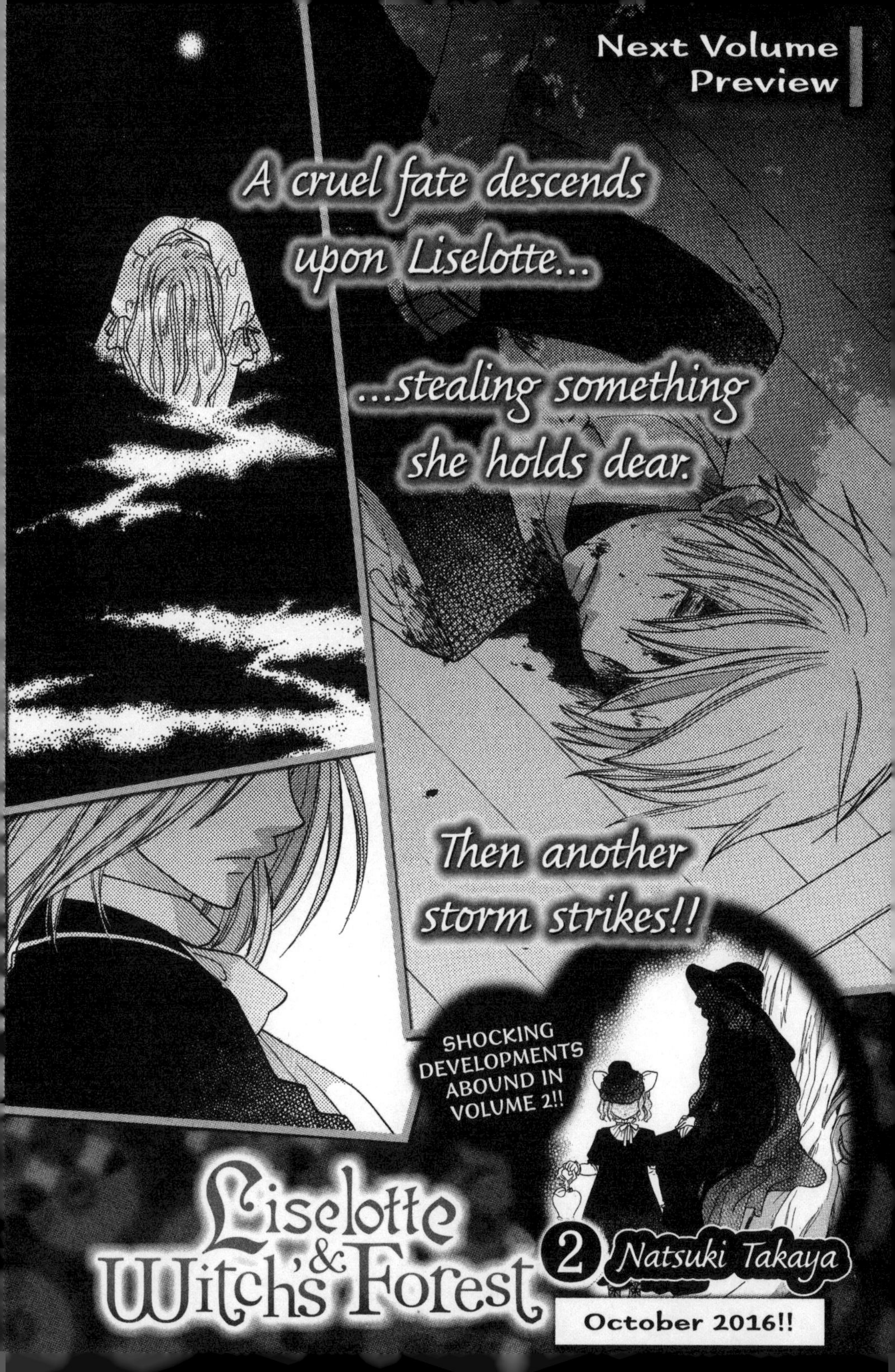

Next Volume Preview
A cruel fate descends upon Liselotte...
...stealing something she holds dear.
Then another storm strikes!!
SHOCKING DEVELOPMENTS ABOUND IN VOLUME 2!!
Liselotte & Witch's Forest
2
Natsuki Takaya
October 2016!!

Liselotte & Witch's Forest

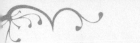 

Liselotte & Witch's

Natsuki Takaya

Translation: Sheldon Drzka

Lettering: Lys Blakeslee

LISELOTTE TO MAJO NO MORI Vol. 1 by Natsuki Takaya
© Natsuki Takaya 2012
All rights reserved.
First published in Japan in 2012 by HAKUSENSHA, INC., Tokyo.
English language translation rights in U.S.A., Canada and U.K. arranged with
HAKUSENSHA, INC., Tokyo through Tuttle-Mori Agency, Inc., Tokyo.

English Translation © 2016 by Yen Press, LLC

Yen Press
1290 Avenue of the Americas
New York, NY 10104

Visit us at yenpress.com
facebook.com/yenpress
twitter.com/yenpress
yenpress.tumblr.com

First Yen Press Edition: July 2016

Yen Press is an imprint of Yen Press, LLC.
The Yen Press name and logo are trademarks of Yen Press, LLC.

The publisher is not responsible for websites (or their content) that are not owned by the publisher.

Library of Congress Control Number: 2016936533

ISBN: 978-0-316-36019-7

10 9 8 7 6 5 4 3 2 1

BVG

Printed in the United States of America